Kaplan Publishing are constantly finding new ways to make a difference to your studies and our exciting online resources really d[...] different to students looking for [...]

D0246162

This book comes with free MyKaplan online resources so that you can study anytime, anywhere. This free online resource is not sold separately and is included in the price of the book.

Having purchased this book, you have access to the following online study materials:

CONTENT	ACCA (including FFA,FAB,FMA)		FIA (excluding FFA,FAB,FMA)	
	Text	Kit	Text	Kit
Electronic version of the book	✓	✓	✓	✓
Check Your Understanding Test with instant answers	✓			
Material updates	✓	✓	✓	✓
Latest official ACCA exam questions*		✓		
Extra question assistance using the signpost icon**		✓		
Timed questions with an online tutor debrief using clock icon***		✓		
Interim assessment including questions and answers	✓		✓	
Technical answers	✓	✓	✓	✓

*   Excludes F1, F2, F3, F4, FAB, FMA and FFA; for all other papers includes a selection of questions, as released by ACCA

**   For ACCA P1-P7 only

*** Excludes F1, F2, F3, F4, FAB, FMA and FFA

How to access your online resources

Kaplan Financial students will already have a MyKaplan account and these extra resources will be available to you online. You do not need to register again, as this process was completed when you enrolled. If you are having problems accessing online materials, please ask your course administrator.

If you are not studying with Kaplan and did not purchase your book via a Kaplan website, to unlock your extra online resources please go to www.mykaplan.co.uk/addabook (even if you have set up an account and registered books previously). You will then need to enter the ISBN number (on the title page and back cover) and the unique pass key number contained in the scratch panel below to gain access.

You will also be required to enter additional information during this process to set up or confirm your account details.

If you purchased through Kaplan Flexible Learning or via the Kaplan Publishing website you will automatically receive an e-mail invitation to MyKaplan. Please register your details using this email to gain access to your content. If you do not receive the e-mail or book content, please contact Kaplan Publishing.

Your Code and Information

This code can only be used once for the registration of one book online. This registration and your online content will expire when the final sittings for the examinations covered by this book have taken place. Please allow one hour from the time you submit your book details for us to process your request.

Please scratch the film to access your MyKaplan code.

Please be aware that this code is case-sensitive and you will need to include the dashes within the passcode, but not when entering the ISBN. For further technical support, please visit www.MyKaplan.co.uk

ACCA

Applied Skills

Audit and Assurance (AA)

Study Text

British library cataloguing-in-publication data

A catalogue record for this book is available from the British Library.

Published by:
Kaplan Publishing UK
Unit 2 The Business Centre
Molly Millars Lane
Wokingham
Berkshire
RG41 2QZ

ISBN 978-1-78740-396-3

© Kaplan Financial Limited, 2019

Acknowledgements

These materials are reviewed by the ACCA examining team. The objective of the review is to ensure that the material properly covers the syllabus and study guide outcomes, used by the examining team in setting the exams, in the appropriate breadth and depth. The review does not ensure that every eventuality, combination or application of examinable topics is addressed by the ACCA Approved Content. Nor does the review comprise a detailed technical check of the content as the Approved Content Provider has its own quality assurance processes in place in this respect.

This product includes content from the International Auditing and Assurance Standards Board (IAASB) and the International Ethics Standards Board for Accountants (IESBA), published by the International Federation of Accountants (IFAC) in 2017 and is used with permission of IFAC.

This product contains material that is ©Financial Reporting Council Ltd (FRC). Adapted and reproduced with the kind permission of the Financial Reporting Council. All rights reserved. For further information, please visit www.frc.org.uk or call +44 (0)20 7492 2300.

The IFRS Foundation logo, the IASB logo, the IFRS for SMEs logo, the "Hexagon Device", "IFRS Foundation", "eIFRS", "IAS", "IASB", "IFRS for SMEs", "IFRS", "IASs", "IFRSs", "International Accounting Standards" and "International Financial Reporting Standards", "IFRIC" and "IFRS Taxonomy" are Trade Marks of the IFRS Foundation.

Trade Marks

The IFRS Foundation logo, the IASB logo, the IFRS for SMEs logo, the "Hexagon Device", "IFRS Foundation", "eIFRS", "IAS", "IASB", "IFRS for SMEs", "NIIF" IASs" "IFRS", "IFRSs", "International Accounting Standards", "International Financial Reporting Standards", "IFRIC", "SIC" and "IFRS Taxonomy".

Further details of the Trade Marks including details of countries where the Trade Marks are registered or applied for are available from the Foundation on request.

Contents

Introduction

This document references IFRS® Standards and IAS® Standards, which are authored by the International Accounting Standards Board (the Board), and published in the 2018 IFRS Standards Red Book.

How to use the materials

These Kaplan Publishing learning materials have been carefully designed to make your learning experience as easy as possible and to give you the best chances of success in your examinations.

The product range contains a number of features to help you in the study process. They include:

(1)　Detailed study guide and syllabus objectives

(2)　Description of the examination

(3)　Study skills and revision guidance

(4)　Study text

(5)　Question practice

The sections on the study guide, the syllabus objectives, the examination and study skills should all be read before you commence your studies. They are designed to familiarise you with the nature and content of the examination and give you tips on how best to approach your learning.

The **Study text** comprises the main learning materials and gives guidance as to the importance of topics and where other related resources can be found. Each chapter includes

- The **learning objectives** contained in each chapter, which have been carefully mapped to the examining body's own syllabus learning objectives or outcomes. You should use these to check you have a clear understanding of all the topics on which you might be assessed in the examination.

- The **chapter diagram** provides a visual reference for the content in the chapter, giving an overview of the topics and how they link together.

- The **content** for each topic area commences with a brief explanation or definition to put the topic into context before covering the topic in detail. You should follow your studying of the content with a review of the illustration/s. These are worked examples which will help you to understand better how to apply the content for the topic.

- **Test your understanding** sections provide an opportunity to assess your understanding of the key topics by applying what you have learned to short questions. Answers can be found at the back of each chapter.

- **Summary diagrams** complete each chapter to show the important links between topics and the overall content of the syllabus. These diagrams should be used to check that you have covered and understood the core topics before moving on.

- **Question practice** is provided at the back of each text.

Quality and accuracy are of the utmost importance to us so if you spot an error in any of our products, please send an email to mykaplanreporting@kaplan.com with full details, or follow the link to the feedback form in MyKaplan.

Our Quality Coordinator will work with our technical team to verify the error and take action to ensure it is corrected in future editions.

Icon Explanations

 Supplementary reading –These sections will help to provide a deeper understanding of core areas. The supplementary reading is **NOT** optional reading. It is vital to provide you with the breadth of knowledge you will need to address the wide range of topics within your syllabus that could feature in an exam question. **Reference to this text is vital when self-studying**.

 Definition – Key definitions that you will need to learn from the core content.

 Key point – Identifies topics that are key to success and are often examined.

 New – Identifies topics that are brand new in exams that build on from earlier exams.

 Test your understanding – Exercises for you to complete to ensure that you have understood the topics just learned.

 Illustration – Worked examples help you understand the core content better.

 Tricky topic – When reviewing these areas care should be taken and all illustrations and Test your understanding exercises should be completed to ensure that the topic is understood.

 Tutorial note – Included to explain some of the technical points in more detail.

 Footsteps – Helpful tutor tips.

References to ISA paragraph numbers are for copyright purposes only. Students are not required to learn this level of detail.

On-line subscribers

Our on-line resources are designed to increase the flexibility of your learning materials and provide you with immediate feedback on how your studies are progressing.

If you are subscribed to our on-line resources you will find:

(1)   On-line reference ware: reproduces your Study Text on-line, giving you anytime, anywhere access.

(2)   On-line testing: provides you with additional on-line objective testing so you can practice what you have learned further.

(3)   On-line performance management: immediate access to your on-line testing results. Review your performance by key topics and chart your achievement through the course relative to your peer group.

Syllabus for September 2019 to June 2020

Syllabus background

The aim of ACCA Audit and Assurance is to develop knowledge and understanding of the process of carrying out the assurance engagement and its application in the context of the professional regulatory framework.

Objectives of the syllabus

- Explain the concept of audit and assurance and the functions of audit, corporate governance, including ethics and professional conduct.

- Demonstrate how the auditor obtains and accepts audit engagements, obtains an understanding of the entity and its environment, assesses the risk of material misstatement (whether arising from fraud or other irregularities) and plans an audit of financial statements.

- Describe and evaluate internal controls, techniques and audit tests, including IT systems to identify and communicate control risks and their potential consequences, making appropriate recommendations. Describe the scope, role and function of internal audit.

- Identify and describe the work and evidence obtained by the auditor and others required to meet the objectives of audit engagements and the application of the International Standards on Auditing.

- Explain how consideration of subsequent events and the going concern principle can inform the conclusions from audit work and are reflected in different types of auditor's report, written representations and the final review and report.

Core areas of the syllabus

- Audit framework and regulation.
- Planning and risk assessment.
- Internal control.
- Audit evidence.
- Review and reporting.

ACCA Performance Objectives

In order to become a member of the ACCA, as a trainee accountant you will need to demonstrate that you have achieved nine performance objectives. Performance objectives are indicators of effective performance and set the minimum standard of work that trainees are expected to achieve and demonstrate in the workplace. They are divided into key areas of knowledge which are closely linked to the exam syllabus.

There are five Essential performance objectives and a choice of fifteen Technical performance objectives which are divided into five areas.

The performance objectives which link to this exam are:

(1)	Ethics and professionalism (Essential)

(2)	Governance risk and control (Essential)

(3)	Prepare for and plan the audit process (Technical)

(4)	Collect and evaluate evidence for an audit (Technical)

(5)	Review and report on the findings of an audit (Technical)

The following link provides an in depth insight into all of the performance objectives:

https://www.accaglobal.com/content/dam/ACCA_Global/Students/per/PER-Performance-objectives-achieve.pdf

Progression

There are two elements of progression that we can measure: first how quickly students move through individual topics within a subject; and second how quickly they move from one course to the next. We know that there is an optimum for both, but it can vary from subject to subject and from student to student. However, using data and our experience of student performance over many years, we can make some generalisations.

A fixed period of study set out at the start of a course with key milestones is important. This can be within a subject, for example 'I will finish this topic by 30 June', or for overall achievement, such as 'I want to be qualified by the end of next year'.

Your qualification is cumulative, as earlier papers provide a foundation for your subsequent studies, so do not allow there to be too big a gap between one subject and another. We know that exams encourage techniques that lead to some degree of short term retention, the result being that you will simply forget much of what you have already learned unless it is refreshed (look up Ebbinghaus Forgetting Curve for more details on this). This makes it more difficult as you move from one subject to another: not only will you have to learn the new subject, you will also have to relearn all the underpinning knowledge as well. This is very inefficient and slows down your overall progression which makes it more likely you may not succeed at all.

In addition, delaying your studies slows your path to qualification which can have negative impacts on your career, postponing the opportunity to apply for higher level positions and therefore higher pay.

You can use the following diagram showing the whole structure of your qualification to help you keep track of your progress.

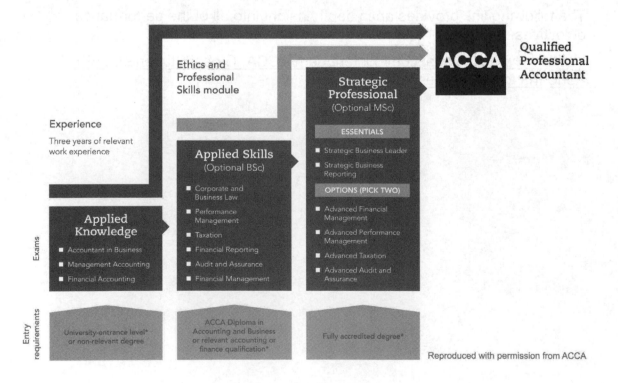

Reproduced with permission from ACCA

Syllabus objectives and chapter references

We have reproduced the ACCA's syllabus below, showing where the objectives are explored within this book. Within the chapters, we have broken down the extensive information found in the syllabus into easily digestible and relevant sections, called Content Objectives. These correspond to the objectives at the beginning of each chapter.

Syllabus learning objective	Chapter reference
A AUDIT FRAMEWORK AND REGULATION	
1 The concept of audit and other assurance engagements	
(a) Identify and describe the objective and general principles of external audit engagements. [2]	1
(b) Explain the nature and development of audit and other assurance engagements. [1]	1
(c) Discuss the concepts of accountability, stewardship and agency. [2]	1
(d) Define and provide the objectives of an assurance engagement. [1]	1
(e) Explain the five elements of an assurance engagement. [2]	1
(f) Describe the types of assurance engagement. [2]	1
(g) Explain the level of assurance provided by an external audit and other review engagements and the concept of true and fair presentation. [1]	1
2 External audits	
(a) Describe the regulatory environment within which external audits take place. [1]	2
(b) Discuss the reasons and mechanisms for the regulation of auditors. [1]	2
(c) Explain the statutory regulations governing the appointment, rights, removal and resignation of auditors. [1]	2
(d) Explain the regulations governing the rights and duties of auditors. [1]	2
(e) Describe the limitations of external audits. [1]	1
(f) Explain the development and status of International Standards on Auditing (ISAs). [1]	2
(g) Explain the relationship between International Standards on Auditing and national standards. [1]	2

Syllabus learning objective			Chapter reference
3	**Corporate governance**		
	(a)	Discuss the objectives, relevance and importance of corporate governance. [2]	3
	(b)	Discuss the provisions of international codes of corporate governance (such as OECD) that are most relevant to auditors. [2]	3
	(c)	Describe good corporate governance requirements relating to directors' responsibilities (e.g. for risk management and internal control) and the reporting responsibilities of auditors. [2]	3
	(d)	Evaluate corporate governance deficiencies and provide recommendations to allow compliance with international codes of corporate governance. [2]	3
	(e)	Analyse the structure and roles of audit committees and discuss their benefits and limitations. [2]	3
	(f)	Explain the importance of internal control and risk management. [1]	3
4	**Professional ethics and ACCA's Code of Ethics and Conduct**		
	(a)	Define and apply the fundamental principles of professional ethics of integrity, objectivity, professional competence and due care, confidentiality and professional behaviour. [2]	4
	(b)	Define and apply the conceptual framework, including the threats to the fundamental principles of self-interest, self-review, advocacy, familiarity, and intimidation. [2]	4
	(c)	Discuss the safeguards to offset the threats to the fundamental principles. [2]	4
	(d)	Describe the auditor's responsibility with regard to auditor independence, conflicts of interest and confidentiality. [1]	4
B	**PLANNING AND RISK ASSESSMENT**		
1	**Obtaining, accepting and continuing audit engagements**		
	(a)	Discuss the requirements of professional ethics and ISAs in relation to the acceptance/continuance of audit engagements. [2]	4
	(b)	Explain the preconditions for an audit. [2]	4
	(c)	Explain the process by which an auditor obtains an audit engagement. [2]	4

Syllabus learning objective			Chapter reference
	(d)	Discuss the importance of engagement letters and their contents. [1]	4
	(e)	Explain the overall objectives and importance of quality control procedures in conducting an audit. [2]	6
	(f)	Explain the quality control procedures that should be in place over engagement performance, monitoring quality and compliance with ethical requirements. [2]	6
2	**Objective and general principles**		
	(a)	Identify the overall objectives of the auditor and the need to conduct an audit in accordance with ISAs. [2]	1 & 6
	(b)	Explain the need to plan and perform audits with an attitude of professional scepticism, and to exercise professional judgment. [2]	5
3	**Assessing audit risks**		
	(a)	Explain the components of audit risk. [1]	5
	(b)	Describe the audit risks in the financial statements and explain the auditor's response to each risk. [2]	5
	(c)	Define and explain the concepts of materiality and performance materiality. [2]	5
	(d)	Explain and calculate materiality levels from financial information. [2]	5
4	**Understanding the entity and its environment**		
	(a)	Explain how auditors obtain an initial understanding of the entity and its environment. [2]	5
	(b)	Describe and explain the nature and purpose of analytical procedures in planning. [2]	5
	(c)	Compute and interpret key ratios used in analytical procedures. [2]	5
5	**Fraud, laws and regulations**		
	(a)	Discuss the effect of fraud and misstatements on the audit strategy and extent of audit work. [2]	6
	(b)	Discuss the responsibilities of internal and external auditors for the prevention and detection of fraud and error. [2]	6
	(c)	Explain the auditor's responsibility to consider laws and regulations. [2]	6

Syllabus learning objective			Chapter reference

6 Audit planning and documentation

(a) Identify and explain the need for and importance of planning an audit. [2] — 6

(b) Identify and describe the contents of the overall audit strategy and audit plan. [2] — 6

(c) Explain and describe the relationship between the overall audit strategy and the audit plan. [2] — 6

(d) Explain the difference between interim and final audit. [1] — 6

(e) Describe the purpose of an interim audit, and the procedures likely to be adopted at this stage in the audit. [2] — 6

(f) Describe the impact of the work performed during the interim audit on the final audit. [2] — 6

(g) Explain the need for and the importance of audit documentation. [1] — 6

(h) Describe the form and contents of working papers and supporting documentation. [2] — 6

(i) Explain the procedures to ensure safe custody and retention of working papers. [1] — 6

C INTERNAL CONTROL

1 Internal control systems

(a) Explain why an auditor needs to obtain an understanding of internal control relevant to the audit. [1] — 8

(b) Describe and explain the five components of internal control. [2] — 8

(i) the control environment

(ii) the entity's risk assessment process

(iii) the information system, including the related business processes, relevant to financial reporting, and communication

(iv) control activities relevant to the audit

(v) monitoring of controls.

Syllabus learning objective			Chapter reference

2 The use and evaluation of internal control systems by auditors

(a) Explain how auditors record internal control systems including the use of, narrative notes, flowcharts and questionnaires. [2]   8

(b) Evaluate internal control components, including deficiencies and significant deficiencies in internal control. [2]   8

(c) Discuss the limitations of internal control components. [2]   8

3 Tests of controls

(a) Describe computer systems controls including general IT controls and application controls. [2]   8

(b) Describe control objectives, control procedures, control activities, key controls and tests of control in relation to: 8

   (i) The sales system

   (ii) The purchases system

   (iii) The payroll system

   (iv) The inventory system

   (v) The cash system

   (vi) Non-current assets.

4 Communication on internal control

(a) Discuss the requirements and methods of how reporting significant deficiencies in internal control are provided to management and those charged with governance. [2]   8

(b) Explain, in a format suitable for inclusion in a report to management significant deficiencies within an internal control system and provide recommendations for overcoming these deficiencies to management. [2]   8

(c) Discuss the need for auditors to communicate with those charged with governance. [2]   8 & 12

5 Internal audit and governance, and the differences between external audit and internal audit

(a) Discuss the factors to be taken into account when assessing the need for internal audit. [2]   9

(b) Discuss the elements of best practice in the structure and operations of internal audit. [2]   9

(c) Compare and contrast the role of external and internal audit. [2]   9

Syllabus learning objective			Chapter reference

6 The scope of the internal audit function, outsourcing and internal audit assignments

(a) Discuss the scope of internal audit and the limitations of the internal audit function. [2]   9

(b) Explain outsourcing and the associated advantages and disadvantages of outsourcing the internal audit function. [1]   9

(c) Discuss the nature and purpose of internal audit assignments including value for money, IT, financial, regulatory compliance, fraud investigations and customer experience. [2]   9

(d) Discuss the nature and purpose of operational internal audit assignments. [2]   9

(e) Describe the format and content of internal audit review reports and make appropriate recommendations to management and those charged with governance. [2]   9

D AUDIT EVIDENCE

1 Financial statement assertions and audit evidence

(a) Explain the assertions contained in the financial statements about: [2]   7

    (i) Classes of transactions and events and related disclosures

    (ii) Account balances and related disclosures at the period end.

(b) Describe audit procedures to obtain audit evidence, including inspection, observation, external confirmation, recalculation, re-performance, analytical procedures and enquiry. [2]   7

(c) Discuss the quality and quantity of audit evidence. [2]   7

(d) Discuss the relevance and reliability of audit evidence. [2]   7

2 Audit procedures

(a) Discuss substantive procedures for obtaining audit evidence. [2]   7

(b) Discuss and provide examples of how analytical procedures are used as substantive procedures. [2]   7

(c) Discuss the problems associated with the audit and review of accounting estimates. [2]   10

Syllabus learning objective			Chapter reference
	(d)	Describe why smaller entities may have different control environments and describe the types of evidence likely to be available in smaller entities. [1]	10
	(e)	Discuss the difference between tests of control and substantive procedures. [2]	7
3	**Audit sampling and other means of testing**		
	(a)	Define audit sampling and explain the need for sampling. [1]	7
	(b)	Identify and discuss the differences between statistical and non-statistical sampling. [2]	7
	(c)	Discuss and provide relevant examples of, the application of the basic principles of statistical sampling and other selective testing procedures. [2]	7
	(d)	Discuss the results of statistical sampling, including consideration of whether additional testing is required. [2]	7
4	**The audit of specific items**		

For each of the account balances stated in this sub-capability:

Explain the audit objectives and the audit procedures to obtain sufficient, appropriate evidence in relation to:

(a)	Receivables: [2]		10
	(i)	direct confirmation of accounts receivable	
	(ii)	other evidence in relation to receivables and prepayments	
	(iii)	other evidence in relation to current assets	
	(iv)	completeness and occurrence of revenue.	
(b)	Inventory: [2]		10
	(i)	inventory counting procedures in relation to year-end and continuous inventory systems	
	(ii)	cut-off testing	
	(iii)	auditor's attendance at inventory counting	
	(iv)	direct confirmation of inventory held by third parties	
	(v)	valuation	
	(vi)	other evidence in relation to inventory.	

Syllabus learning objective			Chapter reference
4	**Audit finalisation and the final review**		
	(a)	Discuss the importance of the overall review in ensuring that sufficient, appropriate evidence has been obtained. [2]	11
	(b)	Describe procedures an auditor should perform in conducting their overall review of financial statements. [2]	11
	(c)	Explain the significance of uncorrected misstatements. [1]	11
	(d)	Evaluate the effect of dealing with uncorrected misstatements. [2]	11
5	**The Independent Auditor's Report**		
	(a)	Identify and describe the basic elements contained in the independent auditor's report. [1]	12
	(b)	Explain unmodified audit opinions in the auditor's report. [2]	12
	(c)	Explain modified audit opinions in the auditor's report. [2]	12
	(d)	Describe the format and content of key audit matters, emphasis of matter and other matter paragraphs. [2]	12

The superscript numbers in square brackets indicate the intellectual depth at which the subject area could be assessed within the examination. Level 1 (knowledge and comprehension) broadly equates with the Knowledge module, Level 2 (application and analysis) with the Skills module and Level 3 (synthesis and evaluation) to the Professional level. However, lower level skills can continue to be assessed as you progress through each module and level.

For a list of examinable documents, see the ACCA website:

accaglobal.com/audit-and-assurance

The Examination

Examination format

The syllabus is assessed by computer-based examination (CBE).

The CBE will contain 100 marks of exam content that needs to be completed within 3 hours. Prior to the start of the exam candidates are given an extra 10 minutes to read the exam instructions.

All questions are compulsory. The exam will contain both computational and discursive elements.

Some questions will adopt a scenario/case study approach.

Section A

Section A of the exam comprises three 10 mark case-based questions. Each case has five objective test questions worth 2 marks each.

There are no dependencies between the individual questions. Therefore, if you get one question wrong, it will not affect your ability to get the others correct.

OT questions in section A will be of varying styles as follows:

- Multiple choice – where you are required to choose one answer from a list of options provided by clicking on the appropriate 'radio button'.

- Multiple response – where you are required to select more than one response from the options provided by clicking on the appropriate tick boxes. The question will specify how many answers need to be selected, but the system won't stop you from selecting more answers than this.

- Fill in the blank – where you are required to type an answer into a box (usually numerical, but may be text). Any specific rounding requirements will be displayed.

- Drag and drop – where you are required to drag an answer and drop it into place. Some questions could involve matching more than one answer to a response area and some questions may have more answer choices than response areas, which means not all available answer choices need to be used.

- Drop down list – where you are required to select one answer from a drop down list. Some questions may contain more than one drop down list and an answer has to be selected from each one.

- Hot spot – where you are required to select one point on an image as your answer. When the cursor is hovered over the image, it will display as an 'X'. To answer, place the X on the appropriate point on the diagram.

- Hot area – these are similar to hot spot questions, but instead of selecting a specific point, you are required to select one or more areas in an image.

Section B

Section B of the exam comprises one 30 mark question and two 20 mark questions.

This section of the exam will predominantly examine one or more aspects of audit and assurance from planning and risk assessment, internal control or audit evidence, although topics from other syllabus areas may also be included.

Examination tips

Be sure you understand how to use the software before you start the exam. If in doubt, ask the assessment centre staff to explain it to you.

Questions are displayed on the screen and answers are entered using keyboard and mouse.

We recommend that 10 minutes should be spent reviewing the format and content of the requirements so that you understand what you need to do. Pay particular attention to section B, where questions will be based on longer scenarios than the 2 mark OT cases in section A.

Read each question carefully.

- Divide the time you spend on questions in proportion to the marks on offer.

- One suggestion for this examination is to allocate 1.8 minutes to each mark available (180 minutes/100 marks), so a 20 mark question should be completed in approximately 36 minutes.

Section A

You should begin by reading the OT questions that relate to the case, so that when you read through the information for the first time, you know what it is that you are required to do.

Once you have read through the information, you should first answer any of the OT questions that can be quickly answered. You should then attempt the other OT questions utilising the remaining time for that case.

If you don't know the answer, eliminate those options you know are incorrect and see if the answer becomes more obvious. After you have eliminated the options that you know to be wrong, if you are still unsure, guess.

Answer every question.

Each OT question is worth two marks. Therefore you have 18 minutes (1.8 minutes per mark) to answer the five OT questions relating to each case. It is likely that all of the cases will take the same length of time to answer, although some of the OT questions within a case may be quicker than other OT questions within that same case.

Work steadily. Rushing leads to careless mistakes and the OT questions are designed to include answers which result from careless mistakes.

Section A questions can be found at the end of each chapter.

Section B

The constructed response questions in section B will require a written response rather than being OT questions. Therefore, different techniques need to be used to score well.

Unless you know exactly how to answer the question, spend some time planning your answer. Stick to the question and tailor your answer to what you are asked. Pay particular attention to the verbs in the question e.g. 'Describe', 'State', 'Explain'.

If you get completely stuck with a question leave it and return to it later.

If you do not understand what a question is asking, state your assumptions. Even if you do not answer in precisely the way the examining team hoped, you may be given some credit, provided that your assumptions are reasonable.

When answering the constructed response questions, be concise. DO NOT write an essay.

Make sure that each point is clearly identifiable by leaving a line space between each of your points.

Some questions ask you to present your answer in the form of a report or letter. Use the correct format as there are easy marks to gain here for presentation.

Section B style questions can be found in most chapters and also in Chapter 15.

All sections

Don't skip parts of the syllabus. The AA syllabus has 18 different questions so the examination can cover a very broad selection of the syllabus each sitting.

Spend time learning definitions.

Practice plenty of questions to improve your ability to apply the techniques.

Spend the last few minutes reading through your answers and making any additions or corrections.

Don't panic if you realise you've answered a question incorrectly. Try to remain calm, continue to apply examination technique and answer all questions required within the time available.

ACCA support

For additional support with your studies please also refer to the ACCA Global website.

Study skills and revision guidance

This section aims to give guidance on how to study for your ACCA exams and to give ideas on how to improve your existing study techniques.

Preparing to study

Set your objectives

Before starting to study decide what you want to achieve i.e. the type of pass you wish to obtain. This will decide the level of commitment and time you need to dedicate to your studies.

Devise a study plan

Determine which times of the week you will study.

Split these times into sessions of at least one hour for study of new material. Any shorter periods could be used for revision or practice.

Put the times you plan to study onto a study plan for the weeks from now until the exam and set yourself targets for each period of study. In your sessions make sure you cover the course, course assignments and revision.

If you are studying for more than one exam at a time, try to vary your subjects as this can help you to keep interested and see subjects as part of wider knowledge.

When working through your course, compare your progress with your plan and, if necessary, re-plan your work (perhaps including extra sessions) or, if you are ahead, do some extra revision/practice questions.

Effective studying

Active reading

You are not expected to learn the text by rote, rather, you must understand what you are reading and be able to use it to pass the exam and develop good practice. A good technique to use is SQ3Rs – Survey, Question, Read, Recall, Review:

(1) **Survey the chapter** – look at the headings and read the introduction, summary and objectives, to get an overview of what the chapter deals with.

(2) **Question** – whilst undertaking the survey, ask yourself the questions that you hope the chapter will answer for you.

(3) **Read** through the chapter thoroughly, answering the questions and making sure you can meet the objectives. Attempt the exercises and activities in the text, and work through all the examples.

KAPLAN PUBLISHING

(4)   **Recall** – at the end of each section and at the end of the chapter, try to recall the main ideas of the section/chapter without referring to the text. This is best done after a short break of a couple of minutes after the reading stage.

(5)   **Review** – check that your recall notes are correct.

You may also find it helpful to re-read the chapter to try to see the topic(s) it deals with as a whole.

Note-taking

Taking notes is a useful way of learning, but do not simply copy out the text. The notes must:

- be in your own words
- be concise
- cover the key points
- be well-organised
- be modified as you study further chapters in this text or in related ones.

Trying to summarise a chapter without referring to the text can be a useful way of determining which areas you know and which you don't.

Summarise the key points of a chapter.

Three ways of taking notes:

(1)   **Make linear notes** – a list of headings, divided up with subheadings listing the key points. If you use linear notes, you can use different colours to highlight key points and keep topic areas together. Use plenty of space to make your notes easy to use.

(2)   **Try a diagrammatic form** – the most common of which is a mind-map. To make a mind-map, put the main heading in the centre of the paper and put a circle around it. Then draw short lines radiating from this to the main subheadings, which again have circles around them. Then continue the process from the sub-headings to sub-sub-headings, advantages, disadvantages, etc.

(3)   **Highlighting and underlining** – you may find it useful to underline or highlight key points in your study text – but do be selective. You may also wish to make notes in the margins.

Revision

The best approach to revision is to revise the course as you work through it. Also try to leave four to six weeks before the exam for final revision. Make sure you cover the whole syllabus and pay special attention to those areas where your knowledge is weak. Here are some recommendations:

Read through the text and your notes again and condense your notes into key phrases. It may help to put key revision points onto index cards to look at when you have a few minutes to spare.

Review any assignments you have completed and look at where you lost marks – put more work into those areas where you were weak.

Practise exam standard questions under timed conditions. If you are short of time, list the points that you would cover in your answer and then read the model answer, but do try to complete at least a few questions under exam conditions.

Also practise producing answer plans and comparing them to the model answer.

If you are stuck on a topic find somebody (a tutor) to explain it to you.

Read good newspapers and professional journals, especially ACCA's **Student Accountant**, this can give you an advantage in the exam.

Ensure you **know the structure of the exam** – how many questions and of what type you will be expected to answer.

During your revision attempt all the different styles of questions you may be asked.

Further reading

You can find further reading and technical articles under the student section of ACCA's website.

Technical update

This text has been updated to reflect Examinable Documents September 2019 to June 2020 issued by ACCA.

KAPLAN PUBLISHING

Introduction to assurance

Chapter learning objectives

This chapter covers syllabus areas:

- A1 – The concept of audit and other assurance engagements

- A2e – Limitations of external audits

Detailed syllabus objectives are provided in the introduction section of the text book.

PER

One of the PER performance objectives (PO4) is governance risk and control. You contribute to effective governance in your area. You evaluate, monitor and implement risk management procedures, complying with the spirit and the letter of policies, laws and regulations. Working through this chapter should help you understand how to demonstrate that objective.

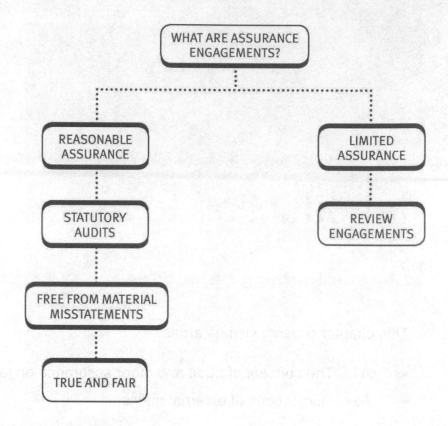

1 What is assurance?

An assurance engagement is: 'An engagement in which a practitioner obtains sufficient appropriate evidence in order to express a conclusion designed to enhance the degree of confidence of the intended users other than the responsible party about the outcome of the evaluation or measurement of a subject matter against criteria.'

[International Framework for Assurance Engagements, 10]

Giving assurance means offering an opinion about specific information so the users of that information are able to make **confident decisions** knowing that the **risk** of the information being 'incorrect' is **reduced**.

There are **five elements of an assurance engagement**:

	Element	Explanation	In relation to an audit
(i)	Three party involvement	Practitioner (the reviewer of the subject matter who provides the assurance)	Auditor
		Intended users (of the information)	Shareholders
		Responsible party (those responsible for preparing the subject matter)	Directors
(ii)	Appropriate subject matter	The information subject to examination by the practitioner	Financial statements
(iii)	Suitable criteria	The subject matter is evaluated against the suitable criteria	Financial reporting framework
(iv)	Sufficient appropriate evidence	Sufficient appropriate evidence is needed to provide a basis for the opinion/conclusion	Sufficient appropriate evidence is obtained by performing audit procedures
(v)	Written assurance report in an appropriate form	The output of the assurance engagement expressing a conclusion/opinion about the subject matter	Independent auditor's report providing an opinion as to whether the financial statements give a true and fair view

[International Framework for Assurance Engagements]

Illustration 1 – Buying a house

Consider someone who is buying a house. There is a risk that someone pays a large sum of money to purchase a structurally unsafe property which needs further expenditure to make it habitable. To reduce this risk, it is normal for house buyers (the users) to pay a property surveyor (the practitioner) to perform a structural assessment of the house (the subject matter). The surveyor would then report back (written report) to the house buyer identifying any structural deficiencies (measured against building regulations/best practice and other criteria). With this information the potential buyer can then make their decision whether or not to buy the house with the confidence that they know its structural condition. In this example, the responsible party is the current house owner, and the evidence would largely be obtained through visual inspection of the property.

Assurance engagements

Examples of assurance engagements include:

- Audit of financial statements
- Review of financial statements
- Systems reliability reports
- Verification of social and environmental information
- Review of internal controls
- Value for money audit in public sector organisations.

General principles the assurance provider must follow when performing such engagements include:

- Comply with ethical requirements.
- Apply professional scepticism and judgment.
- Perform acceptance and continuance procedures to ensure only work of acceptable risk is accepted.
- Agree the terms of engagement.
- Comply with quality control requirements (ISQC 1).
- Plan and perform the engagement effectively.
- Obtain sufficient appropriate evidence.
- Consider the effect of subsequent events on the subject matter.
- Form a conclusion expressing either reasonable or limited assurance as appropriate.
- The evidence should be documented to provide a record of the basis for the assurance report.

Types of assurance engagement

Two types of assurance engagement are permitted:

- Reasonable
- Limited.

Reasonable assurance engagements	Limited assurance engagement
The practitioner:	The practitioner:
Gathers **sufficient appropriate evidence** to be able to draw **reasonable conclusions**	Gathers **sufficient appropriate evidence** to be able to draw **limited conclusions**
Concludes that the subject matter **conforms in all material respects** with identified suitable criteria	Concludes that the subject matter, with respect to identified suitable criteria, is **plausible in the circumstances**
Gives a **positively** worded assurance **opinion**	Gives a **negatively** worded assurance **conclusion**
Gives a **high level** of assurance (confidence)	Gives a **moderate or lower level** of assurance than that of an audit
Performs very thorough procedures to obtain sufficient appropriate evidence – tests of controls and substantive procedures	Performs significantly fewer procedures – mainly enquiries and analytical procedures
In our opinion, the financial statements give a true and fair view of (or *present fairly, in all material respects*) the financial position of Murray Company as at December 31, 20X4, and of its financial performance and its cash flows for the year then ended in accordance with International Financial Reporting Standards.	**Nothing has come to our attention** that causes us to believe that the financial statements of Murray Company as of 31 December, 20X4 are not prepared, in all material respects, in accordance with an applicable financial reporting framework.

The confidence inspired by a reasonable assurance report is designed to be greater than that inspired by a limited assurance report.

Therefore:

- There are more regulations/standards governing a reasonable assurance assignment.

- The procedures carried out in a reasonable assurance assignment will be more thorough.

- The evidence gathered will need to be of a higher quality.

2 External audit engagements

An external audit is an example of a **reasonable assurance** engagement.

Purpose of an external audit engagement

ISA 200 *Overall Objectives of the Independent Auditor and the Conduct of an Audit in Accordance with International Standards on Auditing* states the purpose of an external audit engagement is to **'enhance the degree of confidence of intended users in financial statements.'**

This is achieved by the auditor expressing an opinion on whether the financial statements:

- Give a true and fair view (or present fairly in all material respects).

- Are prepared, in all material respects, in accordance with an applicable financial reporting framework.

[ISA 200, 3]

 The financial reporting framework to be applied will vary from country to country. In Audit & Assurance, it is assumed that International Financial Reporting Standards are the basis for preparing the financial statements.

True and fair

- **True:** factually correct information which conforms with accounting standards and relevant legislation, and agrees with the underlying records.

- **Fair:** clear, impartial and unbiased information which reflects the commercial substance of the transactions of the entity.

Objectives of the auditor

The objectives of an **auditor** are to:

- Obtain reasonable assurance about whether the financial statements as a whole are free from material misstatement, whether due to fraud or error.

- Express an opinion on whether the financial statements are prepared, in all material respects, in accordance with an applicable financial reporting framework.

- Report on the financial statements, and communicate as required by ISAs, in accordance with the auditor's findings.

[ISA 200, 11]

Need for external audit

- Shareholders provide the finance for a company and may or may not be involved in the day to day running of the company.

- Directors manage the company on behalf of the shareholders in order to achieve the objectives of that company (normally the maximisation of shareholder wealth).

- The directors must prepare financial statements to provide information on performance and financial position to the shareholders.

- The directors have various incentives to manipulate the financial statements and show a different level of performance.

- Hence the need for an independent review of the financial statements to ensure they give a true and fair view – the external audit.

In most developed countries, publicly quoted companies and large companies are required by law to produce annual financial statements and have them audited by an external auditor.

Companies that are not required to have a statutory audit may choose to have an external audit because the company's shareholders or other influential stakeholders want one and because of the benefits of an audit.

Benefits of an audit

- Higher quality information which is more reliable improving the reputation of the market.

- Independent scrutiny and verification may be valuable to management.

- Reduces the risk of management bias, fraud and error by acting as a deterrent. An audit may also detect bias, fraud and error.

- Enhances the credibility of the financial statements, e.g. for tax authorities or lenders.

- Deficiencies in the internal control system may be highlighted by the auditor.

Expectation gap

Some users incorrectly believe that an audit provides absolute assurance – that the audit opinion is a guarantee the financial statements are 'correct'. This and other misconceptions about the role of an auditor are referred to as the **'expectation gap'**.

Examples of the expectation gap

- A belief that auditors test **all** transactions and balances – they test on a sample basis.

- A belief that auditors are required to detect **all** fraud – auditors are required to provide reasonable assurance that the financial statements are free from **material** misstatement, which may be caused by fraud.

- A belief that auditors are responsible for **preparing** the financial statements – this is the responsibility of management.

Limitations of an audit

- **F**inancial statements include subjective estimates and other judgmental matters.

- **I**nternal controls may be relied on which have their own inherent limitations.

- **R**epresentations from management may have to be relied upon as the only source of evidence in some areas.

- **E**vidence is often persuasive not conclusive.

- **D**o not test all transactions and balances. Auditors test on a sample basis.

 Auditors provide reasonable assurance which is not absolute assurance. The **limitations of an audit** mean that it is not possible to provide a 100% guarantee.

Limitations of an audit
• Nature of financial reporting – financial statement amounts are affected by management judgment and therefore subject to bias.
• Nature of audit procedures – information provided by the client may be incomplete or falsified documents may be provided.
• Timeliness of financial reporting – the relevance of information diminishes over time and the auditor cannot investigate every matter exhaustively.
[ISA 200, A48 – A50]

3 Review engagements

A review engagement is an example of a **limited assurance** engagement.

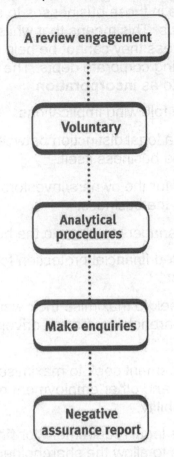

Purpose and objective of a review engagement

A company which is not legally required to have an audit may choose to have a review of their financial statements instead. The review will still provide some assurance to users but is likely to cost less and be less disruptive than an audit.

The procedures will mainly focus on analytical procedures and enquiries of management. In particular, no tests of controls will be performed.

As only limited assurance is being expressed, the work does not need to be as in depth as for an audit.

The **objective of a review of financial statements** is to enable an auditor to state whether, on the basis of procedures which do not provide all the evidence required in an audit, anything has come to the auditor's attention that causes the auditor to believe that the financial statements are not prepared in accordance with the applicable financial reporting framework.

Incorporation and the separation of ownership and control

Businesses can operate through a number of different vehicles. It is common for investors in those businesses to seek the protection of limited company status. This means that whilst they could lose the funds they invest in a business they cannot be held personally responsible for satisfying the remaining corporate debts. The creation of a limited company is referred to as **incorporation**.

Incorporation has the following implications:

- The creation of a legal distinction between the owners of the business and the business itself.

- The opportunity for the owners/investors to detach themselves from the operation of the business.

- The need for managers to operate the business on a daily basis.

Whilst this has provided financial protection for shareholders it does lead to a significant conflict:

- Shareholders seek to maximise their wealth through the increasing value of their shareholding. This is driven by the profitability of the company.

- Directors/management seek to maximise their wealth through salary, bonuses and other employment benefits. This reduces company profitability.

This conflict led to the legal requirement for **financial statements** to be produced by directors to allow the shareholders to assess the performance of management.

Accountability, agency and stewardship

Key definitions:

Accountability means that people in a position of power can be held to account for their actions, i.e. they can be compelled to explain their decisions and can be criticised or punished if they have abused their position.

Accountability is central to the concept of good corporate governance – the process of ensuring that companies are well run – which we will look at in more detail in the chapter 'Corporate governance'.

Agency occurs when one party, the principal, employs another party, the agent, to perform a task on their behalf.

KAPLAN PUBLISHING

Stewardship is the responsibility to take good care of resources. A steward is a person entrusted with management of another person's property, for example, when one person is paid to look after another person's house while the owner goes abroad on holiday. The steward is accountable for the way he carries out his role.

This relationship, where one person has a duty of care towards someone else is known as a **'fiduciary relationship'**.

A **fiduciary relationship** is a relationship of 'good faith' such as that between the directors of a company and the shareholders of the company. There is a 'separation of ownership and control' in the sense that the shareholders own the company, while the directors make the decisions. The directors must make their decisions in the interests of the shareholders rather than in their own selfish personal interests.

Therefore:

- The directors are the stewards of the company.

- The shareholder is the principal, employing the directors (the agents) to run the company on their behalf.

- The directors are accountable to the shareholders for the way in which they run the company.

Examples of stakeholders groups

Stakeholder groups with an interest in the financial statements

- Shareholders can decide whether to alter their shareholdings.

- Employees may be able to judge whether they think their levels of pay are adequate compared to the directors. They may also be interested in the results of the company as this may impact their employment decisions.

- Those charged with governance can see whether they think management have struck the right balance between their own need for reward (remuneration, share options, etc) and the needs of other stakeholders.

- Customers can make judgments about whether the company has sufficient financial strength (i.e. liquidity) to justify future trading.

- Suppliers and lenders can assess financial stability before giving credit.

- The government can decide whether the right amounts of tax have been paid and whether the company appears to be compliant with the relevant laws and regulations.

Test your understanding 1

List and explain the elements of an assurance engagement.

(5 marks)

Test your understanding 2

Explain the term 'limited assurance' in the context of an examination of a company's cash flow forecast and explain how this differs from the assurance provided by an external audit.

(5 marks)

Test your understanding 3

Your firm has been approached to perform the external audit of Perth Co. Perth Co has grown over the last two years and has now reached the audit threshold. As this is the first year the company has required an audit, the directors are unsure about the purpose of the audit. They have been informed that an audit need not be as inconvenient or intrusive as they expect it to be as there are additional benefits that may arise from having an audit. The directors have indicated that they expect your firm to detect every fraud and error in their accounting records so that when they need to apply for finance to help them grow further, they can use the audited financial statements to support the loan application and this should make it easier to get the loan.

(1) **What level of assurance will be provided by the independent auditor's report?**

A   Absolute

B   Reasonable

C   Moderate

D   Limited

(2) **Which of the following is NOT one of the five elements of an assurance engagement?**

A   Subject matter

B   Suitable criteria

C   Assurance file

D   Written report

(3) **Which of the following is NOT a benefit of an audit?**

A   Increased credibility of the financial statements

B   Deficiencies in controls may be identified during testing

C   Fraud may be detected during the audit

D   Sampling is used

(4) **Which of the following statements is false?**

A   The auditor will express an opinion as to whether the financial statements give a true and fair view

B   The auditor must obtain sufficient appropriate evidence to be able to form an audit opinion

C   If the financial statements are found to contain material misstatements a negative audit opinion will be given

D   An audit may not detect all fraud and error in the financial statements

(5) **Which of the following are examples of the expectation gap?**

(i)   The independent auditor's report confirms the financial statements are accurate.

(ii)   An unmodified opinion means the company is a going concern.

(iii)   The auditor tests all transactions.

(iv)   The auditor can be sued for negligence if they issue an inappropriate opinion.

A   (i), (ii) and (iii)

B   (i), (ii) and (iv)

C   (i) and (ii) only

D   (ii) and (iii) only

4 Chapter summary

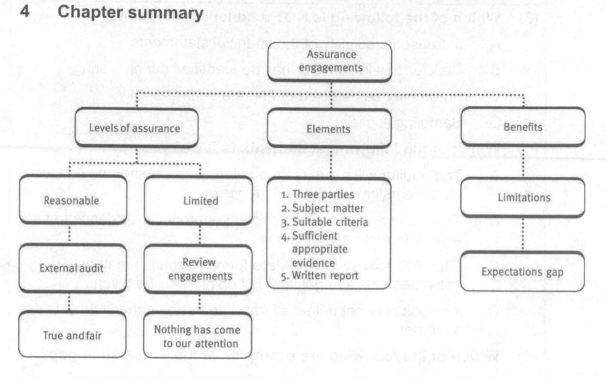

Test your understanding answers

Test your understanding 1

(1) An assurance engagement will involve three separate parties:

    (i) Intended user who is the person who requires the assurance report.

    (ii) Responsible party, which is the person or organisation responsible for preparing the subject matter to be reviewed.

    (iii) Practitioner (i.e. an accountant) who is the professional, who will review the subject matter and provide the assurance.

(2) A suitable subject matter. The subject matter is the data that the responsible party has prepared and which requires verification.

(3) Suitable criteria. The subject matter is compared to the criteria in order for it to be assessed and an opinion provided.

(4) Sufficient appropriate evidence has to be obtained by the practitioner in order to give the required level of assurance.

(5) An assurance report contains the opinion that is given by the practitioner to the intended user.

Test your understanding 2

Limited Assurance	Assurance provided by an external audit
Limited assurance is a moderate level of assurance.	An audit provides reasonable assurance, which is a high level.
The objective of a limited assurance engagement is to obtain sufficient appropriate evidence that the cash flow forecast is plausible in the circumstances i.e. prepared on the basis of reasonable assumptions.	The objective of an audit is to obtain sufficient appropriate evidence that the financial statements conform in all material respects with the relevant financial reporting framework.

A limited assurance report provides a negative conclusion. The practitioner will state that nothing has come to their attention which indicates that the assumptions used to prepare the cash flow forecast are not reasonable. The assurance is therefore given on the absence of any indication to the contrary.	More evidence will need to be obtained to provide reasonable assurance, and a wider range of procedures performed, including tests of controls.
With limited assurance, limited procedures are performed. In the context of a forecast, procedures will be limited as the transactions and events haven't occurred yet.	More evidence will need to be obtained to provide reasonable assurance, and a wider range of procedures performed, including tests of controls.
A forecast relates to the future, which is inherently uncertain, and therefore it would not be possible to obtain assurance that it is free from material misstatement.	Financial statements relate to the past, and so the auditor should be able to obtain sufficient appropriate evidence.
Less reliance can therefore be placed on the forecast than the financial statements.	

Test your understanding 3

(1)	B	Reasonable assurance is given in an independent auditor's report.
(2)	C	Assurance file.
(3)	D	Sampling provides a limitation of the audit process, not a benefit.
(4)	C	A negative conclusion is used for limited assurance engagements.
(5)	A	The auditor cannot confirm the accuracy of the financial statements as they contain estimates and judgments of management. The company may not be a going concern and the financial statements may correctly reflect this resulting in an unmodified audit opinion. The auditor does not test all transactions.

Rules and regulation

Chapter learning objectives

This chapter covers syllabus areas:

* A2 – External audits

Detailed syllabus objectives are provided in the introduction section of the text book.

PER

One of the PER performance objectives (PO4) is governance risk and control. You contribute to effective governance in your area. You evaluate, monitor and implement risk management procedures, complying with the spirit and the letter of policies, laws and regulations. Working through this chapter should help you understand how to demonstrate that objective.

1 The need for regulation

The role of the auditor has come under increased scrutiny over the last thirty years due to an increase in high profile audit failures. The most high profile case, and the catalyst for regulatory change, was the collapse of Enron and its auditor Arthur Andersen.

In order to try and regain trust in the auditing profession, national and international standard setters and regulators have tried to introduce three initiatives:

- **Harmonisation** of auditing procedures, so that users of audit services are confident in the nature of audits being conducted around the world.

- Focus on **audit quality,** so that the expectations of users are met.

- Adherence to a strict **ethical code** of conduct, to try and improve the perception of auditors as independent, unbiased service providers.

In order to achieve this, practitioners have to follow regulatory guidance:

- **National corporate law (e.g. The Companies Act 2006 in the UK and The Sarbanes Oxley Act in the US).**

- **Auditing Standards** (the basis of this text is International Standards on Auditing).

- **Code of Ethics.** Covered in the chapter 'Ethics and acceptance'.

2 Legal requirements for audits and auditors

In this section, the law referred to in most cases is UK law and the Companies Act 2006. Different countries may have different requirements but generally the same principles will apply across the world.

National law includes:

- Which companies are required to have an audit

- Who can and cannot carry out an audit

- Auditor appointment, resignation and removal

- The rights and duties of an auditor.

Who needs an audit and why?

In most countries, companies are required by law to have an audit.

Small or owner-managed companies are often exempt. This is because there is less value in an audit for these companies.

Note that these exemptions often do not apply to companies in certain regulated sectors, e.g. financial services companies or companies listed on a stock exchange.

Reasons for exempting small companies from audit

- The owners and managers of the company are often the same people.

- The advice and value which accountants can add to a small company is more likely to concern other services, such as accounting and tax.

- The impact of misstatements in the financial statements of small companies is unlikely to be material to the wider economy.

- The audit fee and disruption of an audit are seen as too great a cost for any benefits the audit might bring.

Who may act as auditor?

To be **eligible** to act as **auditor,** a person must be:

- A member of a Recognised Supervisory Body (RSB), e.g. ACCA, and allowed by the rules of that body to be an auditor **or**

- Someone directly authorised by the state.

Conducting audit work

Individuals who are authorised to conduct audit work may be:	To be eligible to offer audit services, a firm must be:
• Sole practitioners • Partners in a partnership • Members of a limited liability partnership • Directors of an audit company.	• Controlled by members of a suitably authorised supervisory body or • A firm directly authorised by the state.

Note: In some countries only individuals can be authorised to act as auditor and need to be directly authorised by the state.

Who may not act as auditor?

Excluded by law: The law in most countries excludes those who manage or work for the company, and those who have business or personal connections with them from auditing that company.

Excluded by the Code of Ethics: Auditors must also comply with a Code of Ethics. The Code of Ethics requires the auditor to consider any factors that would prevent them acting as auditor, such as independence, competence or issues regarding confidentiality. This is considered in more detail in the next chapter.

Who appoints the auditor?

Members (shareholders) – of the company appoint the auditor by voting them in.

Directors – can appoint the first auditor or to fill a 'casual vacancy'. This requires the members' approval at a members' meeting. In some countries the auditors may be appointed by the directors as a matter of course.

Secretary of State – if no auditors are appointed by the members or directors.

Auditors of public companies are appointed from one AGM to the next one.

Auditors of private companies are appointed until they are removed.

Removing the auditor

Arrangements for removing the auditor have to be structured in such a way that:

- the auditor has sufficiently secure tenure of office, to maintain independence of management.

- auditors can be removed if there are doubts about their continuing abilities to carry out their duties effectively.

Removal of the auditor can usually be achieved by a simple majority at a general meeting of the company. There are some safeguards, such as a specified notice period, to prevent the resolution to remove the auditors being 'sprung' on the meeting.

The auditor can circulate representations stating why they should not be removed if applicable.

A statement of circumstances must be sent to the company and the regulatory authority to set out issues surrounding the cessation of office.

Resigning as auditor

In practice, if the auditor and management find it difficult to work together, the auditor will usually resign.

The auditor issues written notice of the resignation and a statement of circumstances to the members and regulatory authority.

Notifying ACCA

If an auditor resigns or is removed from office before the end of their term of office, they must notify the ACCA.

The auditors responsibilities on removal/resignation

The following is taken from UK law, but provides an example of the typical responsibilities of the auditor.

- Deposit at the company's registered office:
  - A statement of the circumstances connected with the removal/resignation or
  - A statement that there are no such circumstances.
- Deal promptly with requests for clearance from new auditors.

The auditor's rights

During appointment as auditor

- Access to the company's books and records at any reasonable time.
- To receive information and explanations necessary for the audit.
- To receive notice of and attend any general meeting of members of the company.
- To be heard at such meetings on matters of concern to the auditor.
- To receive copies of any written resolutions of the company.

On resignation

- To request a General Meeting of the company to explain the circumstances of the resignation.
- To require the company to circulate the notice of circumstances relating to the resignation.

The auditor's duties

The external auditor's primary duty is to audit the financial statements and provide an opinion on whether the financial statements give a true and fair view (or are fairly presented in all material respects).

They may have additional reporting responsibilities required by local national law, such as confirming that the financial statements are properly prepared in accordance with those laws.

3 International regulation

The International Federation of Accountants (IFAC)

The International Federation of Accountants (IFAC) is the global organisation for the accountancy profession.

IFAC promotes international regulation of the accountancy profession. By ensuring minimum requirements for accountancy qualifications, post qualification experience and guidance on accounting and assurance for accountants around the world, there will be greater public confidence in the profession as a whole.

International Standards on Auditing (ISAs)

One of the subsidiary boards of IFAC is the International Audit and Assurance Standards Board (IAASB). It is their responsibility to develop and promote International Standards on Auditing (ISAs).

There are currently 37 ISAs and one International Standard of Quality Control, although not all are examinable for this syllabus. A list of examinable documents is available on the ACCA website. You do not need to learn the names or numbers of the ISAs but you do need to know and be able to apply the key principles and requirements of the standards.

Main features of ISAs

- ISAs are professional guidance that the auditor must follow to ensure each audit is performed consistently and to a required standard of quality.

- ISAs are not legal requirements. If a country has a law in place which is inconsistent with the requirements of the ISAs, local law should be followed.

- ISAs are written in the context of an audit of the financial statements but can be applied to the audit of other historical financial information.

- ISAs must be applied in all but exceptional cases. Where the auditor deems it necessary to depart from an ISA to achieve the overall aim of the audit, this departure must be justified.

- The ISAs contain basic principles and requirements followed by application and other explanatory material to aid the auditor on how to follow the requirements.

Development of ISAs

For an ISA to be issued, a lengthy process of discussion and debate occurs to ensure the members affected by the guidance have had an input.

An exposure draft (ED) is issued for public comment and these comments may result in revisions to the ED.

Approval of two thirds of IAASB members is required for the ISA to come into force.

The relationship between international and national standards and regulation

IFAC is simply a grouping of accountancy bodies, therefore it has no legal standing in individual countries. Countries therefore need to have their own arrangements in place for:

- Regulating the audit profession
- Implementing auditing standards.

National standard setters

- May develop their own auditing standards and ethical standards
- May adopt and implement ISAs, possibly after modifying them to suit national needs.

In the event of a conflict between the two sets of guidance, local regulations will apply.

UK as an example

In the UK, the Financial Reporting Council (FRC) is the national regulator responsible for overseeing the accountancy profession.

The Audit and Actuarial Regulation Division within the FRC is responsible for the development of auditing standards and guidance in the UK, monitoring of auditors of public interest entities, and oversight and regulation of Recognised Supervisory Bodies (such as ACCA).

The Audit and Assurance team within the Audit Division take the ISAs as issued by the IAASB and modify them for UK use.

The Audit and Assurance team has also developed its own ethical standard which must be followed. The safeguards within the ethical standard are either the same as those required by IFAC's Code of Ethics or more comprehensive. For example, partner rotation rules in the UK are more stringent than those required by IFAC.

The Audit Quality Review (AQR) team monitors the quality of work performed by audit firms that perform audits of public interest entities in the UK. The AQR performs inspections of audit files to ensure firms are following the requirements of the ethical standard, auditing standards and quality control standard. Inspection reports are available to view on the FRC website.

The accountancy profession in the UK is therefore primarily self-regulated by the FRC. There is little government involvement in the regulation of accountancy firms.

Whilst self-regulation is working effectively it is likely to continue. However, if a major audit failure occurs which damages the reputation of the profession as a whole, then it is likely that the government will get involved. In European countries, there is considerably more government involvement.

4 The role of professional bodies

Professional bodies (such as the ACCA and ICAEW) promote quality within the profession through provision of:

- Rigorous qualifications to acquire the knowledge and skills needed to provide a competent service

- Support to members to demonstrate high professional and ethical values

- Technical expertise to governments on accounting and business matters. This input may help shape the introduction of new laws and regulations affecting the profession.

To obtain membership to a professional body, a person must:

- Successfully complete the exams provided by that body

- Be able to demonstrate appropriate practical experience (usually a minimum of three years)

- Complete an ethical assessment.

To maintain membership a member must demonstrate continuing professional development (CPD) to ensure knowledge and skills are kept up to date. In addition, members must comply with a code of ethics and conduct to ensure they act in a professional manner at all times.

If a member is found not to have complied with the rules of the professional body, disciplinary action will be taken which may involve fines, reprimands, suspension from membership for a limited time or withdrawal of membership. Most disciplinary matters will be dealt with internally by the relevant professional body. However, if the behaviour of the person or the firm is considered very serious, the matter can be referred to the national regulator (e.g. the FRC in the UK) and action can be taken at a higher level. This will generally be the case for significant public interest issues.

By having such rigorous membership requirements and disciplinary proceedings the public can be assured that professional accountants are performing work of a high standard which increases trust in the profession as a whole.

Test your understanding 1

Explain THREE rights that enable auditors to carry out their duties.

(3 marks)

Test your understanding 2

You have been asked to conduct a training workshop for your firm's new trainees which will cover the rules and regulations surrounding the auditing profession. You have prepared a short test for the trainees to take at the end of the workshop to assess whether they have understood the content covered.

(1) **Which of the following statements is false?**

A   Auditing standards are laws which must be followed during all audits

B   Auditing standards should be followed during all audits unless there are exceptional circumstances which would mean the audit objective would not be met

C   Auditing standards are professional regulations

D   Auditing standards may be different in different countries, even those using ISAs

(2) **Which of the following are reasons for the audit profession issuing auditing standards?**

(i) To ensure consistency of audits across different firms.

(ii) To provide bureaucracy for auditors.

(iii) To ensure quality in the standard of audits performed.

A All of them

B (i) and (ii) only

C (i) and (iii) only

D (ii) and (iii) only

(3) **Which of the following people may act as auditor for a company?**

A The company's previous finance director who left the company five years ago to join the audit firm

B A director of the company being audited who holds a valid audit certificate

C An employee of the company being audited who holds a valid audit certificate

D The wife of the finance director who works for a reputable audit firm

(4) **In most jurisdictions, the auditors of a company will be appointed by which party?**

A Directors

B Audit committee

C Government

D Shareholders

(5) **Which of the following statements is true?**

A The shareholders of most companies will also be the directors

B The directors are the stewards of the company responsible for looking after the company on behalf of the owners

C Directors will always have a vested interest in the company doing well because they own shares in the company they work for

D Auditors are allowed to be business partners of the company directors

5   Chapter summary

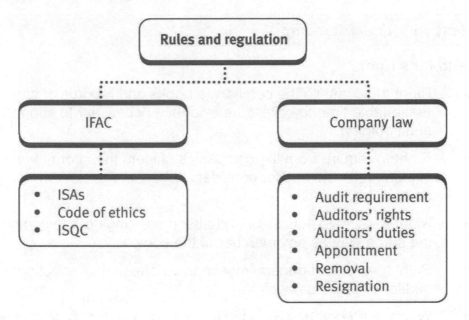

Test your understanding answers

Test your understanding 1

Auditor's rights

- Right of access to the company's books and records at any reasonable time to collect the evidence necessary to support the audit opinion.

- Right to require from the company's officers the information and explanations the auditor considers necessary to perform their duties as auditors.

- Right to receive notices of and attend meetings of the company in the same way as any member of the company.

- Right to speak at general meetings on any matter affecting the auditor or previous auditor.

- Where the company uses written resolutions, a right to receive a copy of those resolutions.

Test your understanding 2

(1)	A	Auditing standards are professional guidance, not law.
(2)	C	By issuing standards, audits should be performed more consistently which should improve quality.
(3)	A	An auditor cannot be an employee or director of the company or someone with a close personal relationship with someone that could influence the audit. An ex-employee or director can be involved with the audit once a cooling-off period has passed.
(4)	D	Shareholders.
(5)	B	Whilst directors may be shareholders of the company they work for, large public companies will have a significant number of shareholders who are not involved in the operations of the company. The auditors are not allowed to be business partners of the directors of a company they audit.

KAPLAN PUBLISHING

Corporate governance

Chapter learning objectives

This chapter covers syllabus areas:

- A3 – Corporate governance

Detailed syllabus objectives are provided in the introduction section of the text book.

PER

One of the PER performance objectives (PO4) is governance risk and control. You contribute to effective governance in your area. You evaluate, monitor and implement risk management procedures, complying with the spirit and the letter of policies, laws and regulations. Working through this chapter should help you understand how to demonstrate that objective.

1 Objectives and importance of corporate governance

 Corporate governance is the means by which a company is operated and controlled.

The aim of corporate governance is to ensure that companies are run well in the interests of their shareholders, employees, and other key stakeholders such as the wider community.

The aim is to try and prevent company directors from abusing their power which may adversely affect these stakeholder groups. For example, the directors may pay themselves large salaries and bonuses whilst claiming they have no money to pay a dividend to shareholders. Similarly, they may be making large numbers of staff redundant but awarding themselves a pay rise.

In response to major scandals (e.g. Enron), regulators sought to change the rules surrounding the governance of companies, particularly publicly owned ones.

In the US the Sarbanes Oxley Act (2002) introduced a set of rigorous corporate governance laws. The UK Corporate Governance Code introduced a set of best practice corporate governance initiatives into the UK.

Advantages of a company following good corporate governance principles:

- Greater transparency
- Greater accountability
- Efficiency of operations
- Better able to respond to risks
- Less likely to be mismanaged.

High profile corporate failures

Carillion

In 2018, construction company Carillion was placed into liquidation after building up debts of £1.5 billion. The company was a major contractor for the UK government with contracts to build hospitals and schools as well as facilities management and ongoing maintenance. It was the second largest construction company in the UK and employed more than 43,000 people. The company took on too many projects and failed to realistically price the contracts resulting in huge cost overruns and losses being made. In December 2017 the major banks refused to lend more money to Carillion and in 2018 the company went into liquidation.

The collapse of the company caused significant problems, not just for the shareholders, but for the significant number of employees who lost their jobs, the government contracts that were in progress that would not be completed and for the suppliers who would not be paid.

One of the issues highlighted by Carillion was that of executive pay. Executive directors were earning significant amounts of money despite running the company into the ground. In 2016, the former chief executive director earned more than £2 million. The Institute of Directors has said that the collapse of Carillion is due to a lack of effective governance. Directors' remuneration allowed them to benefit despite the collapse of the company as there were no claw back conditions. The company could only request claw back from directors if there was gross misconduct or misstatement of financial results. The directors also received payoffs despite being responsible for the collapse.

The collapse of Carillion has also returned focus to the big accounting firms and their part in allowing companies to fail by not having raised the alarm much earlier.

Enron

In the year 2000 Enron, a US based energy company, employed 22,000 people and reported revenues of $101 billion. In late 2001 they filed for bankruptcy protection. After a lengthy investigation it was revealed that Enron's financial statements were sustained substantially by systematic, and creatively planned, accounting fraud.

In the wake of the fraud case the shares of Enron fell from over $90 each to just a few cents each, a number of directors were prosecuted and jailed and their auditors, Arthur Andersen, were accused of obstruction of justice and forced to stop auditing public companies. This ruling against Arthur Andersen was overturned at a later date but the damage was done and the firm ceased trading soon after.

This was just one of a number of high profile frauds to occur at that time.

The Enron scandal is an example of the abuse of the trust placed in the management of publicly traded companies by investors. This abuse of trust usually takes one of two forms:

- Direct extraction from the company of excessive benefits by management, e.g. large salaries, pension entitlements, share options, use of company assets (jets, apartments etc.)

- Manipulation of the share price by misrepresenting the company's profitability, usually so that shares in the company can be sold or options 'cashed in'.

In response, regulators sought to change the rules surrounding the governance of companies, particularly publicly owned ones. In the US the Sarbanes Oxley Act (2002) introduced a set of rigorous corporate governance laws and at the same time the Combined Code (now called the UK Corporate Governance Code) introduced a set of best practice corporate governance initiatives into the UK.

2 The Corporate Governance Code

The Organisation for Economic Co-operation and Development (OECD) has produced a set of six principles of corporate governance to guide policy makers when setting regulations for their own country.

The six OECD Principles are:

- Ensuring the basis of an effective corporate governance framework
- The rights and equitable treatment of shareholders and key ownership functions
- Institutional investors, stock markets, and other intermediaries
- The role of stakeholders in corporate governance
- Disclosure and transparency
- The responsibilities of the board.

The UK Corporate Governance Code reflects the OECD principles.

The UK Corporate Governance Code is particularly important for publicly traded companies because large amounts of money are invested in them, either by 'small' shareholders, or from pension schemes and other financial institutions. The wealth of these companies significantly affects the health of the economies where their shares are traded.

The code is split into five parts:

- Board leadership and company purpose
- Division of responsibilities
- Composition, succession and evaluation
- Audit, risk and internal control
- Remuneration.

The Code does not set out a rigid set of rules; instead it offers flexibility through the application of Principles and 'comply or explain' provisions and supporting guidance.

The main requirements provisions of the Code are given below.

Board leadership and company purpose

Principles

- A successful company is led by an effective board whose role is to promote long-term sustainable success thereby generating value for shareholders.

- The board should establish the company's purpose, values and strategy. The directors should lead by example and promote the desired culture.

- The board should ensure that the necessary resources are in place for the company to meet its objectives. The board should establish a framework of effective controls to enable risk to be assessed and managed.

- The board should ensure effective engagement with, and encourage participation from shareholders and stakeholders.

- The board should ensure that workforce policies and practices are consistent with the company's values. The workforce should be able to raise matters of concern.

Main provisions

- The board should describe in the annual report how opportunities and risks to the future success of the business have been considered and addressed.

- The board should assess and monitor culture. Where behaviour throughout the business is not consistent with the purpose, values or strategy, the board should ensure management have taken corrective action.

- In addition to formal general meetings, the chair should seek regular engagement with major shareholders. The board as a whole should understand the views of the shareholders.

- When 20% or more of votes have been cast against the board recommendation for a resolution, the company should explain what actions it intends to take to understand the reasons behind the result.

- The board should understand the views of the company's other key stakeholders and describe how their interests have been considered in board discussions. For engagement with the workforce, the company should use a director appointed from the workforce, a workforce advisory panel or a designated non-executive director (NED).

- The workforce should be able to raise concerns in confidence and anonymously ('whistleblowing').

- The board should take action to manage conflicts of interest.

- Directors' concerns about the operation of the board or management of the company that cannot be resolved should be minuted. On resignation, a NED should provide a written statement to the chair for circulation to the board if they have any concerns.

Board roles

The chair's role

- Leads the board of directors.
- Enables flow of information and discussion at board meetings.
- Ensures satisfactory channels of communication with the external auditors.
- Ensures effective operation of board sub-committees.
- The chair should be independent to enhance effectiveness.

The chief executive's role

- Ensures the effective operation of the company.
- Head of the executive directors.

Executive directors

The executive directors have responsibility for running the company on a day to day basis.

Non-executive directors (NEDs)

The NEDs monitor the executive directors and contribute to the overall strategy and direction of the organisation. They are usually employed on a part-time basis and do not take part in the routine executive management of the company.

NEDs will:

- participate at board meetings.
- bring experience, insight and contacts to assist the board.
- sit on sub-committees as independent, knowledgeable parties.

Advantages of participation by NEDs

- Oversight of the whole board.
- As they are independent they act as a 'corporate conscience'.
- They bring external expertise to the company.

Disadvantages

- It may be difficult to find the right NEDs who have the relevant skills and experience required by the company.
- They, and the sub-committees, may not be sufficiently well-informed or have time to fulfil the role competently.

- They are subject to the accusation that they are staffed by an 'old boy' network and may fail to report significant problems and approve unjustified pay rises.

- The cost. NEDs are normally remunerated and their fees can be quite expensive.

Division of responsibilities

Principles

- The chair leads the board and is responsible for its overall effectiveness.

- The chair should ensure effective contribution of all board members.

- The chair should ensure that directors receive clear, accurate and timely information.

- The board should be balanced so that no individual or small group of individuals can dominate board decisions.

- NEDs should have sufficient time to meet their board responsibilities and should hold management to account.

- The board should ensure it has the policies, processes, information, time and resources it needs to function effectively and efficiently.

Main provisions

- The chair should be independent on appointment.

- The chair and chief executive roles should not be taken by the same individual and the chief executive should not become the chair of the same company.

- At least half the board, excluding the chair should be independent NEDs.

- The board should identify the independent NEDs in the annual report. Independence would be deemed to be affected if a director:

  - is, or has been, an employee of the company or group within the last five years

  - has, or has had within the last three years, a material business relationship with the company either directly, or as a partner, shareholder, director or senior employee of a body that has such a relationship with the company

  - has received or receives remuneration from the company in addition to a director's fee, participates in the company's share option or a performance-related pay scheme, or is a member of the company's pension scheme

  - has close family ties with any of the company's advisers, directors or senior employees

- holds cross-directorships or has significant links with other directors through involvement in other companies or bodies

- represents a significant shareholder

- has served on the board for more than nine years from the date of their first appointment.

- One of the independent NEDs should be appointed as a senior independent director to provide a sounding board for the chair.

- The NEDs and the senior independent director should meet without the chair present at least annually to appraise the chair's performance.

- NEDs appoint and remove executive directors and scrutinise performance against agreed performance objectives.

- The responsibilities of the chair, chief executive, senior independent director, board and committees should be set out in writing and publicly available.

- The annual report should set out the number of meetings of the board and its committees and the attendance of each director.

- New appointments to the board should take into account other demands on the director's time. Full time executive directors should not take on more than one NED role in a FTSE 100 company or other significant appointment. Appointments should not be made without prior approval of the board.

- Appointment and removal of the company secretary should be a matter for the whole board.

Composition, succession and evaluation

Principles

- Appointments to the board should be subject to a formal, rigorous and transparent procedure.

- An effective succession plan should be maintained for board and senior management.

- Appointments and succession should be based on merit and objective criteria and should promote diversity.

- The board and its committees should have a combination of skills, experience and knowledge.

- Annual evaluation of the board should consider its composition, diversity and how effectively members work together to achieve objectives.

Main provisions

- A nomination committee should be established to appoint board members.

- A majority of the committee members should be independent NEDs.

- The chair should not be a member of the committee when the committee is dealing with the appointment of their successor.

- All directors should be subject to annual re-election.

- The chair should not remain in post for more than nine years from the date of their first appointment. This period can be extended for a limited time to facilitate effective succession planning.

- Open advertising and/or an external search consultancy should be used for the appointment of the chair and NEDs.

- There should be a formal and rigorous annual evaluation of the performance of the board, its committees, the chair and the individual directors.

- The chair should consider having a regular external board evaluation at least every three years for FTSE 350 companies, and the external evaluator should be identified in the annual report.

- The annual report should describe the work of the nomination committee including the process used in making appointments, how the board evaluation has been conducted, the policy on diversity and inclusion and the gender balance of those in senior management.

 Nomination committee

The role of the nomination committee is to decide on appointments of board directors and senior management. This is to ensure the best person for the job is recruited. The majority of this committee should be independent NEDs.

Advantages

- Reduces the risk of 'jobs for the boys'. Executive directors might appoint other directors with whom they are friends or used to work with but wouldn't necessarily have the skills required.

- Reduces the risk of improperly affecting board decisions. Executives might appoint people to the board they know will vote in favour of the same decisions as them and can therefore influence board decisions which may not be in the best interests of the company.

Audit, risk and internal control including audit committees

Principles

- The board should establish formal and transparent policies and procedures to ensure the independence and effectiveness of internal and external audit functions and satisfy itself on the integrity of financial and narrative statements.

- The board should present a fair, balanced and understandable assessment of the company's position and prospects.

- The board should establish procedures to manage risk, oversee the internal control framework, and determine the nature and extent of the principal risks the company is willing to take in order to achieve its long-term strategic objectives.

Main provisions

- The board should establish an audit committee of independent NEDs, with a minimum membership of three, or in the case of smaller companies, two.

- The chair of the board should not be a member of the audit committee.

- At least one member must have recent and relevant financial experience.

- The committee as a whole must have competence relevant to the sector in which the company operates.

- The main roles and responsibilities of the audit committee include:

  - Monitoring the integrity of the financial statements.

  - Providing advice on whether the annual report and accounts are fair, balanced and understandable.

  - Reviewing the company's internal financial controls and risk management systems.

  - Monitoring and reviewing the effectiveness of the internal audit function.

  - If there is no internal audit function in place, they should consider annually whether there is a need for one and make a recommendation to the board.

  - Making recommendations in relation to the appointment and removal of the external auditor and their remuneration.

  - Reviewing and monitoring the external auditor's independence and objectivity and the effectiveness of the audit process.

  - Developing and implementing policy on the engagement of the external auditor to supply non-audit services.

- The annual report should describe the work of the audit committee including:

    - Significant issues considered relating to the financial statements.

    - How it has assessed the independence and effectiveness of the external audit process.

    - Where there is no internal audit function, an explanation for the absence and how internal assurance is achieved.

    - An explanation of how auditor independence and objectivity are safeguarded, if the external auditor provides non-audit services.

- The directors should explain in the annual report their responsibility for preparing the annual report and accounts.

- The board should carry out a robust assessment of the company's emerging and principal risks.

- The board should confirm in the annual report that it has completed this assessment, including a description of its principal risks, what procedures are in place to identify emerging risks, and an explanation of how these are being managed or mitigated.

- The board should monitor the company's risk management and internal control systems and, at least annually, carry out a review of their effectiveness and report on that review in the annual report. The monitoring and review should cover all material controls, including financial, operational and compliance controls.

- The board should state whether it considers it appropriate to adopt the going concern basis of accounting in preparing the financial statements, and identify any material uncertainties to the company's ability to continue to do so over a period of at least 12 months from the date of approval of the financial statements.

- The board should explain in the annual report how it has assessed the prospects of the company, over what period it has done so and why it considers that period to be appropriate.

- The board should state whether it has a reasonable expectation that the company will be able to continue in operation and meet its liabilities as they fall due over the period of their assessment.

Audit committees

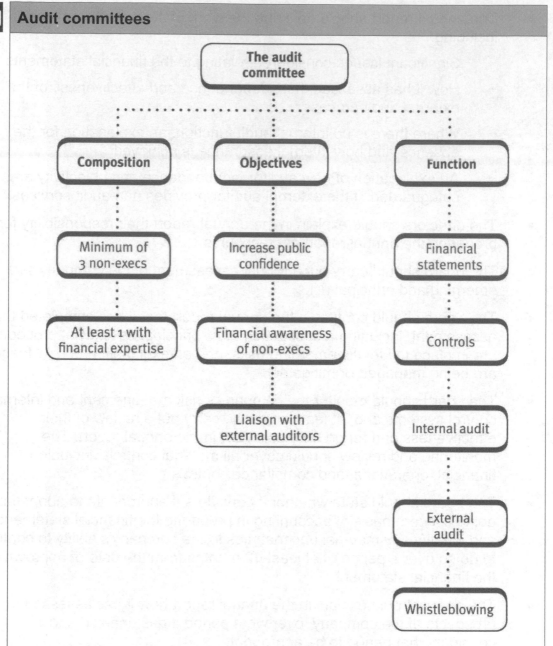

The audit committee will take responsibility for financial reporting and internal control matters. The audit committee is able to view a company's affairs in a detached and independent way and liaise effectively between the main board of directors and the internal and external auditors.

The objectives of the audit committee

- Increasing public confidence in the credibility and objectivity of published financial information (including unaudited interim statements).

- Assisting directors (particularly executive directors) in meeting their responsibilities in respect of financial reporting.

- Strengthening the independent position of a company's external auditor by providing an additional channel of communication.

Benefits of an audit committee

- Improved credibility of the financial statements through an impartial review of the financial statements and discussion of significant issues with the external auditors.

- Increased public confidence in the audit opinion as the audit committee will monitor the independence of the external auditors.

- Stronger control environment as the audit committee help to create a culture of compliance and control.

- The skills, knowledge and experience (and independence) of the audit committee members can be an invaluable resource for a business.

- It may be easier and cheaper to arrange finance, as the presence of an audit committee can give a perception of good corporate governance.

- It will be less of a burden to meet listing requirements if an audit committee (which is usually a listing requirement) is already established.

- The internal audit function will report to the audit committee increasing their independence and adding weight to their recommendations.

Problems

- Difficulties recruiting the right non-executive directors who have relevant skills, experience and sufficient time to become effective members of the committee.

- The cost. Non-executive directors are normally remunerated and their fees can be quite expensive.

FRC Guidance on audit committees

- This guidance is designed to assist company boards when implementing the Corporate Governance Code.

- Companies with a premium listing are required to comply with the Code or explain why they have not done so.

- Audit committee arrangements should be proportionate to the task and will vary according to size and complexity of the company.

- There should be a frank, open working relationship and a high level of mutual respect between audit committee chair and board chair, the chief executive and the finance director.

- Management must ensure the audit committee is kept properly informed. All directors must cooperate with the audit committee.

- The core functions of audit committees are oversight, assessment and review. It is not the duty of the audit committee to carry out functions that belong to others. For example, they should make sure there is a proper system in place for monitoring of internal controls but should not do the monitoring themselves.

- The board should review the audit committee's effectiveness annually.

The audit committee should:

- Receive induction and training for new members and continuing training as required.

- Hold as many meetings as the roles and responsibilities require and it is recommended that no fewer than three meetings are held.

- Meet the external and internal auditors without management at least annually to discuss any issues arising from the audit.

- Report to the board on how it has discharged its responsibilities.

- Ensure the interests of the shareholders are properly protected in relation to financial reporting and internal control.

- Review and report to the board on the significant financial reporting issues and judgments in connection with the preparation of the financial statements.

- Consider the appropriateness of significant accounting policies, significant estimates and judgments.

- Receive reports from management on the effectiveness of systems and the conclusions of any testing carried out by internal and external auditors.

- Review the systems established by management to identify, assess, manage and monitor financial risks.

- Monitor and review the effectiveness of the company's internal audit function. Where there is no internal audit function the audit committee should consider annually the need for one and make a recommendation to the board.

- Review whistleblowing arrangements for staff of the company to raise concerns in confidence.

Annual report

A separate section of the annual report should describe the work of the committee. Specifically:

- A summary of the role of the audit committee.

- The names and qualifications of all members of the audit committee.

- The number of audit committee meetings.

- The significant issues that the committee considered in relation to the financial statements and how these issues were addressed.

- An explanation of how it has assessed the effectiveness of the external audit process and the approach taken to the appointment or reappointment of the external auditor.

- If the external auditor provides non-audit services, how auditor objectivity and independence is safeguarded.

- Where there is a disagreement between the audit committee and the board which cannot be resolved, the audit committee should have the right to report the issue to shareholders as part of its report within the annual report.

- The audit committee chair should be present at the AGM to answer questions.

External audit matters

The audit committee is responsible for making a recommendation on the appointment, reappointment and removal of the external auditors.

FTSE 350 companies should put the audit out to tender at least once every ten years to enable the audit committee to compare the quality and effectiveness of the services provided by the incumbent auditor with those of other firms.

The audit committee should:

- Annually assess and report to the board on the qualification, expertise and resources, and independence of the external auditors and the effectiveness of the audit process.

- Investigate reasons for the resignation of the external auditor and consider whether any action is required.

- Assess the independence and objectivity of the external auditor annually.

- Set and apply a formal policy for non-audit service which are pre-approved, require approval or are not allowed.

- Agree a policy for employment of former employees of the external auditor taking into account the Ethical Standards, paying particular attention to people who were part of the audit team. The audit committee should consider whether there has been any impairment of the auditor's independence and objectivity in respect of the audit.

- Monitor the external audit firm's compliance with ethical standards relating to partner rotation and fee levels.

Internal audit

Internal audit has an important role to play in assisting the board, and audit committee, fulfil their corporate governance responsibilities.

Internal audit will work closely with the audit committee. The audit committee will:

- Ensure that the internal auditor has direct access to the board chair and to the audit committee and is accountable to the audit committee.

- Review and assess the annual internal audit work plan.

- Receive periodic reports on the results of internal audit work.

- Review and monitor management's responsiveness to the internal auditor's findings and recommendations.

- Meet with the head of internal audit at least once a year without the presence of management.

- Monitor and assess the effectiveness of internal audit in the overall context of the company's risk management system.

The roles and functions of internal audit are covered in the chapter 'Internal audit'.

Risk management in practice

The main aim of risk management is to protect the business from unforeseen circumstances that could negatively impact the profitability of the company and stop it achieving its strategic goals.

The board must monitor the company's risk assessment and internal control systems annually. A risk committee may be established to perform this role. The risk committee will be responsible for advising the board on the company's risk appetite, reviewing and approving the risk management strategy and advising the board on risk exposures.

Companies face many risks, for example:

- The risk that products may become technologically obsolete.

- The risk of losing key staff.

- The risk of a catastrophic failure of IT systems.

- The risk of changes in government policy.

- The risk of fire or natural disaster.

Companies need mechanisms in place to identify and then assess those risks. In so doing, companies can rank risks in terms of their relative importance by scoring them with regard to their likelihood and potential impact. This could take the form of a 'risk map'.

A risk map enables the company to assess the likelihood or probability of a risk occurring and the likely impact to the company.

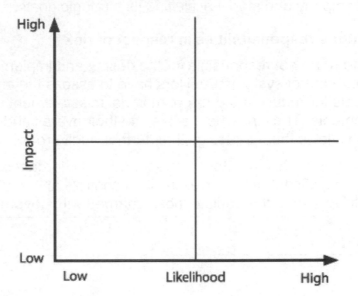

Once identified and assessed, the company must decide on appropriate ways to manage those risks.

Risk management can involve:

- Transferring the risk to another party e.g. by taking out insurance or outsourcing part of the business.

- Avoiding the risk by ceasing the risky activity.

- Reducing the risk by implementing effective systems and controls.

- Accepting the risk and bearing the cost and consequence if the risk happens. This may be likely for risks which are deemed low in terms of probability or impact on the company.

A risk that ranked as highly likely to occur and high potential impact on the business would be prioritised as requiring immediate action. A risk that was considered both low likelihood and low impact might be ignored or insured against.

Internal controls and risk management

One way of minimising risk is to incorporate internal controls into a company's systems and procedures.

Director's responsibilities in respect of risk

It is the director's responsibility to implement internal controls and monitor their application and effectiveness.

The risks considered by management are numerous. They come from both external, environmental sources and internal, operational ones.

> The main aim of risk management is to protect the business from unforeseen circumstances that could negatively impact the profitability of the company and stop it achieving its strategic goals.
>
> **Auditor's responsibilities in respect of risk**
>
> Auditors are not responsible for the design and implementation of their clients' control systems. Auditors have to assess the effectiveness of controls for reducing the risk of material misstatement of the financial statements. They incorporate this into their overall audit risk assessment, which allows them to design their further audit procedures.
>
> In addition to this, auditors are required, in accordance with ISA 265, to report significant deficiencies in client controls and any significant risks identified during the audit to those charged with governance.

Remuneration

Principles

- Remuneration should be designed to promote the long-term sustainable success of the company. Executive remuneration should be aligned to the company purpose, values and long-term strategy.

- The board should establish formal and transparent procedures for developing the policy for executive directors' remuneration.

- No director should be involved in setting his own pay.

- Directors should exercise independent judgment and discretion when authorising remuneration, taking account of company and individual performance, and wider circumstances.

Main provisions

- A remuneration committee comprising a minimum of three independent NEDs should be established.

- The chair cannot chair the committee and can only be a member if they were independent on appointment.

- The remuneration committee should determine the policy for executive director remuneration and set remuneration for the chair, executive directors and senior management.

- The committee should review workforce remuneration and related policies taking these into account when setting the policy for executive director remuneration.

- NED remuneration should be determined by the board. It should reflect time commitment and responsibilities of the role and should not include share options or other performance related elements.

- Remuneration schemes should promote long-term shareholdings by executive directors. Shares awards should be released for sale on a phased basis and be subject to a total vesting and holding period of five years or more.

- Remuneration schemes should include provisions that enable a company to recover or withhold sums or share awards and specify the circumstances in which it would be appropriate to do so.

- Only basic salary should be pensionable and pension contribution rates should be aligned with those available to the workforce.

- Notice or contract periods should be one year or less. If it is necessary to offer longer periods to new directors the period should reduce to one year or less after the initial period.

- When determining the executive director remuneration policy and practices the committee should ensure remuneration arrangements are transparent, easy to understand, predictable, proportionate, and aligned to culture. The risks from excessive rewards should be identified and mitigated and the range of possible values of rewards should be identified and explained at the time of approving the policy.

- The work of the remuneration committee should be described in the annual report.

Remuneration committee

The role of the remuneration committee is to set the remuneration packages for the chair, executive directors and senior management. This is to ensure that they are not paid excessive amounts but are paid fairly for their role.

Advantages

- Decisions are based on agreement of several people, reducing the risk of bribes from directors in return for a higher package.

- No director is involved in setting his own pay which could lead to excessive amounts being paid.

- Long-term performance related elements will be included to avoid the risk that directors are rewarded for poor performance or rewarded for taking decisions which may have a positive outcome in the short-term but would not be good for long-term success of the company.

3 Relevance of corporate governance to external auditors

If a company complies with corporate governance best practice, the control environment of the company is likely to be stronger. There will be a greater focus on financial reporting and internal controls which should reduce control risk and inherent risk which together reduce the risk of material misstatements in the financial statements. In some jurisdictions, external auditors are required to report on whether companies are compliant with corporate governance principles.

There is significantly more communication between audit committees and external auditors in the current environment. If the company, including the audit committee, demonstrates good corporate governance, this should result in the company taking more responsibility for its actions, the independence of the auditor being greater, and the overall quality of the audit being higher.

Auditor reporting responsibilities

ISA (UK) 700 requires the auditor to report by exception in the auditors' reports of companies disclosing compliance with the UK Corporate Governance Code where the annual report includes:

- A statement given by the directors that they consider the annual report and accounts taken as a whole is fair, balanced and understandable and provides the information necessary for shareholders to assess the entity's performance, business model and strategy, that is inconsistent with the knowledge acquired by the auditor in the course of performing the audit.

- A section describing the work of the audit committee that does not appropriately address matters communicated by the auditor to the audit committee.

- An explanation, as to why the annual report does not include such a statement or section that is materially inconsistent with the knowledge acquired by the auditor in the course of performing the audit.

- Other information that, in the auditor's judgment, contains a material inconsistency.

Other countries may have different reporting requirements in accordance with local legislation and regulations.

Test your understanding 1

The directors of Murray Co are interested in being able to report that they comply with best practice corporate governance principles and have asked for your thoughts.

The finance director has provided you with the following information:

The board consists of the chief executive officer, finance director, HR director, production director and sales director. In addition there are two non-executive directors who were appointed last year by the chief executive as they are his aunt and uncle. Previously they ran their own small café and used a firm of accountants for all financial matters due to their own lack of expertise in that area.

The contracts signed by the non-executive directors state that they are in place until they decide to leave or unless they are found guilty of misconduct. They receive an annual fee and a number of share options in Murray Co as their remuneration.

Since appointment, the two non-executives have formed an audit committee consisting of themselves and the human resources director as it was felt that the finance director would not be an independent member of the committee.

They have also formed a remuneration committee with the finance director and are currently in the process of proposing and approving the salaries for all of the directors for the coming year.

Required:

(a) **Explain whether Murray Co is required to comply with a code of corporate governance.**

(b) **Explain the strengths of Murray Co's current governance arrangements.**

(c) **Identify and explain the weaknesses in Murray Co's current governance arrangements and for each weakness recommend an action the company should take to remedy the weakness.**

Test your understanding 2

You are the audit manager of Tela & Co, a medium sized firm of accountants. Your firm has just been asked for assistance from Jumper & Co, a firm of accountants in an adjacent country. This country has just implemented the internationally recognised codes on corporate governance and Jumper & Co has a number of clients where the codes are not being followed. One example of this, from SGCC, a listed company, is shown below. As your country already has appropriate corporate governance codes in place, Jumper & Co have asked for your advice regarding the changes necessary in SGCC to achieve appropriate compliance with corporate governance codes.

Extract from financial statements regarding corporate governance:

Mr Sheppard is the chief executive officer and board chair of SGCC. He appoints and maintains a board of five executive and two non-executive directors. While the board sets performance targets for the senior managers in the company, no formal targets are set for the board and no review of board policies is carried out. Board salaries are therefore set and paid by Mr Sheppard based on his assessment of all the board members, including himself, and not their actual performance.

Internal controls in the company are monitored by the senior accountant, although a detailed review is assumed to be carried out by the external auditors. SGCC does not have an audit committee or an internal audit department.

Annual financial statements are produced, providing detailed information on past performance.

Required:

(i)   Explain SIX corporate governance deficiencies in SGCC, and

(ii) Recommend the changes necessary to overcome each deficiency. **(12 marks)**

Test your understanding 3

Cocklebiddy Co, a listed company, is currently reviewing its corporate governance practices to ensure they are compliant with regulations. The following is a description of the corporate governance policies they have in place:

- A remuneration committee comprising 3 non-executive directors.

- An audit committee comprising the finance director, the chief executive and 2 non-executive directors.

- Separate people taking on the roles of chair and chief executive.

(1) **Which of the following best defines Corporate Governance?**

    A   Corporate governance refers to the importance a company attaches to systems and controls.

    B   Corporate governance is the means by which a company is operated and controlled.

    C   Corporate governance is the extent to which a company is audited, both internally and externally.

    D   Corporate governance is an appraisal activity as a service to the entity.

(2) **In terms of the structure of the audit committee of Cocklebiddy Co, which of the following actions should be taken to become compliant with corporate governance regulations?**

    A   A minimum of one non-executive director should be recruited

    B   A minimum of one non-executive director should be recruited and the finance director should be removed

    C   A minimum of one non-executive director should be recruited and the finance director and chief executive should be removed

    D   No action necessary

(3) **Which TWO of the following are functions of audit committees?**

 (i) Planning the annual external audit.

 (ii) Reviewing the effectiveness of internal financial controls.

 (iii) Reviewing and monitoring the external auditor's independence.

 (iv) Processing year-end journal adjustments to the financial statements.

 A (i) and (iv)

 B (i) and (iii)

 C (ii) and (iv)

 D (ii) and (iii)

(4) **Cocklebiddy Co does not currently have an internal audit function. Which of the following summarises the requirements of corporate governance regulations in respect of internal audit?**

 A The audit committee must review the need for an internal audit function on an annual basis

 B The audit committee must establish an internal audit committee as soon as possible

 C There must either be an audit committee or internal audit function in place but there is no requirement to have both

 D The finance director must review the need for an internal audit function and should make a request to the audit committee if it is decided that an internal audit function would be beneficial

(5) **Which of the following is the main purpose of the remuneration committee?**

 A To ensure that the costs of the company are kept under control

 B To ensure no director is involved in setting his own pay and the pay that is set is at an appropriate level

 C To ensure decision making power for the company is not concentrated in the hands of one individual

 D To ensure executives are paid a large basic salary irrespective of performance

4 Chapter summary

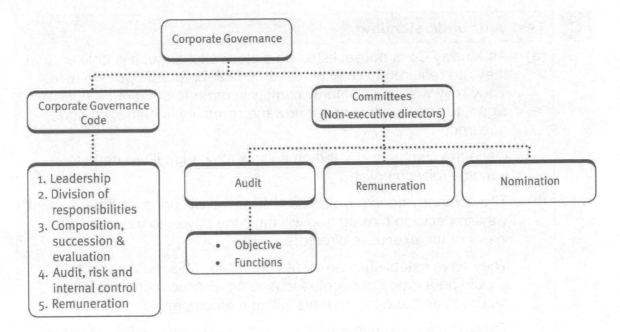

Test your understanding answers

Test your understanding 1

(a) As Murray Co is not yet listed on a stock exchange, it is unlikely that they are required to comply with a code of corporate governance. They may wish to voluntarily comply in order to send out a positive signal to stakeholders about how the company is managed and governed.

Once the company is listed on a stock exchange it will need to become fully compliant.

(b) The company does have some NEDs who will bring an independent view to decision making and will have the power to balance the views of the executive directors.

They have established an audit committee. This means that there should be a group of people focused on all accounting, financial reporting and auditing matters within the company.

There is also a remuneration committee which should bring some independence and fairness into the decisions on salaries and rewards of the directors.

(c)

Weakness	Recommendation
There are not enough non-executive directors. Corporate governance principles require the board to be balanced, and currently the executive directors outweigh the NEDs. This means that the executives could ensure all of their proposals are passed at board meetings which reduces the effectiveness of the NEDs.	At least three more NEDs need to be recruited to ensure a balanced board.

There does not appear to be a chair. Corporate governance principles require that there is an independent chair to run the board and a chief executive in charge of running the company. This is to ensure there is not too much power in the hands of one person and so these two roles cannot be fulfilled by the same person.	An independent person should be appointed as chair.
The current NEDs do not appear to be independent. The logic for NEDs is to being an independent view to the board and to feel comfortable challenging the decisions of the executive directors. As the two current NEDs are related to the CEO, it is unlikely they would challenge any of their decisions making them ineffective.	The two NEDS need to be replaced by independent people.
The NEDs appear to have a continuous contract. In order to make sure they work in the company's best interests, all directors should be subject to re-election at regular intervals. This does not appear to be the case here.	All directors should be subject to re-election on an annual basis.
The NEDs have share options as part of their remuneration. Corporate governance principles make it clear that in order to maintain their independence, NEDs should be paid a flat fee for their services and it should not be related to company performance.	All new NED contracts should have remuneration based on time commitment and responsibilities of the role.

An executive director sits on the audit committee. The sub-committees are meant to be independent and so it is required that only NEDs sit on the audit committee.	The HR director should be removed from the audit committee and one of the newly appointed NEDs should take their place.
Nobody on the audit committee has financial experience. In order to provide valuable input into the accounting and auditing process, at least one member of the audit committee should have financial experience.	When recruiting the new NEDs the company should look for at least one person with a financial background to sit on the audit committee.
An executive director sits on the remuneration committee. It is a requirement of corporate governance principles that no director should be involved in setting their own remuneration as this could lead to excessive pay being awarded.	The finance director should be removed from the remuneration committee and one of the newly appointed NEDs should take their place. The remuneration committee should set the salaries for the executives, senior management and chair. The board should determine the remuneration of the NEDs.

Test your understanding 2

Why the corporate governance code is not met and why this may cause problems	Recommendation
Mr Sheppard is chief executive and chair of the company. Mr Sheppard has too much power over the key decisions of the company.	An independent person should be appointed as chair.
The board ratio is 5:2 in favour of the executive directors. Executive directors can dominate board decisions which may not be in the best interests of the shareholders.	Three more NEDs should be appointed to balance the board.

Mr Sheppard appoints all directors to the board. Mr Sheppard may appoint directors who will support his voting at board decisions. There may be no clear and transparent process for determining appointments.	A nomination committee comprising a majority NEDs should be established to appoint directors and ensure there is no bias.
Mr Sheppard sets the pay of the directors as well as setting his own pay. Mr Sheppard may pay directors more if they agree to back his decisions. He may pay himself more than he deserves.	A remuneration committee comprising independent NEDs should be established to set the pay of the executive directors. The committee should make sure the pay promotes long-term, sustainable success.
The board's performance is not reviewed. If performance is not reviewed there is no accountability for poor performance. The board may not be as effective as it could be at maximising shareholder wealth.	Performance targets should be set and performance against these targets monitored on a regular basis. Directors should be required to explain any under-performance.
It is believed that the external auditor monitors the internal controls. The external auditor will only look at controls relevant to the audit but this cannot be relied on to determine the effectiveness of the internal control systems across the company.	The audit committee should consider the need for an internal audit function. If the audit committee considers an internal audit function is not required they should describe in the annual report how internal assurance is achieved.
There is no audit committee. Corporate governance codes require an audit committee to be established to take responsibility for the oversight of financial reporting and audit matters.	An audit committee should be established comprising independent NEDs and they will be the main point of contact for internal auditors and external auditors.

Test your understanding 3

(1)	B	The means by which a company is operated and controlled.
(2)	C	The audit committee should comprise 3 non-executive directors. The chief executive and finance director should not be members of the audit committee. In addition, it should be confirmed that the NEDs currently sitting on the audit committee are independent.
(3)	D	Reviewing the effectiveness of internal financial controls and reviewing and monitoring the external auditor's independence.
(4)	A	There is no requirement for a company to have an internal audit function. The audit committee should review the need for one on an annual basis if the company does not have one.
(5)	B	Directors should not be involved in setting their own pay. Remuneration should be performance related. Remuneration should be sufficient to attract, retain and motivate but should not be excessive.

Ethics and acceptance

Chapter learning objectives

This chapter covers syllabus areas:

- A4 – Professional ethics and ACCA's Code of Ethics and Conduct

- B1 – Obtaining, accepting and continuing audit engagements

Detailed syllabus objectives are provided in the introduction section of the text book.

PER

One of the PER performance objectives (PO1) is ethics and professionalism. The fundamental principles of ethical behaviour mean you should always act in the wider public interest. You need to take into account all relevant information and use professional judgement, your personal values and scepticism to evaluate data and make decisions. You should identify right from wrong and escalate anything of concern. You also need to make sure that your skills, knowledge and behaviour are up-to-date and allow you to be effective in your role. Working through this chapter should help you understand how to demonstrate that objective.

1 The need for professional ethics

Professional accountants have a responsibility to act in the public interest. The purpose of assurance engagements is to increase the confidence of the intended users; therefore the users need to trust the professional who is providing the assurance.

In order to be trusted the assurance provider needs to be independent of their client.

 Independence can be defined as having 'freedom from situations and relationships where objectivity would be perceived to be impaired by a reasonable and informed third party.'

 Practitioners need to **behave and be seen to behave** in an ethical, professional manner. This means taking active steps to comply with the Code of Ethics in every professional situation.

2 The IFAC and ACCA codes and the conceptual framework

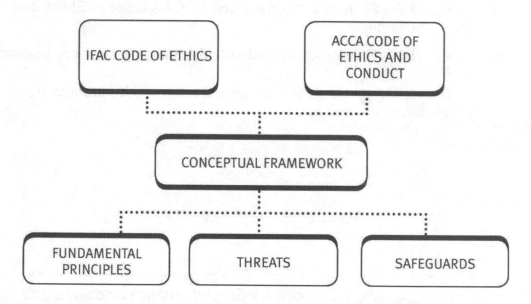

IFAC, through the IESBA, has issued a code of ethics, as has the ACCA. The ACCA Code of Ethics is covered in this chapter. However, both of these Codes have the same roots and are, to all intents and purposes identical.

Both follow a conceptual framework which identifies:

- Fundamental principles of ethical behaviour

- Potential threats to compliance with these fundamental principles

- Possible safeguards which can be implemented to eliminate the threats identified, or reduce them to an acceptable level.

Ethical guidance can take either a principles-based approach or rules-based approach.

A conceptual framework relies on a principles-based approach.

Both IFAC and the ACCA adopt a principles-based approach.

Principles-based approach	Rules-based approach
• Flexible, so can be applied to new, unusual or rapidly changing situations. • Principles may be applied across national boundaries where laws may not. • Requires the accountant to use professional judgment. • Requires compliance with the spirit of the guidance. • Can still incorporate specific rules for ethical situations likely to affect many firms.	• May be easier to follow because rules are clearly defined. • Needs frequent updating to ensure the guidance applies to new situations. • May encourage accountants to interpret requirements narrowly in order to get round the spirit of the requirements. • Virtually impossible to be able to deal with every situation that may arise, particularly across various national boundaries and in a dynamic industry.

Consequences

Practitioners should apply the spirit of the code to everyday practice. Professional bodies such as the ACCA have the right to discipline members who fail to comply with the code of ethics through a process of disciplinary hearings which can result in:

- Fines
- Suspension of membership
- Withdrawal of membership.

3 The fundamental principles

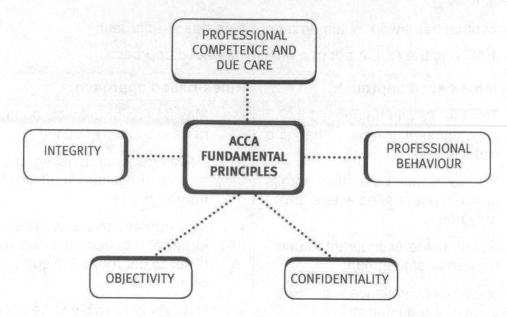

The formal definitions of the fundamental principles are as follows:

- **Objectivity:** Members should <u>not allow bias</u>, <u>conflicts</u> of interest or <u>undue influence of others</u> to override professional or business judgments.

- **Professional behaviour:** Members should <u>comply with relevant laws and regulations</u> and should <u>avoid</u> any <u>conduct that discredits the profession</u>.

- **Professional competence and due care**: Members should <u>maintain</u> professional <u>knowledge and skill</u> at the level required to ensure that a client or employer receives <u>competent professional services</u> based on current developments in practice, legislation and techniques.

  Members should <u>act diligently</u> and in accordance with applicable technical and professional standards.

- **Integrity:** Members should be <u>straightforward</u> and <u>honest</u> in all professional and business relationships.

- **Confidentiality:** Members should respect the confidentiality of information acquired as a result of professional and business relationships and should <u>not disclose</u> any such information to third parties <u>without</u> proper and specific <u>authority</u>, <u>unless there is a legal or professional right or duty to disclose</u>. Such confidential information <u>should not be used for the personal advantage</u> of members or third parties.

[ACCA Code of Ethics and Conduct 2018, Section 100.5]

Illustration 1 – Fundamentals principles

The following are real précis hearings held and decisions made and published by the ACCA Disciplinary Committee:

(1) A member was found guilty of misconduct because they signed the auditor's report without conducting any audit work, contrary to the fundamental principle of **integrity**.

(2) A member was found guilty of misconduct because they failed to advise a client to have an audit when an audit was required by law, contrary to the fundamental principle of **professional competence and due care**.

(3) A member was found guilty of misconduct because they 'failed to reply to correspondence sent by a third party and ACCA' contrary to the fundamental principle of **professional behaviour**.

(4) A member was found guilty of misconduct because they 'lost possession of a client's books and records to a third party' contrary to the fundamental principle of **confidentiality**.

(5) A member was found guilty of misconduct because they 'carried out an audit of a company' in which they owned shares 'without implementing appropriate safeguards' contrary to the fundamental principle of **objectivity**.

As a result, a combination of the following sanctions were ordered by the ACCA Disciplinary Committee in each case:

- Suspension of membership

- Exclusion from ACCA

- A fine

- Ordered to pay costs

- Publication of the results of the decision and the member's name on the ACCA website

- Publication of the results of the decision and the member's name in the local press.

4 Threats and safeguards

Firms must establish procedures to:

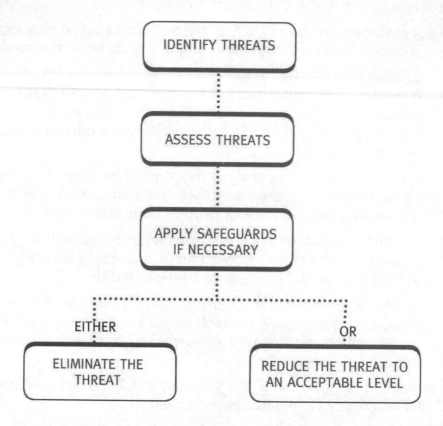

A **safeguard** is an action or measure that eliminates a threat, or reduces it to an acceptable level.

The Code of Ethics divides safeguards into two broad categories:

- **Safeguards created by the profession, legislation or regulation,** these include: requirements for entry into the profession, continuing professional development, corporate governance, professional standards, monitoring and disciplinary procedures, etc.

- **Safeguards created by the work environment,** these include: rotation/removal of relevant staff from the engagement team, independent quality control reviews, using separate teams, etc.

[Section 100.13]

Identifying threats

Self Interest

- Own shares
- Fee dependency
- Gifts & hospitality
- Loans
- Business and personal relationships
- Employment with client
- Overdue fees
- Contingency fees
- Litigation with a client

Self Review

- Accounts preparation
- Internal audit
- Tax computations
- Valuation services
- Client staff joins the audit firm

Familiarity

- Long association
- Personal relationships
- Movement of staff between the firm and client
- Gifts & hospitality

Threats to objectivity

Intimidation

- Fee dependency
- Personal relationships
- Audit partner leaves to join client
- Litigation with a client

Advocacy

- Representing the client
- Promoting the client
- Negotiating on behalf of the client

Self-interest threats

Where the auditor has a financial or other interest that will inappropriately influence their judgment or behaviour.

Threat	Safeguards
Fee dependency Over-dependence on an audit client could lead the auditor to ignore adjustments required in the financial statements for fear of losing the client.	*Non-listed clients* If fees from an audit client represent a large proportion of the firm's total fees, the firm should implement safeguards such as: • Reducing dependency on the client • Consulting with a third party on key audit judgments • Having an external quality control review. [Section 290.215] *Listed clients* A firm's independence is threatened, and should be reviewed if total fees from a listed audit client exceed 15% of the firm's total fees for two consecutive years. • The firm should disclose the issue to those charged with governance at the client. • An independent engagement quality control review should be performed by a person not a member of the audit firm expressing the opinion, or by the professional regulatory body. This can be performed as either a pre-issuance review, before the 2nd year audit opinion is issued or a post-issuance review on the 2nd year audit before the 3rd year audit opinion is issued. [Section 290.217]

Gifts and hospitality Acceptance of goods, services or hospitality from an audit client can create self-interest and familiarity threats as the auditor may feel indebted to the client.	Gifts and hospitality may not be accepted unless: • the value is trivial and inconsequential. • offered in the normal course of business without intention to influence decision-making. [Section 260.2] The offer of gifts and hospitality must be documented in the audit file even if refused.
Owning shares/financial interests The auditor will want to maximise return from the investment and overlook audit adjustments which would affect the value of their investment.	Any member of the audit team or their immediate family must not have a financial interest in the audit client therefore they must dispose of the shares immediately or be removed from the team. [Section 290.104] Any member of the audit team who has a close family member who owns shares should be removed from the audit team or the family member should dispose of their shares. [Section 290.105] A partner of the firm in the office connected with the audit engagement, or any partner providing non-audit services to the audit client should not have a financial interest in the client. [Section 290.110]
Overdue fees The overdue fees may be regarded as a loan (loans are not permitted to an audit client).	Do not perform any further work for, or issue any reports to, the client until the outstanding fees are paid or arrangements have been agreed with the client for payment. An independent review of the work should be performed if the fees remain unpaid after the report has been issued. [Section 290.218]

Loans and guarantees A loan or guarantee from (or deposit with) an assurance client that is a bank or similar institution will not create a threat to independence provided that: • it is on commercial terms, and • made in the normal course of business.	Loans and guarantees between audit clients and audit team members and their immediate family that are not in the normal course of business or not on commercial terms are not permitted. [Section 290.117] If the loan is made to the firm (rather than a member of the audit team), it must be immaterial to both the firm and the client. If it is material, appropriate safeguards should be put into place, e.g. an external review of the work performed. [Section 290.118]
Business relationships If audit firms (or members) enter into business relationships with clients (e.g. joint ventures, marketing arrangements), this leads to self-interest because the auditor would have an interest in the successful operation of the client. The purchase of goods and services from an assurance client would not normally give rise to a threat to independence, provided the transaction is in the normal course of business and on commercial terms.	In the case of audit firms, or partners of those firms, unless immaterial, no safeguard can reduce this threat to an acceptable level. In the case of audit team members, the individual with the connection to the audit client should be removed from the audit team. [Section 290.123] If the purchase of goods and services by an audit team member represents a material amount, that person should be removed from the audit team or they should reduce the magnitude of the transactions. [Section 290.125]
Potential employment with an audit client If a member of the engagement team has reason to believe they may become an employee of the client they will not wish to do anything to affect their potential future employment.	The policies and procedures of the firm should require such individuals to notify the firm of the possibility of employment with the client. Remove the individual from the assurance engagement. Perform an independent review of any significant judgments made by that individual. [Section 290.136]

Contingent fees The auditor would have incentive to ensure a particular outcome is achieved in order to maximise the audit fee. E.g. overlook audit adjustments that would reduce profit if the fee is a percentage of the profit.	Fees based on a particular outcome, e.g. level of profits of the company, are not permitted for assurance services. [Section 290.220]
Compensation and evaluation policies A self-interest threat is created when a member of the audit team is evaluated on or compensated for selling non-assurance services to that audit client. The significance of the threat will depend on: • The proportion of the individual's compensation or performance evaluation that is based on the sale of such services. • The role of the individual on the audit team. • Whether promotion decisions are influenced by the sale of such services. [Section 290.223]	A key audit partner shall not be evaluated on or compensated based on their success in selling non-assurance services to their audit client. [Section 290.224] For other staff the firm shall either revise the compensation plan or evaluation process for that individual or apply safeguards such as: • Removing such members from the audit team. • Having a professional accountant review the work of the member of the audit team. [Section 290.223]
Actual or threatened litigation Litigation could represent a breakdown of trust in the relationship between auditor and client. This may affect the impartiality of the auditor, and lead to a reluctance of management to disclose relevant information to the auditor. The significance of the threat depends on the materiality of the litigation and whether the litigation relates to a prior assurance engagement.	It may be possible to continue other assurance engagements, depending on the significance of the threat by: • Discussing the matter with the client's audit committee. • If the litigation involves an individual, removing that individual from the engagement team. • Obtaining an external review of the work done. If adequate safeguards cannot be implemented the firm must withdraw from or decline the engagement. [Section 290.226]

Familiarity threats

When the auditor becomes too sympathetic or too trusting of a client and loses professional scepticism, or where the relationship between the auditor and client goes beyond professional boundaries.

Threat	Safeguards
Long association of senior personnel Using the same senior personnel in an engagement team over a long period may cause the auditor to become too trusting/less sceptical of the client resulting in material misstatements going undetected. The firm should consider: • The length of time on the audit team. • The structure of the firm. • Whether the client's management team has changed. • Whether the complexity of the subject matter has changed. [Section 290.148]	*Non-listed clients* • Rotate senior personnel. • Independent partner/quality control reviews. [Section 290.148] *Listed clients* • Key audit partners must be rotated after no more than seven years with a minimum break of two years. If the client becomes listed, the length of time the partner has served before becoming listed is taken into account. [Section 290.149] • In exceptional circumstances, a maximum one year extension is permitted where necessary to maintain audit quality. [Section 290.150] **Tutorial note:** Large listed companies must put the audit out to tender at least every ten years. However, this is the responsibility of the company not the audit firm.
Family and personal relationships A familiarity threat (and self-interest threat or intimidation threat) may occur when a member of the engagement team has a family or personal relationship with someone at the client who is able to exert significant influence over the financial statements (or subject matter of another assurance engagement).	Remove the individual from the engagement team. Structure the engagement team so that the individual does not deal with matters that are the responsibility of the close family member. [Section 290.128]

Consideration should be given to the possibility that such a threat may also arise when a partner (or employee) of the firm has a family or personal relationship with someone at the client who is able to exert significant influence over the subject matter, even when the individual is not a member of the engagement team. [Section 290.130]	
Recruitment services Familiarity, self-interest or intimidation threats may arise if the firm is involved in recruiting senior personnel for the client. The firm may also be considered to be assuming management responsibilities. Reviewing qualifications and interviewing applicants to advise on financial competence is allowed. [Section 290.209]	*Listed clients* The firm cannot provide recruitment services in respect of directors or senior management who would be in a position to exert significant influence over the financial statements. [Section 290.210]
Employment with an audit client A self-interest, familiarity or intimidation threat may arise where an employee of the firm becomes a director or employee of an assurance client (in a position to exert significant influence over the financial statements or other subject matter). The threat is significant if significant connection remains between the employee and the firm such as entitlement to benefits or payments from the firm, or participation in the firm's business and professional activities. [Section 290.133] The firm should consider: • The position taken at the client. • The involvement the person is likely to have with the audit team. • The length of time since the individual was a member of the audit team. [Section 290.134]	Assign individuals to the audit team who have sufficient experience in relation to the individual who has joined the client. Perform a quality control review of the engagement. [Section 290.134] *Listed clients* For partners joining public interest entities, independence would be deemed to be compromised unless, subsequent to the partner ceasing to be a key audit partner or senior partner, the client had issued audited financial statements covering a period of not less than 12 months and the partner was not a member of the audit team with respect to the audit of those financial statements. [Section 290.137]

Self-review threats

Where non-audit work is provided to an audit client and is then subject to audit, the auditor will be unlikely to admit to errors in their own work, or may not identify the errors in their own work.

Threat	Safeguards
Accounting and bookkeeping services Preparing accounting records or financial statements for an audit client creates a self-review threat.	*Non-listed clients* • A firm can provide a non-listed audit client with accounting and bookkeeping services, including payroll services, of a routine or mechanical nature. • Separate teams must be used. • Managerial decisions must not be made by the firm, and the source data, underlying assumptions, and subsequent adjustments must be originated or approved by the client. [Section 290.168] *Listed clients* • A firm cannot provide a listed audit client with accounting and bookkeeping services. [Section 290.169] • A firm can provide accounting services for divisions or related entities of a listed client if separate teams are used and the service relates to matters immaterial to the division/related entity. [Section 290.170]
Internal audit services In addition to the self-review threat, the auditor needs to be careful not to assume management responsibilities.	A firm cannot provide internal audit services for a listed audit client, where the service relates to internal controls over financial reporting, financial accounting systems, or in relation to amounts or disclosures that are material to the financial statements. [Section 290.195] Where services are provided, separate teams must be used. [Section 290.194]

Taxation services	Non-listed clients
Tax calculations for inclusion in the financial statements and tax planning advice create a self-review threat. Completion of tax returns does **not** generally create a self-review threat. [Section 290.179]	• Advice should be obtained from an external tax professional. • Where an audit team member performs the tax calculation, the work should be reviewed by a senior person with appropriate expertise that has not been involved with the audit. [Section 290.180] *Listed clients* • A firm cannot prepare tax calculations (current or deferred) for a listed audit client. [Section 290.181]
Tax advice	The firm should not provide tax advice that depends on a particular accounting treatment and is material to the financial statements. [Section 290.185] Other tax advice is allowable with safeguards. [Section 290.184]
IT services IT services may create a self-review threat and also be considered to be assuming management responsibilities.	The firm can only provide IT services which involve: • Design or implementation of IT systems unrelated to internal controls or financial reporting. • Implementation of off-the-shelf accounting software. • Evaluating and making recommendations on a system designed or operated by another service provider or by the entity. [Section 290.197]

Valuation services	*Non-listed clients*
	• Valuation of matters that are material to the financial statements and involve a significant degree of subjectivity should not be provided. • Where the threat is not deemed significant, different personnel should be used. [Section 290.172] *Listed clients* • Valuation services that are material to the financial statements (regardless of subjectivity) should not be provided to listed audit clients. [Section 290.176]
Temporary staff assignments A self-review threat will be created if staff are loaned from the audit firm to the client. If the person was assigned to the audit they would be evaluating work for which they had been responsible during the temporary assignment and may not detect errors in their work.	Staff may be loaned to the client provided: • The loan period is short. • The person does not assume management responsibilities. • The client is responsible for directing and supervising the person. • The loaned staff member is not a member of the audit team. [Section 290.140]
Corporate finance services Self-review and advocacy threats may be created if a firm: • Assists an audit client in developing corporate strategies • Identifies possible targets for the audit client to acquire • Advises on disposal transactions • Assists finance raising transactions • Provides structuring advice.	If there is doubt over the accounting treatment or if the outcome will materially affect the financial statements, the service should not be provided. [Section 290.213] Where services can be provided, the firm should: • Use professionals who are not members of the audit team to perform the service, or

Factors affecting the existence and significance of any threat include: • The degree of subjectivity involved. • Whether the outcome will have a material impact on the financial statements. • Whether the effectiveness of the corporate finance advice depends on a particular accounting treatment.	• Have a professional who was not involved in providing the corporate finance service to the client advise the audit team on the service and review the accounting treatment and any financial statement treatment. [Section 290.212]
Client staff joins audit firm A self-interest, self-review, or familiarity threat may arise where a director or employee of an assurance client (in a position to exert significant influence over the financial statements or subject matter of another assurance engagement) becomes an employee of the firm.	Such individuals should not be assigned to the audit if that person would be evaluating elements of the financial statements for which they had prepared accounting records. [Section 290.141] An employee or partner of a firm cannot also be an employee or director of an assurance client, as the self-interest and self-review threats created would be so significant that no safeguard could reduce the threats to an acceptable level. [Section 290.142]

Advocacy threats

Promoting the position of a client or representing them in some way would mean the audit firm is seen to be 'taking sides' with the client.

Examples include:

• Representing the client in court or in any dispute where the matter is material to the financial statements.

• Negotiating on the client's behalf for finance.

Where the amounts are material, the audit firm must not act for the audit client in this way. Any request for such services must be politely declined.

[Section 290.206]

Where the matter is not material to the financial statements the firm should:

- Use professionals who are not members of the audit team to perform the service, or

- Have a professional who was not involved in providing the legal services advise the audit team on the service and review any financial statement treatment.

[Section 290.207]

Providing services involving promoting, dealing in, or underwriting an audit client's shares would create an advocacy or self-review threat so significant that no safeguards could reduce the threat to an acceptable level. Accordingly, a firm shall not provide such services to an audit client.
[Section 290.214]

Intimidation threats

Actual or perceived pressures from the client or attempts to exercise undue influence over the assurance provider create an intimidation threat.

Intimidation can arise from some of the same situations mentioned above, for example:

- Fee dependency

- Personal relationships

- Audit partner joining the client

- Litigation between the audit firm and client.

The safeguards to address these threats are the same as to address the other threats.

If the threat cannot be eliminated or reduced to an acceptable level, the assurance provider must decline or resign from the engagement.

5 Confidentiality

External auditors are in a unique position of having a legal right of access to all information about their clients. The client must be able to trust the auditor not to disclose anything about their business to anyone as it could be detrimental to their operations.

Confidential information may be obtained from:

- The firm or employing organisation

- Business relationships i.e. current clients

- Prospective clients and employers.

 Members of an assurance team should not disclose any information to anyone outside of the engagement team, whether or not they work for the same firm.

Information should only be disclosed with proper and specific authority or when there is a legal or professional right or duty to disclose.

Disclosure of confidential information should only be made if:

(a) Disclosure is permitted by law and is authorised by the client or the employer.

(b) Disclosure is required by law, for example:

- Production of documents or other provision of evidence in the course of legal proceedings.

- Disclosure to the appropriate public authorities of infringements of the law that come to light.

(c) There is a professional duty or right to disclose, when not prohibited by law:

- To comply with the quality review of ACCA or another professional body.

- To respond to an inquiry or investigation by ACCA or a regulatory body.

- To protect the professional interests of a professional accountant in legal proceedings.

- To comply with technical standards and ethics requirements.

[ACCA Code of Ethics and Conduct 2018, Section 140]

Disclosure of confidential information: specific examples

Permitted or required by law

The most common offences members are likely to encounter in their professional work are in relation to:

- Fraud or theft including fraudulent financial reporting, falsification or alteration of accounting records or other documents and misappropriation of assets

- Taxation law

- Money laundering

- Insider dealing, market abuse, and bribery

- Health and safety law

- Employment law

- Environmental offences.

Public interest

An auditor may disclose information if they consider it to be in the public interest. There is no official definition of 'public interest'. The auditor must employ a combination of judgment and legal advice. A good rule of thumb is that if a member of the public could incur physical or financial damage that the auditor could knowingly have prevented it is likely that the auditor has failed in their public duty.

In determining the need to disclose matters in the public interest the auditor should consider:

- Whether those charged with governance have rectified the matter or are taking effective corrective action

- Whether members of the public are likely to be affected

- The gravity of the matter

- The likelihood of repetition

- The reasons for the client's unwillingness to make the disclosures

- Relevant legislation, accounting standards and auditing standards

- Legal advice obtained.

The auditor will be protected from the risk of liability provided that disclosure is made in the public interest, disclosure is made to an appropriate body or person, and there is no malice motivating the disclosure.

Conflicts of interest

A conflict of interest arises when the same audit firm is appointed for two companies that interact with each other, for example:

- Companies which compete in the same market

- Companies which trade with each other

A conflict of interest may create a threat to the fundamental principles of objectivity and confidentiality.

It may be perceived that the auditor cannot provide objective services and advice to a company where it also audits a competitor.

Professional accountants should always act in the best interests of the client. However, where conflicts of interest exist, the firm's work should be arranged to **avoid the interests of one being adversely affected** by those of another and to prevent a breach of **confidentiality**.

In order to ensure this, the firm must notify all affected clients of the conflict and **obtain their consent to act**.

The following additional safeguards should be considered:

- Separate engagement teams (with different engagement partners and team members).

- Procedures to prevent access to information, e.g. physical separation of the team members and confidential/secure data filing.

- Signed confidentiality agreements by the engagement team members.

- Regular review of the application of safeguards by an independent person of appropriate seniority.

- Advise the clients to seek independent advice.

If adequate safeguards cannot be implemented (i.e. where the acceptance/ continuance of an engagement would, despite safeguards, materially prejudice the interests of any clients) the firm must decline or resign from one or more conflicting engagements.

[ACCA Code of Ethics and Conduct 2018, Section 220]

Test your understanding 1

Murray case study: Ethical issues

You are an audit manager in Wimble & Co, a large audit firm which specialises in providing audit and accountancy services to manufacturing companies. Murray Co has asked your firm to accept appointment as external auditor. Murray Co manufactures sports equipment. Your firm also audits Barker Co, another manufacturer of sports equipment, and therefore your firm is confident it has the experience to carry out the audit.

You have been asked to take on the role of audit manager for Murray Co, should your firm accept the engagement. You own a small number of shares in Murray Co, as you used to be an employee of the company. Don Henman, who has been the engagement partner for Barker Co for twelve years, will take the role of engagement partner for Murray Co. The audit senior will be Tim Andrews, as his sister is the financial controller at Murray Co and therefore he knows the business well.

Your firm recently purchased some bibs, footballs and other equipment from Murray Co for the firm's annual football tournament. Murray Co has offered to provide this equipment free of charge to the firm if they accept the role as auditor.

Murray Co would also like your firm to provide taxation and accounting services. Specifically, the company would like you to prepare the financial statements and represent the company in a dispute with the taxation authorities.

The fees for last year's audit of Barker Co have not yet been paid, and you have been asked by Don Henman to look into the matter.

Required:

(a) Describe the steps Wimble & Co should take to manage the conflict of interest arising from performing the audit of Murray Co and Barker Co.

(b) Explain SIX ethical threats which may affect the independence of Wimble & Co in respect of the audit of Murray Co or Barker Co, and for each threat identify ways in which the threat might be reduced.

6 Accepting/continuing an audit engagement

An audit firm should only take on clients and work of an appropriate level of risk. For this reason, the firm will perform 'client screening'. The firm will consider the following matters before accepting a new engagement or client:

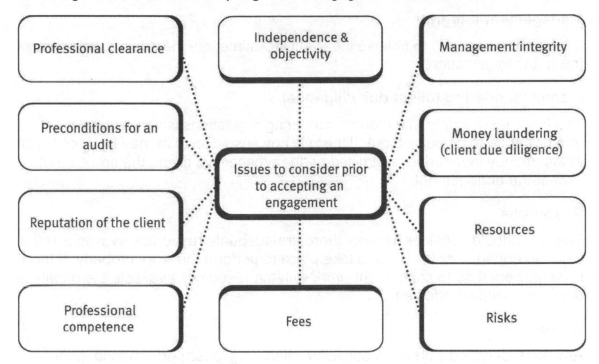

Professional clearance

If offered an audit role, the prospective audit firm must:

- Ask the client for permission to contact the existing auditor (and refuse the engagement if the client refuses).

- Contact the outgoing auditor, asking for all information relevant to the decision whether or not to accept appointment (e.g. overdue fees, disagreements with management, breaches of laws & regulations).

- If a reply is not received, the prospective auditor should try and contact the outgoing auditor by other means e.g. by telephone.

- If a reply is still not received, the prospective auditor may still choose to accept but must proceed with care.

- If a reply is received, consider the outgoing firm's response and assess if there are any ethical or professional reasons why they should not accept appointment.

- The existing auditor must ask the client for permission to respond to the prospective auditor.

- If the client refuses permission, the existing auditor should notify the prospective auditor of this fact.

Independence and objectivity

If the assurance provider is aware, prior to accepting an engagement, that the threats to objectivity cannot be managed to an acceptable level, the engagement should not be accepted.

Management integrity

If the firm has reason to believe the client lacks integrity there is a greater risk of fraud and intimidation.

Money laundering (client due diligence)

The firm must comply with money laundering regulations which require client due diligence to be carried out. If there is any suspicion of money laundering, or actual money laundering committed by the prospective client, the firm cannot accept the engagement.

Resources

The firm should consider whether there are adequate resources available at the time the engagement is likely to take place to perform the work properly. If there is insufficient time to conduct the work with the resources available the quality of the work could be affected.

Risks

Any risks identified with the prospective client (e.g. poor performance, poor controls, unusual transactions) should be considered. These risks can increase the level of engagement risk, i.e. the risk of issuing an inappropriate report.

Fees

The firm should consider the acceptability of the fee. The fee should be commensurate with the level of risk.

In addition, the creditworthiness of the prospective client should be considered as non-payment of fees can create a self-interest threat.

Professional competence

An engagement should only be accepted if the audit firm has the necessary skill and experience to perform the work competently.

Reputation of the client

The audit firm should consider the reputation of the client and whether its own reputation could be damaged by association.

If there are any reasons why the firm believes they may not be able to issue an appropriate report, they should not accept the engagement.

Preconditions for an audit

ISA 210 *Agreeing the Terms of Audit Engagements* and the Code of Ethics and Conduct provides guidance to the professional accountant when accepting new work.

Before accepting (or continuing with) an engagement the auditor must establish whether the preconditions for an audit are present and that there is a common understanding between the auditor and management and, where appropriate, those charged with governance. [ISA 210, 3]

The preconditions for an audit are that management acknowledges and understands its responsibility for:

- Preparation of the financial statements in accordance with the applicable financial reporting framework.

- Internal control necessary for the financial statements to give a true and fair view.

- Providing the auditor with access to all relevant information and explanations.

[ISA 210, 6b]

If the client imposes a limitation on the scope of the auditor's work to the extent that the auditor believes it likely that a disclaimer of opinion will ultimately be issued then the auditor shall not accept the engagement, unless required to do so by law. [ISA 210, 7]

Continuance

Once the engagement is complete, the audit firm must revisit the acceptance considerations again to ensure it is appropriate to continue for the following year. If any significant issues have arisen during the year such as disagreements with management or doubts over management integrity, the firm may consider resigning.

7 Engagement letters

Purpose

The engagement letter specifies the nature of the contract between the firm and client. The letter will be **sent before the audit commences**.

Its purpose is to:

- Minimise the risk of any misunderstanding between the practitioner and client

- Confirm acceptance of the engagement

- Set out the terms and conditions of the engagement.

Changes to the engagement letter

The engagement letter should be **reviewed every year** to ensure that it is up to date but does not need to be reissued every year unless there are changes to the terms of the engagement.

ISA 210 requires the auditor to consider whether there is a need to remind the entity of the existing terms of the audit engagement for recurring audits. Some firms choose to send a new letter every year to emphasise its importance to clients.

The auditor should issue a new engagement letter if the scope or context of the assignment changes after initial appointment, or if there is a need to remind the client of the existing terms.

Reasons for changes would include:

- Changes to statutory duties due to new legislation

- Changes to professional duties, for example, due to new or updated ISAs

- Changes to other services as requested by the client.

[ISA 210, A30]

The contents of the engagement letter

The auditor will agree the terms of the audit engagement with management or those charged with governance, as appropriate.
[ISA 210, 9]

The terms are recorded in a written audit engagement letter and should include:

- The objective and scope of the audit of the financial statements

- The responsibilities of the auditor

- The responsibilities of management

- Identification of the applicable financial reporting framework for the preparation of the financial statements

- Reference to the expected form and content of any reports to be issued by the auditor.

[ISA 210, 10]

In addition the following items will be included:

- Reference to professional standards, regulations and legislation applicable to the audit

- Limitations of an audit

- Expectation that management will provide written representations

- Basis on which the fees are calculated

- Agreement of management to notify the auditor of subsequent events after the auditor's report is signed

- Agreement of management to provide draft financial statements in time to allow the audit to be completed by the deadline

- Form (and timing) of any other communication during the audit.

[ISA 210, A24]

Other matters that the engagement letter may cover include:

- Arrangements concerning the involvement of internal auditors and other staff of the entity

- Limitations to the auditor's liability.

[ISA 210, A26]

The content of the engagement letter should be agreed with the client before any engagement related work commences.

The client's acknowledgement of the terms of the letter should be formally documented in the form of a director's signature.

| Illustration 2 – Murray Co engagement letter |

Wimble & Co
14 The Grove
Kingston
KI4 6AP

25 November 20X4

To the Board of Directors of Murray Company.

This letter and the attached terms of business dated 25 November 20X4 set out the basis on which we are to provide services as auditors and your and our respective responsibilities.

The objective and scope of the audit: You have requested that we audit the financial statements of Murray Company, which comprise the statement of financial position as at December 31, and the statement of profit or loss, statement of changes in equity and statement of cash flows for the year then ended, and a summary of significant accounting policies and other explanatory information.

We are pleased to confirm our acceptance and our understanding of this audit engagement by means of this letter. Our audit will be conducted with the objective of our expressing an opinion on the financial statements.

The responsibilities of the auditor: We will conduct our audit in accordance with International Standards on Auditing (ISAs). Those standards require that we comply with ethical requirements and plan and perform the audit to obtain reasonable assurance about whether the financial statements are free from material misstatement. An audit involves performing procedures to obtain audit evidence about the amounts and disclosures in the financial statements. The procedures selected depend on the auditor's judgment, including the assessment of the risks of material misstatement of the financial statements, whether due to fraud or error. An audit also includes evaluating the appropriateness of accounting policies used and the reasonableness of accounting estimates made by management, as well as evaluating the overall presentation of the financial statements.

Because of the inherent limitations of an audit, together with the inherent limitations of internal control, there is an unavoidable risk that some material misstatements may not be detected, even though the audit is properly planned and performed in accordance with ISAs.

In making our risk assessments, we consider internal control relevant to Murray Company's preparation of the financial statements in order to design audit procedures that are appropriate in the circumstances, but not for the purpose of expressing an opinion on the effectiveness of Murray Company's internal control. However, we will communicate to you in writing concerning any significant deficiencies in internal control relevant to the audit of the financial statements that we have identified during the audit.

The responsibilities of management: Our audit will be conducted on the basis that management acknowledge and understand that they have responsibility:

(a) For the preparation and fair presentation of the financial statements in accordance with International Financial Reporting Standards.

(b) For such internal control as management determines is necessary to enable the preparation of financial statements that are free from material misstatement, whether due to fraud or error.

(c) To provide us with:

    (i) Access to all information of which management is aware that is relevant to the preparation of the financial statements such as records, documentation and other matters.

    (ii) Additional information that we may request from management for the purpose of the audit.

    (iii) Unrestricted access to persons within the entity from whom we determine it necessary to obtain audit evidence.

As part of our audit process, we will request from management written confirmation concerning representations made to us in connection with the audit. We look forward to full cooperation from your staff during our audit.

Report: We will report to the members of Murray Company as a body, whether in our opinion the financial statements present fairly in all material respects, the financial position of Murray Company as at December 31, and its financial performance and its cash flows for the year then ended in accordance with International Financial Reporting Standards. The form and content of our report may need to be amended in the light of our audit findings.

Fees: Our fees, which will be billed as work progresses, are based on the time required by the individuals assigned to the engagement plus out-of-pocket expenses. Individual hourly rates vary according to the degree of responsibility involved and the experience and skill required.

Limitation of liability: To the fullest extent permitted by law, we will not be responsible for any losses, where you or others supply incorrect or incomplete information, or fail to supply any appropriate information or where you fail to act on our advice or respond promptly to communications from us.

Our work is not, unless there is a legal or regulatory requirement, to be made available to third parties without our written permission and we will accept no responsibility to third parties for any aspect of our professional services or work that is made available to them.

Confirmation of your agreement: Please sign and return the attached copy of this letter to indicate your acknowledgement of, and agreement with, the arrangements for our audit of the financial statements including our respective responsibilities.

If this letter and the attached terms of business are not in accordance with your understanding of our terms of appointment, please let us know.

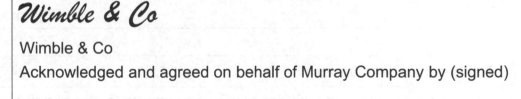

Wimble & Co

Acknowledged and agreed on behalf of Murray Company by (signed)

....

Date

Further explanation of engagement letter contents

To the Board of Directors of Murray Company...

- Although the auditor's report is issued to the shareholders, the engagement letter is addressed to and signed by the directors of a company.

The responsibilities of the auditor... The responsibilities of management...

- It is important to set out the directors' and auditor's responsibilities for clarity and to reduce any expectation gap.

- The responsibilities of the auditor include the scope of the audit, i.e. the process by which the auditor will form their opinion. The same description of the scope of an audit is included in the auditor's report.

We will report to the members of Murray Company as a body...

- It is important to define who the intended users of the report are, i.e. who can place reliance on it.

Confirmation of your agreement...

- Both the client and the auditor must sign and retain a copy of the engagement letter for reference and to support the contract agreed.

Test your understanding 2

Explain each of the FIVE fundamental principles of ACCA's Code of Ethics and Conduct.

(5 marks)

Test your understanding 3

(a) There are legal and professional arrangements for the appointment and removal of auditors.

    (i) **State the circumstances in which a person is not eligible to act as an auditor.**

(2 marks)

    (ii) **Describe the steps required to remove an auditor from an engagement.**

(3 marks)

(b) You are a manager in the audit department of Whilling and Abel. A potential new client, Truckers Co, a haulage company, has approached your firm to do the external audit in addition to some other non-audit services for the year-ended 30 September. Your audit firm was recommended to Truckers Co by an existing client, O&P, a shipping company who is also a major customer of Truckers Co.

You have been chosen to lead the engagement as you have experience of auditing haulage companies and you also manage the audit of O&P.

Whilst arranging the initial meeting with the directors of Truckers Co you discover that you studied accountancy with the finance director at university.

Truckers Co has not made a profit for the last 2 years. The directors explain that this is largely due to escalating costs in the industry including fuel price rises. They are confident they have now controlled their costs for the current year. They have also been approached to tender for a large profitable contract which would improve their financial performance going forward. They would like you to assist them with the preparation of this tender and present with them on the day.

The current year's financial statements and audit are being finalised with another audit firm. The finance director tells you that the current auditors have identified material misstatements but the board of directors are refusing to make these adjustments. If adjusted, it would turn the break-even position into a loss.

The current auditors have replied to your professional clearance letter and have informed you that they are still owed fees relating to the prior year. This is under dispute with the client.

You calculate that the potential fees from Truckers Co would amount to approximately 14% of your firm's total fee income.

Required:

Identify and explain the threats to independence if Whilling and Abel accept Truckers Co as a new audit client. For each threat, recommend how the threat can be managed.

(15 marks)

(Total: 20 marks)

Test your understanding 4

You are holding a training course for your firm's new recruits covering the topic of ethics. The training will focus on the fundamental principles of ethical behaviour which accountants must follow. You have compiled the following quiz for the end of the session to test their understanding of the course content.

(1) **Which of these is NOT a fundamental ethical principle?**

A   Integrity

B   Independence

C   Objectivity

D   Professional competence and due care

(2) **Which of these statements provides the best explanation of integrity?**

A   Members should act diligently and in accordance with applicable technical and professional standards

B   Members should not bring the profession into disrepute

C   Members should not use client information for personal advantage

D   Members should be straightforward and honest in all professional and business relationships

(3) **A member was found guilty of ethical misconduct by failing to respond to the professional clearance requests from another audit firm. This is a breach of which fundamental principle?**

A   Integrity

B   Independence

C   Professional behaviour

D   Professional competence and due care

(4) **Which of the following statements best describes the conceptual framework approach to ethics?**

A   A set of rules which must be followed in all circumstances

B   A set of principles which the auditor applies based on professional judgment

C   The conceptual framework is set out in company law

D   A set of principles which the auditor applies at their discretion

(5) Why do auditors need to be independent?

A To ensure users of the auditor's report can place reliance on it and have faith it is not biased

B To ensure the financial statements give a true and fair view

C To provide more regulation for auditors to increase the perception of quality

D The law requires it

Test your understanding 5

You are the audit manager responsible for the audit of Broome Co, a listed company. You have been informed by one of the audit juniors that the finance director has offered to take the audit team to a World Cup Final at the expense of the client as a thank you for an efficient audit with minimal disruption.

The finance director has requested that you attend a social event where the company will outline a new rights issue of ordinary shares to shareholders. The finance director believes that the presence of the external auditor will add credibility to the rights issue and increase the chance of raising the required finance.

(1) Which of the following is NOT a threat to objectivity?

A Independence

B Self-review

C Advocacy

D Intimidation

(2) Which ethical threat would be created if the audit manager attends the social event where the client will outline a new rights issue to shareholders?

A Familiarity

B Advocacy

C Self-review

D Self-interest

(3) The offer of tickets to the World Cup Final creates which type of threat?

A Intimidation

B Advocacy

C Self-review

D Self-interest

(4) **What is the restriction, if any, on the level of fee income that can be received from recurring work from Broome Co before a situation of dependency is presumed to exist?**

A   5%

B   10%

C   15%

D   No restriction

(5) **For clients where the level of fees must be monitored, what safeguard can the firm apply to reduce the threat to an acceptable level?**

(i)   Rotation of audit team members on an annual basis.

(ii)   Discussion of the matter with the audit committee.

(iii)   Assign an engagement quality control review partner.

A   (i) and (ii) only

B   (i) and (iii) only

C   (ii) and (iii) only

D   (i), (ii) and (iii)

8   Chapter summary

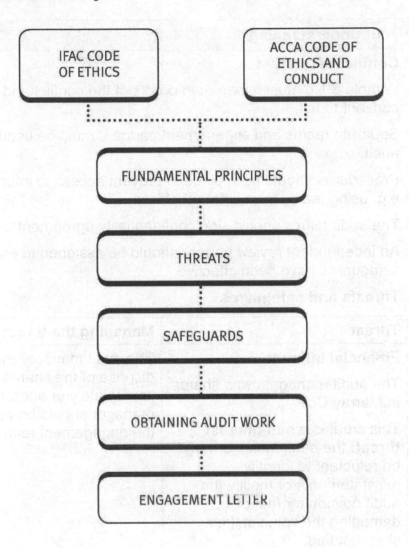

Test your understanding answers

Test your understanding 1

(a) Conflict of interest

Wimble & Co must inform both clients of the conflict and obtain their consent to act.

Separate teams and engagement partners must be used for each audit.

Procedures should be in place to prevent access to information e.g. using teams from different offices.

The audit teams should sign confidentiality agreements.

An independent review partner should be assigned to ensure the safeguards have been effective.

(b) Threats and safeguards

Threat	Managing the threat
Financial interest The audit manager owns shares in Murray Co. This creates a **self-interest threat:** the audit manager may be reluctant to identify misstatements or modify the audit opinion for fear of damaging the value of their shareholding.	The audit manager must dispose of the shares immediately or another audit manager should be appointed to the engagement team instead.
Previous employment with the client The audit manager used to work for Murray Co. This creates a **self-review threat**.	The audit manager should not be assigned to the audit of Murray Co if they would be audited accounting records they had prepared whilst employed at the client.

If employment with the client was recent, the audit manager may be auditing work for which they were responsible when working for Murray Co. They may not identify errors in their own work, or if they are identified, they may not be brought to the client's attention. In addition, a familiarity threat may arise as the audit manager is likely to have friendships with previous colleagues which could result in the audit manager not applying sufficient professional scepticism and trusting the client too much.	
Gifts and hospitality Murray Co has offered free equipment to the auditor. Accepting gifts or hospitality from an audit client may create **self-interest** and familiarity threats. The auditor may feel indebted to the client or the offer may be seen to be a bribe from the client for a clean audit opinion.	The firm should evaluate the gift offered and unless trivial and inconsequential, the audit team must not accept the equipment.
Long association The engagement partner for Barker Co has been in place for twelve years. **Familiarity** and **self-interest** threats are created by using the same senior personnel on an assurance engagement for a long period of time. The audit partner may be too trusting of the client and may lack professional scepticism.	• Rotate the senior personnel. • Independent review of the senior personnel's work. • Independent quality control reviews of the engagement.

Personal relationship The audit senior's sister is the financial controller at Murray Co and is therefore in a position to exert significant influence over the financial statements. Family and personal relationships between a member of an assurance team and a director of the client, or an employee of the client in a position to exert significant influence over the subject matter, may create **familiarity, self-interest or intimidation threats**. The audit senior may be too trusting of his sister and not apply sufficient professional scepticism.	Tim Andrews should not be on the audit team for Murray Co.
Representing the client Murray Co would like the audit firm to represent the company in a dispute with the taxation authorities. This would create **advocacy** and **self-review** threats as the audit firm would be seen to be taking sides with their client.	Firms must not represent audit clients in such disputes. The request should be politely declined.
Overdue fees The fee for last year's audit of Barker Co has not yet been paid. Overdue fees create a **self-interest threat** where they remain unpaid for some time. The auditor may be reluctant to raise issues with the client in case they refuse to pay. In addition, overdue fees could be perceived to be a loan. An audit firm must not enter into any loan arrangement with a client.	Do not perform any more work for the client until the outstanding have been paid, or arrangements for payment have been agreed with the client.

Provision of other services	
Murray Co would like the audit firm to prepare the financial statements. Preparing the financial statements and then auditing them creates a significant self-review threat. If the auditor reviews work they were responsible for, they may not identify errors they have made.	• The firm must only perform work of a routine or mechanical nature. • Use staff who are not part of the audit team to prepare the financial statements. • If performed by a member of the audit team, arrange an independent partner or senior staff member to review the work performed. **Tutorial note:** If an audit client is a listed or other public interest entity, the firm must not provide any accounting or bookkeeping services.

Test your understanding 2

Fundamental principles

Integrity. A professional accountant should be honest and straightforward in performing professional services.

Objectivity. A professional accountant should be fair and not allow personal bias, conflict of interest or influence of others to override objectivity.

Professional competence and due care. When performing professional services, a professional accountant should show competence and due care by acting diligently when performing their work and keeping up-to-date with developments in practice, legislation and techniques.

Confidentiality. A professional accountant should respect the confidentiality of information acquired during the course of providing professional services and should not use or disclose such information without obtaining client permission.

Professional behaviour. A professional accountant should act in a manner consistent with the good reputation of the profession and refrain from any conduct which might discredit the profession.

Test your understanding 3

(a)   (i)   A person is not eligible to act as an auditor in the following circumstances:

– They are not a member of an RSB (recognised supervisory body) or not allowed to practise under the rules of an RSB.

– They are an officer or employee of the company.

– They are a business partner or employee of such a person.

(ii)   Steps required to remove an auditor from an engagement

– A decision must be made by the shareholders at a general meeting usually with a majority vote being required.

– Advance notice must be given to the company and the auditors prior to any general meeting.

– Auditors have the right to attend and speak at the general meeting or have representations read out on their behalf.

(b)   **Threats and independence**

Threat	Managing the threat
Audit manager knows one of the directors socially. This creates a familiarity threat. The auditor may be too trusting of the client or too sympathetic to the client's needs.	A different audit manager should be assigned to the audit of Truckers Co.
You are the audit manager of one of Trucker Co's major customers. This creates a conflict of interest and a risk that confidential information may be passed between the clients.	A different audit manager should be assigned to the audit of Truckers Co. Different teams should be used for the audit of Truckers Co and O&P.
The audit manager has been asked to present at the tender for a contract. This would give rise to an advocacy threat as the audit firm would be promoting the client.	The auditor should politely decline the invitation to present at the tender explaining their reasons.

There are outstanding fees still owed to the previous auditors. This situation could arise again for the new auditor leading to a self-interest threat where the auditor may not wish to identify misstatements or modify the audit opinion for fear of not receiving the outstanding fees.	Discuss reasons for non-payment with the client and consider whether you should accept the assignment.
The audit firm will provide non-audit services in addition to the external audit. This represents a self-review threat. The audit firm may ignore or overlook their own errors when auditing the financial statements.	The audit firm should ensure separate teams work on each engagement. An independent partner review of the files for each engagement should be arranged.
Total fees received from Trucker Co will represent 14% of the audit firm's total income. Fee dependence creates a self-interest threat. The firm may not wish to raise issues with the client for fear of losing them.	Whilling & Abel should consider declining additional non-audit services from Trucker Co to reduce fee dependence. An independent partner review of the audit work should be arranged. **Tutorial note:** If the client is a listed company, fee dependency is presumed when fees exceed 15% for two consecutive years.

Test your understanding 4

(1)	B	Whilst independence is an important characteristic for an auditor it is not one of the fundamental principles.
(2)	D	Integrity means straightforward and honest.
(3)	C	Professional behaviour incorporates professional courtesy e.g. responding promptly to requests from other auditors.
(4)	B	The conceptual framework approach requires the auditor to assess each situation individually and act in a manner that would be seen as appropriate for a professional accountant. Principles rather than rules are used as principles can apply across national boundaries. The Code of ethics is professional guidance but not a legal requirement.
(5)	A	Independence means freedom from bias and influence.

Test your understanding 5

(1)	A	Independence.
(2)	B	The audit manager may be seen to be promoting the company and encouraging the shareholders to subscribe to the rights issue.
(3)	D	Self-interest. The auditor may feel they owe the client something in return if they accept such an expensive gift.
(4)	C	15%.
(5)	C	Independence matters should be discussed with the audit committee and an engagement quality review partner should be assigned. Rotation of the audit team would not provide a safeguard for this self-interest threat.

Risk

Chapter learning objectives

This chapter covers syllabus areas:

- B2b – Explain the need to plan and perform audits with an attitude of professional scepticism and to exercise professional judgment

- B3 – Assessing audit risks

- B4 – Understanding the entity and its environment

Detailed syllabus objectives are provided in the introduction section of the text book.

PER

One of the PER performance objectives (PO18) is to is to prepare for and plan the audit process. You plan and control the engagement process, including the initial investigation. You also plan and monitor the audit programme – legally and ethically. Working through this chapter should help you understand how to demonstrate that objective.

1 Audit risk

One of the main requirements of the audit is for the auditor to:

'...obtain sufficient appropriate evidence to reduce audit risk to an acceptably low level...'

[ISA 200 *Overall Objectives of the Independent Auditor and the Conduct of an Audit in Accordance with ISAs*, 17]

 Audit risk is the risk that the auditor expresses an inappropriate opinion when the financial statements are materially misstated.
[ISA 200, 13c]

This means that they give an unmodified audit opinion when the financial statements are materially misstated.

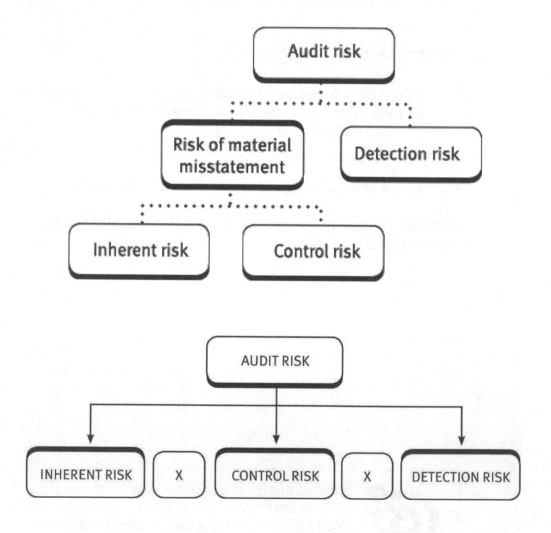

Audit risk comprises the risk of material misstatement and detection risk.

 Risk of material misstatement is the risk that the financial statements are materially misstated prior to the audit. [ISA 200, 13ni]

This will be due to fraud or errors occurring during the year when transactions have been processed or when the financial statements have been prepared.

ISA 315 (Revised) *Identifying and Assessing the Risks of Material Misstatement Through Understanding the Entity and its Environment states:*

'The objective of the auditor is to identify and assess the risk of material misstatement, whether due to fraud or error, at the financial statement and assertion levels, through understanding the entity and its environment, including the entity's internal control, thereby providing a basis for designing and implementing responses to the assessed risks of material misstatement.' [ISA 315, 3]

What is a misstatement?

 'A **difference between** the reported amount, classification, presentation, or disclosure of a **financial statement** item and the amount, classification, presentation, or disclosure that is required for the item to be in accordance with the applicable financial reporting framework. Misstatements can arise from error or fraud.'

[ISA 450 *Evaluation of Misstatements Identified During The Audit*, 4a]

In conducting a thorough assessment of risk, auditors will be able to:

- Identify areas of the financial statements where misstatements are likely to occur early in the audit.

- Plan procedures that address the significant risk areas identified.

- Carry out an efficient, focused and effective audit.

- Reduce the risk of issuing an inappropriate audit opinion to an acceptable level.

- Minimise the risk of reputational and punitive damage.

Categories of misstatement

There are three categories of misstatements:

(i)   Factual misstatements: a misstatement about which there is no doubt.

(ii) Judgmental misstatements: a difference in an accounting estimate that the auditor considers unreasonable, or the selection or application of accounting policies that the auditor considers inappropriate.

(iii) Projected misstatements: a projected misstatement is the auditor's best estimate of the total misstatement in a population through the projection of misstatements identified in a sample.

[ISA 450, A6]

The risk of material misstatement comprises inherent risk and control risk.

Inherent risk

Inherent risk is the susceptibility of an assertion about a class of transaction, account balance or disclosure to misstatement that could be material, before consideration of any related controls.
[ISA 200, 13ni]

- Complex accounting treatment is an example of an inherent risk. For example, where an accounting standard provides guidance on a specific accounting treatment this might not be understood by the client and material misstatement could result.

- Inherent risk may arise due to the nature of the industry, entity or the nature of the balance itself. For example, inventory is inherently risky if it quickly becomes obsolete as it may not be valued appropriately at the lower of cost and NRV as required by IAS 2 *Inventories*.

Control risk

Control risk is the risk that a misstatement that could occur and that could be material will not be prevented, or detected and corrected on a timely basis by the entity's internal controls.
[ISA 200, 13nii]

Control risk may be high either because the design of the internal control system is insufficient in the circumstances of the business or because the controls have not been applied effectively during the period. This is covered in more detail in the chapter 'Systems and controls'.

Detection risk

 Detection risk is the risk that the procedures performed by the auditor to reduce audit risk to an acceptably low level will not detect a misstatement that exists and that could be material.
[ISA 200, 13e]

Detection risk comprises **sampling risk** and **non-sampling risk:**

- **Sampling risk** is the risk that the auditor's conclusion based on a sample is different from the conclusion that would be reached if the whole population was tested, i.e. the sample was not representative of the population from which it was chosen. [ISA 530 *Audit Sampling*, 5c]

- **Non-sampling risk** is the risk that the auditor's conclusion is inappropriate for any other reason, e.g. the application of inappropriate procedures or the failure to recognise a misstatement. [ISA 530, 5d]

The auditor must amend the audit approach in response to risk assessment to ensure they detect the material misstatements in the financial statements. They can achieve this by:

- Emphasising the need for professional scepticism.

- Assigning more experienced staff to complex or risky areas of the engagement.

- Providing more supervision.

- Incorporating additional elements of unpredictability in the selection of further audit procedures.

- Making changes to the nature, timing or extent of audit procedures, e.g.

  - Placing less reliance on the results of systems and controls testing.

  - Performing more substantive procedures.

  - Consulting external experts on technically complex or contentious matters.

  - Changing the timing and frequency of review procedures.

[ISA 330 *The Auditor's Response to Assessed Risks*, A1]

Professional scepticism

 Professional scepticism is: 'An attitude that includes a **questioning mind,** being alert to conditions which may indicate possible misstatement due to fraud or error, and a **critical assessment of audit evidence.**'
[ISA 200, 13l]

This requires the audit team to have a good knowledge of how the client's activities are likely to affect its financial statements. The audit team should discuss these matters in a **planning meeting** before deciding on the detailed approach and audit work to be used.

How to apply professional scepticism

Professional scepticism requires the auditor to **be alert to:**

- Audit **evidence that contradicts other** audit **evidence.**

- Information that brings into question **the reliability of documents and responses to enquiries** to be used as audit evidence.

- Conditions that may indicate **possible fraud.**

- Circumstances that suggest **the need for audit procedures in addition to those required by ISAs.**

[ISA 200, A20]

Exercising professional scepticism

The auditor identifies a customer of a client is having financial difficulties and has not paid any invoices for 6 months when the client's credit terms are 10 days. The auditor may make an enquiry of management regarding the outstanding debt and their view on whether it should be written off. Management may inform the auditor that they believe the debt will be paid as they have never experienced irrecoverable debts with this customer in the past. As a result they do not intend to write it off or make any allowance for it. Application of professional scepticism would require the auditor to seek alternative, corroborative evidence to support management's claim as management may not want to allow for the debt as this will reduce profit. The auditor could review bank statements post year-end to identify if payment has been made. The auditor could also review any correspondence between the customer and the client indicating when payment might be made. Both of these procedures provide more reliable evidence than an enquiry with management who may tell the auditor what they think the auditor wants to hear to avoid an adjustment to the financial statements being suggested. Similarly, obtaining a written representation from management would not be appropriate as this is only marginally more reliable than an enquiry. Client generated evidence is always the least reliable form of evidence and the auditor should always look for better quality evidence where possible due to the risk of management bias.

2 Materiality

What is materiality?

 'Misstatements, including omissions, are considered to be material if they, individually or in the aggregate, could reasonably be expected to influence the economic decisions of users taken on the basis of the financial statements.'
[ISA 320 *Materiality in Planning and Performing an Audit*, 2]

What is the significance of materiality?

If the financial statements contain material misstatement they cannot be deemed to show a true and fair view.

As a result, the focus of an audit is identifying the significant risks of material misstatement in the financial statements and then designing procedures aimed at identifying and quantifying them.

How is materiality determined?

The determination of materiality is a **matter of professional judgment**. The auditor must consider:

- Whether the misstatement would affect the economic decision of the users
- Both the size and nature of misstatements
- The information needs of the users as a group.

Materiality is a subjective matter and as such should be considered in light of the client's circumstances.

Material by size

ISA 320 recognises the need to establish a financial threshold to guide audit planning and procedures. For this reason the following benchmarks may be used as a starting point:

- ½ – 1 % of revenue
- 5% – 10% of profit before tax
- 1 – 2% of total assets.

The above are common benchmarks but different audit firms may use different benchmarks or different thresholds for each client.

Material by nature

Materiality is not just a purely financial concern. Some items may be material by nature.

Examples of items which are material by nature or material by impact include:

- Misstatements that affect compliance with regulatory requirements.

- Misstatements that affect compliance with debt covenants.

- Misstatements that, when adjusted, would turn a reported profit into a loss for the year.

- Misstatements that, when adjusted, would turn a reported net-asset position into a net-liability position.

- Transactions with directors, e.g. salary and benefits, personal use of assets, etc.

- Disclosures in the financial statements relating to possible future legal claims or going concern issues, for example, could influence users' decisions and may be purely narrative. In this case a numerical calculation is not relevant.

Illustration 1 – Murray Co materiality

Financial Statement Extracts	20X4	20X3
	$000	$000
Revenue	21,960	19,580
Total assets	9,697	7,288
Profit before tax	1,048	248

Materiality	Lower	Upper
Revenue	½%	1%
	110	220
Profit before tax	5%	10%
	52	105
Total assets	1%	2%
	97	194

A suitable range for **preliminary materiality** is **$97,000 – $105,000**.

Materiality is not normally based on revenue, except in circumstances when it would not be meaningful to base materiality on profit, e.g. because the entity being audited is a not-for-profit entity or where there is a small profit (or a loss) as this will result in over-auditing of the financial statements (such as was the case for Murray Co in the prior year).

More than $105,000 profit is material to the statement of profit and loss; therefore preliminary materiality is likely to be set lower than this amount. Less than $52,000 is not material to profit (or to the statement of financial position) so preliminary materiality should not be less than this amount.

A suitable preliminary materiality level is most likely to be one that lies within the overlap of the ranges calculated for profit and total assets. $97,000 (1% of total assets) represents 9% profit. As this is at the lower end of the assets range, this would be a relatively prudent measure of materiality (resulting in a higher level of audit work).

$105,000 (10% of profit) represents 1.1% of total assets. Preliminary materiality might be set at this end of the range had this been a recurring audit. However, as this is a first audit, preliminary materiality is likely to be lower.

The financial statements are draft and therefore greater errors should be expected than if they were actual figures. Consequently, sample sizes for audit testing should be increased (i.e. preliminary materiality should be set at a relatively lower level).

Preliminary materiality is therefore likely to be set at $97,000.

Performance materiality

It is unlikely, in practice, that auditors will be able to design tests that identify individual material misstatements. It is much more common that misstatements are material in aggregate (i.e. in combination).

For this reason, ISA 320 introduces the concept of **performance materiality**.

 Performance materiality is 'The amount set by the auditor at less than materiality for the financial statements as a whole to reduce to an appropriately low level the probability that the aggregate of uncorrected and undetected misstatements exceeds materiality for the financial statements as a whole.' [ISA 320, 9]

- The auditor sets **performance materiality** at a **value lower than overall materiality**, and uses this lower threshold when designing and performing audit procedures.

- This **reduces** the **risk** that the auditor will fail to identify misstatements that are material when added together.

3 Risk assessment procedures

The auditor should perform the following risk assessment procedures:

- **Enquiries** with management, of appropriate individuals within the internal audit function (if there is one), and others (with relevant information) within the client entity (e.g. about external and internal changes the company has experienced)

- **Analytical procedures**

- **Observation** (e.g. of control procedures)

- **Inspection** (e.g. of key strategic documents and procedural manuals).

[ISA 315, 6]

Understanding the entity and its environment

In order to identify the risks of material misstatement in the financial statements the auditor is required to obtain an understanding of: their clients; their clients' environments; and their clients' internal controls. This generally includes:

- Relevant industry, regulatory and other external factors, including:
  - Financial reporting framework
  - Legislation and regulations
  - Competition
  - Economic conditions.

- Nature of the entity, including:
  - Nature of products and services
  - Ownership and governance structures
  - Investment and financing activities
  - Key customers and suppliers.

- Entity's selection and application of accounting policies.

- Entity's objectives, strategies and related business risks
  - Industry developments
  - New products and services
  - New accounting requirements
  - Current and future financing requirements.

- Measurement and review of the entity's financial performance

  - Performance measures and related incentives to commit fraud through management bias

  - Budgets, forecasts and variance analyses and performance reports

  - Comparison of performance with competitors

  - Consideration of performance related bonuses.

- Internal controls relevant to the audit (covered in more detail in the Systems and controls chapter).

[ISA 315, 11, A25 – A48]

If the entity has an internal audit function, obtaining an understanding of that function also contributes to the auditor's understanding, in particular, the role that the function plays in the entity's monitoring of internal control over financial reporting. [ISA 315, A113]

The information used to obtain this understanding can come from a wide range of sources, including:

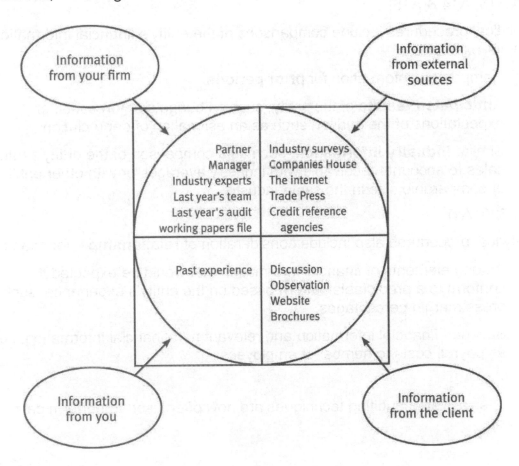

Analytical procedures

 'Evaluations of financial information through analysis **of plausible relationships** among both financial and non-financial data and investigation of identified fluctuations, inconsistent relationships or amounts that differ from expected values by a significant amount.' [ISA 520 *Analytical Procedures*, 4]

Analytical procedures are fundamental to the auditing process.

The auditor is **required to perform analytical procedures as risk assessment procedures in accordance with ISA 315** in order to:

- Identify aspects of the entity of which the auditor was unaware.

- Assist in **assessing the risks of material misstatement**.

- Help **identify unusual transactions or events, and amounts, ratios, and trends** that might have audit implications.

- Help identify **risks of material misstatement due to fraud**.

[ISA 315, A14 & A15]

Analytical procedures include comparisons of the entity's financial information with, for example:

- Comparable information for **prior periods.**

- **Anticipated results** of the entity, such as budgets or forecasts, or expectations of the auditor, such as an estimation of depreciation.

- Similar **industry information,** such as a comparison of the entity's ratio of sales to accounts receivable with industry averages or with other entities of comparable size in the same industry.

[ISA 520, A1]

Analytical procedures also include consideration of **relationships**, for example:

- Among elements of financial information that would be expected to conform to a predictable pattern based on the entity's experience, such as gross margin percentages.

- Between financial information and relevant non-financial information, such as payroll costs to number of employees.

[ISA 520, A2]

Computer-assisted auditing techniques are now often used to perform data analysis.

Analytical procedures during the audit

Analytical procedures can be used at all stages of an audit.

ISA 315 requires the auditor to perform analytical procedures as risk assessment procedures in order to help the auditor to obtain an understanding of the entity and assess the risk of material misstatement.

ISA 500 *Audit Evidence* allows the auditor to use analytical procedures as a substantive procedure during the final audit to help detect misstatement.

In addition, ISA 500 requires the auditor to use analytical procedures at the completion stage of the audit when forming an overall conclusion as to whether the financial statements are consistent with the auditor's understanding of the entity.

Key ratios

Profitability ratios

Gross margin: gross profit/sales revenue × 100%

Net margin: profit before tax/sales revenue × 100%

Auditors would expect the relationships between costs and revenues to stay relatively stable. Things that can affect these ratios include: changes in sales prices, bulk purchase discounts, economies of scale, new marketing initiatives, changing energy costs, wage inflation.

Therefore, any unusual fluctuation in the profitability ratio could mean that the figures are materially misstated. For example, if gross profit margin improves, this could be caused by any or all of the following:

- Overstated revenue because of inappropriate revenue recognition or cut-off issues.

- Understated cost of sales because of incomplete recording of purchases.

- Understated cost of sales because of overvaluation of closing inventory.

Efficiency ratios

Receivables collection period: receivables/revenue × 365

Payables payment period: payables/purchases × 365

Inventory holding period: inventory/cost of sales × 365

These ratios show how long, on average, companies take to collect cash from customers and pay suppliers and how many days inventory is held before being sold.

Any changes can indicate significant issues, such as:

- Worsening credit control and increased need for receivables allowance

- Slow-moving and possible obsolete inventory that could be overvalued

- Poor cash flow leading to going concern problems which would require disclosure.

Liquidity ratios

Current ratio: current assets/current liabilities

Quick ratio: (current assets-inventory)/current liabilities

These ratios indicate the ability of a company to meet its short term debts. As a result these are key indicators when assessing going concern. If there are indicators of going concern uncertainties the financial statements must include disclosure which the auditor must assess for adequacy.

Investor ratios

Gearing: borrowings/(share capital + reserves)

Return on capital employed (ROCE): profit before interest and tax/(share capital + reserves + borrowings)

Gearing is a measure of external debt finance to internal equity finance. ROCE indicates the returns those investments generate.

Any change in gearing or ROCE could indicate a change in the financing structure of the business or it could indicate changes in overall performance of the business. These ratios are important for identifying potentially material changes to the statement of financial position (new/repaid loans or share issues) and for obtaining an overall picture of the annual performance of the business.

4   Exam focus – Audit risk questions

Audit risk identification and explanation

Audit risk is regularly examined and it is important to answer the question from an auditor's perspective rather than the perspective of the client.

The auditor is trying to detect material misstatements in the financial statements to avoid issuing the wrong opinion. The auditor is not looking to identify risks which affect the profitability of the client, they are not business consultants.

A common mistake that students make in exams is to explain business risks rather than audit risks. Business risks are not examinable in this syllabus. Therefore take care to ensure your answer is relevant to the requirement.

For example:

Identification of risk from the scenario	Audit risk explanation	NOT Audit risk (business risk)
Customers are struggling to pay debts.	Receivables may be overstated if irrecoverable debts are not written off.	Irrecoverable debts may arise reducing the profits of the company.
The client operates in a fast paced industry.	Inventory may be overstated if the inventory is obsolete and NRV is lower than cost.	Inventory may have to be written off reducing the profits of the company.
Revenue is falling due to recession. The cash flow forecast shows negative cash flows for the next 12 months.	If other factors are present, this could mean the company is unable to continue to trade for the foreseeable future and going concern disclosures may be required. There is a risk that adequate disclosure is not made.	Falling revenue will result in reduced profits and possible going concern issues.

In the exam make sure you explain the risk by stating the area of the financial statements which is at risk of material misstatement. A risk of material misstatement will affect either a balance in the financial statements, a disclosure in the notes to the financial statements or the basis of preparation.

This can be achieved in several ways:

- State the financial statement assertion affected, e.g. cut-off, valuation, completeness, etc.

- State the risk to the balance, e.g. overstatement, understatement or misstatement.

- State the component of audit risk affected, e.g. inherent, control or detection risk.

Auditor responses to risks

Once the risks are identified, you must suggest a **relevant** audit response to the risk identified.

The response must specifically deal with the risk. You should not suggest audit responses that address the balance generally.

Audit risk	Relevant response	Irrelevant response	Explanation
Customers are struggling to pay debts. Overstatement of receivables if irrecoverable debts are not written off.	Inspect after date cash receipts from customers to see if paid post year-end proving the debt is appropriately valued.	Obtain the receivables listing and cast it to verify arithmetical accuracy.	The risk identified is overvaluation. Obtaining the listing does not provide evidence that the debts are appropriately valued.
	Review the aged receivables listing for old debts which may not be recoverable and discuss the need for an allowance to be made with management.	Obtain external confirmation from customers to confirm existence.	External confirmation is providing evidence of existence but not valuation.
		The company should improve their credit control procedures.	This is a client response not an auditor response.
The client operates in a fast paced industry. Overstatement of inventory due to obsolete items not written off.	Obtain the aged inventory listing and review for old items. Discuss with management the need for these to be written down in the financial statements.	The company should discount the inventory in order to sell it.	This is a client response not an auditor response.

		Attend the inventory count to confirm existence of the inventory.	As written, the response of attending the inventory count is confirming existence, not valuation. This should be reworded to say attend the inventory count and look out for old or obsolete items that should be written down in the financial statements.
Revenue is falling due to recession. The cash flow forecast shows negative cash flows for the next 12 months. Going concern disclosures may not be adequate if the company has trading difficulties.	Assess the client's ability to continue as a going concern by examining the forecasts prepared by management and assess the reasonableness of the assumptions used in the forecasts.	Perform an analysis of past performance and assess the profitability of the company. Calculate liquidity ratios.	Analysing past performance does not help indicate how the company will perform in the future. Profitability is not the best indicator of going concern. Profits can be distorted by accounting policies. A company can be profitable but not have sufficient cash available to pay its suppliers and employees.
			Calculation of ratios can help identify indicators of going concern problems but further procedures would need to be performed to obtain evidence of the company's ability to continue to trade.

Test your understanding 1

Murray case study: Audit risks

Your firm Wimble & Co has recently accepted appointment as auditor of Murray Co (a manufacturer of sports equipment).

Having sold your shares in Murray Co, you have been assigned as audit manager and you have started planning the audit (although you were an employee of Murray Co, this was many years ago and you did not have any involvement in the preparation of the financial statements). You have held a meeting with the client and have ascertained the following:

Murray Co manufactures sports equipment. Most items of equipment, such as tennis rackets, hockey sticks and goals, take less than one day to manufacture. Murray Co's largest revenue generating product, ergometers (rowing machines), takes up to one week to manufacture. Murray Co refurbished the assembly line for the ergometers during the year. Murray Co uses a third party warehouse provider to store the manufactured ergometers and approximately one quarter of the other equipment.

Historically, Murray Co has only sold to retailers. For the first time this year, Murray Co has made sales directly to consumers, via a new website. The website is directly linked to the finance system, recording sales automatically. Website customers pay on ordering. The website development costs have been capitalised. This initiative was implemented to respond to market demands, as retailer sales have fallen dramatically in the last two years. Some of Murray Co's retail customers are struggling to pay their outstanding balances. Several of the sales team were made redundant last month as a result of the falling retailer sales.

Murray Co is planning to list on the stock exchange next year.

Required:

Using the information provided, describe SIX audit risks and explain the auditor's response to each risk in planning the audit of Murray Co.

(12 marks)

Test your understanding 2

Murray Case Study: Analytical procedures

Draft Statement of Financial Position as at 31 December 20X4

	20X4	20X3
	$000	$000
Non-current assets		
Property plant and equipment	5,350	4,900
Website development	150	0
	5,500	4,900
Current assets		
Inventory	2,109	1,300
Trade receivables	2,040	1,050
Cash and cash equivalents	48	38
	4,197	2,388
	9,697	7,288
Equity		
Share capital (50c shares)	2,100	2,100
Retained earnings	2,959	2,156
	5,059	4,256
Non-current liabilities		
Long term loan	2,800	1,500
Current liabilities		
Provisions	240	195
Trade and other payables	1,400	1,205
Accruals	18	12
Bank overdraft	180	120
	1,838	1,532
	9,697	7,288

Draft Statement of Profit or Loss for the year ended 31 December 20X4

	20X4	20X3
	$000	$000
Revenue	21,960	19,580
Cost of sales	(18,560)	(17,080)
Gross profit	3,400	2,500
Operating expenses	(2,012)	(2,012)
Finance cost	(340)	(240)
Profit before tax	1,048	248
Taxation	(245)	(24)
Profit for the period	803	224

Required:

Using the financial information provided, and the information from TYU 1, perform analytical procedures on the draft financial statements of Murray Co and explain the audit risks that arise.

Test your understanding 3

You are an audit senior at JPR Edwards & Co and you are currently planning the audit of Hook Co for the year ending 30 June. Your firm was appointed as auditor in January after a successful tender to provide audit and tax services. JPR Edward & Co were asked to tender after the lead partner, Neisha Selvaratalm, met Hook Co's CEO, Pete Tucker, at a charity cricket match. Neisha explained that they were unhappy with the previous auditors as Pete Tucker felt their audit didn't add much value to Hook Co.

Hook Co manufactures electrical goods such as MP3 players, smart phones and personal computers for larger companies with established brands. Their key client, who represents 70% of their revenue, was the market leader in smart phones and MP3 players last year with 60% market share.

Hook Co uses a number of suppliers to source components for their products. Most suppliers are based in the UK however Hook Co imports microchips, a key component in all their goods, from a number of suppliers based in San Jose, Costa Rica. They assemble their goods in their one factory in Staines, UK, and package their products for their customers before distribution across the UK. The work-in-progress balance is expected to be material at the year end.

During the year Hook Co started developing applications which can be downloaded onto their smart phones. They have spent $1 million on an application called 'snore-o-meter' which allows the users to record the sounds they make while they are asleep. There was a technical difficulty in production which meant the launch of 'snore-o-meter' was delayed from the 31 March to its anticipated release on the 31 July.

To fund their expansion into Smartphone applications Hook is seeking a listing on the London Stock Exchange in the fourth quarter of the year.

Required:

Using the information provided, describe FIVE audit risks and explain the auditor's response to each risk in planning the audit of Hook Co.

(10 marks)

Test your understanding 4

Define materiality and explain how the level of materiality is assessed.

(5 marks)

Test your understanding 5

You have received the latest management accounts from your client, Esperence Co, to help with your risk assessment for the forthcoming audit. The management accounts show actual results for the year to date, January to October inclusive. In October Esperence Co received a claim from a customer as a result of a defective product.

(1) **Which of the following is an example of an audit risk for Esperence Co?**

   A   The client is being sued by a customer for a defective product and if they lose, the compensation awarded is likely to be significant

   B   The client is being sued by a customer for a defective product. The publicity of the case could damage their reputation

   C   The client will have to spend a significant amount of money on improving their quality control procedures to avoid the same defects occurring again

   D   Provisions may be understated if the probable payment resulting from the court case is not recognised as a liability in the financial statements

(2) **Which of the following is the correct formula for calculating the payables payment period using the management accounts of Esperence Co?**

   A   Payables/Cost of sales × 304

   B   Payables/Cost of sales × 365

   C   Payables/Revenue × 304

   D   Payables/Revenue × 365

(3) **Which of the following is not an analytical procedure?**

   A   Calculation of gross profit margin and comparison with prior year

   B   Recalculation of a depreciation charge

   C   Comparison of revenue month by month

   D   Comparison of expenditure for current year with prior year

(4) **Which of the following is not a ratio?**

   A   Gross profit margin

   B   Acid test

   C   Inventory turnover

   D   Revenue growth

(5)　**You have used the management accounts to calculate the gross profit margin and found it to be higher than the prior year figure. Which of the following would provide a possible explanation?**

A　Sales prices have been reduced to increase sales volumes

B　Prices charged by suppliers have increased but the company has not increased sales prices to customers to cover the increased costs

C　Closing inventory has been overvalued

D　Administration expenses have reduced increasing profitability of the company

Test your understanding 6

You are the audit manager responsible for planning the audit of Fremantle Co. The draft financial statements show profit before tax of $3m and total assets of $50m. You have held a planning meeting with the client and have performed preliminary analytical procedures on the draft financial statements. You are currently assessing preliminary materiality for the audit and performing further risk assessment procedures.

(1)　**Which of the following statements is false in relation to materiality?**

A　Materiality can be assessed by size or nature

B　A balance which is omitted from the financial statements cannot be material

C　Materiality is a matter of professional judgment for the auditor

D　There is an inverse relationship between risk and materiality. If audit risk is high, the materiality level set by the audit will be lower

(2)　**Which of the following procedures are NOT required to be performed in accordance with ISA 315 (Revised)** *Identifying and Assessing the Risks of Material Misstatement Through Understanding the Entity and its Environment* **to identify risks of material misstatements?**

A　Inspection

B　Observation

C　External confirmation

D　Enquiry

(3) **Based on the above draft figures, what would be an appropriate level at which to set preliminary materiality?**

A $150,000 for the statement of profit and loss and $500,000 for the statement of financial position

B $500,000 for the statement of profit and loss and $150,000 for the statement of financial position

C $1,500 for the statement of profit and loss and $50,000 for the statement of financial position

D $50,000 for the statement of profit and loss and $1,500 for the statement of financial position

(4) **Performance materiality should be used by the auditor when performing substantive testing during the audit. Which of the following best describes performance materiality?**

A The maximum amount of misstatement the auditor is willing to accept

B The amount at which the auditor deems the misstatement to be trivial

C An amount which could influence the economic decisions of the users taken on the basis of the financial statements

D An amount set below materiality for the financial statements as a whole to reduce, to an acceptably low level, the risk that misstatements could be material in aggregate

(5) **Professional scepticism must be applied by auditors during the audit. Which of the following is NOT an application of professional scepticism?**

A A critical evaluation of the evidence

B An open and questioning mind

C The auditor should not believe anything the client tells them

D The auditor must be alert to fraud and error

5 Chapter summary

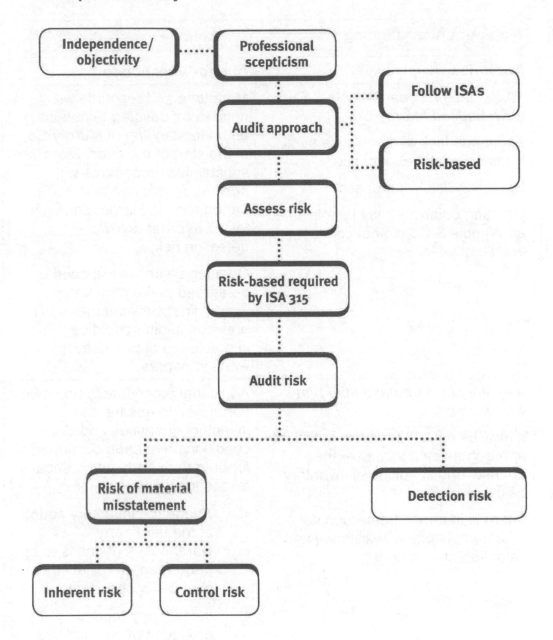

Test your understanding answers

Test your understanding 1

Audit risks	Auditor's response
This is the first year Wimble & Co have audited Murray Co. There is a lack of cumulative audit knowledge and experience. Detection risk is increased. Opening balances may be misstated as Wimble & Co did not conduct the audit last year.	More time and resource will need to be devoted to obtaining an understanding of Murray Co at the start of the audit. More substantive procedures will need to be planned and performed, and larger samples tested in order to lower detection risk. Opening balances will need to be agreed to the prior year signed financial statements. The previous auditor could be contacted to obtain relevant working papers.
Inventory is stored at a third party warehouse. It may be difficult to obtain sufficient appropriate evidence over the quantity and condition of inventory held. There is increased detection risk over completeness, existence and valuation of inventory.	Additional procedures should be performed to ensure that inventory quantities and condition have been confirmed for both third party and company owned locations, e.g. • Attend the inventory count at the third party warehouses (if one is to be performed) to review the controls in operation. • Inspect any reports produced by the auditors of third party warehouses in relation to the adequacy of controls over inventory. • Obtain external confirmation from the third party regarding the quantity and condition of the inventory.

Ergometers take up to one week to manufacture. There is likely to be a material work in progress (WIP) inventory balance at the year-end. Determining the value and quantity of WIP is complex. There is a risk of misstatement of WIP inventory.	The percentage of completion basis should be discussed with the client and assessed for reasonableness. The WIP calculation should be agreed to supporting documentation such as purchase invoices for materials and timesheets and payroll records for labour. The overhead calculation should be recalculated and reviewed for any non-production overheads.
Murray Co refurbished the assembly line for the ergometers during the year. Expenditure incurred may have been incorrectly capitalised or incorrectly expensed as repairs. There is a risk that that non-current assets are over or understated.	Review a breakdown of the costs and agree to invoices to assess the nature of the expenditure. Agree capital expenditure to inclusion within the asset register, and agree repairs to expenses in the statement of profit or loss.
There is a new website directly linked to the finance system which records sales automatically. There is increased risk over completeness of income if the system fails to record all sales made on the website. There is a risk that revenue is understated.	Extended controls testing to be performed over the sales cycle. Use test data to confirm that sales entered into the website are automatically transferred to the finance system. Detailed testing to be performed over the completeness of income by tracing orders through to GDNs, sales invoices and into the sales day book.
The website development costs have been capitalised. In order to be capitalised, it must meet all of the criteria under IAS ® 38 *Intangible Assets*. Research costs should be expensed rather than capitalised. There is a risk that intangible assets and profits are overstated.	A breakdown of the development expenditure should be reviewed and tested in detail to ensure that only projects which meet the capitalisation criteria are included as an intangible asset, with the balance being expensed.

Retailer sales have fallen dramatically in the last two years. If retailer sales continue to fall and direct consumer sales do not compensate for the loss of retailer revenue, Murray Co may not be able to continue to operate for the foreseeable future. There is a risk that disclosures of material uncertainties relating to going concern may be inadequate.	Perform a detailed going concern review, including: Obtain and review the company's cash flow forecast and evaluate the reasonableness of the assumptions used to understand if management will have sufficient cash. Review the post year-end order book from retailers and post year-end direct consumer sales to assess if the revenue figures in the cash flow are reasonable.
Several of the sales team were made redundant last month as a result of the falling retailer sales. Under IAS 37 *Provisions, Contingent Liabilities and Contingent Assets*, a redundancy provision will be required for any staff not yet paid at the year-end. There is a risk of understated liabilities.	Discuss with management the progress of the redundancy programme. Review post year-end bank statements for any redundancy payments made and agree to the year-end provision.
Some retail customers are struggling to pay their outstanding balances to Murray Co. The balances may be irrecoverable debts that should be written off. There is a risk of overstatement of receivables and understatement of the irrecoverable debt allowance.	Extended post year-end cash receipts testing to assess valuation. Review of the aged receivables ledger to identify long outstanding debts. The allowance for receivables should be discussed with management if it is considered inadequate.
Murray Co is planning to list on the stock exchange next year. There is an increased risk of manipulation of the financial statements. There is a risk of overstatement of assets and profits, and understatement of expenses and liabilities.	Increase the level of professional scepticism and be alert to the risks identified in order to achieve a successful listing. Plan and perform procedures to ensure accounting estimates and judgmental areas are reasonable.

Test your understanding 2

Audit risks identified using analytical procedures

Revenue has increased by 12%.	Retailer sales at Murray Co have fallen dramatically in the last two years. The increase in revenue is not consistent with this. Although Murray Co has started selling directly to consumers for the first time this year, it is unlikely that these sales will have compensated for the loss in retailer sales at this early stage. In addition, revenue may be deliberately overstated by Murray Co in order to increase the chances of a successful listing. There is a risk that revenue is overstated.
Gross profit margin has increased from 13% (2,500/19,580) to 15% (3,400/21,960).	The margins for direct consumer sales are likely to be higher than retailer sales, which may explain this increase. However, the increase could also be caused by overstatement of revenue, as explained above, or understatement of cost of sales due to incomplete recording of costs or overvaluation of closing inventory.
Operating expenses has no movement.	This is unusual given the increase in revenue and cost of sales. There is a risk that the prior year figure has been incorrectly presented In the current year column.
Net margin has increased from 1.3% (248/19,580) to 4.8% (1,048/21,960).	Net margin has increased at a greater rate than gross profit margin. Given that this is the first year of direct consumer sales, the net margin would not be expected to increase significantly as the level of operating expenses would normally be higher at this early stage. This indicates potential overstatement of revenue and understatement of operating expenses.
Inventory holding period has increased from 28 (1,300/17,080 × 365) to 41 (2,109/18,560 × 365) days.	As sales have increased, this could be because of an increase in demand and therefore the need to hold more inventory. However, as retailer sales at Murray Co have fallen dramatically, there is a risk that some of the inventory is bespoke, and may therefore be obsolete. There is a risk that inventory is overstated.

Trade receivables collection period has increased from 20 (1,050/19,580 × 365) to 34 (2,040/21,960 × 365) days.	Given that website customers pay on ordering, the collection period would be expected to fall. However, some of Murray Co's retail customers are struggling to pay their outstanding balances. Trade receivables may be overstated, and the allowance for doubtful debts understated.
Trade payables payment period has increased from 26 (1,205/17,080 × 365) to 28 (1,400/18,560 × 365) days.	An increase in the payables payment period could be caused by understatement of cost of sales. The increase in gross profit margin also highlighted this as a potential risk.
Current ratio has improved from 1.6:1 to 2.3:1. Quick ratio has improved from 0.71: 1 to 1.14:1.	Murray Co appears to be managing its working capital effectively. However, given the plans to list on the stock exchange next year, this may be indicative of manipulation of the financial statements in order to increase the chances of a successful listing. In addition, Murray Co has increased its long and short-term finance during the year.

Test your understanding 3

Audit risks and effect on audit approach

Risk and explanation	Effect on audit approach
This is the first year JPR Edwards & Co have audited Hook Co. There may not be as deep an understanding of Hook Co's business as if they had audited in previous years. Detection risk is increased. Opening balances may be misstated as JPR Edwards & Co were not the auditors last year and cannot rely on their own previous work.	More time should be devoted to understanding the business at the start of the audit. More substantive procedures may be planned to lower detection risk. JPR Edwards & Co will have to design specific audit procedures to obtain sufficient evidence regarding opening balances. This includes agreeing the opening balances to the prior year signed financial statements and obtaining relevant working papers from the prior year auditors.

Hook Co is expected to have a material work-in-progress balance at the year end. The calculation and valuation of work in progress is subjective. There is a risk of overstatement of inventory.	Appropriate time should be allocated to attending the inventory count and understanding the inventory valuation process for work in progress. The basis for assessing the percentage of completion of WIP should be discussed with management to ensure it is reasonable. Purchase invoices should be inspected to verify cost; payroll records and job cards should be inspected to verify the labour element of WIP and finished goods. Overheads included in WIP and finished goods should be recalculated and reviewed to ensure only production overheads are included.
Hook Co manufactures electrical goods for the entertainment market. This is a rapidly changing market and goods can become obsolete quickly which may result in the NRV falling below cost. There is a risk of overstatement of inventory.	The aged inventory listing should be reviewed for old or obsolete items and compared with the allowance made to write the inventory down to NRV to ensure the allowance is adequate. If the allowance does not appear adequate, it should be discussed with management.
Their key client represents 70% of their revenue. Hook Co may be over reliant on this client which could threaten its going concern status if this key client was lost. There is a risk that disclosures of material uncertainties relating to going concern are inadequate.	Procedures should be designed at the planning stage to allow the auditor to assess the going concern risk faced by Hook Co. Contracts and other correspondence from the key customer should be reviewed to identify any specific risks that the client may be lost. Analytical procedures should be designed to assess the impact on Hook Co's financial position if the contract is not renewed.

Hook Co spent $1m on developing a new product. There is a risk that Hook Co has capitalised development expenditure which should have been expensed through the statement of profit or loss as research costs. If the application does not meet the criteria required to classify as development costs they should be expensed to the statement of profit or loss in the year they were incurred. There is a risk of overstatement of intangible assets.	Enquiries should be made as to how Hook Co identifies whether the criteria for capitalisation have been met in accordance with accounting standards. Where amounts have been capitalised further procedures should be performed to assess whether the criteria of IAS 38 have been met e.g. review budgets to ensure resources have been allocated to the development, review project plans to ensure the development is expected to be completed, and review forecasts to ensure the product is expected to generate a profit.
Hook Co is aiming to list on the London Stock Exchange this year. The directors may have greater incentive to 'window dress' the accounts to show a more favourable position in order to increase the proceeds generated from flotation. Assets and profits may be overstated and liabilities understated to make the company appear a more attractive investment.	Increased professional scepticism is required when performing the audit. Procedures should be planned to ensure areas of judgment and estimates exercised by the directors are reasonable and can be justified. Special consideration should be given to sales cut-off testing.

Test your understanding 4

Materiality is defined as follows:

'Misstatements, including omissions, are considered to be material if they, individually or in aggregate, could reasonably be expected to influence the economic decisions of users taken on the basis of the financial statements.'

In assessing the level of materiality there are a number of areas that should be considered. Firstly the auditor must consider both the amount (quantity) and the nature (quality) of any misstatements, or a combination of both. The quantity of the misstatement refers to the relative size of it and the quality refers to an amount that might be low in value but due to its prominence could influence the user's decision, for example, directors' transactions.

The assessment of what is material is ultimately a matter of the auditors' professional judgment, and it is affected by the auditor's perception of the financial information needs of users of the financial statements.

Materiality is often calculated using benchmarks such as 5% of profit before tax or 1% of assets. These values are useful as a starting point for assessing materiality.

In assessing materiality the auditor must consider that a number of errors each with a low value may, when aggregated, amount to a material misstatement.

In calculating materiality the auditor should also consider setting the performance materiality level. This is the amount set by the auditor, below materiality for the financial statements as a whole, and is used for particular transactions, account balances and disclosures.

Test your understanding 5

(1)	D	Options A, B and C are business risks. An audit risk must be described in terms of a risk of material misstatement (i.e. the impact on the financial statements) or a detection risk (why the auditor may not detect the misstatement).
(2)	A	Payables/Cost of sales × 304. There are 304 days in the period January to October.
(3)	B	Recalculation is not an analytical procedure. An analytical procedure evaluates relationships between data.
(4)	D	Revenue growth is a trend rather than a ratio. Acid test is another name for the quick ratio.
(5)	C	If closing inventory is overvalued, a larger figure will be deducted from cost of sales and, therefore, cost of sales will be lower and gross profit will be higher. A and B would both cause gross profit margin to fall. D would have no impact as administrative expenses do not affect gross profit.

Test your understanding 6		
(1)	B	The financial statements can be materially misstated by the omission of a balance or disclosure.
(2)	C	External confirmation is not listed in ISA 315 as a risk assessment procedure. It is usually used as a substantive procedure.
(3)	A	Using 5% of PBT and 1% of total assets an appropriate level of materiality would be $150,000 for the statement of profit or loss and $500,000 for the statement of financial position.
(4)	D	A and B both refer to tolerable misstatement. C is a description of materiality for the financial statements as a whole.
(5)	C	Professional scepticism involves being alert to possible frauds and errors but does not require complete mistrust of the client.

Planning

Chapter learning objectives

This chapter covers syllabus areas:

- B1e – Objectives and importance of quality control procedures in conducting an audit

- B1f – Quality control procedures over engagement performance, monitoring quality and compliance with ethical requirements

- B2 – Planning and risk assessment: objective and general principles

- B5 – Fraud, laws and regulations

- B6 – Audit planning and documentation

Detailed syllabus objectives are provided in the introduction section of the text book.

PER

One of the PER performance objectives (PO18) is to is to prepare for and plan the audit process. You plan and control the engagement process, including the initial investigation. You also plan and monitor the audit programme – legally and ethically. Working through this chapter should help you understand how to demonstrate that objective.

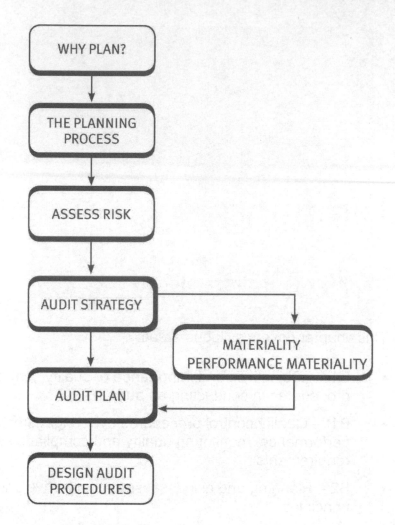

1 Purpose of planning

'The objective of the auditor is to plan the audit so that it will be performed in an effective manner.'
[ISA 300 *Planning an Audit of Financial Statements*, 4]

Audits are potentially complex, risky and expensive processes. Although firms have internal manuals and standardised procedures, it is vital that engagements are planned to ensure that the auditor:

- Devotes appropriate attention to important areas of the audit.

- Identifies and resolves potential problems on a timely basis.

- Organises and manages the audit so that it is performed in an effective and efficient manner.

- Selects team members with appropriate capabilities and competencies.

- Directs and supervises the team and reviews their work.

- Effectively coordinates the work of others, such as experts and internal audit.

[ISA 300, 2]

Planning ensures that the risk of performing a poor quality audit (and ultimately giving an inappropriate audit opinion) is reduced to an acceptable level.

In order to achieve the overall objectives of the auditor, the audit must be conducted in accordance with ISAs.

Conducting the audit in accordance with ISAs:

- Ensures that the auditor is fulfilling all of their responsibilities.

- Allows a user to have as much confidence in one auditor's opinion as another's and therefore to rely on one audited set of financial statements to the same extent that they rely on another.

- Ensures that the quality of audits internationally, is maintained to a high standard (thereby upholding the reputation of the profession).

- Provides a measure to assess the standard of an auditor's work (necessary when determining their suitability as an authorised practitioner).

Professional scepticism and professional judgment

Auditors are also required to perform audits with an attitude of professional scepticism. Professional scepticism was explained in the previous chapter. Having an enquiring mind in itself is not sufficient to comply with a risk based method of auditing, the auditor must also use professional judgment.

 Professional judgment – the application of relevant training, knowledge and experience in making informed decisions about the courses of action that are appropriate in the circumstances of the audit engagement. [ISA 200, 13k]

Therefore the use of a risk based approach requires skill, knowledge, experience and an inquisitive, open mind.

 Although risk assessment is a fundamental element of the planning process, risks can be uncovered at any stage of the audit and procedures must be adapted in light of revelations that indicate further risks of material misstatement. It is, ultimately, the responsibility of the most senior reviewer (usually the engagement partner) to confirm that the risk of material misstatement has been reduced to an acceptable level.

The planning process

Planning consists of a number of elements. They can be summarised as:

- Preliminary engagement activities:

  - Perform procedures regarding the continuance of the client engagement.

  - Evaluating compliance with ethical requirements.

  - Ensuring there are no misunderstandings with the client as to the terms of the engagement.

  [ISA 300, 6]

  The preliminary engagement activities were covered in the previous chapter.

- Planning activities:

  - Developing the audit strategy

  - Developing an audit plan.

  [ISA 300, 7]

The audit strategy and the audit plan must be documented in the audit working papers. Any updates to them must also be documented.

2 The audit strategy

The audit strategy sets the scope, timing and direction of the audit.

The diagram below summarises some of the matters the auditor may consider in establishing the strategy.

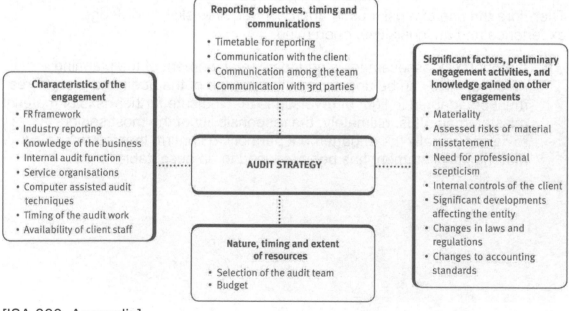

[ISA 300, Appendix]

The audit strategy allows the auditor to determine:

- The resources to deploy for specific audit areas (e.g. experience level, external experts).

- The amount of resources to allocate (i.e. number of team members).

- When these resources are to be deployed.

- How the resources are managed, directed and supervised, including the timings of meetings, debriefs and reviews.

[ISA 300, A8]

3 The audit plan

Once the audit strategy has been established, the next stage is to develop a specific, detailed plan to address how the various matters identified in the overall strategy will be applied.

The strategy sets the overall approach to the audit; the plan fills in the operational details of how the strategy is to be achieved.

The audit plan should include specific descriptions of:

- The nature, timing and extent of risk assessment procedures.

- The nature, timing and extent of further audit procedures, including:

    – **What** audit procedures are to be carried out

    – **Who** should do them

    – **How** much work should be done (sample sizes, etc.)

    – **When** the work should be done (interim vs. final)

- Any other procedures necessary to conform to ISAs.

[ISA 300, 9]

The relationship between the audit strategy and the audit plan

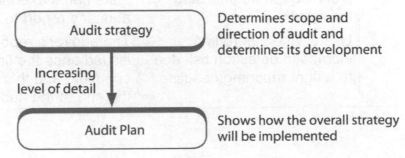

4   Interim and final audit

The auditor must consider the timing of audit procedures such as whether to carry out an interim audit and a final audit, or just a final audit.

For an interim audit to be justified the client normally needs to be of a sufficient size because this may increase costs. However, an interim audit should improve risk assessment and make final procedures more efficient.

 It is important to note that the interim audit and final audit are two stages of the same audit. One set of financial statements are audited. One auditor's report will be issued. The audit work however is being performed in two stages – some work before the year-end and some work after the year-end.

	Interim audit	**Final audit**
Timing	Completed part way through a client's accounting year (i.e. before the year-end). Early enough not to interfere with year-end procedures at the client and to give adequate warning of specific problems that need to be addressed in planning the final audit. Late enough to enable sufficient work to be done to ease the pressure on the final audit.	Takes place after the year-end at a time agreed with the client which enables them to file their financial statements with the relevant authorities by the required deadline. Generally a client would not want the auditor to be performing the audit at the year-end as this will cause disruption for the client's year-end procedures.
Purpose	Allows the auditor to spread out their procedures and enables more effective planning for the final stage of the audit. Useful when there is increased detection risk due to a tight reporting deadline.	To obtain sufficient appropriate evidence in respect of the financial statements to enable the auditor's report to be issued. The auditor's report will be issued once the final audit complete and this signifies the end of the audit.

Work performed	• Documenting systems • Evaluating controls. Additional activities that can be performed include: • Test specific and complete material transactions, e.g. purchasing new non-current assets. • Test transactions such as sales, purchases and payroll for the year to date. • Assess risks that will impact work conducted at the final audit. • Attend perpetual inventory counts.	• Statement of financial position balances which will only be known at the year-end. • Transaction testing for transactions that have occurred since the interim audit took place. • Year-end journals which may include adjustments to the transactions tested at the interim audit. • Obtaining evidence that the controls tested at the interim audit have continued to operate during the period since the interim audit took place. • Completion activities such as the going concern and subsequent events reviews, overall review of the financial statements and communication of misstatements with management and those charged with governance.

Impact of interim audit work on the final audit

- If the controls tested at the interim stage provided evidence that control risk is low, fewer substantive procedures can be performed.

- If substantive procedures were performed at the interim stage, fewer procedures will be required at the final audit in general.

- As fewer procedures are being performed, the final audit will require less time to perform.

- The auditor's report can be signed closer to the year-end resulting in more timely reporting to shareholders.

- If the interim audit identified areas of increased risk, for example, controls were found not to be working effectively, increased substantive procedures will be required at the final audit.

5 Fraud and error

Fraud

 Fraud is an **intentional** act by one or more individuals among management, those charged with governance, employees or third parties, involving the use of **deception** to obtain an unjust or illegal advantage. [ISA 240 *the Auditor's Responsibilities Relating to Fraud in an Audit of Financial Statements*, 11a]

Fraud can be split into two types:

- Fraudulent financial reporting – deliberately misstating the financial statements to make the company's performance or position look better/worse than it actually is.

- Misappropriation – the theft of a company's assets such as cash or inventory.

[ISA 240, 3]

Error

An error can be defined as an unintentional misstatement in financial statements, including the omission of amounts or disclosures, such as the following:

- A mistake in gathering and processing data from which financial statements are prepared.

- An incorrect accounting estimate arising from oversight or a misinterpretation of facts.

- A mistake in the application of accounting principles relating to measurement, recognition, classification, presentation or disclosure.

[ISA 450 *Evaluation of Misstatements Identified During the Audit*, A1]

Directors' responsibilities in respect of fraud

The primary responsibility for the prevention and detection of fraud rests with those charged with governance and the management of an entity. This is achieved by:

- Implementing an **effective system of internal control,** reducing opportunities for fraud to take place and increasing the likelihood of detection (and punishment).

- Creating a **culture** of honesty, ethical behaviour, and active oversight by those charged with governance.

The directors should be aware of the potential for fraud and this should feature as an element of their risk assessment and corporate governance procedures.

The audit committee should review these procedures to ensure that they are in place and working effectively.

This will normally be done in conjunction with the internal auditors.

[ISA 240, 4]

Internal auditors

Internal auditors can help management fulfil their responsibilities in respect of fraud and error. Typical functions the internal auditor can perform include:

- Testing the effectiveness of the internal controls at preventing and detecting fraud and error and provide recommendations for improvements to the controls.

- Performing fraud investigations to identify:
  - how the fraud was committed
  - the extent of the fraud
  - provide recommendations on how to prevent the fraud from happening again.

- Performing surprise asset counts to identify misappropriation.

The presence of an internal audit department may act as a deterrent to fraud in itself as there is a greater chance of being discovered.

External auditor's responsibilities in respect of fraud

Misstatement in the financial statements can arise from either fraud or error. The distinguishing factor is whether the underlying action that resulted in the misstatement was intentional or unintentional. [ISA 240, 2]

There is an unavoidable risk that some material misstatements may not be detected even if properly planned in accordance with ISAs as fraud is likely to be concealed. [ISA 240, 5]

The ability to detect fraud depends on the skill of the perpetrator, collusion, relative size of amounts manipulated, and the seniority of the people involved. [ISA 240, 6]

The auditor's role is two-fold:

- Assess the risk of material misstatement due to fraud, and

- Respond to the assessed risks.

Assessing the risk of fraud

The auditor should:

- Obtain reasonable assurance that the financial statements are free from material misstatement, whether caused by fraud or error. [ISA 240, 5]

- Apply professional scepticism and remain alert to the possibility that fraud could take place. [ISA 240, 8]

  This means that the auditor must recognise the possibility that a material misstatement due to fraud could occur, regardless of the auditor's prior experience of the client's integrity and honesty.

- Consider the potential for management override of controls and recognise that audit procedures that are effective for detecting error may not be effective for detecting fraud. [ISA 240, 8]

This can be achieved by performing the following procedures:

- Discuss the susceptibility of the client's financial statements to material misstatement due to fraud with the engagement team. [ISA 240, 15]

  - Consider any incentives to commit fraud such as profit related bonuses or applications for finance.

  - Opportunities to commit fraud such as ineffective internal controls.

  - Management's attitude e.g. disputes with the auditor over auditing matters or failure to remedy known deficiencies.

  [ISA 240, Appendix 1]

- Enquire of management about their processes for identifying and responding to the risk of fraud. [ISA 240, 17]

- Enquire of management, internal auditors and those charged with governance if they are aware of any actual or suspected fraudulent activity. [ISA 240, 18, 19, 20]

- Consideration of relationships identified during analytical procedures. [ISA 240, 22]

Responding to the assessed risks

The following procedures must be performed:

- Review journal entries made to identify manipulation of figures recorded or unauthorised journal adjustments:

  - Enquire of those involved in financial reporting about unusual activity relating to adjustments.

  - Select journal entries and adjustments made at the end of the reporting period.

  - Consider the need to test journal entries throughout the period. [ISA 240, 32a]

- Review management estimates for evidence of bias:

  - Evaluate the reasonableness of judgments and whether they indicate any bias on behalf of management.

  - Perform a retrospective review of management judgments reflected in the prior year.
    [ISA 240, 32b]

- Review transactions outside the normal course of business, or transactions which appear unusual and assess whether they are indicative of fraudulent financial reporting.
  [ISA 240, 32c]

- Obtain written representation from management and those charged with governance that they:

  - acknowledge their responsibility for internal controls to prevent and detect fraud.

  - have disclosed to the auditor the results of management's fraud risk assessment.

  - have disclosed to the auditor any known or suspected frauds.

  - have disclosed to the auditor any allegations of fraud affecting the entity's financial statements.
    [ISA 240, 39]

Reporting of fraud and error

- If the auditor identifies a fraud they must communicate the matter on a timely basis to the appropriate level of management (i.e. those with the primary responsibility for prevention and detection of fraud). [ISA 240, 40]

- If the suspected fraud involves management the auditor must communicate the matter to those charged with governance. [ISA 240, 41]

- If the auditor has doubts about the integrity of those charged with governance they should seek legal advice regarding an appropriate course of action. [ISA 240, A63]

- In addition to these responsibilities the auditor must also consider whether they have a responsibility to report the occurrence of a suspicion to a party outside the entity. Whilst the auditor does have an ethical duty to maintain confidentiality, it is likely that any legal responsibility will take precedence. In these circumstances it is advisable to seek legal advice. [ISA 240, 43]

- If the fraud has a material impact on the financial statements the audit opinion will be modified. When the opinion is modified, the auditor will explain why it has been modified and this will make the shareholders aware of the fraud.

6 Laws and regulations

Guidance relating to laws and regulations in an audit of financial statements is provided in ISA 250 (Revised) *Consideration of Laws and Regulations in an Audit of Financial Statements.*

 Non-compliance – Acts of omission or commission, either intentional or unintentional, committed by the entity, which are contrary to the prevailing laws or regulations. Non-compliance does not include personal misconduct unrelated to the business activities of the entity. [ISA 250, 12]

Responsibilities are considered from the perspective of both auditors and management.

Responsibilities of management

It is the responsibility of management, with the oversight of those charged with governance, to ensure that the entity's operations are conducted in accordance with relevant laws and regulations, including those that determine the reported amounts and disclosures in the financial statements. [ISA 250, 3]

Responsibilities of the auditor

The auditor must perform audit procedures to help identify non-compliance with laws and regulations that may have a material impact on the financial statements.

The auditor must obtain sufficient, appropriate evidence regarding compliance with laws and regulations generally recognised to have a **direct effect** on the determination of material amounts and disclosures in the financial statements (e.g. completeness of a tax provision in accordance with tax law, or the presentation of the financial statements in accordance with the applicable financial reporting framework). [ISA 250, 6a]

The auditor must perform audit procedures to help identify non-compliance with **other laws and regulations** that may have a material impact on the financial statements (e.g. data protection, environmental legislation, public health and safety). Non-compliance in respect of such matters could affect the company's ability to continue as a going concern or could result in the need for material liabilities to be recognised or disclosed. [ISA 250, 6b]

Audit procedures to identify instances of non-compliance

- **Obtaining a general understanding** of the legal and regulatory framework applicable to the entity and the industry, and of how the entity is complying with that framework. [ISA 250, 13]

- **Enquiring of management and those charged with governance** as to whether the entity is in compliance with such laws and regulations. [ISA 250, 15a]

- **Inspecting correspondence** with relevant licensing or regulatory authorities. [ISA 250, 15b]

- **Remaining alert** to the possibility that other audit procedures applied may bring instances of non-compliance to the auditor's attention. [ISA 250, 16]

- **Obtaining written representation** from the directors that they have disclosed to the auditors all those events of which they are aware which involve possible non-compliance, together with the actual or contingent consequences which may arise from such non-compliance. [ISA 250, 17]

Investigations of possible non-compliance

When the auditor becomes aware of information concerning a possible instance of **non-compliance** with laws or regulations, they should:

- Understand the **nature of the act and circumstances** in which it has occurred.

- Obtain further information to **evaluate** the possible effect on the financial statements.

[ISA 250, 19]

Audit procedures when non-compliance is identified

- Enquire of management of the penalties to be imposed.

- Inspect correspondence with the regulatory authority to identify the consequences.

- Inspect board minutes for management's discussion on actions to be taken regarding the non-compliance.

- Enquire of the company's legal department as to the possible impact of the non-compliance.

Reporting non-compliance

- The auditor should report non-compliance to management and those charged with governance, unless prohibited by law or regulation. [ISA 250, 23]

- If the auditor believes the non-compliance is intentional and material the matter should be reported to those charged with governance. [ISA 250, 24]

- If the auditor suspects management or those charged with governance are involved in the non-compliance, the matter should be reported to the audit committee or supervisory board. [ISA 250, 25]

- If the non-compliance has a material effect on the financial statements, a qualified or adverse opinion should be issued. [ISA 250, 26]

- The auditor should also consider whether they have any legal or ethical responsibility to report non-compliance to third parties (e.g. to a regulatory authority). [ISA 250, 29]

NOCLAR: Auditor responsibilities in addition to ISA 250

The IESBA *Code of Ethics for Professional Accountants* sets out new ethical requirements in relation to an entity's compliance with laws and regulations.

The ethical standard, *Responding to Non-compliance with Laws and Regulations* (NOCLAR), provides guidance to accountants as to the actions that should be taken if they become aware of an illegal act committed by a client or employer.

The additional requirements have been introduced to address concerns that the duty of confidentiality was acting as a barrier to the disclosure of potential NOCLAR to public authorities in the appropriate circumstances. Auditors were resigning from client relationships without NOCLAR issues being appropriately addressed.

NOCLAR sets out responsibilities in relation to:

- Responding to identified or suspected non-compliance

- Communicating identified or suspected non-compliance with other auditors

- Documenting identified or suspected non-compliance.

The aim is to generate an earlier response by management or those charged with governance, thereby mitigating adverse consequences for stakeholders and the general public and timelier intervention from public authorities on reports of potential NOCLAR to mitigate any adverse consequences for stakeholders and the general public.

7 Quality control

ISA 220 *Quality Control for an Audit of Financial Statements* requires the firm to establish a system of quality control to ensure the firm complies with professional standards and issues reports that are appropriate in the circumstances.

Policies and procedures should be established which address:

- Leadership responsibilities for quality within the firm
- Relevant ethical requirements
- Acceptance and continuance of client relationships and specific engagements
- Human resources
- Engagement performance
- Monitoring.

[ISA 220, A1]

Leadership

The engagement partner takes overall responsibility for the overall quality of the engagement. [ISA 220, 8]

The engagement partner should emphasise the importance of:

- Performing work that complies with professional standards.
- Complying with the firm's quality control policies and procedures.
- Issuing auditor's reports that are appropriate in the circumstances.
- The engagement team's ability to raise concerns without fear of reprisal.

[ISA 220, A3a]

Relevant ethical requirements

The firm should ensure compliance with the requirements of the ACCA Code of Ethics. This is covered in Chapter 4.

Acceptance and continuance of client relationships

The firm should ensure only clients and work of an acceptable level of risk are accepted. This requires consideration of:

- Integrity of management
- Competence of the engagement team

- Compliance with ethical requirements
- Significant matters that have arisen during the current or previous audit engagement and their implications for continuing the relationship.

[ISA 220, A8]

Human resources

The engagement partner should ensure that the engagement team collectively have the competence and capabilities to perform the audit in accordance with professional standards. This includes knowledge of professional standards, knowledge of relevant industries in which the client operates, the ability to apply judgment and an understanding of the firm's quality control policies and procedures. [ISA 220, A11]

Engagement performance

Engagement performance comprises direction, supervision and review of the engagement.

Direction involves informing team members of:

- Their responsibilities
- Objectives of the work to be performed
- The nature of the business
- Risks
- Problems that may arise
- The detailed approach to the performance of the engagement.

[ISA 220, A13]

Supervision includes:

- Tracking the progress of the audit to ensure the timetable can be met
- Considering the competence of the team
- Addressing significant matters arising and modifying the planned approach accordingly
- Identifying matters for consultation. Consultation may be required where the firm lacks appropriate internal expertise.

[ISA 220, A15]

Review responsibilities include consideration of whether:

- The work has been performed in accordance with professional standards

- Appropriate consultations have taken place

- The work performed supports the conclusions reached

- The evidence obtained is sufficient and appropriate to support the auditor's report.

- The objectives of the engagement procedures have been achieved.

[ISA 220, A17]

The engagement partner should perform a review of critical areas of judgment, significant risks and other areas of importance throughout the audit. The extent and timing of the partner's reviews should be documented. [ISA 220, A18]

Engagement Quality Control Review

Listed entities and other high risk clients should be subject to an engagement quality control review (EQCR). [ISA 220, 19]

This is also referred to as a pre-issuance review or 'Hot' review.

High risk clients include those which are in the public interest, those with unusual circumstances and risks, and those where laws or regulations require an EQCR.

An EQCR includes:

- Discussion of significant matters with the engagement partner.

- Review of the financial statements and proposed auditor's report.

- Review of selected audit documentation relating to significant judgments and conclusions reached. This includes:

  - Significant risks and responses to those risks

  - Judgments with respect to materiality and significant risks

  - Significance of uncorrected misstatements

  - Matters to be communicated to management and those charged with governance, and where applicable, other parties such as regulatory bodies.

- Evaluation of conclusions reached in forming the audit opinion.

[ISA 220, 20]

For listed entity audits, the EQCR should also consider:

- Independence of the engagement team.

- Whether appropriate consultation has taken place on contentious matters or differences of opinion.

- Whether documentation reflects the work performed in relation to significant judgments.

[ISA 220, 21]

Eligibility criteria

The engagement quality control reviewer:

- Should have the technical qualifications to perform the role, including the necessary experience and authority, and

- Should be objective. To be objective the reviewer should not be selected by the engagement partner and should not participate in the engagement.

[ISA 220, 7c]

Note: An engagement quality control reviewer may also be referred to as an independent review partner.

Monitoring

Quality control policies alone do not ensure good quality work. The firm must ensure that its policies and procedures relating to the system of quality control are relevant, adequate and operating effectively. [ISA 220, 23]

Firms should carry out post-issuance or 'cold' reviews to ensure that quality control procedures are adequate, relevant and operating effectively.

	Post-issuance (cold) review
Purpose	To assess whether the firm's policies and procedures were implemented during an engagement and to identify any deficiencies therein.
When	After the auditor's report has been signed.
Which files	A selection of completed audit files.
Conducted by	A dedicated compliance or quality department/a qualified external consultant/an independent partner.
Matters considered	Working papers should demonstrate that: • Sufficient appropriate evidence has been obtained. • All matters were resolved before issuing the auditor's report. All working papers should be: • On file • Completed • Signed as completed • Evidence as reviewed.
Outcomes	A report of the results will be provided to the partners of the firm flagging deficiencies that require corrective action. Recommendations will be made including: • Communication of findings • Additional quality control reviews • Training • Changes to the firm's policies and procedures • Disciplinary action.

8 Audit documentation

Purposes of audit documentation

ISA 230 *Audit Documentation* requires auditors to prepare and retain written documentation that:

- Provides evidence of the auditor's basis for their report.

- Provides evidence that the audit was planned and performed in accordance with ISAs and applicable legal and regulatory requirements.

[ISA 230, 2]

In addition, audit documentation:

- Assists the engagement team to plan and perform the audit.

- Assists members of the engagement team responsible for supervision to direct, supervise and review the audit work.

- Enables the engagement team to be accountable for its work.

- Retains a record of matters of continuing significance to future audits.

- Enables the quality control reviews to be performed.

- Enables the external quality inspections to be performed.

[ISA 230, 3]

Form and content of audit documentation

Documentation should be sufficient to enable an experienced auditor, with no previous connection to the audit, to understand:

- The nature, timing and extent of audit procedures performed

- The results of the procedures performed and the evidence obtained

- The significant matters arising during the course of the audit and the conclusions reached thereon, and significant professional judgments made in reaching those conclusions.

[ISA 230, 8]

Retention of working papers

Documentation is retained in an audit file, which should be completed in a timely fashion after the date of the auditor's report (normally not more than 60 days after) and retained for the period required by national regulatory requirements (this is normally five years from the date of the auditor's report).

[ISA 230, A21, A23]

Illustration 1 – Wimble & Co working paper

Wimble & Co Audit and Accounting Practitioners: Working Paper

Client:	*Murray Co*	Reference:	*RA1*
Period end:	*31/12/X4*	Prepared by:	*Rob Cash*
Subject	*Risk Assessment*	Date	*Dec 1*
		Prepared	*20X4*

Objective:	To identify the risks of material misstatement in the financial statements of Murray Co for the year-ended 31 December 20X4, in order to provide a basis for designing and performing audit procedures that respond to the assessed risks.
Work performed:	Discussion among the engagement team of the susceptibility of the financial statements to material misstatement: RA1/1of the financial statements to material misstatement: **RA1/1**
	A summary of the understanding of the entity and its environment obtained, detailing the key elements including internal control components, sources of information and risk assessment procedures performed: **RA/2**
	Analytical procedures performed: **RA/3**
Results:	The identified and assessed risks of material misstatement: **RA/4**
Conclusions:	The overall responses to address the risks of material misstatement: **RA/5**
Reviewed by:	*An Audit Manager*
Date reviewed:	*December 5 20X4*

Wimble & Co working paper

Features of Wimble & Co working paper

Name of client: identifies the client being audited.

Period-end date: identifies the period to which the audit work relates.

Subject: identifies the topic of the working paper such as the area of the financial statements being audited, or the overall purpose of the work.

Working paper reference: provides a clear reference to identify the working paper. RA1 is the first working paper in the risk assessment section.

Preparer: identifies the name of the audit team member who prepared the working paper to enable any queries to be directed to the relevant person.

Date prepared: the date the audit work was performed, the end of the time period to which issues were considered.

Objective: this explains the relevance of the work being performed (in relation to financial statement assertions where appropriate).

Work performed: the work done cross-referenced to supporting working papers, including details of the sources of information, and items selected for testing (where relevant).

Results of work performed: any significant issues identified, exceptions or other significant observations including whether further audit work is necessary.

Conclusions: key points (including whether the area is true and fair where relevant).

Reviewer: the name of the audit team member who reviewed the work. This provides evidence of the review as required by ISAs.

Date of review: this must be before the audit opinion is signed.

Types of audit documentation

Audit documentation includes:

- Planning documentation
  - overall audit strategy
  - audit plan
  - risk analysis
- Audit programmes
- Summary of significant matters
- Written representation from management
- Checklists
- Correspondence
- Copies of client records.

Example contents of a permanent audit file

For large audits much of the knowledge of the business information may be kept on a **permanent file** and the audit plan may contain a summary or simply cross refer to the permanent file. Typical information on a permanent file includes:

- Names of management, those charged with governance, shareholders
- Systems information
- Background to the industry and the client's business
- Title deeds
- Directors' service agreements
- Copies of contract and agreements.

Example contents of a current audit file

The audit work for a specific period is kept on a **current file.**

Typically, there are at least three sections:

- Planning
- Performance
- Completion.

Planning

The main element of this section is likely to be the Audit Planning Memorandum.

This document is the written audit plan and will be read by all members of the audit team before work starts. Its contents are likely to include:

- Background information about the client, including recent performance
- Changes since last year's audit (for recurring clients)
- Key accounting policies
- Important laws and regulations affecting the company
- Client's trial balance (or draft financial statements)
- Preliminary analytical procedures
- Key audit risks
- Overall audit strategy
- Materiality assessment
- Timetable of procedures
- Deadlines
- Staffing and a budget (hours to be worked × charge out rates)
- Locations to be visited.

Performance

Working papers are likely to consist of:

- Lead schedule – showing total figures, which agree to the financial statements.
- Back-up schedules – breakdowns of totals into relevant sub-totals.
- Audit work programme detailing:
    - The objectives being tested
    - Work completed
    - How samples were selected
    - Conclusions drawn
    - Who did the work
    - Date the work was completed
    - Who reviewed it.

Completion

The completion (also known as review) stage of an audit has a number of standard components:

- Going concern review

- Subsequent events review

- Final analytical procedures

- Accounting standards (disclosure) checklist

- Written representation from management

- Summary of adjustments made since trial balance produced

- Summary of unadjusted misstatements

- Draft final financial statements

- Draft report to those charged with governance and management letter.

Security of working papers

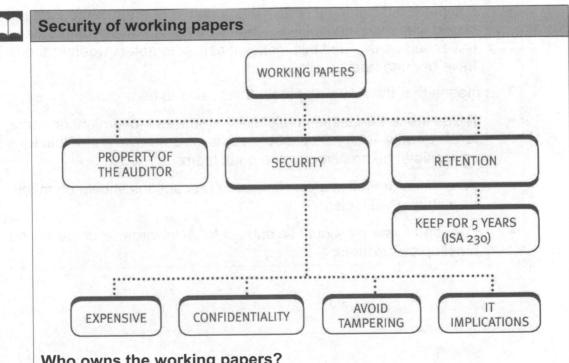

Who owns the working papers?

The auditor owns the audit working papers. This is important because:

- Access to the working papers is controlled by the auditor, not the client, which is an element in preserving the auditor's independence.

- In some circumstances care may need to be taken when copies of client generated schedules are incorporated into the file.

Security

Working papers must be kept secure.

- By its nature, audit evidence will comprise confidential, sensitive information. If the files are lost or stolen, the auditor's duty of confidentiality will be compromised.

- Audits are expensive. If the files are lost or stolen, the evidence they contain will need to be recreated, so the work will need to be done again. The auditors may be able to recover the costs from their insurers, but otherwise it will simply represent a loss to the firm.

- There have been cases of unscrupulous clients altering auditors' working papers to conceal frauds.

The implications of IT-based audit systems are also far reaching.

- By their nature, laptops are susceptible to theft, even though the thief may have no interest in the contents of the audit file. Nevertheless, all the problems associated with re-performing the audit and breaches of confidentiality remain.

- It is more difficult to be certain who created or amended computer based files than manual files – handwriting, signatures and dates have their uses – and this makes it harder to detect whether the files have been tampered with.

This means that the following precautions need to be taken.

- If files are left unattended at clients' premises – overnight or during lunch breaks – they should be securely locked away, or if this is impossible, taken home by the audit team.

- When files are left in a car, the same precautions should be taken as with any valuables.

- IT-based systems should be subject to passwords, encryption and back up procedures.

Test your understanding 1

You are an audit senior responsible for understanding the entity and its environment and assessing the risk of material misstatements for the audit of Rock Co for the year-ending 31 December. Rock Co is a company listed on a stock exchange. Rock Co is engaged in the wholesale import, manufacture and distribution of basic cosmetics and toiletries for sale to a wide range of stores, under a variety of different brand names. You have worked on the audit of this client for several years as an audit junior.

Required:

(a) **Describe the information you will seek, and procedures you will perform in order to understand the entity and its environment and assess risk for the audit of Rock Co.**

(10 marks)

(b) You are now nearing the completion of the audit of Rock Co. Draft financial statements have been produced. You have been given the responsibility of performing a review of the audit files before they are passed to the audit manager and the audit partner for their review. You have been asked to concentrate on the proper completion of the audit working papers. Some of the audit working papers have been produced electronically but all of them have been printed out for you.

Required:

Describe the types of audit working papers you should expect to see in the audit files and the features of those working papers that show that they have been properly completed.

(10 marks)

(Total: 20 marks)

Test your understanding 2

You are the audit manager responsible for planning the audit of Rottnest Co. During the planning of the audit you have identified an increased risk of material misstatement due to fraud. The audit strategy and audit plan reflect this increased risk.

(1) **Which of the following statements regarding fraud is correct?**

A   The auditor may not detect all material fraud in the financial statements but this won't necessarily mean the auditor has been negligent due to the nature of fraud and the likelihood of concealment

B   The auditor must detect all material fraud in the financial statements

C   The auditor must detect every fraud in the financial statements

D   The auditor is not responsible for detecting fraud as this is management's responsibility

(2) **If material misstatement as a result of fraud is detected during the audit, and is not corrected by management, how will this be communicated to the shareholders?**

A   The auditor must send a letter to the shareholders informing them of the fraud

B   The auditor must speak at the annual general meeting and specifically inform them

C   The auditor will report it to the police and the police will notify the shareholders

D   Through the auditor's report as the opinion will be modified

(3) **Which of the following procedures must the auditor perform to respond to the risk of fraud?**

(i)   The auditor must obtain written representation from management confirming they have disclosed all known and suspected frauds to the auditor.

(ii)   The auditor must incorporate an unpredictable element into the design of their audit procedures.

(iii) The auditor must test year-end journal entries and estimates which may be used to manipulate the financial statements.

A   (i) and (ii) only

B   (i) and (iii) only

C   (ii) and (iii) only

D   (i), (ii) and (iii)

(4)   **Which of the following statements is true in respect of the audit plan?**

    A   The audit plan sets out the scope, direction and framework for the audit

    B   The audit plan contains the detailed audit procedures designed to obtain sufficient appropriate evidence including the objective of each procedure and the sample size to be tested

    C   The plan includes preliminary engagement activities such as materiality and risk assessment

    D   The audit plan is developed before the audit strategy

(5)   **Which matters will not be included in the audit strategy?**

    A   Risk assessment and materiality

    B   Communications with the client

    C   Specific audit procedures to respond to the risks assessed

    D   The need for professional scepticism

Test your understanding 3

Your firm has recently been appointed auditor of Albany Co, a large company with sophisticated computer systems. The planning is due to commence shortly. It has been agreed with the client that an interim and final audit will be performed.

(1)   **Which of the following is NOT a benefit of planning the audit?**

    A   It ensures the audit is performed efficiently and effectively

    B   It helps identify the resources to be allocated

    C   It ensures the financial statements will be correct

    D   It minimises the risk of issuing an inappropriate audit opinion

(2)   **Which of the following is NOT part of the planning stage of the audit?**

    A   Preliminary materiality assessment

    B   Risk assessment

    C   Developing the audit strategy

    D   Final analytical procedures

(3) **Which of the following is the most appropriate time to perform an interim audit?**

A   After the year-end before the auditor's report is signed

B   Before the year-end

C   At the same time as the final audit

D   After the auditor's report has been signed

(4) **Which of the following will NOT be performed at the interim audit?**

A   Obtaining written representation from management

B   Tests of controls

C   Transaction testing for transactions that have occurred to date

D   Performing risk assessment procedures

(5) **What are the main reasons for performing an interim audit?**

(i)   To increase fee income for the firm.

(ii)   To reduce time pressure at the final audit.

(iii) To assess the level of control risk and determine the amount of substantive testing required at the final audit.

A   (i) and (ii) only

B   (i) and (iii) only

C   (ii) and (iii) only

D   (i), (ii) and (iii)

Test your understanding 4

You are the partner within Mosaic Co. Your firm has an established reputation for performing high quality audits. Your firm has a quality control procedures document which is updated regularly. The procedures document is published in the employee handbook which each employee receives a copy of on joining the firm. The procedures are also available on your firm's intranet site so staff are able to access it at any time. The firm's procedures have been designed to ensure compliance with ISA 220 *Quality Control for an Audit of Financial Statements*.

(1) At the start of an audit, all audit team members are required to attend a planning meeting where they are informed of the nature of the client, the risks identified to date and any other issues of which they should be aware when performing the audit.

This is an example of which element of quality control?

A Direction

B Consultation

C Review

D Supervision

(2) **Which of the following is NOT an element of a quality control system?**

A Human resources

B Engagement performance

C Engagement quality control review

D Monitoring

(3) **Which of the following are primary reasons why a firm should perform audits to a high standard of quality?**

(i) To maintain confidence in the audit profession.

(ii) To ensure auditor's reports issued are appropriate.

(iii) To avoid punishment.

(iv) To ensure clients receive a competent and professional service.

A (i) and (ii)

B (i), (iii) and (iv)

C (iii) and (iv)

D (i), (ii) and (iv)

(4) **Which of the following should NOT perform an Engagement Quality Control Review?**

A   External consultant

B   Engagement partner of the client subject to review

C   Engagement partner of the audit firm not involved with the client subject to review

D   Senior manager or director of the audit firm not involved with the client subject to review

(5) **Which of the following statements regarding quality control is false?**

A   Where deficiencies in quality control procedures are identified the firm should take action such as providing additional training or increasing the frequency of quality control reviews.

B   The firm only needs to act on quality control deficiencies identified by an external quality control review such as that performed by the ACCA.

C   The firm should monitor its quality control procedures and policies on a regular basis to ensure they are working effectively.

D   Every person within the audit firm has a responsibility to ensure quality control is adhered to.

9 Chapter summary

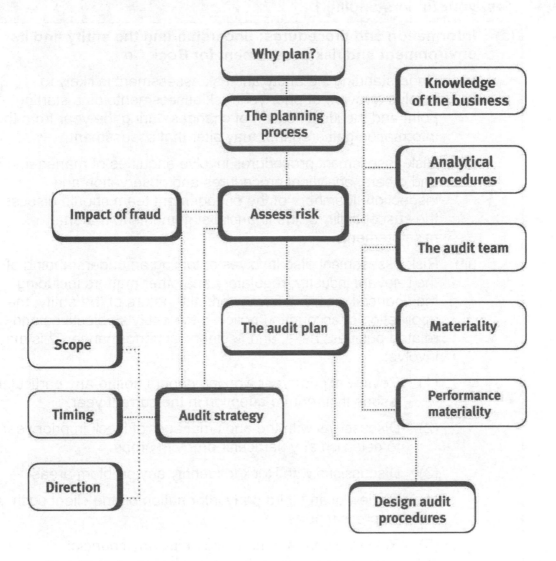

Test your understanding answers

Test your understanding 1

(a) **Information and procedures: understanding the entity and its environment and risk assessment for Rock Co**

(i) Understanding the entity and risk assessment is likely to involve a review of prior year risk assessments as a starting point and the identification of changes during the year from the information gathered that may alter that assessment.

(ii) Risk assessment procedures involve enquiries of management and others, analytical procedures and observation and inspection. Members of the engagement team should discuss the susceptibility of the financial statements to material misstatements.

(iii) Risk assessment also involves obtaining an understanding of the relevant industry, regulatory and other matters including the financial reporting framework, the nature of the entity, the application of accounting policies, the entity's objectives and related business risks, and its financial performance. This may involve:

(1) Review of prior year working papers noting any particular issues that require attention in the current year.

(2) Discussions with the audit manager of Rock in prior years to establish any particular problem areas.

(3) Discussions with Rock to identify any problem areas.

(4) Review of any third party information on the client such as press reports.

(5) Review of management accounts, any financial information provided to the stock exchange or draft financial statements that may be available to establish trends in the business.

(6) Review of any changes in stock exchange requirements.

(7) Review of systems documentation (either generated by Rock Co or held by the firm) to see if it needs updating.

(iv) Auditors should obtain an understanding of the control environment, the entity's process for identifying and dealing with risks, information systems, control activities and monitoring of contents.

(v)   Risks should be assessed at the financial statements level, and at the assertion level, and identify significant risks that require special audit consideration, and risks for which substantive procedures alone do not provide sufficient, appropriate audit evidence.

(vi)   Analytical procedures are often used to highlight areas warranting particular audit attention. In the case of Rock Co, they are likely to focus on inventory which is likely to have a significant effect on profit (there may be slow-moving or obsolete inventory that needs to be written down) and on property, plant and equipment which (as a manufacturer and distributor) is likely to be a significant item on the statement of financial position.

(vii)   Risk assessment will facilitate the determination of materiality and tolerable error (calculations are normally based on revenue, profit and assets) that will be used in determining the sample sizes and in the evaluation of errors.

(b)   **Types and features of audit working papers**

(i)   Types of audit working papers include:

(1)   Systems documentation (flowcharts, systems manuals, narrative notes, checklists and questionnaires, etc.)

(2)   Constitutional documents

(3)   Agreements with banks and other providers of finance

(4)   Details of other advisors used by the entity such as lawyers

(5)   Regulatory documentation relating to the stock exchange listing

(6)   Audit planning documentation

(7)   Audit work programs

(8)   Working papers showing the work performed

(9)   Lead schedules showing summaries of work performed and conclusions on individual account areas and the amounts to be included in the financial statements

(10) Trial balances, management accounts and financial statements

(11) Standard working papers relating to the calculation of sample sizes, for example

(12) Schedules of unadjusted differences

(13) Schedules of review points

(14) Letters of deficiency and written representation letters.

(ii) Features of audit working papers. All working papers (without exception) should show:

(1) By whom they were prepared and when.

(2) When they were reviewed and/or updated, and by whom, by means of signatures and dates – these may be electronic in the case of electronic working papers.

(3) Audit planning documentation should include the risk assessment which should be cross referenced to the audit program, and the audit program should be cross referenced to the audit working papers and vice versa.

(4) Working papers showing the work performed should be cross referenced to the audit program and the lead schedule on that particular section of the audit file, and should describe the nature of the work performed, the evidence obtained, and the conclusions reached.

(5) Each section of the audit file should have a lead schedule which should be cross referenced back to the relevant working papers.

(6) Trial balances should be cross referenced back to the relevant section of the audit file, and cross referenced forward to the financial statements.

(7) The financial statements should be cross referenced to the trial balance.

(8) Schedules of unadjusted differences should be cross referenced to the sections of the file to which they relate.

(9) Schedules of review points should all be 'cleared' to show that all outstanding matters have been dealt with.

Test your understanding 2

(1)	A	The auditor should plan and perform the audit to have a reasonable expectation of detecting material fraud and error. However, if a fraud is very well concealed, even a very thorough audit may not detect it.
(2)	D	Material misstatements are brought to the attention of the shareholders by modifying the audit opinion.
(3)	D	All three procedures must be performed to respond to the risk of fraud.
(4)	B	Options A and C describe aspects of the audit strategy The audit strategy is developed before the audit plan.
(5)	C	Specific procedures are included in the audit plan.

Test your understanding 3

(1)	C	Financial statements cannot be verified as being correct due to the inclusion of estimates and judgments.
(2)	D	'Final' analytical procedures are performed at the completion stage of the audit.
(3)	B	The interim audit helps to develop the audit strategy. It should take place before the year-end to avoid interfering with the client's year-end procedures but should not be so early to be of little use.
(4)	A	Written representations are obtained at the end of the audit, just before the auditor's report is signed.
(5)	C	An interim audit may result in increased fees for the firm if a greater amount of work is performed. However, this is not a reason for performing an interim audit. The interim audit is a means of spreading the workload over a longer period to avoid time pressure.

Test your understanding 4

(1)	A	Briefing of the audit teams forms part of the direction of the audit.
(2)	C	Engagement quality control review is part of engagement performance and monitoring.
(3)	D	Quality is important for upholding the reputation of the profession and the firm in order to maintain investor confidence. Avoiding punishment is not the primary reason for ensuring a quality audit is performed.
(4)	B	An EQCR should be performed by someone independent of the engagement and someone of suitable authority such as a senior manager, director or partner.
(5)	B	The firm should perform its own quality control reviews and take action as necessary to ensure quality control procedures are followed.

Evidence

Chapter learning objectives

This chapter covers syllabus areas:

- C1a – The need to obtain an understanding of internal control relevant to the audit

- D1 – Financial statement assertions and audit evidence

- D2 – Audit procedures

- D3 – Audit sampling and other means of testing

- D5 – Computer assisted audit techniques

- D6 – The work of others

Detailed syllabus objectives are provided in the introduction section of the text book.

PER

One of the PER performance objectives (PO19) is to collect and evaluate evidence for an audit. Carry out an internal or external audit from collecting evidence, through to forming an opinion. You demonstrate professional scepticism and make sure judgements are based on sufficient valid evidence. Working through this chapter should help you understand how to demonstrate that objective.

1 Audit evidence

 In order for the auditor's opinion to be considered trustworthy, auditors must come to their conclusions having completed a thorough examination of the books and records of their clients and they must document the procedures performed and evidence obtained, to support the conclusions reached.

ISA 500 *Audit Evidence* states the objective of the auditor, in terms of gathering evidence, is:

'to design and perform audit procedures in such a way to enable the auditor to obtain **sufficient appropriate audit evidence** to be able to draw reasonable conclusions on which to base the auditor's opinion.' [ISA 500, 4]

- **Sufficiency** relates to the **quantity** of evidence.

- **Appropriateness** relates to the **quality** or relevance and reliability of evidence.

[ISA 500, 5b, 5e]

Sufficient evidence

There needs to be 'enough' evidence to support the auditor's conclusion. This is a matter of professional judgment. When determining whether there is enough evidence the auditor must consider:

- The risk of material misstatement
- The materiality of the item
- The nature of accounting and internal control systems
- The results of controls tests
- The auditor's knowledge and experience of the business
- The size of a population being tested
- The size of the sample selected to test
- The reliability of the evidence obtained.

Sufficient evidence

Consider, for example, the audit of a bank balance:

Auditors will confirm year-end bank balances directly with the bank. This is a good source of evidence but on its own is not sufficient to give assurance regarding the completeness and final valuation of bank and cash amounts. The key reason is timing differences. The client may have received cash amounts or cheques before the end of the year, or may have paid out cheques before the end of the year, that have not yet cleared the bank account.

For this reason the auditor should also review and reperform the client's year-end bank reconciliation.

In combination these two pieces of evidence will be sufficient to give assurance over the bank balances.

Appropriate evidence

Appropriateness of evidence breaks down into two important concepts:

- Reliability
- Relevance.

Reliability

Auditors should always attempt to obtain evidence from the most trustworthy and dependable source possible.

- Evidence obtained from an independent external source is more reliable than client generated evidence.

- Evidence obtained directly by the auditor is more reliable than evidence obtained indirectly.

- Client generated evidence is the least reliable source of evidence. If the client is manipulating the financial statement figures they may produce fictitious evidence to support the figures. Client generated evidence is more reliable if effective controls are in place. This doesn't mean the auditor should not rely on client generated evidence. It simply means that where more reliable evidence is available, the auditor should obtain it.

- In addition, written evidence is more reliable than oral evidence as oral representations can be withdrawn or challenged. Original documents are more reliable than copies or documents transformed into electronic form as it may be difficult to see if these have been tampered with.

[ISA 500, A31]

Broadly speaking, the more reliable the evidence the less of it the auditor will need. However, if evidence is unreliable it will never be appropriate for the audit, no matter how much is gathered. [ISA 500, A4]

Relevance

Relevance means the evidence relates to the financial statement assertions being tested. [ISA 500, A27]

For example, when attending an inventory count, the auditor will:

- Select a sample of items from physical inventory and trace them to inventory records to confirm the **completeness** of accounting records

- Select a sample of items from inventory records and trace them to physical inventories to confirm the **existence** of inventory assets.

Whilst the procedures are similar in nature, their purpose (and relevance) is to test different **assertions** regarding inventory balances.

2 Financial statements assertions

The objective of audit testing is to assist the auditor in coming to a conclusion as to whether the financial statements are free from material misstatement.

Auditors perform a range of tests on the significant classes of transaction and account balances. These tests focus on what are known as **financial statements assertions**:

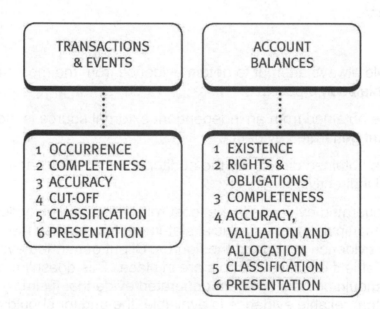

Assertions about classes of transactions and events, and related disclosures, for the period under audit

Occurrence – the transactions and events recorded and disclosed actually occurred and pertain to the entity.

Completeness – all transactions and events that should have been recorded have been recorded, and all related disclosures that should have been included have been included.

Accuracy – amounts and other data have been recorded appropriately and related disclosures have been appropriately measured and described.

Cut-off – transactions and events have been recorded in the correct accounting period.

Classification – transactions and events have been recorded in the proper accounts.

Presentation – transactions and events are appropriately aggregated or disaggregated and clearly described, and related disclosures are relevant and understandable in the context of the applicable financial reporting framework.

[ISA 315, A129a]

Assertions about account balances and related disclosures at the period end

Existence – assets, liabilities and equity interests exist.

Rights and obligations – the entity holds or controls the rights to assets and liabilities are the obligations of the entity.

Completeness – all assets, liabilities and equity interests that should have been recorded have been recorded, and all related disclosures that should have been included have been included.

Accuracy, valuation and allocation – assets, liabilities and equity interests have been included in the financial statements at appropriate amounts and any resulting valuation or allocation adjustments have been appropriately recorded, and related disclosures have been appropriately measured and described.

Classification – assets, liabilities and equity interests have been recorded in the proper accounts.

Presentation – account balances are appropriately aggregated or disaggregated and clearly described, and related disclosures are relevant and understandable in the context of the applicable financial reporting framework.

[ISA 315, A129b]

Inventory misstatements

There are many ways inventory could be materially misstated:

- Items might not be counted and therefore not be included in the balance. This would mean the inventory balance was not **complete**.

- Items delivered after the year-end could be included in this accounting period. This would mean the inventory did not **exist** at the year-end date.

- Damaged or obsolete inventory might not be valued at the lower of cost and net realisable value. This would mean the inventory was **valued** incorrectly.

- Purchase costs might not be recorded accurately. This would also affect **valuation**.

- Inventory stored at the client's site may belong to a 3rd party. The client would not have the **right** to include this inventory in their financial statements.

Addressing disclosures in the audit of financial statements

Disclosures are an important part of the financial statements and seen as a way for communicating further information to users. Poor quality disclosures may obscure understanding of important matters.

Concerns have been raised about whether auditors are giving sufficient attention to disclosures during the audit. The IAASB believes that where the term financial statements is used in the ISAs it should be clarified that this is intended to include all disclosures subject to audit.

Recent changes to ISAs include:

- Emphasis on the importance of giving appropriate attention to addressing disclosures.

- Focus on matters relating to disclosures to be discussed with those charged with governance, particularly at the planning stage.

- Emphasis on the need to agree with management their responsibility to make available information relevant to disclosures, early in the audit process.

3 Sources of audit evidence

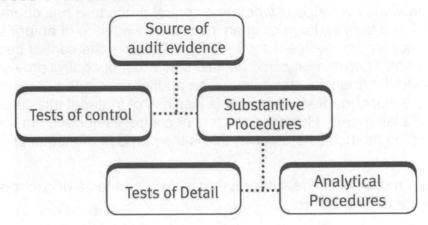

Auditors can obtain assurance from:

 Tests of control: Tests of control are designed to evaluate the operating effectiveness of controls in preventing or detecting and correcting material misstatement.

Substantive procedures: Substantive procedures are designed to detect material misstatement at the assertion level.

[ISA 330, 4]

Tests of controls

In order to design further audit procedures the auditor must assess the risk of material misstatement in the financial statements.

 Remember: Audit risk = Inherent risk × Control risk × Detection risk

Internal controls are a vital component of this risk model, they are the mechanisms that clients design in an attempt to prevent, detect and correct misstatement. This is not only necessary for good financial reporting, it is necessary to safeguard the assets of the shareholders and is a requirement of corporate governance.

 The stronger the control system the lower the control risk and as a result, there is a lower risk of material misstatement in the financial statements.

In order to be able to rely on controls the auditor will need to:

- Ascertain how the system operates

- Document the system in audit working papers

- Test the operation of the system

- Assess the design and operating effectiveness of the control system

- Determine the impact on the audit approach for specific classes of transactions, account balances and disclosures.

The focus of a test of control is not the monetary amount of a transaction. A test of control provides evidence of whether a control procedure has operated effectively. For example, inspecting an invoice for evidence of authorisation. It is irrelevant whether the invoice is for $100 or $1000 as it the control being tested, not the amount. Therefore, it could be said that a test of control provides indirect evidence over the financial statements. The auditor makes the assumption that if controls are working effectively there is less risk of material misstatement in the financial statements. However, the test of control itself does not test the figure within the financial statements, this is the purpose of a substantive procedure.

We will learn more about the systems themselves and tests of controls in the chapter 'Systems and controls'.

Substantive procedures

Substantive procedures consist of:

- **Tests of detail:** tests of detail to verify individual transactions and balances.

- **Substantive analytical procedures:** analytical procedures (as seen in the chapter 'Risk') involve analysing relationships between information to identify unusual fluctuations which may indicate possible misstatement.

Tests of detail v analytical procedures

A test of detail looks at the supporting evidence for an individual transaction such as inspection of a purchase invoice to verify the amount/date/classification of a specific purchase. If there are 5000 purchase invoices recorded during the accounting period, this one test of detail has only provided evidence for one of those transactions.

An analytical procedure would be used to assess the reasonableness of the purchases figure in total. For example, calculate the percentage change in purchases from last year and then compare this with the percentage change in revenue to see if they move in line with each other as expected.

The analytical procedure is not looking at the detail of any of the individual purchases but at the total figure. It is possible that there are a number of misstatements within the purchases population which would only be discovered by testing the detail as they may cancel each other out. An analytical procedure would not detect these misstatements.

Because of this, analytical procedures should only be used as the main source of substantive evidence where the internal controls have been found to be reliable as there is less chance of misstatements being present as the control system would have detected and corrected them.

In some circumstances the auditor may rely solely on substantive testing:

- The auditor may choose to rely solely on substantive testing where it is considered to be a more efficient or more effective way of obtaining audit evidence, e.g. for smaller organisations.

- The auditor may have to rely solely on substantive testing where the client's internal control system cannot be relied on.

The auditor must always carry out substantive procedures on material items. [ISA 330 *The Auditor's Response to Assessed Risks*, 18].

The auditor is required to carry out the following substantive procedures:

- Agreeing the financial statements to the underlying accounting records.

- Examination of material journals and other adjustments made in preparing the financial statements.

[IAS 330, 20]

4 Types of audit procedure

The auditor can adopt the following procedures to obtain audit evidence:

- Inspection of records, documents or physical assets.

- Observation of processes and procedures, e.g. inventory counts.

- External confirmation obtained in the form of a direct written response to the auditor from a third party.

- Recalculation to confirm the numerical accuracy of documents or records.

- Re-performance by the auditor of procedures or controls.

- Analytical procedures.

- Enquiry of knowledgeable parties.

[ISA 500, A14 – A22]

In the chapter 'Procedures' we will look in detail at how these procedures are applied to specific items in the financial statements.

Explanation of audit procedures

Inspection of documents and records: examining records or documents, in paper or electronic form.

- May give evidence of rights and obligations, e.g. title deeds.

- May give evidence that a control is operating, e.g. invoices stamped paid or authorised for payment by an appropriate signature.

- May give evidence about cut-off, e.g. the dates on invoices, despatch notes, etc.

- Confirms sales values and purchases costs.

Inspection of tangible assets: physical examination of an asset.

- To obtain evidence of existence of that asset.

- May give evidence of valuation, e.g. evidence of damage indicating impairment of inventory or non-current assets.

Observation: looking at a process or procedure being performed by others.

- May provide evidence that a control is being operated, e.g. segregation of duties or a cheque signatory.

- Only provides evidence that the control was operating properly at the time of the observation. The auditor's presence may have had an influence on the operation of the control.

- Observation of a one-off event, e.g. an inventory count, may well give good evidence that the procedure was carried out effectively.

Enquiry: seeking information from knowledgeable persons, both financial and non-financial, within the entity or outside.

Whilst a major source of evidence, the results of enquiries will usually need to be corroborated in some way through other audit procedures. This is because responses generated by the audit client are considered to be of a low quality due to their inherent bias.

The answers to enquiries may themselves be corroborative evidence. In particular they may be used to corroborate the results of analytical procedures.

Written representations from management are part of overall enquiries. These involve obtaining written statements from management to confirm oral enquiries. These are considered further in the chapter 'Completion and review'.

External confirmation: obtaining a direct response (usually written) from an external, third party.

- Examples include:
    - Circularisation of receivables
    - Circularisation of payables where supplier statements are not available
    - Confirmation of bank balances in a bank letter
    - Confirmation of actual/potential penalties from legal advisers
    - Confirmation of inventories held by third parties.

- May give good evidence of existence of balances, e.g. receivables confirmation.

- May not necessarily give reliable evidence of valuation, e.g. customers may confirm receivable amounts but, ultimately, be unable to pay in the future.

Recalculation: manually or electronically checking the arithmetical accuracy of documents, records, or the client's calculations, e.g. recalculation of the translation of a foreign currency transaction.

Reperformance: the auditor's independent execution of procedures or controls that were originally performed as part of the entity's internal control system, e.g. reperformance of a bank reconciliation.

Analytical procedures: analysis of plausible relationships between data. See below.

Analytical procedures as substantive tests

We have already come across analytical procedures as a risk procedure at the planning stage. Later in the text we will also see that they are a component of the completion of an audit. Here we consider their use as substantive procedures, i.e. procedures designed to detect material misstatement.

Analytical procedures are used to identify trends and understand relationships between sets of data. This in itself will not detect misstatement but will identify possible areas of misstatement. As such, analytical procedures cannot be used in isolation and should be coupled with other, corroborative, forms of testing, such as enquiry of management.

When performing analytical procedures, auditors do not simply look at current figures in comparison to last year. Auditors may consider other points of comparison, such as budgets and industry data.

Other techniques are also available, including:

- Ratio analysis

- Trend analysis

- Proof in total, for example: an auditor might create an expectation of payroll costs for the year by taking last year's cost and inflating for pay rises and changes in staff numbers.

Analytical procedures are useful for assessing several assertions at once as the auditor is effectively auditing a whole account balance or class of transaction to see if it is reasonable.

They can be used to corroborate other audit evidence obtained, such as statements by management about changes in cost structures.

By using analytical procedures the auditor may identify unusual items that can then be further investigated to ensure that a misstatement doesn't exist in the balance.

However, in order to use analytical procedures effectively the auditor needs to be able to create an expectation. It would be difficult to do this if operations changed significantly from the prior year. If the changes were planned, the auditor could use forecasts as a point of comparison, although these are inherently unreliable due to the number of estimates involved. In this circumstance it would be pointless comparing to prior years as the business would be too different to be able to conduct effective comparison.

It would also be difficult to use analytical procedures if a business had experienced a number of significant one-off events in the year as these would distort the year's figures making comparison to both prior years and budgets meaningless.

The suitability of analytical procedures as substantive tests

The suitability of this approach depends on four factors:

- The assertion(s) under scrutiny

- The reliability of the data

- The degree of precision possible

- The amount of variation which is acceptable.

For example:

(1) Assertions under scrutiny

– Analytical procedures should be suitable for the assertion being tested. They are clearly unsuitable for testing the existence of inventories. They are, however, suitable for assessing the value of inventory in terms of the need for allowances against old inventories, identified using the inventory holding period ratio.

– Analytical procedures are more suitable for testing balances which are likely to be predictable over time meaning relationships between data can be analysed to identify usual fluctuations.

(2) Reliability of data

If controls over financial data are weak, the data is likely to contain misstatement and is therefore not suitable as a basis for assessment.

(3) Precision required

– As analytical procedures are a high level approach to test a balance as a whole, if the auditor needs to test with precision, analytical procedures are unlikely to identify the misstatements.

– Precision will be improved if disaggregated information is obtained and analysed. For example, when performing analytical procedures over revenue, it may produce more reliable results if sales by month/customer/product/region are analysed rather than the revenue figure as a whole.

(4) Acceptable variation

The amount of acceptable variation between the expected figure and the actual figure will impact whether analytical procedures provide sufficient appropriate evidence. If the level of variation from actual is higher than the level of variation the auditor is willing to accept, further procedures will be necessary to ensure the balance in the financial statements is not materially misstated.

5 Relying on the work of others

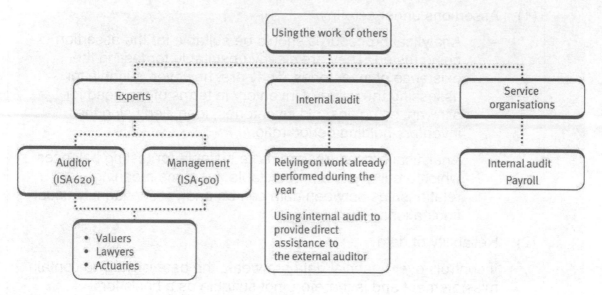

There are two types of expert an auditor may use:

(1) Management's expert – an employee of the client or someone engaged by the audit client who has expertise that is used to assist in the preparation of the financial statements.

(2) Auditor's expert – an employee of the audit firm or someone engaged by the audit firm to provide sufficient appropriate evidence.

Relying on the work of a management's expert

ISA 500 *Audit Evidence* provides guidance on what the auditor should consider before relying on the work of a management's expert. This guidance is very similar to that given for relying on the work of an auditor's expert.

The auditor must:

• Evaluate the competence, capabilities and objectivity of that expert.

• Obtain an understanding of the work of that expert.

• Evaluate the appropriateness of that expert's work as audit evidence for the relevant assertion.

[ISA 500, 8]

The rest of this section focuses on the work of an auditor's expert.

Relying on the work of an auditor's expert

ISA 620 *Using the Work of an Auditor's Expert* provides guidance to auditors.

If the auditor lacks the required technical knowledge to gather sufficient appropriate evidence to form an opinion, they may have to rely on the work of an expert.

Examples of such circumstances include:

- The valuation of complex financial instruments, land and buildings, works of art, jewellery and intangible assets.

- Actuarial calculations associated with insurance contracts or employee benefit plans.

- The estimation of oil and gas reserves.

- The interpretation of contracts, laws and regulations.

- The analysis of complex or unusual tax compliance issues.

[ISA 620, A1]

The auditor must determine if the expert's work is adequate for the auditor's purposes. [ISA 620, 5b]

To fulfil this responsibility the auditor must **evaluate whether the expert has the necessary competence, capability and objectivity for the purpose of the audit**. [ISA 620, 9]

Evaluating competence [ISA 620, A15]

Information regarding the competence, capability and objectivity on an expert may come from a variety of sources, including:

- Personal experience of working with the expert.

- Discussions with the expert.

- Discussions with other auditors.

- Knowledge of the expert's qualifications, memberships of professional bodies and licences.

- Published papers or books written by the expert.

- The audit firm's quality control procedures.

Evaluating objectivity [ISA 620, A20]

Assessing the objectivity of the expert is particularly difficult, as they may not be bound by a similar code of ethics as the auditor and, as such, may be unaware of the ethical requirements and threats with which auditors are familiar.

It may therefore be relevant to:

- Make enquiries of the client about known interests or relationships with the chosen expert.

- Discuss applicable safeguards with the expert.

- Discuss financial, business and personal interests in the client with the expert.

- Obtain written representation from the expert.

Agreeing the work [ISA 620, 11]

Once the auditor has considered the above matters they must then obtain written agreement from the expert of the following:

- The nature, scope and objectives of the expert's work.

- The roles and responsibilities of the auditor and the expert.

- The nature, timing and extent of communication between the two parties.

- The need for the expert to observe confidentiality.

Evaluating the work [ISA 620, 12]

Once the expert's work is complete the auditor must scrutinise it and evaluate whether it is appropriate for audit purposes.

In particular, the auditor should consider:

- The reasonableness of the findings and their consistency with other evidence.

- The significant assumptions made.

- The use and accuracy of source data.

Reference to the work of an expert

Auditors cannot devolve responsibility for forming an audit opinion. The auditor has to use their professional judgment whether the evidence produced by the expert is sufficient and appropriate to support the audit opinion.

The use of an auditor's expert is not mentioned in an unmodified auditor's opinion unless required by law or regulation. Reference to the work of an expert may be included in a modified opinion if it is relevant to the understanding of the modification. This does not diminish the auditor's responsibility for the opinion. [ISA 620, 14 & 15]

Relying on internal audit

ISA 610 *Using the Work of Internal Auditors* provides guidance.

An internal audit department forms part of the client's system of internal control. If this is an effective element of the control system it may reduce control risk, and therefore reduce the need for the auditor to perform detailed substantive testing.

Additionally, auditors may be able to co-operate with a client's internal audit department and place reliance on their procedures in place of performing their own.

Before relying on the work of internal audit, the external auditor must assess the effectiveness of the internal audit function and assess whether the work produced by the internal auditor is adequate for the purpose of the audit.

Evaluating the internal audit function [ISA 610, 15]

- The extent to which the internal audit function's **organisational status** and relevant policies and procedures support the **objectivity** of the internal auditors.

- The **competence** of the internal audit function.

- Whether the internal audit function applies a systematic and disciplined **approach**.

Evaluating objectivity [ISA 610, A7]

- Whether the internal audit function reports to those charged with governance or has direct access to those charged with governance.

- Whether the internal audit function is free from operational responsibility.

- Whether those charged with governance are responsible for employment decisions such as remuneration.

- Whether any constraints are placed on the internal function by management or those charged with governance.

- Whether the internal auditors are members of a professional body which requires compliance with ethical requirements.

Evaluating competence [ISA 610, A8]

- Whether the resources of the internal audit function are appropriate and adequate for the size of the organisation and nature of its operations.

- Whether there are established policies for hiring, training and assigning internal auditors to internal audit engagements.

- Whether internal auditors have adequate technical training and proficiency, including relevant professional qualifications and experience.

- Whether the internal auditors have the required knowledge of the entity's financial reporting and the applicable financial reporting framework and possess the necessary skills to perform work related to the financial statements.

- Whether the internal auditors are members of a professional body which requires continued professional development.

Evaluating the systematic and disciplined approach

- Existence, adequacy and use of internal audit procedures and guidance.

- Application of quality control standards such as those in ISQC 1.

[ISA 610, A11]

If the auditor considers it appropriate to use the work of the internal auditors they then have to determine the areas and extent to which the work of the internal audit function can be used (by considering the nature and scope of work) and incorporate this into their planning to assess the impact on the nature, timing and extent of further audit procedures. [ISA 610, 17]

Evaluating the internal audit work

- The work was properly planned, performed, supervised, reviewed and documented.

- Sufficient appropriate evidence has been obtained.

- The conclusions reached are appropriate in the circumstances.

- The reports prepared are consistent with the work performed.

[ISA 610, 23]

To evaluate the work adequately, the external auditor must re-perform some of the procedures that the internal auditor has performed to ensure they reach the same conclusion. [ISA 610, 24]

The extent of the work to be performed on the internal auditor's work will depend on the amount of judgment involved and the risk of material misstatement in that area. [ISA 610, 24]

When reviewing and re-performing some of the work of the internal auditor, the external auditor must consider whether their initial expectation of using the work of the internal auditor is still valid. [ISA 610, 25]

Note that the auditor is not required to rely on the work of internal audit. In some jurisdictions, the external auditor may be prohibited or restricted from using the work of the internal auditor by law.

Responsibility for the auditor's opinion cannot be devolved and no reference should be made in the auditor's report regarding the use of others during the audit.

Using the internal audit to provide direct assistance

External auditors can consider whether the internal auditor can provide direct assistance with gathering audit evidence under the supervision and review of the external auditor. ISA 610 provides guidance to aim to reduce the risk that the external auditor over uses the internal auditor.

The following considerations will be made:

- Direct assistance cannot be provided where laws and regulations prohibit such assistance, e.g. in the UK. [ISA 610, 26]

- The competence and objectivity of the internal auditor. Where threats to objectivity are present, the significance of them and whether they can be managed to an acceptable level must be considered. [ISA 610, 27]

- The external auditor must not assign work to the internal auditor which involves significant judgment, a high risk of material misstatement or with which the internal auditor has been involved. [ISA 610, 30]

- The planned work must be communicated with those charged with governance so agreement can be made that the use of the internal auditor is not excessive. [ISA 610, 31]

Where it is agreed that the internal auditor can provide direct assistance:

- Management must agree in writing that the internal auditor can provide such assistance and that they will not intervene in that work.
  [ISA 610, 33a]

- The internal auditors must provide written confirmation that they will keep the external auditors information confidential. [ISA 610, 33b]

- The external auditor will provide direction, supervision and review of the internal auditor's work. [ISA 610, 34]

- During the direction, supervision and review of the work, the external auditor should remain alert to the risk that the internal auditor is not objective or competent. [ISA 610, 35]

Documentation [ISA 610, 37]

The auditor should document:

- The evaluation of the internal auditor's objectivity and competence.

- The basis for the decision regarding the nature and extent of the work performed by the internal auditor.

- The name of the reviewer and the extent of the review of the internal auditor's work.

- The written agreement of management mentioned above.

- The working papers produced by the internal auditor.

Use of service organisations

Many companies use service organisations to perform business functions such as:

- Payroll processing

- Receivables collection

- Pension management.

If a company uses a service organisation this will impact the audit as audit evidence will need to be obtained from the service organisation instead of, or in addition to, the client. This needs to be taken into consideration when planning the audit.

ISA 402 *Audit Considerations Relating to an Entity Using a Service Organisation* provides guidance to auditors.

Planning the audit

The service organisation is an additional element to be taken into account when planning the audit and greater consideration needs to be made regarding obtaining sufficient appropriate evidence.

The auditor will need to:

- Obtain an understanding of the service organisation sufficient to identify and assess the risks of material misstatement.

- Design and perform audit procedures responsive to those risks.

[ISA 402, 1]

This requires the auditor to obtain an understanding of the service provided:

- Nature of the services and their effect on internal controls.

- Nature and materiality of the transactions to the entity.

- Level of interaction between the activities of the service organisation and the entity.

- Nature of the relationship between the service organisation and the entity including contractual terms.

[ISA 402, 9]

The auditor should determine the effect the use of a service organisation will have on their assessment of risk. The following issues should be considered:

- Reputation of the service organisation.

- Existence of external supervision.

- Extent of controls operated by service provider.

- Experience of errors and omissions.

- Degree of monitoring by the user.

Sources of information about the service organisation

- Obtaining a type 1 or type 2 report from the service organisation's auditor.

  A Type 1 report provides a description of the design of the controls at the service organisation prepared by the management of the service organisation. It includes a report by the service auditor providing an opinion on the description of the system and the suitability of the controls. [ISA 402, 8b]

  A Type 2 report is a report on the description, design and operating effectiveness of controls at the service organisation. It contains a report prepared by management of the service organisation. It includes a report by the service auditor providing an opinion on the description of the system, the suitability of the controls, the effectiveness of the controls and a description of the tests of controls performed by the auditor. [para 8c]

  If the auditor intends to use a report from a service auditor they should consider:

  - The competence and independence of the service organisation auditor.

  - The standards under which the report was issued.

- Contacting the service organisation through the client.

- Visiting the service organisation.

- Using another auditor to perform tests of controls.

[ISA 402, 12]

Responding to assessed risks

The auditor should determine whether sufficient appropriate evidence is available from the client and if not, perform further procedures or use another auditor to perform procedures on their behalf. [ISA 402, 15]

If controls are expected to operate effectively:

- Obtain a type 2 report if available and consider:

  - Whether the date covered by the report is appropriate for the audit.

  - Whether the client has any complementary controls in place.

  - The time elapsed since the tests of controls were performed.

  - Whether the tests of controls performed by the auditor are relevant to the financial statement assertions.

  [ISA 402, 17]

- Perform tests of controls at the service organisation.

- Use another auditor to perform tests of controls.

[ISA 402, 16]

The auditor should enquire of the client whether the service organisation has reported any frauds to them or whether they are aware of any frauds.
[ISA 402, 19]

Impact on the auditor's report

If sufficient appropriate evidence has not been obtained, a qualified or disclaimer of opinion will be issued. [ISA 402, 20]

The use of a service organisation auditor is not mentioned in the auditor's report unless required by law or regulation. Reference to the work of a service organisation auditor may be included in a report containing a modified opinion if it is relevant to the understanding of the modification. This does not diminish the auditor's responsibility for the opinion. [ISA 402, 21]

Benefits to the audit

- Independence: because the service organisation is external to the client, the audit evidence derived from it is regarded as being more reliable than evidence generated internally by the client.

- Competence: because the service organisation is a specialist, it may be more competent in executing its role than the client's internal department resulting in fewer errors.

- Possible reliance on the service organisation's auditors: it may be possible for the client's auditors to confirm information directly with the service organisation's auditors.

Drawbacks

The main disadvantage of outsourced services from the auditor's point of view concerns access to records and information.

Auditors generally have statutory rights of access to the client's records and to receive answers and explanations that they consider necessary to enable them to form their opinion.

They do not have such rights over records and information held by a third party such as a service organisation.

If access to records and other information is denied by the service organisation, this may impose a limitation on the scope of the auditor's work. If sufficient appropriate evidence is not obtained this will result in a modified auditor's report.

6   Selecting items for testing

The auditor has 3 options for selecting items to test:

(1)   Select all items to test (100% testing) [ISA 500, A53]

This may be chosen where the population may be very small and it is easy for the auditor to test all items. Alternatively, if it is an area over which the auditor requires greater audit confidence, for example an area that is material by nature or is considered to be of significant risk, the auditor may decide to test all items within the population.

(2) Selecting specific items for testing [ISA 500, A54]

Items with specific characteristics may be chosen for testing such as:

- High value items within a population
- All items over a certain amount
- Items to obtain information.

Although less than 100% of the population is being tested, this does not constitute sampling. As explained below, sampling requires all items in the population to have a chance of selection. In the categories above, only the items with the specific characteristics have a chance of selection.

(3) Sampling [ISA 500, A56]

The definition of sampling, as described in ISA 530 *Audit Sampling* is:

 'The application of audit procedures to less than 100% of items within a population of audit relevance such that all sampling units have a chance of selection in order to provide the auditor with a reasonable basis on which to draw conclusions about the entire population.' [ISA 530, 5a]

The need for sampling

It will usually be impossible to test every item in an accounting population because of the costs involved.

It is also important to remember that auditors give reasonable not absolute assurance and therefore do not certify that the financial statements are 100% accurate.

Selecting an appropriate sample

When sampling, the auditor must choose a representative sample.

- If a sample is representative, the same conclusion will be drawn from that sample as would have been drawn had the whole population been tested.
- For a sample to be representative, it must have the same characteristics as the other items in the population from which it was chosen. [ISA 530, A12]
- In order to reduce sampling risk and ensure the sample is representative, the auditor can increase the size of the sample selected or use stratification.

Stratification [ISA 530, Appendix 1]

Stratification is used in conjunction with sampling. Stratification is the process of breaking down a population into smaller subpopulations. Each subpopulation is a group of items (sampling units) which have similar characteristics.

The objective of stratification is to enable the auditor to reduce the variability of items within the subpopulation and therefore allow sample sizes to be reduced without increasing sampling risk.

For example the auditor may stratify the population of revenue into three subpopulations: revenue from Product A, revenue from Product B and revenue from Product C. The auditor may select a sample of revenue from Product A. The results of the testing of that sample can be extrapolated across the whole subpopulation of revenue from Product A. A sample may be selected of revenue from Product B and again, the results of that testing can be extrapolated across that subpopulation. Revenue from Product C may not be tested if it is considered immaterial.

Statistical and non-statistical sampling

 Statistical sampling means any approach to sampling that uses:

- Random selection of samples, and
- Probability theory to evaluate sample results.

Any approach that does not have both these characteristics is considered to be non-statistical sampling. [ISA 530, 5g]

The approach taken is a matter of auditor judgment. [ISA 530, A9]

Statistical sampling methods [ISA 530, Appendix 4]

- **Random selection** – this can be achieved through the use of random number generators or tables.

- **Systematic selection** – where a constant sampling interval is used (e.g. every 50th balance) and the first item is selected randomly.

- **Monetary unit selection** – selecting items based upon monetary values (usually focusing on higher value items).

Non-statistical sampling methods

- **Haphazard selection** – auditor does not follow a structured technique but avoids bias or predictability.

- **Block selection** – this involves selecting a block of contiguous (i.e. next to each other) items from the population. This technique is used for cut-off testing.

When non-statistical methods (haphazard and block) are used the auditor uses judgment to select the items to be tested. Whilst this lends itself to auditor bias it does support the risk based approach, where the auditor focuses on those areas most susceptible to material misstatement.

Designing a sample

When designing a sample the auditor has to consider:

- The purpose of the procedure
- The combination of procedures being performed
- The nature of evidence sought
- Possible misstatement conditions.

[ISA 530, A5, A6]

Illustration 1 – Murray Co sampling

Sampling

Murray Co deals with large retail customers, and therefore has a low number of large receivables balances on the receivables ledger. Given the low number of customers with a balance on Murray Co's receivables ledger, all balances would probably be selected for testing. However, for illustrative purposes the following shows how a sample of balances would be selected using systematic and Monetary Unit Sampling.

Credit and zero balances on the receivables ledger have been removed. The number of items to be sampled has been determined as 6. The customer list has been alphabetised.

Systematic Sampling

There are 19 customers with balances in the receivables ledger. The sampling interval is calculated by taking the total number of balances and dividing it by the sample size. The sampling interval (to the nearest whole number) is therefore 3. The first item is chosen randomly, in this case item 10. Every third item after that is then also selected for testing until 6 items have been chosen.

$000

Customer Ref	Customer Name	Balance $	Item number	Sampling Item
A001	Anfield United Shop	176	1	
B002	The Beautiful Game	84	2	
B003	Beckham's	42	3	(5)
C001	Cheryl & Coleen Co	12	4	
D001	Dream Team	45	5	
E001	Escot Supermarket	235	6	(6)
G001	Golf is Us	211	7	
G002	Green Green Grass	61	8	
H001	HHA Sports	59	9	
J001	Jilberts	21	10	(1)
J002	James Smit Partnership	256	11	
J003	Jockeys	419	12	
O001	The Oval	92	13	(2)
P001	Pole Vaulters	76	14	
S001	Stayrose Supermarket	97	15	
T001	Trainers and More	93	16	(3)
W001	Wanderers	89	17	
W003	Walk Hike Run	4	18	
W004	Winners	31	19	(4)

Monetary Unit Sampling

Monetary Unit Sampling can utilise either the random or systematic selection method. This example illustrates the systematic selection method.

The cumulative balance is calculated.

The sampling interval is calculated by taking the total value on the ledger of $2,103,000 (to the nearest $000) and dividing by the sample size of 6. The sampling interval is therefore $351,000.

The first item is chosen randomly (a number between 1 and 2,103,000), in this case 233. Each item after that is selected by adding the sampling interval to the last value, until six items have been selected.

$000

Customer Ref	Customer Name	Balance $	Cumulative	Sampling Item
A001	Anfield United Shop	176	176	
B002	The Beautiful Game	84	260	(1) $233
B003	Beckham's	42	302	
C001	Cheryl & Coleen Co	12	314	
D001	Dream Team	45	359	
E001	Escot Supermarket	235	594	(2) $584
G001	Golf is Us	211	805	
G002	Green Green Grass	61	866	
H001	HHA Sports	59	925	
J001	Jilberts	21	946	(3) $935
J002	James Smit Partnership	256	1,202	
J003	Jockeys	419	1,621	(4) $1,286
O001	The Oval	92	1,713	(5) $1,637
P001	Pole Vaulters	76	1,789	
S001	Stayrose Supermarket	97	1,886	
T001	Trainers and More	93	1,979	
W001	Wanderers	89	2,068	(6) $1,988
W003	Walk Hike Run	4	2,072	
W004	Winners	31	**2,103**	

Evaluating deviations and misstatements in a sample

Deviations

Any issues identified during a test of control are called **deviations**.

If the auditor tests a sample of 100 invoices for evidence of authorisation and 10 have not been authorised, there is a deviation rate of 10%. There is no need to project this across the population as the deviation rate will still be 10%.

The auditor will use professional judgment to determine a level of deviation they are willing to accept – tolerable deviation rate.

The auditor will compare the actual deviation rate to the tolerable deviation rate. If the actual deviation rate exceeds the tolerable deviation rate, the risk of material misstatement is greater and more substantive procedures will be required.

Misstatements

Misstatements are differences between the amounts actually recorded and what should have been recorded. Misstatements are identified when performing substantive tests of detail.

The auditor must first consider the nature and cause of the misstatement. If the misstatement is an anomaly (isolated), no further procedures will be performed as the misstatement is not representative of further misstatements.

If the auditor believes the misstatement could be representative of further misstatements the auditor will project the misstatement found in the sample across the population as a whole, and evaluate the results by considering tolerable misstatement.

Tolerable misstatement is defined as:

 A monetary amount set by the auditor in respect of which the auditor seeks to obtain an appropriate level of assurance that the monetary amount set by the auditor is not exceeded by the actual misstatement in the population. [ISA 530, 5e]

- If the total projected misstatement in the sample is less than tolerable misstatement then the auditor may be reasonably confident that the risk of material misstatement in the whole population is low and no further testing will be required.

- If the total projected misstatement in the sample exceeds tolerable misstatement the auditor will extend the sample in order to determine the total misstatement in the population.

Evaluating misstatements in a sample

A sample of $50,000 has been tested out of a population of $800,000. Misstatements of $2,000 were found. Tolerable misstatement has been set at $10,000.

The auditor needs to consider whether the misstatement is an anomaly and therefore isolated, or whether the misstatement is likely to be representative of further misstatements in the population.

If the misstatement is an anomaly, no further procedures will be necessary.

If it is expected that the misstatement is likely to be representative of further misstatements, the auditor should extrapolate the effect of the misstatement across the population to assess whether the projected misstatement is greater than tolerable misstatement.

Here, the auditor might expect that there are misstatements of $32,000 ($2,000/$50,000 × $800,000) in the population.

As the projected misstatement of $32,000 exceeds tolerable misstatement of $10,000, further audit testing will be required.

7 Computer assisted audit techniques (CAATs)

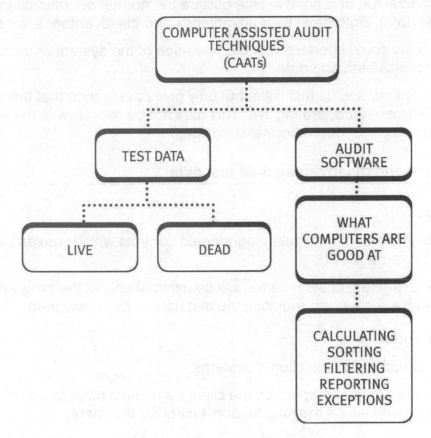

The use of computers as a tool to perform audit procedures is often referred to as a 'computer assisted audit techniques' or CAATs for short.

There are two broad categories of CAAT:

(1)   Test data

(2)   Audit software.

Test data

Test data involves the auditor submitting 'dummy' data into the client's system to ensure that the system correctly processes it and that it prevents or detects and corrects misstatements. The objective of this is to test the operation of application controls within the system.

To be successful test data should include both data with errors built into it and data without errors. Examples of errors include:

*   Codes that do not exist, e.g. customer, supplier and employee.

*   Transactions above predetermined limits, e.g. salaries above contracted amounts, credit above limits agreed with customer.

*   Invoices with arithmetical errors.

*   Submitting data with incorrect batch control totals.

Data may be processed during a normal operational cycle ('live' test data) or during a special run at a point in time outside the normal operational cycle ('dead' test data). Both have their advantages and disadvantages, for example:

- Live tests could interfere with the operation of the system or corrupt master files/standing data.

- Dead testing avoids this issue but only gives assurance that the system works when not operating live. This may not be reflective of the strains the system is put under in normal conditions.

Advantages and disadvantages of test data

Advantages

- Enables the auditor to test programmed controls which wouldn't otherwise be able to be tested.

- Once designed, costs incurred will be minimal unless the programmed controls are changed requiring the test data to be redesigned.

Disadvantages

- Risk of corrupting the client's systems.

- Requires time to be spent on the client's system if used in a live environment which may not be convenient for the client.

Audit software

Audit software is used to interrogate a client's system. It can be either packaged, off-the-shelf software or it can be purpose written to work on a client's system. The main advantage of these programs is that they can be used to scrutinise large volumes of data, which it would be inefficient to do manually. The programs can then present the results so that they can be investigated further.

Specific procedures they can perform include:

- Extracting samples according to specified criteria, such as:
  - random
  - over a certain amount e.g. individually material balances or expenses
  - below a certain amount e.g. debit balances on a payables ledger or credit balances on a receivables ledger
  - at certain dates e.g. receivables or inventory over a certain age

- Calculating ratios and select indicators that fail to meet certain predefined criteria (i.e. benchmarking)

- Casting ledgers and schedules

- Recalculation of amounts such as depreciation

- Preparing reports (budget vs actual)

- Stratification of data (such as invoices by customer or age)

- Identifying changes to standing data e.g. employee or supplier bank details

- Produce letters to send out to customers and suppliers.

These procedures can simplify the auditor's task by selecting samples for testing, identifying risk areas and by performing certain substantive procedures. The software does not, however, replace the need for the auditor's own procedures.

Advantages and disadvantages of audit software

Advantages

- Calculations and casting of reports will be quicker.

- More transactions can be tested as compared with manual testing.

- The computer files are tested rather than printouts.

- Once set up can be a cost effective means of testing.

Disadvantages

- Bespoke software (specific to one client) can be expensive to set up.

- Training of audit staff will be required incurring additional cost.

- The audit software may slow down or corrupt the client's systems.

- If errors are made in the design of the software, issues may go undetected by the auditor.

General advantages and disadvantages of CAATs

General advantages of CAATs

- Enables the auditor to test more items more quickly.

- The auditor is able to test the system rather than printouts.

- Obtain greater evidence as the results of CAATs can be compared with other tests to increase audit confidence.

- Perform audit tests more cost effectively.

Disadvantages of CAATs

- CAATs can be expensive and time consuming to set up.

- Client permission and cooperation may be difficult to obtain.

- Potential incompatibility with the client's computer system.

- The audit team may not have sufficient IT skills and knowledge to create the complex data extracts and programming required.

- The audit team may not have the knowledge or training needed to understand the results of the CAATs.

- Data may be corrupted or lost during the application of CAATs.

The Growing Use of Data Analytics in an Audit

In the past, CAATs have been used to analyse data. As CAATs were tailored to the specific client they required significant investment and, as a result, were not widely used across all audits.

Technological development means it is now possible to capture and analyse entire datasets allowing for the interrogation of 100% of the transactions in a population – data analytics (DA). Whilst DA can be developed for bespoke issues, a key characteristic is that the development of standard tools and techniques allows for more widespread use. Some of the more widely used DA tools started out as bespoke CAATs which have been developed for wider application.

Definitions

Data analytics is the science and art of discovering and analysing patterns, deviations and inconsistencies, and extracting other useful information in the data of underlying or related subject matter of an audit through analysis, modelling, visualisation for the purpose of planning and performing the audit.

Big data refers to data sets that are large or complex.

Big data technology allows the auditor to perform procedures on very large or complete sets of data rather than samples.

Features of data analytics

- DA allows the auditor to manipulate 100% of the data in a population quickly which reduces audit risk.

- Results can be visualised graphically which may increase the user-friendliness of the reports.

- DA can be used throughout the audit to help identify risks, test the controls and as part of substantive procedures. The results still need to be evaluated using the professional skills and judgment of the auditor in order to analyse the results and draw conclusions.

- As for analytical procedures in general, the quality of DA depends on the reliability of the underlying data used.

- DA can incorporate a wider range of data. For example data can be extracted and analysed from social media, public sector data, industry data and economic data.

Example

The auditor may use DA to analyse journals posted. The analysis identifies:

- The total number of journals posted.

- The number of journals posted manually.

- The number of journals posted automatically by the system.

- The number of people processing journals.

- The time of day the journals are posted.

The auditor may conclude there is a higher risk of fraud this year compared with last if:

- The number of manual versus automatic journals increases significantly.

- The number of people processing journals increases.

- Journals are posted outside of normal working hours.

Benefits of data analytics

- Audit procedures can be performed more quickly and to a higher standard. This provides more time to analyse and interpret the results rather than gathering the information for analysis.

- Audit procedures can be carried out on a continuous basis rather than focused on the year end.

- Reporting to the client and users will be more timely as the work may be completed within weeks rather than months after the year-end.

- The use of DA may result in more frequent interaction between the auditor and client over the course of the year.

- A reduction in billable hours as audit efficiency increases. Although this is good news for the client, it will mean lower fees for the auditor.

What it means for the profession

- Larger accountancy firms are developing their own data analytic platforms. This requires significant investment in computer hardware and software, training of staff and quality control.

- Small firms are unlikely to have the resources available to develop their own software as the cost is likely to be too prohibitive. However, external computer software companies have developed audit systems that work with popular accounting systems such as Sage, Xero and Intuit which many clients of small accountancy firms may be using.

- Medium sized firms may also find the level of investment too restrictive and may therefore be unable to compete with the larger audit firms for listed company audits. However, these firms may find that listed companies require systems and controls assurance work which their auditors would not be allowed to perform under ethical standards.

Developments within the profession

Currently, ISAs take a systems-based approach to audit, which seeks to obtain audit evidence by placing reliance on internal controls rather than on carrying out extensive substantive tests of detail. The development of DA represents a significant progression away from traditional auditing methods. Therefore, as they become more widely used, ISAs will need to be updated to reflect this innovation in auditing techniques. ED 315 contains some guidance on the use of DA when performing risk assessment procedures.

The IAASB has a responsibility to develop standards that reflect the current environment and facilitate a high quality audit. Auditors, audit oversight authorities and standard setters need to work together to explore how developments in technology can support enhanced audit quality.

Auditors and businesses operate in an environment with larger volumes of transactions, greater complexity and greater regulation as a result of corporate failures. Technological change means information systems are capable of capturing, analysing and communicating significantly more data than previously. As a result, stakeholders are expecting the auditor to perform an audit that includes greater use of technology including DA.

The quality of the audit can be enhanced by the use of DA. DA enables the auditor to obtain a greater understanding of the entity and its environment. Professional scepticism and professional judgment are improved when the auditor has a better understanding.

Limitations of Data Analytics

There are still limitations to the audit and therefore auditors need to be careful not to place too much confidence into the use of DA which could have a negative impact on audit quality.

- The data may not be complete, well-controlled or from a reliable source.
- Financial statements still contain a significant amount of estimates.
- DA will not replace the need for auditors to use professional scepticism and professional judgment.

Because of these limitations, the auditor is still only able to give reasonable assurance even though 100% of a population may be tested.

Challenges that impact the use of Data Analytics

Data acquisition and retention – The entity's data will need to be transferred to the auditor raising concerns over data security and privacy as well as creating storage problems for such large data sets.

Conceptual challenges – Auditors will be asking questions they have never asked in the past and the client may be hesitant to provide all of the information requested.

Legal and regulatory challenges – Regulations may prohibit data leaving the jurisdiction the entity is located. This may pose a problem if the IT facilities of the client are located in a different country.

Resource availability – Data scientists may form part of a centralised department which supports all engagement teams within the firm. The resources are likely to be limited which will put a strain on resources.

How regulators and audit oversight authorities maintain oversight – These bodies have little experience themselves of inspecting audits using DA.

Investment in retraining and reskilling auditors – Changing the auditor's mind-set from traditional audit methods will require time and investment.

The use of DA and developments in auditing standards will impact:

Risk assessment – DA may improve the risk assessment process.

Quality control – Audit firms will need to consider how specialist teams are supervised and how they interact with the audit teams they support. Firms will need to consider the integrity of the DA software to ensure it does what it is supposed to.

Group audits – DA may help by enabling better analytical procedures to be performed in respect of components that are not significant components. Also, the audit procedures may be more centralised enabling the group auditor to perform more procedures rather than relying on the work of a component auditor.

Estimates and fair values – Due to large volumes of data that feed into the models used to develop accounting estimates, DA may be valuable in addressing audit risks associated with these data sources.

Smaller audit firms – Smaller firms may not be able to make the required investment to develop DA tools. Audits of public sector entities may prove challenging as home-grown systems are more prevalent and data capture may be more difficult.

Education – Auditors and accountants will need to be re-skilled to realise the potential of DA. Training and qualifications will need to reflect the increased use of DA for new entrants to the profession.

Ethics – Due to auditors having access to large volumes of client data, there may be a need to update the Code of Ethics to enhance the requirements for confidentiality.

Other auditing standards – There is also likely to be a need to revise other auditing standards such as ISA 240 (Fraud), ISA 320 (Materiality), ISA 330 (Responses to risks), ISA 500 (Audit Evidence), ISA 520 (Analytical Procedures) and ISA 530 (Audit Sampling).

FRC Audit Quality Thematic Review – The Use of Data Analytics in the Audit of Financial Statements

With the increasing use of data analytics, the FRC has performed a review to identify what is working well with a view of sharing information to promote continuous improvement in audit quality. The Audit Quality Review (AQR) team assessed the use of DA in the six largest audit firms.

Current use of data analytics

- Analyse all transactions in a population, stratify the population and identify outliers for further examination.

- Re-perform calculations

- Match transactions as they pass through the system

- Assist in segregation of duties testing

- Compare client data with externally obtained data

- Perform sensitivity analysis.

Impact on audit quality

Audit quality is a driver for the implementation of DA. DA can:

- Deepen the auditor's understanding of the entity.
- Facilitate testing of the highest risk areas through stratification.
- Enhance the use of professional scepticism.
- Improve consistency on group audits
- Enable the auditor to test entire datasets.
- Improve audit efficiency.
- Increase the possibility of identifying fraud.
- Provide a channel for enhanced communication with audit committees.

Good practices observed during the AQR

- Focused roll out of a DA tool.
- Clear positioning within the audit methodology.
- Testing or trial running the DA tool.
- Using specialist staff and clearly defined roles between the specialists and the core engagement team.
- Central running of DA for group audits.
- Clearly documenting the DA tool using flowcharts.

Summary of key findings

- The introduction of mandatory retendering in the UK has provided incentive for firms to develop DA tools as this acts as a key differentiator.
- UK firms are at the forefront of developing DA tools.
- The pace of change is not as fast as expected by audit committees and investors.
- Whilst some firms are investing heavily in DA tools, they are not monitoring their use by audit teams or effectiveness at providing appropriate evidence.
- Some audit teams have over-emphasised their use to audit committees. In some cases DA have been used to provide insight to the audit committee rather than to generate audit evidence. In another case a firm described a DA tool as launched in a report but was described to the Audit Quality Review team as being in pilot stage.
- All firms used DA to assist with journal entry testing, however, most firms are not using DA tools routinely in other audit areas.

- For complex entities it can take two years to achieve the full benefits of a DA approach.

- The main barrier to effective use relates to difficulties obtaining entity data and audit teams often lack expertise to extract the data required.

- The use of DA techniques was higher at firms where the audit methodology clearly defines the purpose of the DA.

- In the audits tested, insufficient evidence audit evidence was retained on file.

    - Criteria input into the DA tool was not retained.

    - Screenshots omitted important information.

    - Evidence produced by specialists was omitted.

    - Firm's archiving tools were not able to archive DA evidence.

    - It may not be technically, practically or legally possible for the audit firm to retain audit evidence for the file retention period required by auditing standards.

Exploring the Growing Use of Technology in the Audit, with a Focus on Data Analytics

In September 2016, IAASB issued a request for input from accounting firms, regulatory bodies, standard setters, academics and public sector organisations to obtain information about the current use and future direction of the use of data analytics.

The key messages from the Feedback Statement published in January 2018 are:

- ISAs are not 'broken' and should remain principles-based. There should be no rush to change requirements in ISAs at present.

- ISAs should be updated in a way that reflects current technology but remains technologically neutral to provide the ability to accommodate future changes in technology. ISA 500 *Audit Evidence* and ISA 230 *Audit Documentation* were highlighted as priorities for revision.

- Non-authoritative, practical guidance with real-life examples of the use of DA is needed. This process has already commenced.

- The use of DA does not reduce the need to exercise professional scepticism and judgment. Both are integral to understanding the benefits and limitations of using DA in the audit.

Areas of concern

Regulators and oversight authorities are most concerned with data acquisition, auditor skills and compliance with ISAs.

- Audit clients may be reluctant to give access to live systems and this may cast doubt on the reliability of the data being analysed.

- Currently auditors tend to have insufficient understanding of IT to design effective procedures using DA.

- Audit evidence generated from DA must demonstrate that the requirements of the ISAs have been met, particularly the documentation requirements.

Accounting firms are also concerned about retraining and re-skilling not only auditors, but also regulators and audit committees who will need to understand the DA performed as part of assessing the work of the auditor. There is also concern that these authorities have little experience themselves of inspecting audits involving the use of DA.

Other computer-assisted audit techniques

There are other forms of CAAT that are becoming increasingly common as computer technology develops, although the cost and sophistication involved currently limits their use to the larger accountancy firms with greater resources. These include:

Integrated test facilities – this involves the creation of dummy ledgers and records to which test data can be sent. This enables more frequent and efficient test data procedures to be performed live and the information can simply be ignored by the client when printing out their internal records.

Embedded audit software – this requires a purpose written audit program to be embedded into the client's accounting system. The program will be designed to perform certain tasks (similar to audit software) with the advantage that it can be turned on and off at the auditor's wish throughout the accounting year. This will allow the auditor to gather information on certain transactions (perhaps material ones) for later testing and will also identify peculiarities that require attention during the final audit.

Auditing around the computer

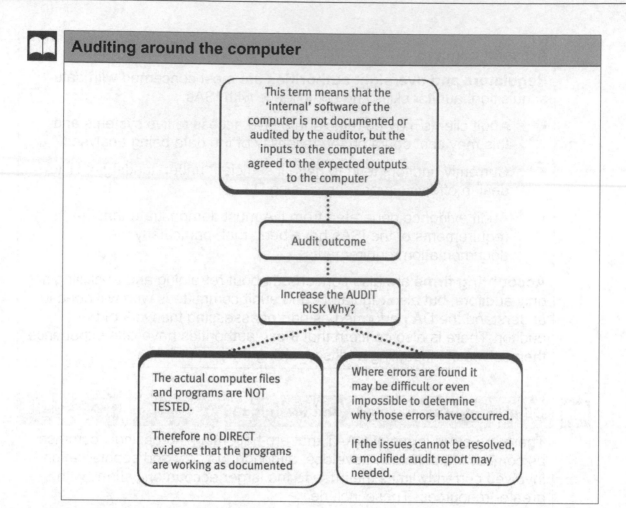

This term means that the 'internal' software of the computer is not documented or audited by the auditor, but the inputs to the computer are agreed to the expected outputs to the computer

Audit outcome

Increase the AUDIT RISK Why?

The actual computer files and programs are NOT TESTED.

Therefore no DIRECT evidence that the programs are working as documented

Where errors are found it may be difficult or even impossible to determine why those errors have occurred.

If the issues cannot be resolved, a modified audit report may needed.

Test your understanding 1

List FOUR factors that influence the reliability of audit evidence.

(4 marks)

Test your understanding 2

List and explain FOUR methods of selecting a sample of items to test from a population in accordance with ISA 530 *Audit Sampling*.

(4 marks)

Test your understanding 3

List and explain FOUR factors that will influence the auditor's judgment regarding the sufficiency of the evidence obtained.

(4 marks)

Test your understanding 4

During the audit, the auditor will use sampling. There are a variety of sampling methods available. Some sampling methods are statistical and some non-statistical. The auditor must use an appropriate method for the item being tested.

(1) **You have identified a higher than expected deviation rate when performing tests of controls over purchases. Which of the following would be an appropriate response?**

    (i)   Pick alternative items to test in place of those just tested and ignore the deviations.

    (ii)   Extend the sample size.

    (iii) Perform more substantive procedures over purchases as tests of controls have not provided sufficient appropriate evidence.

    A   (i) and (ii) only

    B   (iii) only

    C   (ii) and (iii) only

    D   (i), (ii) and (iii)

(2) **Which of the following statements is true?**

    A   Random sampling is a method where the auditor picks the sample with no particular pattern

    B   Deviations must be extrapolated to determine the effect on the population

    C   Block sampling is where the auditor tests all items in a population

    D   Monetary unit sampling is a statistical method of sampling

(3) **Which of the following constitutes sampling?**

    A   Where less than 100% of the items in a population are tested and have an equal chance of selection

    B   Where less than 100% of the items in a population are tested and have a chance of selection

    C   Where items within a population with certain characteristics are chosen for testing

    D   Where every nth item in a population are chosen for testing

(4) **Which of the following statements is true?**

A   Statistical sampling methods are more reliable than non-statistical methods

B   The auditor must always use stratification to ensure a representative sample is tested

C   More than one sampling method may be used to test one population

D   A deviation occurs when a result differs from expectation during a substantive procedure

(5) **The auditor has identified a misstatement in a sample. Which of the following is the most appropriate initial course of action?**

A   Consider whether the misstatement is an anomaly or representative of further possible misstatement

B   Inform the client of the misstatement

C   Calculate the materiality of the misstatement in relation to the financial statements

D   Compare the misstatement to the tolerable misstatement level

Test your understanding 5

You are planning the audit of Wyndham Co. The company sells diamonds and other precious stones. You have decided to use the work of an auditor's expert to provide sufficient appropriate evidence over the valuation of inventory.

(1) **Before appointing an auditor's expert, what factors must the auditor consider?**

   (i)   Competence

   (ii)   Capability

   (iii)   Objectivity

   (iv)   Reliability of the source data

   A   (i), (ii) and (iii)

   B   (ii), (iii) and (iv)

   C   (i) (iii) and (iv) only

   D   (i), (ii), (iii) and (iv)

(2) **How can the auditor assess the competence of an auditor's expert?**

   (i)   Obtain copies of professional certificates and make enquiries of the expert's experience.

   (ii)   Ask for confirmation from the expert of their independence.

   (iii)   Inspect the register of members of the relevant professional body for the name of the expert.

   A   (i) and (ii) only

   B   (ii) and (iii) only

   C   (i) and (iii) only

   D   (i), (ii) and (iii)

(3) **What must be agreed with the auditor's expert in writing before the work is performed?**

   (i)   Responsibilities of each party

   (ii)   Inherent limitations of the audit

   (iii)   Deadline for the work

   (iv)   Scope and objectives

   A   (i), (ii), (iii) and (iv)

   B   (i), (iii) and (iv) only

   C   (iii) and (ii) only

   D   (i), (ii) and (iv) only

(4) **Which of the following statements is true in respect of the expert's work?**

A   The auditor can rely on the expert's work and does not need to review it

B   The auditor may choose not to review the expert's work if it is an area in which the auditor has knowledge or experience

C   The auditor must review the assumptions and source data used by the expert to ensure they were reasonable and reliable

D   The auditor will engage a second expert to review the work of the first to ensure sufficient appropriate evidence has been obtained

(5) **Which of the following statements best describes a management's expert?**

A   A management's expert is an employee of the company

B   A management's expert is someone appointed by the company to provide evidence for the auditor

C   A management's expert is someone recommended by the auditor which management appoints to provide evidence for the audit

D   A management's expert is someone appointed by the company to provide evidence for management which may be relied upon by the auditor

8　Chapter summary

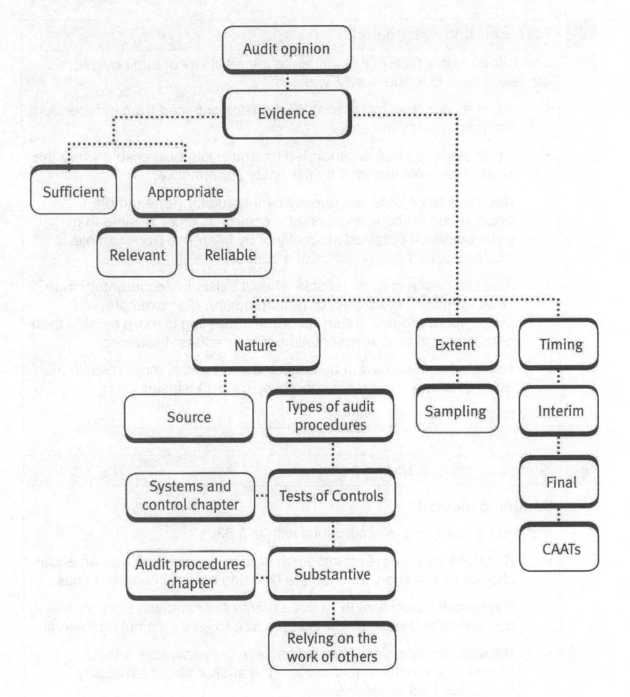

Test your understanding answers

Test your understanding 1

The following five factors that influence the reliability of audit evidence are taken from ISA 500 *Audit Evidence*:

- Audit evidence is more reliable when it is obtained from independent sources outside the entity.

- Audit evidence that is generated internally is more reliable when the related controls imposed by the entity are effective.

- Audit evidence obtained directly by the auditor (for example, observation of the application of a control) is more reliable than audit evidence obtained indirectly or by inference (for example, inquiry about the application of a control).

- Audit evidence is more reliable when it exists in documentary form, whether paper, electronic, or other medium. (For example, a contemporaneously written record of a meeting is more reliable than a subsequent oral representation of the matters discussed.)

- Audit evidence provided by original documents is more reliable than audit evidence provided by photocopies or facsimiles (fax).

Only four examples are required.

Test your understanding 2

Sampling methods

Methods of sampling in accordance with ISA 530:

- **Random** selection. Ensures each item in a population has an equal chance of selection, for example by using random number tables.

- **Systematic** selection. In which a number of sampling units in the population is divided by the sample size to give a sampling interval.

- **Haphazard** selection. The auditor selects the sample without following a structured technique – the auditor would avoid any conscious bias or predictability.

- **Sequence** or block. Involves selecting a block(s) of contiguous items from within a population.

- **Monetary unit sampling.** This selection method ensures that each individual $1 in the population has an equal chance of being selected.

Note: Only four sampling methods were required.

Test your understanding 3

Sufficiency of evidence

- Assessment of risk at the financial statement level and/or the individual transaction level. As risk increases then more evidence is required.

- The materiality of the item. More evidence will normally be collected on material items whereas immaterial items may simply be reviewed to ensure they appear materially correct.

- The nature of the accounting and internal control systems. The auditor will place more reliance on good accounting and internal control systems limiting the amount of audit evidence required.

- The auditor's knowledge and experience of the business. Where the auditor has good knowledge of the business and trusts the integrity of staff then less evidence will be required.

- The findings of audit procedures. Where findings from related audit procedures are satisfactory (e.g. tests of controls over revenue) then less substantive evidence will be collected.

- The source and reliability of the information. Where evidence is obtained from reliable sources (e.g. written evidence) then less evidence is required than if the source was unreliable (e.g. verbal evidence).

Test your understanding 4

(1)	C	Extend the sample size and perform more substantive tests. The auditor should never disregard deviations or misstatements identified during testing.
(2)	D	Option A describes haphazard sampling. Deviations are not extrapolated as the deviation rate will be the same across the population. Misstatements are extrapolated across the population. Block sampling is where items next to each other in the population are tested. If the auditor tests all items in the population the auditor is not using sampling.
(3)	B	Sampling is when each item in a population has a chance of selection. They do not need to have an equal chance.
(4)	C	An auditor may use multiple sampling methods to test items from the same population for example if the population has been stratified into three sub-populations the auditor may use random sampling to test one sub-population, haphazard to test the second and monetary unit to test the third.
(5)	A	If the misstatement is considered to be an anomaly there is no need to perform any further testing and a conclusion can be drawn. If the misstatement was considered to be representative of further misstatements the auditor should extend the sample before assessing whether the misstatement exceeds tolerable misstatement or is material.

Test your understanding 5

(1)	A	Reliability of source data is evaluated after the expert has performed the work.
(2)	C	An independence confirmation from the expert would confirm objectivity but not competence.
(3)	B	Inherent limitations of an audit would not be communicated to the expert. This would be included in an audit engagement letter.
(4)	C	The auditor cannot just rely on the expert's work. They must review it to ensure it provides sufficient appropriate evidence and therefore must consider the assumptions and source data. If the auditor already had knowledge and experience in this area there would be no need to use an auditor's expert. If the auditor has evaluated the competence, capability and objectivity of the expert before using them, there should be no need to appoint a second expert to the review the first expert's work.
(5)	D	A management's expert is appointed by management to produce evidence to be used by management. If the evidence is reliable and relevant to the external audit, the auditor may choose to rely on that work.

Systems and controls

Chapter learning objectives

This chapter covers syllabus areas:

- C1 – Internal control systems

- C2 – The use and evaluation of internal control systems by auditors

- C3 – Tests of controls

- C4 – Communication on internal control

Detailed syllabus objectives are provided in the introduction section of the text book.

PER

One of the PER performance objectives (PO19) is to collect and evaluate evidence for an audit. Carry out an internal or external audit from collecting evidence, through to forming an opinion. You demonstrate professional scepticism and make sure judgements are based on sufficient valid evidence. Working through this chapter should help you understand how to demonstrate that objective.

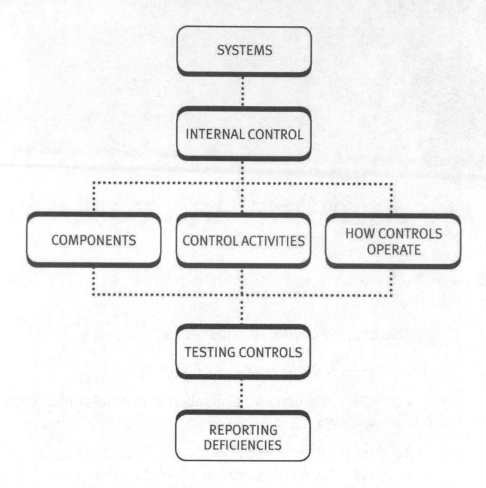

1 Effect of controls on the audit

This chapter considers the basic components of control systems and how the auditor fulfils their objectives for assessing control risk.

The auditor will ascertain the internal control system to assess whether it is likely to be reliable. If so, they will test the controls to ensure they are in place and working effectively.

Impact of tests of controls on the audit strategy and plan

The extent of substantive testing to be carried out will depend on the results of the tests of controls which will affect the auditor's assessment of control risk.

If control risk is low

- The auditor can **place more reliance on internal controls** and evidence generated internally within the entity.

- This increases the appropriateness of interim audit testing and allows the auditor to **reduce the quantity of detailed substantive procedures** performed at the final audit stage.

- The audit strategy and plan will be updated to reflect that fewer substantive procedures will be required or smaller sample sizes can be tested at the final audit stage.

If control risk is high

- Increase the volume of procedures conducted at and after the year-end. [ISA 330, A2]

- Increase the level of substantive procedures, in particular, tests of detail. [ISA 330, A2]

- Increase the locations included in the audit scope. [ISA 330, A2]

- Place less reliance on analytical procedures as the information produced by the client's systems is not reliable.

- Place less reliance on written representations from management if the control environment generally is considered to be weak.

- Obtain more evidence from external sources e.g. external confirmations from customers and suppliers.

- Update the audit strategy and plan to reflect the additional testing required at the final audit stage.

Limitations of internal controls

The auditor can never eliminate the need for substantive procedures entirely because there are inherent limitations to the reliance that can be placed on internal controls due to:

- Human error. [ISA 315, A54]

- Ineffective controls. [ISA 315, A54]

- Collusion of staff in circumventing controls. [ISA 315, A55]

- The abuse of power by those with ultimate controlling responsibility (i.e. management override). [ISA 315, A55]

- Use of management judgment on the nature and extent of controls it chooses to implement. [ISA 315, A56]

As a result, the auditor must always perform substantive testing on material balances in the financial statements. [ISA 330, 18]

2 Components of an internal control system

ISA 315 *Identifying and Assessing the Risks of Material Misstatement Through Understanding the Entity and its Environment*, states that auditors need to understand an entity's internal controls. To assist this process it identifies five components of an internal control system:

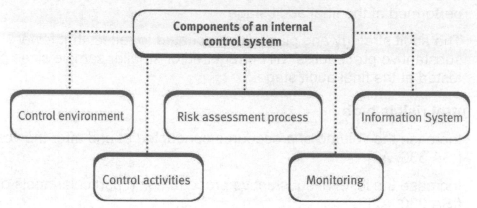

[ISA 315, A59]

(i) The control environment

The control environment includes the **governance and management** function of an organisation.

It focuses largely on the **attitude, awareness and actions** of those responsible for designing, implementing and monitoring internal controls.

[ISA 315, A77]

Elements of the control environment that are relevant when the auditor obtains an understanding include the following:

- Communication and enforcement of integrity and ethical values
- Commitment to competence
- Participation by those charged with governance
- Management's philosophy and operating style
- Organisational structure
- Assignment of authority and responsibility
- Human resource policies and practices.

[ISA 315, A78]

When assessing the control environment, the auditor may also consider how management has responded to the findings and recommendations of the internal audit function regarding identified deficiencies in internal control relevant to the audit, including whether and how such responses have been implemented, and whether they have been subsequently evaluated by the internal audit function. [ISA 315, A80]

Evidence regarding the control environment is usually obtained through a mixture of enquiry and observation, although inspection of key internal documents (e.g. codes of conduct and organisation charts) is possible.

(ii) The risk assessment process

The risk assessment process forms the basis for how management determines the business risks to be managed. These processes will vary depending on the nature, size and complexity of the organisation. [ISA 315, A88]

Business risks are threats to the achievement of ongoing business objectives and can lead to misstatement in the financial statements, e.g. non-compliance with laws and regulations may lead to fines and penalties, which require disclosure or provision in the financial statements.

If the client has robust procedures for assessing the business risks it faces, the risk of misstatement overall will be lower.

(iii) The information system

The information system refers to all of the business processes relevant to financial reporting and communication. It includes the procedures within both information technology and manual systems.

The information system includes all of the procedures and records which are designed to:

- Initiate, record, process and report transactions.

- Maintain accountability for assets, liabilities and equity.

- Resolve incorrect processing of transactions.

- Process and account for system overrides.

- Transfer information to the general/nominal ledger.

- Capture information relevant to financial reporting for other events and conditions.

- Ensure information required to be disclosed is appropriately reported.

[ISA 315, A90]

(iv) Control activities

Control activities are the policies and procedures that help ensure management directives are carried out.

Examples of specific control activities include those relating to:

- Authorisation

- Performance review

- Information processing

- Physical controls

- Segregation of duties.

[ISA 315, A99]

Examples of control activities

Authorisation – approval of transactions prior to being processed

- A manager signing off an employee's timesheet to confirm that the hours stated have been worked and can be paid. This should ensure the employee is not claiming for hours not worked.

- A manager signing a purchase order to confirm the order can be placed with the supplier. This should ensure that the goods are for a valid business use and the items are needed.

Performance review – to identify unusual differences between data

- Managers should compare actual spend against budgeted spend to detect unusual fluctuations. If actual spend is significantly higher than budget, the department may have spent more than it should or it could indicate an error when processing the transactions.

- Management may compare the company's results with those of competitors as a benchmark.

Information processing – to ensure completeness and accuracy of processing

- Preparation of a bank reconciliation to ensure cash transactions have been recorded completely and accurately.

- Batch totals used when inputting data to ensure items are not omitted.

Physical controls – to prevent unauthorised access

- Restrictions on access to assets such as keeping cash in a safe to prevent theft.

- Password restrictions to prevent unauthorised access to computer files.

Segregation of duties – Assigning the responsibility for recording transactions, authorising transactions and maintaining custody of assets to different employees to prevent the risk of fraud and error.

- Warehouse staff should not be responsible for the inventory count as this would not detect if goods were being stolen by staff throughout the year.

- Employees who authorise transactions should not be the ones who originate the transaction.

IT controls

IT affects the way in which control activities are implemented. It is important that auditors assess how controls over IT maintain the integrity and security of information held. Such controls are normally divided into **application** and **general** controls. [ISA 315, A107]

An effective IT system should include both application and general control procedures.

Application controls

Application controls are either manual or automated and typically operate at the business process level. Application controls relate to data integrity and ensure that only valid data is being processed, and is being processed completely and accurately. [ISA 315, A109]

Examples include:

- Batch total checks (e.g. when entering invoices onto the system the system may give a batch total i.e. the number of invoices actually entered. The clerk entering the invoices can then double check that the correct number of invoices has been entered and none have been missed or entered twice).

- Sequence checks (to ensure the number sequence is complete and no items are missing).

- Matching master files to transaction records (e.g. sales invoice discounts to ensure the prices/discount levels being applied are correct).

- Arithmetic checks (to verify arithmetical accuracy).

- Range checks (to ensure that data stays within reasonable ranges).

- Existence checks (e.g. to check employees exist).

- Authorisation of transaction entries (to ensure the transaction is valid and should be processed).

- Exception reporting (the system may generate an exception report when something which isn't usual has occurred e.g. changes to bank details of employees which wouldn't be expected to change often).

General controls

General IT controls are policies and procedures that relate to many applications. They support the effective functioning of application controls by helping to ensure the continued proper operation of information systems.

E.g. controls over:

- Data centre and network operations e.g. preventing non-company issued laptops from connecting to the network.

- System software acquisition – tendering, testing, controls during installation, training.

- Program change – testing, authorisation, restricted access.

- Access security – passwords, door locks, swipe cards.

- Business continuity/disaster recovery – back up procedures to enable data to be restored, backup power supply.

[ISA 315, A108]

(v)   Monitoring of controls

This is the client's process of assessing the effectiveness of controls over time and taking necessary remedial action.

Monitoring can be either ongoing or performed on a separate evaluation basis (or a combination of both).

[ISA 315, A110]

Monitoring of internal controls is often the key role of internal auditors.
[ISA 315, A115]

3 Ascertaining the systems

Procedures used to obtain evidence regarding the design and implementation of controls include:

- Enquiries of relevant personnel.

- Observing the application of controls.

- Tracing a transaction through the system to understand what happens (a walkthrough test).

- Inspecting documents, such as internal procedure manuals.

It should also be noted that enquiry alone is not sufficient to understand the nature and extent of controls.

Auditors can also use existing knowledge of the client and the operation of the systems. However, the auditor cannot simply rely on their knowledge from the prior year audit as changes may have occurred. Systems knowledge must be updated and the systems tested once more.

4 Documenting client systems

The auditor must document the client's control systems before evaluating whether the system is adequate and working effectively.

Possible ways of documenting systems include:

- **Narrative notes** – a written description of a system.

- **Flowcharts** – a diagrammatical representation of the system.

- **Organisation chart** – a diagram showing reporting lines, roles and responsibilities.

- **Questionnaires** – a prepared list of questions in relation to the clients control system. There are two types of questionnaire that can be used:

   Internal Control Questionnaire (ICQ) – a list of controls is given to the client and they are asked whether or not those controls are in place.

   Internal Control Evaluation Questionnaire (ICEQ) – the client is asked to describe the controls they have in place for a given control objective.

 Tutorial note

A control objective identifies the risk that the entity needs to manage i.e. the reason for a control procedure or activity being required.

For example, a risk within a purchasing system is that purchases could be made for personal use and paid by the company. Therefore the control objective is to ensure goods cannot be purchased for personal use.

Most companies would have a control procedure in place to prevent this risk from occurring such as authorisation of purchase orders by a responsible official.

ICQ wording	ICEQ wording
Does a supervisor authorise all weekly timesheets?	How does the company ensure that only hours worked are recorded on timesheets?
Does the company perform a regular credit check on all customers?	How does the company try to minimise the risk of irrecoverable debts?
Does a manager or director authorise purchase orders before an order is placed?	How does the company ensure goods are only purchased for a valid business use?
Is a bank reconciliation performed regularly?	How does the company ensure discrepancies in the cash book are identified and resolved?
Is a regular inventory count performed?	How does the company ensure its inventory system is up to date and discrepancies in the inventory records are identified and corrected?
Is a regular reconciliation performed between the physical non-current assets and the non-current asset register?	How does the company ensure the non-current asset register is up to date and accurate?

The method adopted is a matter of auditor judgment.

Documentation Method	Advantages	Disadvantages
Narrative notes	• Simple to record • Facilitate understanding by all audit staff	• May be time consuming and cumbersome if the system is complex • May be more difficult to identify missing controls
Flow charts	• Easy to view the whole system in one diagram • Easy to spot missing controls due to the use of standard symbols	• May be difficult to amend as the whole diagram may need to be re-drawn • There is still a need for narrative notes to accompany the flow chart increasing the time involved to document the system fully
Internal control questionnaires (ICQs)	• Quick to prepare as a standard questionnaire can be used for all clients • Can ensure all controls are present	• Controls may be overstated as the client knows the answer the auditor is looking for is 'yes' • Unusual controls are unlikely to be included on a standard questionnaire and may not be identified • May contain a number of irrelevant controls
Internal control evaluations (ICEs)	• The client has to respond with the control they have in place rather than a yes/no answer which should mean controls are less likely to be overstated • Quick to prepare	• The client may still overstate controls as they may say a control is in place for the control objective even if it is not • The checklist may contain control objectives not relevant to the client • Unusual risks and therefore objectives may not be identified

5   Testing the system

A test of control involves the auditor obtaining evidence that the client has implemented the controls they say they have, and that they have worked effectively, during the period.

Typical methods of controls testing include:

- Observation of control activities, e.g. observing the inventory count to ensure it is conducted effectively and in accordance with the count instructions.

- Inspection of documents recording performance of the control, e.g. inspecting an order for evidence of authorisation.

- Computer assisted audit techniques (such as test data to ensure the programmed controls are working effectively. See the 'Evidence' chapter).

Designing valid tests of controls

To design a test of control, the auditor must first identify the controls they want to test.

A control is an activity applied in addition to the normal processing of the system to ensure that the system has operated as it should.

Just because errors have not been made does not mean that controls have worked effectively. The person performing the processing may not have made any errors. There may have been no controls in place. A control is an additional activity to ensure the person has not made any errors.

For example, if the client claims to perform bank reconciliations, the auditor should look at the file containing the reconciliations to verify that they are done, and then re-perform the reconciliation to ensure it has been done properly, to test the effectiveness of the control. Simply performing the reconciliation and finding that it reconciles does not prove that the client has done the reconciliation themselves. Therefore, re-performance of the reconciliation on its own is not a valid test of control.

Similarly, performing a sequence check on a set of documents does not mean the client has performed a sequence check. It may just mean that no documents have gone missing. A sequence check is the control to ensure that no documents have gone missing.

6 Communicating control deficiencies

ISA 265 *Communicating Deficiencies in Internal Control to Those Charged with Governance and Management* requires the auditor to:

- Communicate any deficiencies that are of sufficient importance to merit management's attention to management, [ISA 265, 10]

- Communicate significant deficiencies to those charged with governance. [ISA 265, 9]

Deficiencies occur when:

- A control is designed, implemented or operated in such a way that it is unable to prevent, or detect and correct misstatements in the financial statements on a timely basis, or

- A control necessary to prevent, or detect and correct, misstatements in the financial statements on a timely basis is missing.

[ISA 265, 6a]

Significant deficiencies are those which merit the attention of those charged with governance. [ISA 265, 6b]

The external auditor should consider the following when determining if a deficiency in internal controls is significant:

- The likelihood of the deficiencies leading to material misstatements in the financial statements in the future.

- The susceptibility to loss or fraud of the related asset or liability.

- The subjectivity and complexity of determining estimated amounts.

- The financial statement amounts exposed to the deficiencies.

- The volume of activity that has occurred or could occur in the account balance or class of transactions exposed to the deficiency or deficiencies.

- The importance of the controls to the financial reporting process.

- The cause and frequency of the exceptions detected as a result of the deficiencies in the controls.

- The interaction of the deficiency with other deficiencies in internal control.

[ISA 265, A6]

The auditor will communicate the deficiencies in a management letter or report to management. It is usually sent at the end of the audit process.

> In the exam you may be required to prepare extracts for inclusion in a report to management. This requires you to identify and explain the deficiencies within the control system described in a scenario. You will have to suggest a recommendation to overcome each deficiency.

Deficiency	A clear description of what is wrong.
Consequence	What could happen if the deficiency is not corrected?
	Focus on what matters to the client – the risk of a reduction in revenue, extra costs, stolen assets, errors in the accounts.
Recommendation	This must deal with the specific deficiency you have identified. It must also provide greater benefits than the cost of implementation.
	Try to specify exactly how the recommended control should, for example, suggest who should carry out the control procedures, and how frequently it should be performed.

 When the auditor reports deficiencies, it should be made clear that:

- The report is not a comprehensive list of deficiencies, but only those that have come to light during normal audit procedures.

- The report is for the sole use of the company.

- No disclosure should be made to a third party without the written agreement of the auditor.

- No responsibility is assumed to any other parties.

If you are asked for a covering letter in the exam, you should include the above matters within it.

Management letter extract

Deficiency	Consequence	Recommendation
Purchase invoices were missing from the sequentially numbered invoice file.	There is a possibility that purchases and liabilities are not completely recorded. This could result in late payment of invoices which could cause damage to the company's relationship with the supplier resulting in removal of credit terms or discounts.	All invoices should be sequentially filed on receipt by the accounts department. Regular sequence checks should be performed to ensure completeness. Any missing items should be investigated and copies requested if necessary.

7 Sales system

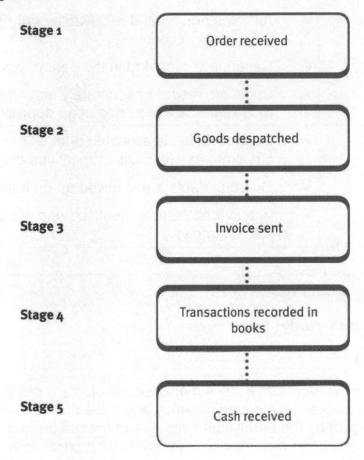

Stage 1 — Order received

Stage 2 — Goods despatched

Stage 3 — Invoice sent

Stage 4 — Transactions recorded in books

Stage 5 — Cash received

Objectives

The objectives of controls in the sales system are to ensure that:

Stage	Objective
Ordering	• Goods are only supplied to customers who pay promptly and in full. • All orders are processed.
Despatch	• Orders are despatched promptly and in full to the correct customer. • All orders are despatched.
Invoicing	• All goods despatched are invoiced. • Invoices are raised accurately.

Recording	• Only valid sales are recorded.
	• All sales and related receivables are recorded and in the correct accounts.
	• Revenue is recorded in the period to which it relates.
	• Sales are recorded accurately and related receivables are recorded at an appropriate value.
Cash received	• Cash received is allocated against the correct customer and invoices to minimise disputes.
	• Overdue debts are followed up on a timely basis.
	• Irrecoverable debts identified and written off appropriately.

Test your understanding 1

Murray case study: Sales cycle

Ordering

For all new customers, a sales manager completes a credit application which is checked with a credit agency and a credit limit is entered into the sales system by the credit controller. Credit checks are not reperformed unless a customer requests an increase to their credit limit. If an increase is requested, a new check will be performed and the credit limit revised.

The orders are entered into the sales system by a sales assistant. After the order has been accepted, the sales assistant checks that the goods are available and that the order will not take the customer over their credit limit.

Goods despatch

When the warehouse receives the order, a goods despatch note (GDN) is generated and a member of the warehouse team packs the goods using the GDN. A second member of the team double checks the details on the GDN to the goods packed, signing the GDN to evidence the check.

Four copies of the GDN are produced. One copy is sent with the goods and retained by the customer. A second is sent with the goods, signed by the customer and returned to Murray Co to confirm receipt of the goods which is filed in the warehouse. A third copy is sent to the sales team who update the system and the fourth copy is sent to the accounts department.

Invoicing

Sales invoices are raised by the accounts department using the GDNs. Sales invoices are not sequentially numbered, and no review is performed to ensure all goods have been invoiced.

Sales invoices are prepared using the approved company price list, which is updated quarterly. Discounts must be requested by a sales manager and authorised by the sales director to allow the accounts team to raise an invoice.

Recording transaction

The receivables ledger is reviewed for credit balances by the senior accountant on a monthly basis and the receivables ledger is reconciled with the receivables ledger control account when the sales ledger manager has time.

Monthly customer statements are sent to customers.

Cash receipt

Receipts are counted by the office assistant, recorded by the cashier in the cash book, and the sales ledger clerk is notified of the receipt. The sales ledger clerk agrees the amount received to the amount invoiced and marks the invoice as paid.

The credit controller reviews the aged receivables analysis on a fortnightly basis to assess the level of slow moving debts and an allowance is made for any debts which are considered doubtful. Debts which are more than six months overdue are chased up.

Required:

(a) In respect of the sales system for Murray Co:

    (i) Identify and explain FIVE KEY CONTROLS which the auditor may seek to place reliance on; and

    (ii) Describe a TEST OF CONTROL the auditor should perform to assess if each of these key controls is operating effectively. **(10 marks)**

(b) Identify and explain FIVE DEFICIENCIES in Murray Co's sales system and provide a recommendation to address each of these deficiencies. **(10 marks)**

(Total: 20 marks)

The key document in the sales cycle is the goods despatch note:

Murray Co

"Supplying Equipment to the Sporting Nation"

Goods Despatch Note

Ref: AB123456MC

www.murraysports.com

Murray Company

1 Murray Mound,
Wimbledon, London
WN1 2LN

Destination

Customer Ref: W004

Customer Name: Winners Co

Customer Address: 2 Edinburgh St,

Dunblaine, Scotland DL2 2ES

Order Number:

ZY987654WS

Line	Product Number	Description	Quantity	Quantity Quality and quantity of goods checked and agreed
001	4378493729	Tennis racket	24	Yes
002	3257845743	Tennis balls (packs of 6)	6	Yes
003	4357849574	Tennis court net	3	Yes
004	3473895789	Tennis scoreboard	3	Yes
005	4574895743	Winner's trophy	1	Yes
006	3457435437	Runner-up trophy	1	Yes
007	4830998543	Participant's medal	24	Yes

Signed:

A Warehouse Packer

8 Purchase system

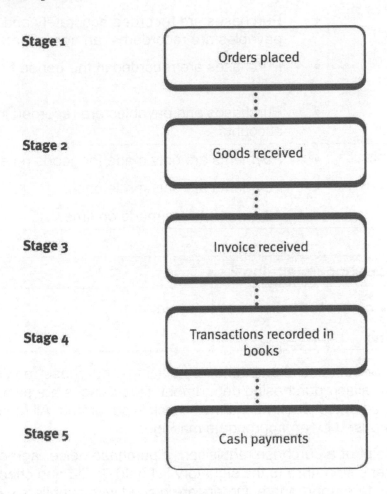

Stage 1 — Orders placed

Stage 2 — Goods received

Stage 3 — Invoice received

Stage 4 — Transactions recorded in books

Stage 5 — Cash payments

Objectives

The objectives of controls in the purchases system are to ensure that:

Stage	Objective
Ordering	• All purchases are made with suppliers who have been checked for quality, reliability and pricing. • Purchases are only made for a valid business use. • Orders are placed taking consideration of delivery lead times to avoid disruption to the business.
Goods received	• Only goods ordered by the company are accepted. • Goods received are recorded promptly.
Invoice received	• Invoices received relate to goods actually received. • Invoices received relate to the company. • Invoices received are correct in terms of quantities, prices, discounts.

Recording	• All purchases and related payables are recorded.
	• Purchases are recorded accurately and related payables are recorded at an appropriate value.
	• Purchases are recorded in the period to which they relate.
	• Purchases and payables are recorded in the correct accounts.
Cash payments	• Payments are only made for goods received.
	• Payments are only made once.
	• All payments are made on time.

Test your understanding 2

Murray case study: Purchases cycle

Ordering

Goods or services are obtained by placing a purchase requisition with the centralised purchasing department. Requisitions are sequentially pre-numbered and a weekly sequence check is performed. All requisitions must be authorised by an appropriate manager.

On receipt of a purchase requisition, a purchase officer agrees the manager's signature to the signatory list held on file and checks inventory levels where appropriate. Orders are placed with suppliers using sequentially pre-numbered purchase orders.

Orders can only be placed with suppliers from the approved supplier list. Suppliers can only be added to the approved suppliers list by the procurement team once the terms of the contract have been agreed, and references obtained. Written confirmation is requested for all orders placed, and the purchase officer agrees the quoted price against the agreed price list and ensures any bulk discounts to which Murray Co is entitled, have been honoured.

Goods receipt

Goods are received into the central warehouse. Goods are inspected for condition and quantity by a warehouse operative, and agreed to the purchase order before the supplier's delivery note is signed to accept the goods.

A sequentially pre-numbered goods received note (GRN) is prepared by the warehouse team manager, and grid-stamped. The grid stamp is signed by the warehouse operative to confirm that the goods have been inspected for condition and quantity and agreed to the purchase order.

The warehouse manager updates the inventory system on a daily basis from the prepared GRNs. The warehouse manager checks the sequence of purchase orders received on a weekly basis and informs the purchasing department of any missing orders so that they can be followed up.

Invoicing

On receipt of an invoice by the head office accounts team, the invoice is matched to and filed with the relevant GRN, using the purchase order number marked on the invoice (if there is no purchase order number marked on the invoice, this must be obtained from the supplier). The invoice number is noted on the GRN grid stamp. The invoice is also checked to the original purchase order to ensure the agreed prices and discounts have been honoured.

A monthly check of GRNs is made by the purchases ledger manager, to identify any GRNs for which no invoice has been received.

Recording transaction

The purchases ledger clerk enters invoices into the system in batches. A batch control sheet is used, which details the number of invoices and the total value. These details are checked to the system batch report.

Each invoice is stamped as 'recorded' once the details have been entered onto the system. The purchase ledger manager inspects the file of invoices on a monthly basis to ensure that all invoices have been recorded.

Suppliers are required to submit monthly supplier statements, which are reconciled to the supplier's ledger account by the purchases ledger manager. The purchase ledger is reconciled to the purchase ledger control account on a monthly basis by the purchase ledger manager, and reviewed by the company accountant.

Cash payment

The list of payments is sent to the company accountant, who agrees the details of each payment to the relevant invoice and signs each invoice to authorise payment and evidence the check. The list of payments is signed by the accountant once all invoices have been checked, and sent to the cashier's office for payment.

If any individual payment is for more than $25,000 or total payments are for more than $250,000 a second signatory is required. These payments must also be checked and signed by either the financial controller, or finance director.

Payments are made by the cashier's office by bank transfer. Invoices are stamped as 'paid', and returned to the purchases ledger team who record the payment and file the invoices (separately from invoices not yet paid).

The purchase ledger manager checks GRNs on a monthly basis to ensure that invoices have been received and paid on a timely basis.

Required:

Identify and explain the controls in Murray Co's purchases system and suggest how the auditor would test those controls.

Illustration 2: Murray Co goods received note

The key document in the purchases cycle is the goods received note:

Murray Co   **Goods Received Note**

Quality of goods checked   **A2012/123478**

Purchase Order number:
MC/34324832809/RC

Date of receipt: 31st August 20X4

Time of receipt: 12:48pm

Description	Quantity ordered	Quantity received	Quality of goods checked
Vectran	75kg	75kg	Yes

Sign to confirm quantity and quality of

goods checked: *Warehouse Operative*

Invoice number:

Problems with fraud

Fraud is specifically designed to mislead people. Consider the following example:

- A company only deals with suppliers on a list authorised by the finance director (FD).

- Payments to suppliers are made after the purchases clerk identifies the monthly payments to be made and prepares the cheques.

- The cheques are signed by the FD, who confirms the amounts paid and supplier names to supporting documentation.

- The cheques are countersigned by the managing director, who does not check the details but has a good knowledge of who the suppliers are.

- This appears like a sensible combination of authorisation controls and segregation of duties. The auditor would place reliance on the control system and reduce substantive testing of purchases.

However, now consider the implication if one of the suppliers is actually controlled by the FD. The supplier regularly overcharges the company and the purchases clerk is being bribed by the FD in return for their silence.

It is for this reason that the auditor must always perform some substantive procedures and must always maintain an attitude of professional scepticism.

Non-current assets

Expenditure on non-current assets should be controlled in a similar way to other purchases. However, because of the significant amounts involved, additional controls should be in place.

Control objectives:

- Assets are only purchased if there is a business need.

- Assets are purchased at an appropriate price.

- The company can afford the capital expenditure proposed.

- Capital expenditure is appropriately treated in the accounting records.

- Capital expenditure is completely and accurately recorded in the accounting records.

- Assets are covered by adequate insurance to prevent loss to the company.
- Documents relating to assets are safeguarded from theft or damage.

Control	Test of control
Requisitions for capital expenditure should be made by an appropriate person.	Inspect the requisition for the signature of the person requisitioning the assets. Ensure this is a person of suitable authority by agreeing the name to a list of people authorised to make such requisitions.
Authorisation for purchases of non-current assets should be at a more senior level.	Inspect the purchase order for signature of appropriate senior person(s).
Several quotations should be obtained before purchase in order to obtain the best price.	Inspect the purchase requisition for the quotations to ensure they have been obtained.
An annual capital expenditure budget for each department should be prepared and authorisation should only be given for purchases which have been budgeted.	Inspect the annual budget to ensure it has been prepared. Inspect board minutes to confirm the budget has been approved by the board. Inspect orders for capital expenditure items to ensure they have been authorised by a responsible official.
Regular review of revenue expenditure should be performed to ensure items of a capital nature have not been expensed in error.	Inspect management accounts/revenue expenditure lists for evidence of review. Enquire of management how discrepancies are dealt with.
A regular reconciliation of the asset register to the physical assets held should be performed.	Inspect the reconciliation of the asset register and evidence of approval by a senior person to ensure the reconciliation has been performed correctly.

KAPLAN PUBLISHING

An asset register should be maintained which includes cost, depreciation, location, responsible employee, insurance details, etc.	Inspect the asset register to ensure details expected to be recorded have been recorded to ensure good control is maintained over assets.
Adequate insurance cover should be purchased.	Inspect insurance policies to ensure they are in place. Review the policies to ascertain the level of cover in place and compare this with the value of assets to ensure it is sufficient.
Documentation such as title deeds, vehicle registration documents, insurance policies, etc. should be stored in a secure, fire-proof location.	Inspect the storage facilities for important documentation to ensure it is appropriately secure and adequate backups have been maintained in case of a fire or flood.

9 Payroll system

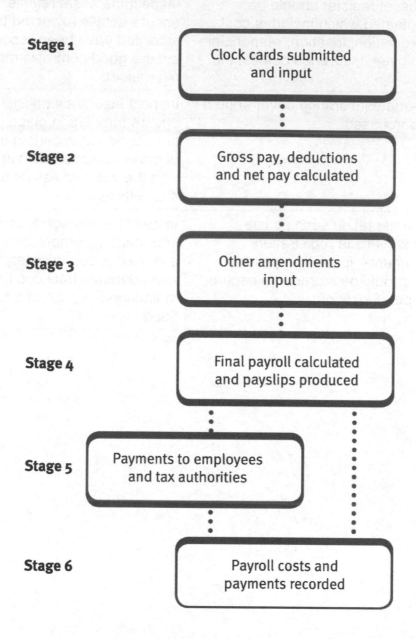

Stage 1 — Clock cards submitted and input

Stage 2 — Gross pay, deductions and net pay calculated

Stage 3 — Other amendments input

Stage 4 — Final payroll calculated and payslips produced

Stage 5 — Payments to employees and tax authorities

Stage 6 — Payroll costs and payments recorded

Objectives

The objectives of controls in the payroll system are to ensure that:

Stage	Objective
Clock cards (or timesheets) submitted.	• Employees are only paid for work actually done.
Payroll calculation	• Only genuine employees are paid. • Employees are paid at the correct rates of pay. • Gross pay is calculated and recorded accurately. • Net pay is calculated and recorded accurately.
Standing data amendments	• Standing data is kept up to date. • Access to standing data is restricted to prevent fraud or error occurring.
Recording	• All payroll amounts are recorded. • Payroll amounts are recorded accurately. • Payroll costs are recorded in the period to which they relate.
Payments to employees and tax authorities	• Correct amounts are paid to the employees and taxation authorities. • Payments are made on time. • Payments are only made to valid employees.

Test your understanding 3

Murray case study: Payroll cycle

Clock cards submitted and input

Murray Co employs a total of 300 people, 200 of these being workers who are paid weekly in cash. Weekly paid workers are required to record their times of arrival and departure at the factory using a clock card which is inserted in a time recording clock. Use of the time recording clock is supervised by the relevant factory manager.

On a weekly basis the cards are collected and passed to the works office where the clerk totals up the hours worked on each card and lists the total hours worked (a 'hash' total). The cards and the total hours list are then passed to the wages clerk who enters the hours worked into the payroll system and agrees the total entered.

Gross pay, deductions and net pay calculated

The payroll system calculates the gross and net pay and a payroll report is generated by the payroll manager. The payroll manager recalculates a sample of employee wages and compares his figures to the amounts calculated by the payroll system. He passes the payroll report to the wages clerk who creates a payment list detailing the payments to be made to the monthly paid employees and the taxation authority.

The payroll report and payment list are passed to the company accountant. The company accountant reviews the payment list for any unusual amounts and compares each employee's net pay on the payroll report to the payment list. He also compares the totals with the previous week as a reasonableness check. Once all of these procedures are complete, the company accountant signs both documents and raises a cheque requisition for the weekly paid workers. The signed payroll report is returned to the payroll clerk who generates the payslips from the payroll system. The payslips, cheque requisition and signed payment list are then passed to the cashier's department for processing.

Payments to employees and tax authorities

The cashier draws a cheque for the net amount of the payroll which is then signed by two directors. The cheque is given to a secure cash transit company who draw the money from the bank and deliver it under guard to the cashier. The cashier then puts the money into pay envelopes along with a pay slip for weekly paid workers.

The sealed envelopes and relevant clock cards are then used for pay-outs. Each worker obtains their money once they have identified themselves and signed their clock card. Unclaimed wages are held for three weeks before being banked.

Monthly paid workers and the tax authorities are paid by bank transfer on the last day of each month, as per the payment list authorised by the company accountant.

Payroll costs and payments recorded

A copy of the payroll list is sent to the head office accounts team who record the payroll expense and payments made. Any unclaimed wages are notified by the wages office to the head office team on an anomalies list completed once all of the clock cards have been returned. The head office accounts team check the bank statements to ensure that this money has been banked.

Standing data and other amendments

Leaver and joiner forms must be completed and authorised by the employee's immediate manager and the finance director at least one month before the amendment is required to the payroll. Other amendments to standing data, e.g. pay rises and hourly rates, are completed on a specific form for this purpose, and authorised in the same way. A monthly report of amendments to standing data is sent to the finance director for review and authorisation. Standing data files are sent to departmental managers on a quarterly basis for review.

Required:

Identify and explain the controls in Murray Co's payroll system and suggest how the auditor would test those controls.

10   Inventory system

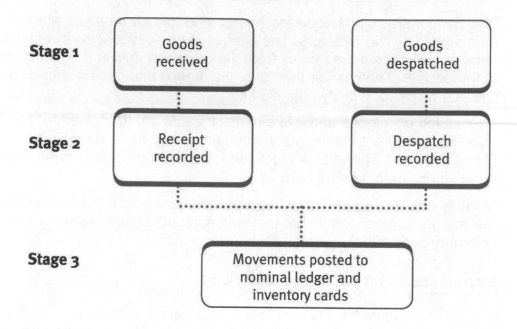

Stage 1 — Goods received | Goods despatched

Stage 2 — Receipt recorded | Despatch recorded

Stage 3 — Movements posted to nominal ledger and inventory cards

Objectives

The objectives of controls in the inventory system are to ensure that:

- Inventory levels meet the needs of production (raw materials and components) and customer demand (finished goods).

- Inventory levels are not excessive, preventing obsolescence and unnecessary storage costs.

- Inventory is safeguarded from theft, loss or damage.

- Inventory received and despatched is recorded on a timely basis.

- All inventory is recorded.

- Inventory should be recorded at the appropriate value.

- Only inventory owned by the company is recorded.

The following controls over inventory relate to the period after purchase and before sale i.e. when the goods are being stored in the warehouse.

Control	Test of control
Inventory should be maintained at an appropriate level through the use of automatic ordering systems when inventory reaches a certain level or by checking inventory levels before orders are placed.	Use test data to place an order to reduce inventory of an item to below the reorder level and trace through the system to see if an order is automatically generated. Observe the ordering clerk checking inventory levels before placing an order.
Inventory should be kept in a warehouse with access restricted to warehouse staff by the use of swipe card or keypad access. CCTV should be in place to monitor people around the entrance to the warehouse to ensure people don't follow other people into the warehouse to avoid the need for a code/swipe card.	Visit the warehouse and attempt to enter. Ensure that doors are kept closed requiring the swipe card or code to gain access. Inspect the warehouse area to see the CCTV in place and visit the location of the camera feed to ensure the cameras are monitored.
Inventory should be kept in appropriate conditions e.g. temperature controlled environment for perishable items.	Visit the warehouse and inspect the conditions of storage. Inspect evidence of monitoring the conditions on a regular basis such as temperature logs.
Fire/smoke/heat detectors and sprinkler systems should be in place to reduce the risk of damage caused by fire.	Inspect the warehouse to see the detectors and sprinkler systems are in place. Inspect certificates confirming they have been checked and tested on a regular basis.
Inventory should be insured in case of theft or damage.	Inspect insurance policies to ensure they cover inventory, that adequate cover is in place by comparing against inventory value, and that the policy has not lapsed.
Inventory movements should be recorded in the system promptly using the GRNs and GDNs. The GRNs and GDNs should be stamped to confirm they have been input and the system is up to date.	Inspect the GRNs and GDNs to see they have been stamped as entered into the system. Compare the date on the stamp to the date on the GRN/GDN to ensure they have been entered promptly.

Inventory counts should take place on a regular basis so that physical inventory quantities can be reconciled with the accounting system on a regular basis to ensure the records are accurate and up to date.	Obtain inventory counting instructions and review to ensure the count will be appropriately organised and controlled. Attend the inventory count to ensure the count is carried out in accordance with the instructions and perform test counts to ensure the client's counts are carried out accurately.
Inventory should be reviewed during the count for damage or obsolescence and valued separately from the other inventory by making an allowance to write the inventory down to net realisable value.	During the count, review the inventory to ensure damaged or obsolete items are separately identified.

See the 'Procedures' chapter for detailed controls over inventory counts.

11 Cash system

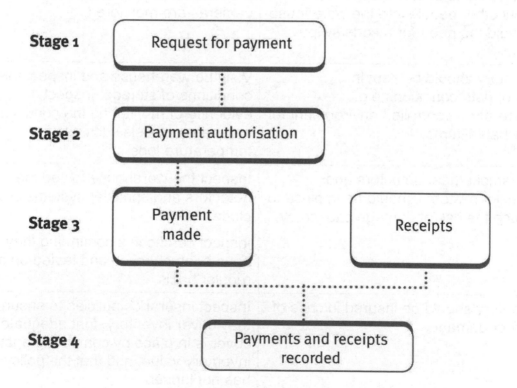

Stage 1 — Request for payment

Stage 2 — Payment authorisation

Stage 3 — Payment made — Receipts

Stage 4 — Payments and receipts recorded

Objectives

The objectives of controls in the cash cycle are to ensure that:

- Petty cash levels are kept to a minimum, preventing theft.

- Payments can only be made for legitimate business expenditure.

- Cash can only be withdrawn for business purposes.

- Cash is safeguarded to prevent theft.

- Receipts are banked on a timely basis to prevent theft.

- Cash movements are recorded on a timely basis.

The following controls over cash relate to the period after receipt from a customer and before being used to pay for expenses. In addition, there should be adequate controls over access to cash and bank records.

Control	Test of control
An imprest system of petty cash should be used for items of expenditure less than $x. All other reimbursements should be made through an expense claim and processed as a bank payment.	In the presence of the client, count the petty cash to ascertain that the level is at the limit set. Inspect the petty cash vouchers to ensure amounts reimbursed are below the limit stated.
Petty cash reimbursements must be supported by an invoice to confirm the expenditure was incurred and is business related before being authorised and paid.	Inspect the petty cash reimbursements for the supporting invoice and the signature of the person authorising the reimbursement.
Cash withdrawals must be authorised by a manager.	Inspect the withdrawal request for evidence of the manager's signature authorising that the money can be taken out of the bank.
Cash and cheque books should be stored in a locked safe with restricted access.	In the presence of the client, inspect where the cash and cheque books are stored to ensure they are secure, e.g. within a safe. Enquire of management who has access to the safe to ensure this is restricted to people with suitable seniority.

Controls over bank transfers and online banking should be in place, e.g. secure passwords and PINs.	Enquire of management who has access to the online banking system. Inspect transactions in the banking system for the username of the person initiating and authorising transactions to ensure this corroborates what has been said. Assess whether the person authorising the transactions is of suitable seniority.
Cash and cheques received should be banked frequently.	Inspect the paying in books or bank statements to identify how frequently deposits are paid in to ensure this is adequate.
Regular bank reconciliations prepared and then reviewed by personnel of appropriate seniority.	Inspect the file of bank reconciliations to ensure they are performed regularly. Inspect the reconciliation for a manager's signature as evidence it has been reviewed and approved. Reperform the reconciliation to ensure it has been carried out effectively.

 Exam question approach

The exam is likely to include one, or both, of the following requirements:

- Identify and explain the **control deficiencies** from the scenario and provide **recommendations** to overcome the deficiencies.

- Identify and explain the **key controls** from the scenario and describe **tests of controls** the auditor would perform to obtain evidence that the control is working effectively.

Control deficiencies

Identification of the deficiencies is usually quite straightforward. You should look for information which indicates:

- Controls are missing e.g. Sales orders are not sequentially numbered.

- Controls are not effective e.g. Bank reconciliations are supposed to be performed but often don't get done due to lack of time.

Work with the information provided. Do not assume that because something isn't mentioned it isn't happening.

Explanation of the deficiency requires you to give a business risk or a risk of misstatement in the accounting records. It is not an explanation if you only say this should not be done or this should be done. You must explain what the control would achieve if it was in place and working effectively. The explanation needs to be sufficiently detailed. If you only explain the deficiency in part you will not earn the explanation marks.

Recommendation

For the recommendation, suggest the control procedure which needs to be implemented. This also needs to be sufficiently detailed. Try and recommend which person within the company should perform the control and how frequently. Sometimes a control requires more than one element to be effective, therefore make sure you suggest everything that needs to happen to make the control effective.

	Control deficiency	Recommendation
Poor answer	Sales orders are not sequentially numbered. *Deficiency is not explained. Why does it matter if the sales orders are not sequentially numbered?*	Orders should be sequentially numbered. *Recommendation is not sufficiently detailed. How does the client know the sequence is complete?*
Better answer	Sales orders are not sequentially numbered. Orders will be difficult to trace and orders may not be fulfilled. *Deficiency is still not fully explained. What are the consequences to the company if they have unfulfilled orders?*	Orders should be sequentially numbered. A sequence check should be performed and any breaks in the sequence investigated and resolved. *Recommendation is now sufficiently detailed.*
Good answer	Sales orders are not sequentially numbered. Orders will be difficult to trace and orders may not be fulfilled. Customers will be dissatisfied if orders are not fulfilled resulting in complaints and loss of future revenue. *Deficiency is now fully explained as a business risk.*	Orders should be sequentially numbered. A sequence check should be performed and any breaks in the sequence investigated and resolved. *Recommendation is sufficiently detailed.*

	Control deficiency	Recommendation
Poor answer	Bank reconciliations are supposed to be performed but often don't get done due to lack of time. *Deficiency is not explained. Why does it matter if the bank reconciliation does not get performed?*	Bank reconciliations should be performed. *Recommendation is not sufficiently detailed. Who should perform the bank reconciliation?* *How often should it be performed?* *How does management know it has actually been done?*
Better answer	Bank reconciliations are supposed to be performed but often don't get done due to lack of time. Errors could occur. *Deficiency is still not fully explained.* *Errors in what?*	Bank reconciliations should be performed weekly. *Recommendation is slightly better but is still not sufficiently detailed.*
Good answer	Bank reconciliations are supposed to be performed but often don't get done due to lack of time. Errors could occur. The cash book may be incorrect resulting in misstatement of the bank and cash figure in the financial statements. *Deficiency is now fully explained as a risk to the accounting records.*	Bank reconciliations should be performed on a weekly basis by someone independent of maintaining the cash book and the reconciliation should be reviewed by a responsible official. *Recommendation is now sufficiently detailed.*

Key controls

Key controls are control procedures which are properly designed, in place and working effectively.

Read the scenario and look for mention of controls such as reconciliations being performed, authorisation of transactions, segregation of duties, restricted access to valuable items, etc.

A control is an activity performed that is **in addition** to the normal processing of the system, to ensure that the system has operated as it should. For example, raising a sales invoice is part of a normal sales system, it is not a control. A control would be someone performing a check to confirm the sales invoice had been raised accurately, or someone performing a check to confirm completeness of sales invoices in relation to GDNs. A control to confirm accuracy of invoices might be a sales manager agreeing the price on the invoice to the company's authorised price list and recalculating the invoices to confirm accuracy before they are sent to the customer. A control to confirm completeness of sales invoices might be that sales invoices are matched to GDNs and every week a sales manager performs a review of sales invoices to identify any unmatched invoices which are then investigated.

Make sure that there is nothing mentioned which would make the control ineffective. For example, duties may be segregated between two individuals who are related. This increases the risk of collusion which would negate the control. Reconciliations might be performed infrequently and not reviewed by anyone. Therefore the control is ineffective as it is not being performed all of the time, and no-one is checking that it has been performed correctly.

Tests of controls

A test of control is an audit procedure which will provide evidence as to whether the control procedure is in place and working effectively.

The focus of a test of control is the control procedure. If a key control identified is segregation of duties between calculating payroll and making the payroll payment, the auditor will need to obtain evidence that these duties are segregated e.g. by observing the procedures and inspecting procedures documents and organisation charts to ensure different people are responsible for each task.

Tests of controls are not substantive procedures. Therefore, when testing the control, the auditor does not need to test the balance which will go into the financial statements.

	Key control	Test of control
Poor answer	GDNs are matched to sales invoices. *There is no explanation of the control objective.*	Agree the amount recorded on the sales invoice and GDN to the sales day book. *This is a substantive procedure, not a test of control. The objective of the test of control is to confirm the control is in place, i.e. that the GDNs are matched to the sales invoices.*
Better answer	GDNs are matched to sales invoices. This reduces the risk of errors. *The control explanation is too vague. Reduces the risk of errors in what?*	Inspect the GDNs and sales invoices. *The test of control does not explain the objective of the test. What are we inspecting the GDNs and invoices for?*
Good answer	GDNs are matched to sales invoices by a finance clerk and signed to confirm the matching has been performed. This ensures the customer is invoiced for the correct goods which will reduce the risk of disputes and ensure sales are recorded accurately. *The control is now fully explained.*	Inspect a sample of GDNs and related invoices to confirm the details match and inspect for evidence of the finance clerk's signature confirming the matching has been performed. *The focus of the test is to confirm the control explained is in place and effective, therefore is a valid test of control.*

Test your understanding 4

Rhapsody Co supplies a wide range of garden and agricultural products to trade and domestic customers. The company has 11 divisions, with each division specialising in the sale of specific products, for example, seeds, garden furniture, and agricultural fertilizers. The company has an internal audit department which provides reports to the audit committee on each division on a rotational basis.

Products in the seed division are offered for sale to domestic customers via an Internet site. Customers review the product list on the Internet and place orders for packets of seeds using specific product codes, along with their credit card details, onto Rhapsody Co's secure server. Order quantities are normally between one and three packets for each type of seed. Order details are transferred manually onto the company's internal inventory control and sales system and a two part packing list is printed in the seed warehouse. Each order and packing list is given a random alphabetical code based on the name of the employee inputting the order, the date and the products being ordered.

In the seed warehouse, the packets of seeds for each order are taken from specific bins and despatched to the customer with one copy of the packing list. The second copy of the packing list is sent to the accounts department where the inventory and sales computer is updated to show that the order has been despatched. The customer's credit card is then charged by the inventory control and sales computer. Irrecoverable receivables in Rhapsody are currently 3% of the total sales.

Finally, the computer system checks that for each charge made to a customer's credit card account, the order details are on file to prove that the charge was made correctly.

Required:

In respect of sales in the seeds division of Rhapsody Co:

(i) **Explain FOUR deficiencies in the sales system, and**

(ii) **For each deficiency provide a recommendation to overcome that deficiency.**

(8 marks)

Test your understanding 5

Whilst performing tests of controls, many control deviations were found. The auditor has therefore concluded that reliance cannot be placed on the internal controls.

Required:

Explain THREE actions that the auditor may now take in response to this problem.

(3 marks)

Test your understanding 6

(a) **Define 'tests of control' and explain the importance of tests of control in the audit of a company.**

(2 marks)

(b) You are an audit senior working at a medium sized firm of auditors. One of your clients is an exclusive hotel called 'Numero Uno' situated in the centre of Big City. As part of your audit procedures you are assessing the controls surrounding payroll. You have read last year's audit file and have obtained the following information:

The hotel employs both full and part time staff. Due to the nature of the business most of the work is done in shifts. All staff are paid on a monthly basis.

New members of staff are given an electronic photo identification card on the day they join by the personnel department. This card is used to 'clock in' and 'clock out' at the start and end of the shift to record the hours worked.

At the end of each week the information recorded on the system is sent automatically to the payroll department and also to the head of each of the three main operating divisions: Rooms, Food & Beverage and Corporate Events. Each division head must reply back to the payroll department by email to authorise the hours worked by their staff.

The payroll clerk collates all the authorised information and then inputs the hours worked into a standardised computerised payroll package. This system is password protected using an alphanumerical password that is only known to the payroll clerk and the finance manager.

Once the hours have been entered, the calculations of gross pay and taxation are calculated automatically along with any other statutory deductions. At the end of the calculations a payroll report is produced and printed. The finance manager reviews the report and compares the data to last month to identify and follow up any unusual variances. When he is satisfied with the information he authorises the payroll run by signing the payroll report and the payroll clerk submits the data.

Payslips are sent to the home address of each employee and payment is made by bank transfer.

Required:

With reference to the scenario:

(i)   **Identify and explain FOUR STRENGTHS within the hotel's internal control system in respect of payroll.**

(4 marks)

(ii)   **For each of the identified strengths, state a test of control the auditor could perform to assess if the controls are operating effectively.**

(4 marks)

(Total: 10 marks)

Test your understanding 7

You are testing the controls over the payroll system of Bunbury Co. You have confirmed that the following controls have operated throughout the year:

- Sample check of payroll calculations by a payroll manager.

- Review of the payroll listing once prepared before details are entered into the banking system.

- Segregation of duties between calculation of monthly payroll and responsibility for changes to standing data.

- Each department manager receives a list of employees in their department for them to sign to confirm those employees should be paid.

(1) **Which of the following is the main reason for the control of segregation of duties between calculation of payroll and responsibility for changes to standing data?**

A Changes to standing data must be performed by a manager whereas payroll calculations can be performed by a payroll clerk

B If one person was responsible for both they would be more likely to make errors due to a high workload

C If one person was responsible for both they could increase their salary and make fraudulent payments to themselves

D Each individual role within an organisation must be carried out by different people

(2) **Which of the following procedures would provide the most reliable evidence that the first control, payroll calculations are checked by a payroll manager, is working effectively?**

A Enquiry with the payroll clerk performing the payroll calculation

B Enquiry with the payroll manager performing the check

C Recalculation of the payroll amounts by the auditor

D Inspection of the payroll report for evidence that a sample of payroll amounts are checked

(3) **Which of the following is NOT a test of control?**

A Inspection of employee contracts to confirm the salary the employee should be paid

B Inspection of payroll reports for evidence of authorisation by the manager

C Inspection of the list of employees for each department for evidence of the department manager's review

D Observation of the payroll function to confirm segregation of duties is in place

(4) **Which of the following is a control objective relevant to the control that each department manager reviews the list of employees?**

A To ensure payroll is accurately calculated

B To ensure only valid employees are paid

C To ensure employees are paid for the correct hours

D To ensure employees are paid at the correct salary

(5) **Which of the following could be used by Bunbury Co to monitor the effectiveness of the company's controls?**

A   Internal audit assignments

B   Performing bank reconciliations

C   Authorisation of payments

D   Segregation of duties

 Test your understanding 8

You are performing the risk assessment for the audit of Kununurra Co, a client your firm has audited for the past two years. From your review of last year's audit file you have found that no significant control deficiencies were identified. The systems are documented on the permanent audit file in the form of flow charts and narrative notes.

(1) **Which of the following best describes the requirement of the auditor in respect of the controls documentation?**

A   The auditor must document the systems this year as they may have changed since last year

B   The auditor may enquire whether the systems have changed since last year and if not no further work is necessary

C   The auditor must perform procedures to ensure the systems work as documented on file e.g. by performing walkthrough tests

D   No work is necessary on systems documentation unless the client informs the auditor that changes have occurred

(2) **Which of the following best describes the auditor's approach in respect of reliance on internal controls?**

A   Tests of controls must be performed over material areas of the financial statements

B   Tests of controls must be performed each year over the areas where the auditor is hoping to place reliance on the controls

C   Tests of controls are not necessary this year as no deficiencies were identified last year

D   Tests of controls must be performed over all areas irrespective of whether the auditor is planning to place reliance on those controls

(3) **Which of the following would NOT be included in an internal control evaluation questionnaire?**

A How does the company ensure sales are only made to creditworthy customers?

B How does the company ensure that purchases are only made for a valid business use?

C How does the company ensure that all purchases are recorded?

D Is access to the warehouse restricted to authorised personnel only?

(4) **Internal controls should be monitored on an ongoing basis to ensure they are adequate, relevant and working effectively. Which of the following will NOT monitor the internal controls of a company?**

A External auditor

B Management

C Consultancy firm hired by management

D Internal auditor

(5) **Match the description to the appropriate method of documenting a control system.**

	ICQ/ICE	Flowchart	Narrative notes
A diagram depicting the controls in place at each stage of a process			
A disadvantage of this method may be that controls are overstated			
An advantage of this method is that they are easy to prepare in advance and therefore efficient			
For larger systems this method may be time consuming and it may be difficult to identify missing controls			

12 Chapter summary

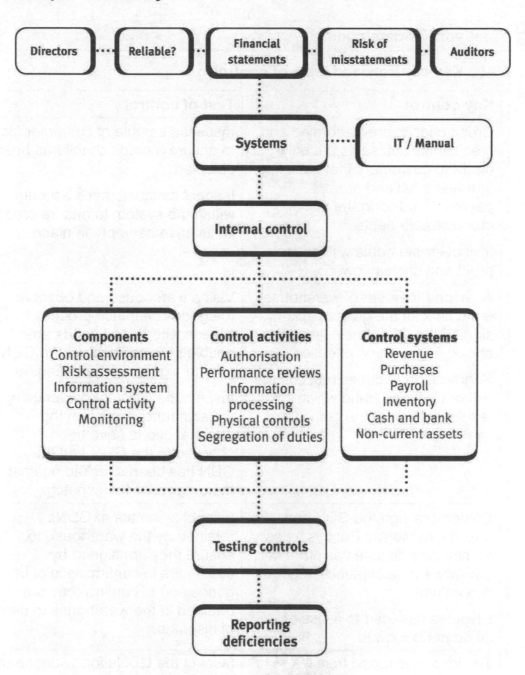

Test your understanding answers

Test your understanding 1

(a) Key controls and tests of control

Key control	Test of control
Credit checks are performed and credit limits set: sales are only made to customers that are likely to make a full and prompt payment, reducing the risk of irrecoverable debts. Irrecoverable debts will reduce profit and cash inflows.	Inspect a sample of customer files to ensure a credit check has been obtained. Inspect the customer's account within the system to ensure credit limits have been put in place.
A second member of warehouse team checks the goods packed, signing the GDN to evidence the check: segregation of duties. Segregation of duties reduces the risk of theft and fraud which results in loss for the company.	Visit a warehouse and observe the goods despatch process to assess whether all goods are double checked against the GDN prior to signing and sending out. Inspect the GDN for evidence of the signature to confirm the physical goods have been checked to the GDN and the GDN has been checked against the order prior to despatch.
Customers sign the GDN and return it to Murray Co: this helps to minimise disputes as proof of delivery and acceptance of goods is obtained. Disputes can lead to a loss of customer goodwill.	Inspect a sample of GDNs retained by the warehouse to ensure they are signed by customers to confirm receipt of goods and to confirm they are retained in the warehouse in case of disputes.
The invoice is raised from the GDN: this ensures the invoice relates to the actual quantity of goods despatched rather than the order which may be different. This reduces the risk of customers being invoiced incorrectly for goods not received which could cause customer dissatisfaction and a loss of customer goodwill.	Inspect the GDNs for evidence of being matched to invoices. Agree the details on both to ensure the control has been effective.

Sales invoices are prepared using the company price list: ensures customers are invoiced correctly. Incorrect invoicing could cause customer dissatisfaction and a loss of customer goodwill.	Inspect the price list for approval by the directors. Obtain a copy of the current price list and, for a sample of invoices, agree that the correct prices have been used. Agree the prices in the system to the approved price list. Enquire of management who has authority to amend standing data such as prices in the system to ensure only persons of suitable authority have access. Try to input a change to the prices in the system using a user ID of a clerk to ensure that the system does not allow access to this standing data.
Discounts must be requested by a sales manager and authorised by the sales director: segregation of duties and authorisation. This reduces the risk of fraud and unauthorised discounts which will result in loss of revenue for the company.	With the client's permission, attempt to process an invoice with a sales discount without authorisation from the sales director. The system should reject the invoice. Inspect sales orders with discounts given for evidence of the sales director's signature authorising the discount.
Review of the receivables ledger for credit balances: identifies possible overpayments or errors within the receivables ledger. Errors in the accounting records can be promptly corrected.	Inspect the receivables ledger for evidence of monthly review for credit balances such as a manager's signature.
Monthly customer statements sent to customers: reminds customers of the invoices they need to pay and enables them to identify errors in invoices which can be notified to Murray Co. This can reduce the risk of irrecoverable debts which will reduce profit and cash inflows.	For a sample of customers, inspect copies of monthly statements sent out to confirm statements are in fact issued.

Receipts are counted by the office assistant, recorded by the cashier, and the sales ledger clerk agrees the amount received to the amount invoiced: segregation of duties. Segregation of duties reduces the risk of fraud which could cause loss for the company.	Observe the cash receipt process to assess the adequacy of segregation of duties.

(b)   **Control deficiencies and recommendations**

Control deficiency	Recommendation
Credit checks are only reperformed if a customer requests an increase to their credit limit. A customer's credit rating may have deteriorated but Murray Co will not know and continue to give the same level of credit which increases the risk of irrecoverable debts, affecting profit and cash flow.	Credit checks should be performed annually to ensure the credit limit originally given to the customer is still appropriate. If the credit status has changed, the credit limit should be revised.
The availability of goods is only checked after the order has been accepted. Orders may not be able to be fulfilled which can result in complaints from customers and a loss of customer goodwill.	Sales assistants should be able to view real time inventory information in the system. The availability of goods should be checked at the time the order is taken so the customer can be made aware of any delay.
Credit limits are checked after the order has been accepted. The customer may not have sufficient credit which may result in irrecoverable debts and a reduction to profit.	Credit limits should be checked before the order is confirmed to ensure the customer has sufficient credit.
Sales invoices are not sequentially numbered. The company will not be able to identify if any invoices are missing. Goods may not have been invoiced which will result in lost revenue and profit for the company.	Sales invoices should be sequentially numbered and a sequence check should be performed by the accounts department on a daily/weekly basis. Any breaks in the sequence should be investigated.

No review is performed to ensure all goods have been invoiced. Goods may not have been invoiced which will result in lost revenue and profit for the company.	A review should be performed to ensure that every GDN has a matching invoice to ensure all goods have been invoiced.
The receivables ledger is only reconciled when the sales manager has time. Errors may exist within the receivables accounting records which will not be identified and resolved on a timely basis.	The receivables ledger should be reconciled to the control account on a monthly basis. The reconciliations should be reviewed by a different, responsible official to ensure the reconciliation has been performed properly.
The credit controller only follows up on balances which are six months overdue. This increases the risk of irrecoverable debts which will reduce profit and cash inflows.	Credit control procedures should be followed to ensure full and prompt payment by customers, e.g. a telephone call to the customer followed by a letter.

Test your understanding 2

Ordering

Control	Test of control
Centralised purchasing department: ensures that purchasing is cost effective and only necessary goods and services are procured, reducing the risk of loss to the company and unnecessary cash outflow.	Inspect the organisation chart to verify that a centralised purchasing department is in place. Enquire of the purchasing director whether all purchases must go through the department, or if some purchases are made within individual departments, to assess the effectiveness of the control. Inspect a sample of purchase orders to ensure they have been generated by the central purchasing department.
Sequentially pre-numbered requisitions and sequence check performed by the purchasing department: ensures that all requisitions are fulfilled, preventing stock outs/ manufacturing delays. Delays will result in dissatisfied customers which will reduce customer goodwill.	Enquire of the staff responsible for the sequence check what they do to evidence the control, e.g. a log in the file with a signature to confirm the sequence check has been performed for that week. Inspect the log and ensure it is completed weekly and is up to date. Inspect the log for a signature to confirm the check has been performed.
Requisitions are authorised and manager's signature agreed: ensures only necessary goods and services are procured, reducing the risk of loss to the company and unnecessary cash outflow.	Inspect a sample of requisitions for the signature of an appropriate manager.
Inventory levels are checked prior to ordering: ensures only necessary goods and services are procured, reducing the risk of loss to the company and unnecessary cash outflow.	Inspect a sample of requisitions for evidence of inventory levels being checked first, such as a signature. Observe the ordering process to see the ordering clerk checking inventory levels first.

Sequentially pre-numbered purchase orders and weekly check by warehouse manager: to ensure that all goods and services ordered are received so any missing purchase orders can be followed up. This reduces the risk of production delays which will result in dis-satisfied customers and a loss of customer goodwill.	Review the purchase orders for evidence of the warehouse manager's weekly sequence check such as a signature to confirm it has been performed.
Approved supplier list: gives assurance about the quality of goods and services and reliability of the suppliers. Poor quality supplies will affect the quality of the product sold resulting in complaints from customers and damage to the company's reputation reducing future sales.	For a sample of purchase orders placed, agree the supplier name to the approved supplier list. Attempt to place an order with an unapproved supplier. The system should not allow it to proceed.
Written confirmation for all orders: ensures all and only necessary goods and services are received. This reduces the risk of disputes with suppliers which could cause production delays resulting in dissatisfied customers and a loss of customer goodwill.	For a sample of purchase requisitions, inspect the purchase order and written confirmation from the supplier.
Price agreed to price list and discounts checked: ensures that the correct prices are being charged by the supplier and discounts are being obtained. This ensures the correct amounts will be paid reducing the risk of loss to the company and unnecessary cash outflow.	Inspect a sample of purchase orders for evidence of prices having been agreed to price list such as a signature of the person checking. Select a sample of orders and agree to the authorised price list to test the effectiveness of the control.

Goods receipt

Control	Test of control
Goods received into the central warehouse. Having one, secure delivery area prevents goods received being lost or stolen reducing the risk of loss to the company.	Visit a warehouse and inspect the delivery area for security of goods e.g. locked area, security guard, CCTV.
Goods are inspected for condition and quantity and agreed to the purchase order. This prevents Murray Co from paying for unnecessary, or poor quality goods which would result in loss for the company and unnecessary cash outflow.	Observe the goods receipt process to ensure goods are inspected for condition and quantity before the supplier's delivery note is signed. Inspect the delivery note for a signature confirming the goods have been checked on arrival.
Sequentially pre-numbered goods received note (GRN) prepared by the warehouse team manager and a sequence check performed by the purchase ledger manager. This ensures that all goods received are recorded which will reduce disputes with suppliers or over payment for goods.	Inspect evidence of the sequence check being performed such as a signature of the warehouse manager.
Grid stamp: a grid stamp is a grid that can be ink-stamped onto any document, with boxes for recording different information such as confirmation the goods have been inspected for condition and agreed to the PO. This prevents Murray Co from paying for unnecessary or poor quality goods reducing the risk of loss to the company and unnecessary cash outflow.	Inspect a sample of GRNs to ensure they are grid-stamped and signed by the warehouse operative to confirm the goods have been inspected and agreed to the PO.

Inventory system updated on a daily basis by the warehouse manager: prevents unnecessary goods being ordered, ensures inventory levels are up-to-date when checked before acceptance of customer orders. This reduces the risk of not being able to fulfil customer orders which could result in dissatisfied customers and a loss of customer goodwill.	Inspect a sample of GRNs for the previous day to ensure the inventory system has been updated for them.

Invoicing

Control	Test of control
The invoice is matched to the GRN: by matching the invoice to the GRN and not the original order it ensures that only goods that have been received are paid for, reducing the risk of loss to the company and unnecessary cash outflow.	Inspect a sample of invoices and ensure they are filed with the relevant GRN, and the invoice number is written on the GRN.
Using the purchase order number marked on the invoice: when placing an order, the supplier will be given the purchase order number. This allows the purchase to be matched to the relevant GRN and requisition and the company can efficiently trace the relevant documentation in case of queries.	Inspect a sample of invoices for the PO number and that it is matched to the relating GRN and requisition.
The invoice number is noted on the GRN grid stamp, and a monthly check of GRNs with no invoice: this prevents goods received being invoiced twice which would cause loss to the company.	Review the GRN for the grid stamp. Inspect evidence of signature to confirm the monthly check has been carried out by the purchase ledger manager.

Recording transaction	
Control	**Test of control**
Batch controls: the system will notify the clerk inputting the data of how many invoices have been input. This will be checked to the physical number of invoices and will highlight if too many or too few invoices have been entered. This ensures accuracy of the purchases and payables figures in the accounting records enabling invoices to be paid on time reducing the risk of disputes with suppliers.	Inspect a sample of batch control sheets for evidence of completion and agreement to the batch system report.
Invoice stamped as 'recorded' and checks to ensure all invoices recorded: Prevents under or overstatement of trade payables reducing the risk of disputes with or late payments to suppliers.	Select a sample of invoices recorded on the system and inspect them to ensure they are marked as 'recorded'.
Supplier statement reconciliations: enables mis-recorded purchases, payments and liabilities to be identified and corrected. This reduces the risk of disputes with suppliers and ensures accuracy of the accounting system relating to purchases and payables.	For a sample of suppliers, inspect the monthly supplier statements received for evidence of the reconciliation being performed. Reperform the reconciliation to confirm it has been reconciled correctly to test the effectiveness of the control.
Control account reconciliation: ensures that credits and payments recorded in individual supplier ledgers have also been recorded in the accounts (and vice versa). Segregation of duties monitors performance of controls and ensures accuracy of the accounting system in relation to purchases and payables.	Inspect the purchase ledger reconciliations for evidence of performance and review on a monthly basis. Reperform the reconciliation to ensure it has been carried out effectively.

Cash payment

Control	Test of control
The company accountant checks and authorises payments: payments should only be authorised by a senior member of the finance department to prevent error or fraud which could result in loss for the company.	For a sample of payments made, inspect the payment list for evidence of the company accountant's review and authorisation.
Individual payments of more than $25,000 or total payments of more than $250,000 require a second signatory: a second signatory prevents fraud on unusual transactions which could result in loss for the company. The additional check by the financial controller or finance director further enhances this control.	Inspect a sample of invoices > $25,000 for evidence of a second signatory and agree that the signature is of someone with authority to authorise such amounts. Inspect the invoices for the additional signature of the financial controller or finance director.
Payments are made by the cashier's office and recorded by the purchase ledger team: segregation of duties prevents fraud which could result in loss for the company.	Observe the process of payments from the cashier's office to ensure segregation of duties is in place.
Invoices are stamped as 'paid' and filed separately from invoices not yet paid: this prevents invoices being paid twice which could result in loss for the company and unnecessary cash outflow.	Inspect the file of paid invoices and ensure they are kept separate from invoices not yet paid. Inspect them stamped as 'Paid'.
GRNs are checked on a monthly basis: to ensure that suppliers are paid on a timely basis, which ensures that early settlement discounts available are obtained, and supplier goodwill is maintained.	Review evidence of the purchase ledger manager's monthly invoice review such as a signature.

Test your understanding 3

Clock cards submitted and input

Control	Test of control
Clock card to record time and supervision of clock card use: ensures that only genuine employees are paid for work done. This reduces the risk of unnecessary additional expense for the company which reduces profit.	Observe the use and supervision of clocking in and out procedures to ensure that employees are not able to clock in for other people.
Hash total and agreement of the total: segregation of duties by performing and checking the procedure reduces the risk of human error and therefore the risk of incorrect payments being made which will affect profit.	Observe the process of the works office clerk totalling the hours and passing the list to the wages clerk to confirm segregation of duties is in place. Inspect a sample of payroll sheets for the wages clerk's signature as evidence they have checked the total hours list.

Payroll calculation and payment list created

Control	Test of control
Payroll is calculated automatically by the payroll system and the payroll manager recalculates a sample of wages: Calculation by the system is less vulnerable to error and a sample check by the payroll manager ensures the system calculates the wages accurately, minimising the risk of incorrect payments being made.	Review a sample of the calculations performed by the payroll manager.
The company accountant's review of payroll: ensures that any anomalies can be identified and resolved. Payroll is a significant cost for most companies and it is important that a responsible individual, independent of preparation of payroll, undertakes this role. This reduces the risk of payments being made to ghost employees or incorrect amounts being paid which would cause unnecessary expense and reduce profit.	Inspect the payroll report and payment list for the signature of the company accountant confirming the reports have been checked to each other and a review has been performed.

Payroll is calculated by the payroll department. The company accountant raises the cheque requisition and authorises the payment list. The cashier's department makes the relevant payments: segregation of duties prevents fraud and error which could result in loss for the company.	Inspect the monthly payment list and payroll report for the company accountant's signature. For a sample of cheques raised for wages, inspect the cheque requisition to ensure it has been completed by the company accountant.

Payments to employees and tax authorities

Control	Test of control
Payroll cheque is signed by two directors: this is likely to be a large amount of money and therefore requires authorisation by two senior personnel to prevent fraud and error which could result in loss to the company.	Inspect the bank mandate to ensure it requires the signature of two directors for large cheques.
Cash is delivered by a secure transit company, under guard: due to the amount of cash likely to be needed to pay the weekly paid workers, it would not be appropriate for Murray Co staff to go to the bank to get the money themselves as this would threaten their personal safety.	Observe the cash being delivered by the security firm. Inspect invoices for services of the security firm to ensure the service is provided weekly.
Workers must identify themselves and sign their clock cards before receiving their money: ensures that only genuine employees are paid, reducing the risk of unnecessary expense for the company which reduces profit.	Observe payment of weekly wages to confirm identification is checked. Inspect a sample of clock cards to ensure they have been signed by the worker.

Payroll costs and payments recorded

Control	Test of control
The head office accounts team record the payroll expense and payments and the wages office notifies the team of unclaimed wages: segregation of duties prevents fraud and error which could result in loss for the company.	Inspect the anomalies list to see it has been prepared. Enquire of the wages office and the head office team that this notification occurs on a weekly basis to corroborate that the control works effectively.
Bank statements are checked for deposit of unclaimed wages: prevents misappropriation which would result in loss for the company.	Inspect the anomalies list or bank statements for evidence that the bank statements are checked to ensure any unclaimed wages have been banked.

Standing data and other amendments

Control	Test of control
Completion and authorisation of standing data forms: ensures that only genuine employees are paid and at authorised rates of pay. This reduces the risk of payments being made to ghost employees or incorrect amounts being paid which would cause unnecessary expense and reduce profit.	Select a sample of employees with pay rises or other amendments from human resources records and inspect the system details to ensure that the relevant payroll form has been completed and authorised on a timely basis.
Use of specific forms, such as for starters and leavers: prevents errors in processing information. This reduces the risk of incorrect payments being made which would result in employee dissatisfaction or payments being made to people no longer working for the company which would result in loss to the company.	Select a sample of leavers and joiners from human resources records and trace the changes to the system to ensure that payroll forms have been completed and authorised on a timely basis.

Monthly review of standing data amendments and quarterly review of standing data files: ensures that any unauthorised amendments to standing data are identified and resolved. This reduces the risk of payments being made to ghost employees or incorrect amounts being paid which would cause unnecessary expense and reduce profit.	Select a sample of amendments made to standing data and trace to the monthly report authorised by the finance director, and the relevant amendment form.
	Inspect the standing data files sent to departmental managers for evidence of review.
	For any anomalies identified by departmental managers, enquire of and corroborate the reasons for the anomaly and what action was taken to resolve the issue.

Test your understanding 4

Deficiency and effect	Recommendation
Recording of orders	
Orders placed on the website are transferred manually into the inventory and sales system. Manual transfer may result in errors.	The computer system should be upgraded so that order details are transferred directly between the two computer systems. This will remove manual transfer of details, limiting the possibility of human error.
Customers will be sent incorrect goods resulting in increased customer complaints and a loss of customer goodwill.	
Control over orders and packing lists	
Each order/packing list is given a random alphabetical code. This type of code makes it difficult to check completeness of orders.	Orders/packing lists should be controlled with a numeric sequence.
Packing lists can be lost resulting in goods not being despatched to the customer which will result in a loss of customer goodwill. The order may be sent but the customer's credit card may not be charged which would result in loss for Rhapsody.	At the end of each day, a sequence check should be performed and any gaps in the sequence should be investigated.

Obtaining payment

The customer's credit card is charged after despatch of goods to the customer, meaning that goods are already sent to the customer before payment is authorised.

Rhapsody Co will not be paid for the goods despatched where the credit company rejects the payment request. Given that customers are unlikely to return seeds, Rhapsody Co will automatically incur an irrecoverable debt which reduces profit and cash inflow.

Authorisation to charge the customer's credit card should be obtained prior to despatch of goods and the card should be charged on despatch to ensure Rhapsody Co is paid for all goods sent to customers.

Completeness of orders

There is no overall check that all orders recorded on the inventory and sales system have actually been invoiced and the customer's credit card charged.

Orders despatched may not have been invoiced resulting in understatement of revenue and profit. If the credit card has not been charged the company will experience a reduction in cash flow.

An exception report of orders not invoiced should be generated each week. Orders where there is no corresponding invoice should be investigated.

Test your understanding 5

The auditor can expand the amount of controls testing in that audit area.

This may indicate that the control deficiency was not as bad as initially thought.

The problem could be raised with those charged with governance to ensure that they are aware of the problem.

The auditor could perform additional substantive procedures on the audit area. If controls have not worked effectively in this area there is a greater risk of misstatement. Substantive procedures will be used to quantify the misstatement.

If the matter is not resolved, then the auditor will also need to consider the implications for the auditor's report.

Test your understanding 6

(a) **Tests of control**

A test of control tests the operating effectiveness of controls in preventing, detecting or correcting material misstatements.

It is important for the external auditor to test controls to ensure their initial understanding obtained when assessing the control environment and internal controls is appropriate.

This will allow the auditor to identify and assess the risks of material misstatements in the financial statements and determine the amount of reliance that can be placed on the internal control system.

The auditor will then be able to design sufficient and appropriate substantive audit procedures to reduce detection risk, and therefore audit risk, to an acceptable level.

(b) **Payroll system strengths and tests of control**

Strengths in the control system at the hotel in respect of payroll are set out below including the test of control to be performed by the auditor.

Strength (i)	Test of control (ii)
All staff are assigned a unique ID card by the personnel department to record hours worked. Segregation of duties between allocating the cards and processing payroll will reduce the risk of the creation of 'ghost' employees by the payroll department which would result in additional cost for the company and a reduction in profit.	Ask a sample of employees to confirm who provided them with their unique ID card on joining the business. Inspect the ID cards for existence. Agree the employee details to HR records.
Hours worked are authorised by divisional heads. There is a reduced risk that hours are overstated as the divisional head is more likely to identify errors or anomalies. This reduces the risk of incorrect payments being made which will affect profit.	Inspect the email sent by the divisional head for a sample of months and agree to the employee's hours recorded on the payroll system.

The payroll system is password protected with an alphanumerical password known only to the payroll clerk and finance manager. The password is difficult to guess and therefore will limit the risk of unauthorised access which could lead to payroll data being manipulated. This reduces the risk of fraud and loss to the company.	The auditor should use test data and enter a 'dummy' password into the payroll system to ensure that access is not granted.
Payroll calculations are automatically calculated by the standardised payroll software. There is a reduced risk of human error as the calculations are automatically performed. This reduces the risk of incorrect payments being made to employees which could result in unnecessary expense for the company or dissatisfied employees.	The auditor should recalculate a sample of employee's monthly pay from across the year and compare to the calculations on the payroll report for those months.
The finance manager reviews the payroll report and compares to last month before the final payroll is processed. The comparison of data to the prior month should highlight any unusual movements, that could be errors, before the payroll is processed. This reduces the risk of incorrect payments being made to employees which could result in unnecessary expense for the company or dissatisfied employees.	For a sample of months, inspect the payroll reports for evidence of the finance manager's signature confirming that the review has been performed.
Payslips are sent to the home address of each employee. This should reduce the risk that payslips are misplaced or manipulated. It would also reduce the risk of a confidentiality breach.	Ask a sample of employees to confirm they receive their monthly payslips via post to their home address.
Payments are sent by bank transfer to each employee. This will reduce the risk of payments being stolen or handed to the wrong employee which could result in loss for the company.	Inspect the bank statements to identify payments made to a sample of employees on the payroll report for a selection of months.

Test your understanding 7

(1)	C	Segregation of duties helps to prevent fraud.
(2)	D	Enquiry is not the most reliable form of evidence as the clerk or the manager could say what they think the auditor wants to hear. Recalculation of payroll by the auditor is a substantive test and does not confirm the manager has performed the necessary checks.
(3)	A	Inspection of employee contracts to confirm salary details is a substantive procedure.
(4)	B	The department manager would identify if any fictitious employees or employees who had left the company were included on the list and could notify the payroll department before any invalid payments were made.
(5)	A	Internal audit can monitor the effectiveness of controls by regularly testing them. B, C and D are all examples of control activities that would be tested for effectiveness.

Test your understanding 8

(1)	C	The auditor must ensure the systems documentation held on file is still correct. This can be achieved through a combination of enquiry and walkthrough tests but enquiry alone is not sufficient appropriate evidence.
(2)	B	Tests of controls are only performed when the auditor is planning to place reliance on those controls. If the auditor has decided that substantive testing is more efficient for a specific balance it is not necessary to test the controls over that area. Reliance cannot be placed on the results of tests of controls performed in previous years as the auditor would need to confirm they had worked effectively in the current year.
(3)	D	An internal control evaluation questionnaire asks the client to respond with the control in place that addresses the risk. Restricted access as given in answer D is a control. This question would be included in an internal control questionnaire rather than an internal control evaluation questionnaire.
(4)	A	The external auditor should not monitor the controls as this requires ongoing involvement in the company on a regular basis. Whilst the external auditor may test the controls and identify deficiencies, this does not constitute monitoring. Management are ultimately responsible for the internal controls including assessing whether they are effective and whether any improvements are required. They may utilise an external consultant or internal audit function to help them fulfil this responsibility.

(5)

	ICQ/ICE	Flowchart	Narrative notes
A diagram depicting the controls in place at each stage of a process		✓	
A disadvantage of this method may be that controls are overstated	✓		
An advantage of this method is that they are easy to prepare in advance and therefore efficient	✓		
For larger systems this method may be time consuming and it may be difficult to identify missing controls			✓

Internal audit

Chapter learning objectives

This chapter covers syllabus areas:

- C5 – Internal audit and governance, and the differences between external audit and internal audit

- C6 – The scope of the internal audit function, outsourcing and internal audit assignments

Detailed syllabus objectives are provided in the introduction section of the text book.

PER

One of the PER performance objectives (PO19) is to collect and evaluate evidence for an audit. Carry out an internal or external audit from collecting evidence, through to forming an opinion. You demonstrate professional scepticism and make sure judgements are based on sufficient valid evidence. Working through this chapter should help you understand how to demonstrate that objective.

1 The need for internal audit

 Internal audit is an independent, objective assurance and consulting activity designed to add value and improve an organisation's operations.

Companies must create a strong system of internal control in order to fulfil their responsibilities.

However, it is not sufficient to simply have mechanisms in place to manage a business, their effectiveness must be regularly evaluated. All systems need some form of monitoring and feedback. This is the role of internal audit.

Having an internal audit department is generally considered to be best practice, but is not required by law. This allows flexibility in the way internal audit is established to suit the needs of a business.

In small, or owner managed businesses there is unlikely to be a need for internal audit because the owners are able to exercise more direct control over operations, and are accountable to fewer stakeholders.

The need for internal audit (IA) therefore will depend on:

- Scale and diversity of activities. In a larger, diversified organisation there is a risk that controls don't work as effectively because of the delegation of responsibility down the organisation. Internal audit can report back to the audit committee if controls are not as effective as they should be.

- Complexity of operations. The more complex the organisation is, the greater the benefit obtained from having an IA function as there is greater risk of things going wrong. With larger organisations the consequences of poor controls/risk management/corporate governance practices are likely to be greater.

- Number of employees. The greater the number of employees the greater the risk of fraud.

- Cost/benefit considerations. It will only be worth establishing an IA function if the benefits outweigh the costs. For example a company might be losing money as a result of fraud, not using the most cost effective or reliable suppliers, or incurring fines for non-compliance with laws and regulations. If these costs outweigh the cost of employing an IA function it will be beneficial to the company to establish a department.

- The desire of senior management to have assurance and advice on risk and control. The directors may wish to have the comfort that there is ongoing monitoring of the organisation to help them discharge their responsibilities.

- The current control environment and whether there is a history of fraud or control deficiencies. If so it will be beneficial for the company to establish an internal audit function to prevent and detect fraud.

2 The difference between internal and external auditors

	External audit	Internal audit
Objective	Express an opinion on the truth and fairness of the financial statements in a written report.	Improve the company's operations by reviewing the efficiency and effectiveness of internal controls.
Reporting	Reports to shareholders.	Reports to management or those charged with governance.
Availability of report	Publicly available.	Not publicly available. Usually only seen by management or those charged with governance.
Scope of work	Verifying the truth and fairness of the financial statements.	Wide in scope and dependent on management's requirements.
Appointment and removal	By the shareholders of the company.	By the audit committee or board of directors.
Relationship with company	Must be independent of the company.	May be employees (which limits independence) or an outsourced function (which enhances independence).

3 The role of the internal audit function

The role of internal audit can vary depending on the requirements of the business.

Key activities of the internal audit function

- Assessing whether the company is demonstrating best practice in corporate governance.

- Evaluating the company's risk identification and management processes.

- Testing the effectiveness of internal controls.

- Assessing the reliability of financial and operating information.

- Assessing the economy, efficiency and effectiveness of operating activities (value for money).

- Assessing compliance with laws and regulations.

- Providing recommendations on the prevention and detection of fraud.

Most of these activities can be seen as helping management comply with corporate governance requirements.

Additional roles

In addition to the above, internal audit will carry out ad hoc assignments, as required by management. For example:

- Fraud investigations – this may involve detecting fraud, identifying the perpetrator of a fraud and quantifying the loss to the company as a result of a fraud.

- IT systems reviews – performing a review of the computer environment and controls.

- Mystery shopper visits – for retail and service companies the internal audit staff can pose as customers to ensure that customer service is at the required level.

- Contract audits – making sure that where material or long term contracts are entered into by the organisation, the contract is written to protect the organisation appropriately and contractual terms are being adhered to by the supplier in line with the service level agreement.

- Asset verification – such as performing cash counts and physical inspection of non-current assets to verify existence.

- Providing direct assistance to the external auditor –internal audit staff can help the external auditor with their procedures under their supervision, in accordance with ISA 610. This is covered in the 'Evidence' chapter.

Qualities of an effective internal audit function

- Sufficiently resourced, both financially and in terms of qualified, experienced staff.

- Well organised, so that it has well developed work practices.

- Independent and objective to provide an unbiased view of the organisation's operations.

- The chief internal auditor should be appointed by the audit committee to reduce management bias.

- The department should have no operational responsibilities to reduce the threat of self-review.

- The audit committee should set the plan of work.

- There should be no limitation on the scope of their work i.e. full access to every part of the organisation.

Limitations of internal audit

- Internal auditors may be employees of the company they are reporting on and therefore may not wish to raise issues in case they lose their job.

- In smaller organisations in particular, internal audit may be managed as part of the finance function. They will therefore have to report on the effectiveness of financial systems of which they form a part and may be reluctant to say their department (and manager) has deficiencies.

- If the internal audit staff have worked in the organisation for a long time, possibly in different departments, there may be a familiarity threat as they will be auditing the work of long standing colleagues and friends.

It is therefore difficult for internal audit to remain truly objective. However, acceptable levels of independence can be achieved through one, or more, of the following strategies:

- Reporting channels separate from the management of the main financial reporting function.

- Reviews of internal audit work by managers independent of the function under scrutiny.

- Outsourcing the internal audit function to a professional third party.

4 Outsourcing the internal audit function

In common with other areas of a company's operations, the directors may consider that outsourcing the internal audit function represents better value than an in-house department.

Outsourcing is where the company uses an external company to perform its internal audit service instead of employing its own staff.

Advantages

- Professional firms follow an ethical code of conduct and should therefore be independent of the client and their management.

- Professional firms should have qualified, competent staff who receive regular development and have a broader range of expertise.

- An outsourcing firm will have specialist skills readily available therefore outsourcing can be used to overcome a skills shortage.

- Professional firms can be employed on a flexible basis, i.e. on an individual engagement basis rather than full time employment which may prove more cost effective.

- Employment costs of permanent staff are avoided.

- The risk of staff turnover is passed to the outsourcing firm.

- Professional firms are responsible for their activities and hold insurance.

- There is likely to be greater focus on cost and efficiency of the internal audit work as this will affect profitability of the assignment.

- The company will obtain access to new market place technologies without the associated costs, e.g. audit methodology software.

- Management time in administering an in-house department will be reduced.

Disadvantages

- Professional firms lack the intimate knowledge and understanding of the organisation that employees have.

- The decision may be based on cost with the effectiveness of the function being reduced.

- Engagements with professional firms are constrained by contractual terms. Flexibility and availability may not be as high as with an in-house function.

- Fees charged by professional firms may be high.

- An ethical threat may arise if the service is provided by the external audit firm. E.g. the ACCA Code of Ethics prohibits external auditors of a listed company from providing internal audit services for the same client where the service relates to internal controls over financial reporting.

- Pressure on the independence of the outsourced function, for example, if management threaten not to renew the contract.

- Lack of control over the quality of service.

5 Internal audit assignments

Internal auditors perform many different types of assignment. Common examples include:

- Value for money assignments

- Operational audits

- The audit of IT systems

- Financial audit.

Value for money

Value for money (VFM) is concerned with obtaining the best possible combination of services for the least resources. It is often referred to as a review of the three Es:

- **Economy** – obtaining the best quality of resources for the minimum cost.

- **Efficiency** – obtaining the maximum departmental/organisational outputs with the minimum use of resources.

- **Effectiveness** – achievement of goals and targets (departmental/organisational etc).

Comparisons of value for money achieved by different organisations (or branches of the same organisation) are often made using performance indicators that provide a measure of economy, efficiency or effectiveness. This is particularly common in the not-for-profit sector (i.e. public services and charities), but it can apply to any company.

For example, a company chooses the cheapest supplier for the materials it needs. The supplier has a lead time for delivery of 6 weeks. If the company needs a supplier that can deliver at short notice on a regular basis this will not be effective.

If a company sources lower quality materials at a price 10% cheaper than their current supplier but uses 50% more as a result of the lower quality, this is not efficient.

Value for money: hospital

Examples of value for money indicators for a hospital might include:

- Economy – cost of medical supplies per annum.

- Efficiency – number of patients treated per year, utilisation rate of beds/operating theatre.

- Effectiveness – recovery rates, number of deaths.

Operational audits

An operational audit is a systematic review of the efficiency and effectiveness of operations within the organisation. The focus of the audit is on the processes which take place within the organisation to identify if they can be streamlined and performed more efficiently. The more efficient a process is the more profitable the organisation should be.

For example during an operational audit the internal auditor may find that orders are manually entered into a sales system to record an order. A copy of the order is passed to the despatch department who manually enter the details into the despatch system. A copy of the goods despatch note is sent to the finance department for invoicing and the details are manually entered into the invoice.

In addition to the risk of error that arises each time the details are manually entered, this is a time consuming and inefficient process.

The internal auditor may recommend that an integrated system is introduced to remove the need for the data to be entered by each department. If the order system links to the despatch system and the despatch system links to the finance system, no manual entry will be required after the order has been entered in the first instance.

The audit of IT systems

The external auditor considers IT systems from the perspective of whether they provide a reliable basis for the preparation of financial statements, and whether there are internal controls which are effective in reducing the risk of misstatement.

Internal audit will also consider this. However, their role is much wider in scope and will also consider whether:

- The company is getting value for money from their IT system.

- The procurement process for the IT system was effective.

- The ongoing management/maintenance of the system is appropriate.

Whilst this is an ongoing role, project auditing can be used to look at whether the objectives of a specific project, such as implementing new IT systems, were achieved.

Financial audit

The main aim of a financial reporting system is to create accurate, complete and timely information which can be used for decision making and business planning. This information is also needed to satisfy the requirements of actual and potential investors and trading partners.

Typical examples of financial information include:

- Financial statements

- Monthly management accounts

- Forecasts and projections.

The main aim of internal financial audits is to ensure that the information produced is reliable and produced in an efficient and timely manner. If not, executive decisions may be based on unreliable information.

The other aim of a financial audit is to assess the financial health of a business. More importantly it is about ensuring there are mechanisms in place for the early identification of financial risk, such as:

- Adverse currency fluctuations

- Adverse interest rate fluctuations

- Cost price inflation.

In both cases the focus of internal audit will be on the processes and controls that underpin the creation of the various financial reports to ensure they are as effective as possible for assisting decision making and the risk management processes of the company.

6 Reporting

Unlike an independent external auditor's report, the internal audit report does not have a formal reporting structure. It is likely that the format is agreed with the audit committee or board of directors prior to commencing the assignment.

These reports will generally be for internal use only. The external auditors may inspect them if they are intending to place reliance on the work of internal audit.

A typical report will include:

- Terms of reference – the requirements of the assignment.

- Executive summary – the key risks and recommendations that are described more fully in the body of the report.

- Body of the report – a detailed description of the work performed and the results of that work.

- Appendix – containing any additional information that doesn't belong in the body of the report but which is relevant to the assignment.

 In the exam you may be asked to take the role of an internal auditor performing an audit assignment to test controls or identify improvements in efficiency that can be made.

The internal audit report can be set out in the same way as the report to management that has been seen in the 'Systems and controls' chapter, describing the deficiencies identified, consequences of those deficiencies and recommendations for improvement.

Test your understanding 1

Murray Co's internal audit function

The internal audit function at Murray Co consists of a head of internal audit, two senior internal audit managers, four internal audit managers, seven internal auditors and an internal audit assistant. The head of internal audit has been in post for twelve years, and the other members of the team have varying lengths of service from two to fifteen years.

The head of internal audit is responsible for recruiting staff into the internal audit team. The head of internal audit was appointed by the audit committee.

The head of internal audit reports to the audit committee and agrees the scope of work for the internal audit function with the audit committee.

The internal audit staff have no operational responsibility. Where the staff have previously transferred from another department within Murray Co, the head of internal audit ensures that another member of the team carries out the audit of that system.

Murray Co's internal audit function follows the International Standards for the Professional Practice of Internal Auditing issued by the Global Institute of Internal Auditors.

Barker Co's internal audit function

The internal audit function at Barker Co consists of a chief internal auditor, one senior internal audit manager, one audit manager, one auditor and an audit assistant. The chief internal auditor has been in post for ten years, and the other members of the team have varying lengths of service from five to nine years.

The finance director is responsible for recruiting all staff into the internal audit function. The chief internal auditor reports to the finance director and agrees the scope of work for the internal audit function with him.

The internal audit team spend 50% of their time carrying out internal audit assignments and 50% of their time working in the finance department. Due to the limited number of staff in the team, this has resulted in the internal auditors reviewing their own work.

Barker Co's internal audit team follow a variety of standards, in accordance with their own professional training.

Required:

Compare and contrast the effectiveness of Murray Co and Barker Co's internal audit functions.

Test your understanding 2

You are the senior manager in the internal audit department of Octball, a limited liability company. You report to the chief internal auditor and have a staff of six junior auditors to supervise, although the budget allows for up to ten junior staff.

In a recent meeting with the chief internal auditor, the difficulty of staff recruitment and retention was discussed. Over the past year, five junior internal audit staff have left the company, but only two have been recruited. Recruitment problems identified include the location of Octball's head office in a small town over 150 kilometres from the nearest major city and extensive foreign travel, often to cold climates.

Together with the chief internal auditor you believe that outsourcing the internal audit department may be a way of alleviating the staffing problems. You would monitor the new outsourced department in a part-time role taking on additional responsibilities in other departments, and the chief internal auditor would accept the post of finance director (FD) on the board, replacing the retiring FD.

Two firms have been identified as being able to provide the internal audit service:

- The NFA Partnership, a large local firm specialising in the provision of accountancy and internal audit services. NFA does not audit financial statements or report to members.

- T&M, Octball's external auditors, who have offices in 75 countries and employ in excess of 65,000 staff.

Required:

(a) **Discuss the advantages and disadvantages of appointing NFA as internal auditors for Octball.**

(8 marks)

(b) **Discuss the matters T&M need to consider before they could accept appointment as internal auditors for Octball.**

(7 marks)

(c) **Assume that an outsourcing company has been chosen to provide internal audit services. Describe the control activities that Octball should apply to ensure that the internal audit service is being maintained to a high standard.**

(5 marks)

(Total: 20 marks)

Test your understanding 3

You are an audit senior working at Monkey, Mia & Co. You have been seconded to your firm's internal audit department to broaden your experience. You have been assigned to an internal audit assignment to test the effectiveness of the computer systems at a large company. Your firm won the contract to provide internal audit services to the company after the company took the decision to outsource its internal audit function and make the existing internal audit staff redundant.

(1) **With which of the following should the internal auditor not be involved?**

    A   Identifying deficiencies in internal controls

    B   Providing recommendations to management on how to overcome the deficiencies identified

    C   Implementing the new controls recommended

    D   Evaluating the effectiveness of the new controls implemented

(2) **Which TWO of the following statements are correct?**

    (i)   Internal auditors always report directly to shareholders.

    (ii)   The format of the independent external auditor's report is determined by management.

    (iii)   The internal auditor's work may be determined by management.

    (iv)   All external audits must be planned and performed in accordance with International Auditing Standards and other regulatory requirements.

    A   (i) and (iv)

    B   (i) and (iii)

    C   (ii) and (iii)

    D   (iii) and (iv)

(3) **Which of the following is NOT part of the role of internal audit?**

    A   Risk identification and monitoring

    B   Expression of opinion to the shareholders on whether the annual financial statements give a true and fair view

    C   Fraud investigations

    D   Assessing compliance with laws and regulations

(4) **Which of the following is NOT a valid reason to outsource the internal audit function?**

A   The external audit will be more efficient as the external audit staff will have a good understanding of the company if they are also involved with the internal audit work

B   Outsourcing may be more cost effective as compared with employing staff and providing training and other employment benefits

C   A professional firm is likely to be more experienced and able to provide better recommendations for improvements

D   Greater independence of an external service provider

(5) **Identify whether the following statements are true or false**

	True	False
Internal audit reports must be produced in a standardised format as set out by the financial reporting framework		
Internal audit reports are issued to shareholders		
There is no legal requirement for companies to have an internal audit department		
The presence of an internal audit function may act as a deterrent for fraud		

7   Chapter summary

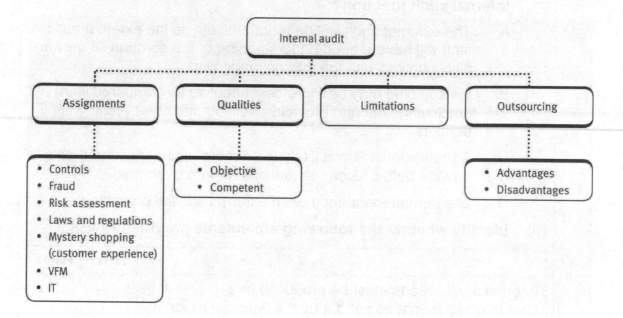

Test your understanding answers

Test your understanding 1

Reporting system

The chief internal auditor at Barker Co reports into the finance director. This limits the effectiveness of the internal audit reports as the finance director will also be responsible for some of the financial systems that the internal audit function is reporting on. Similarly, the chief internal auditor may soften or limit criticism in reports to avoid confrontation with the finance director.

To ensure independence, the chief internal auditor should report into the audit committee, as the head of internal audit at Murray Co does.

Recruitment of staff

All of the internal audit team at Barker Co are recruited by the finance director. The finance director may appoint personnel who are less likely to criticise his work. To ensure independence, the head of internal audit should be appointed by the audit committee, and they should then recruit and appoint the rest of the team, as at Murray Co.

Scope of work

The scope of work of internal audit at Barker Co is decided by the finance director in discussion with the chief internal auditor. This means that the finance director may try and influence the chief internal auditor regarding the areas that the internal audit department is auditing, possibly directing attention away from any contentious areas that the director does not want auditing.

To ensure independence, the scope of work of the internal audit department should be decided by the chief internal auditor, perhaps with the assistance of an audit committee, as at Murray Co.

Audit work

The internal audit team at Barker Co review their own work. This limits independence as the auditor may overlook or fail to identify errors or deficiencies in those areas. This is a self-review threat.

If possible, the internal audit team should not have operational responsibility. However, if this is not possible, the internal audit work should be arranged so that no member of the team reviews areas where they have operational responsibility, as Murray Co does.

Lengths of service of internal audit staff

The internal audit team staff of both companies have been employed for a long time. This may limit their effectiveness as they will be very familiar with the systems being reviewed and therefore may not be sufficiently objective to identify errors in those systems.

However, there are sufficient staff at Murray Co to ensure that the team can be rotated into different areas of internal audit work, and their work can be independently reviewed. Due to the small number of staff in the internal audit team, Barker Co may not be able to achieve this.

Given the extent of limitations, it may be appropriate for Barker Co to outsource its internal audit function.

Variation of standards

Staff at Barker Co follow the auditing standards with which they are familiar. Standards of internal audit are not uniform across the profession. This could lead to inconsistency in the way each internal audit assignment is performed. This can lead to manipulation of internal audit aims and measurement. Barker Co should follow an agreed, recognised set of professional internal audit standards, such as those followed by Murray Co.

Test your understanding 2

(a) **Benefits of outsourcing to NFA**

Expertise available

The NFA partnership will be able to provide the necessary expertise for internal audit work. They may be able to provide a broader range of expertise as they serve many different clients therefore staff may be available for specialist work that Octball could not afford to employ.

Obtain skills as and when required

If internal audit is only required for specific functions or particular jobs each year then the expertise can be purchased as required. Taking this approach will minimise in-house costs.

KAPLAN PUBLISHING

Independence

As an independent firm which does not perform the audit of the financial statements it is likely that they can provide a high level of service with appropriate objectivity. In particular, there will be no self-review threats.

Audit techniques – training

Outsourcing will remove the need for training internal staff. The outsourcing firm will be responsible for providing training for their staff and keeping them up-to-date with new auditing techniques and processes.

Continuity of service – staffing

As provision of internal audit services is the NFA partnership's main activity, they should also be able to budget for client requirements. As a larger internal auditing firm, they may be able to offer staff better career progression which should assist staff retention.

Problems with outsourcing to NFA

Fee pressure

NFA may experience some fee pressure, but only in respect of maintaining cost effectiveness of the internal audit department. The relationship needs to be managed carefully to ensure that NFA do not decrease the quality of their work due to insufficient fees.

Knowledge

The NFA partnership will not have any prior knowledge of Octball. This is a disadvantage as it will mean the partnership will need time to ascertain the accounting systems and controls in Octball before commencing work. However, provision of an independent view may identify control deficiencies that the current internal audit department have missed.

Location

The NFA partnership may not be able to provide this service to Octball as they are a local firm and therefore the issue of travel and working away from home would remain.

(b) **Matters to be considered by T&M**

Independence

T&M need to ensure that independence can be maintained in a number of areas:

– Independence regarding recommending systems or preparing working papers and subsequent checking of those systems or working papers. While the internal audit department may need to carry out these functions, T&M must ensure that separate staff are used to provide the internal and external audit functions.

– Staff from T&M will be expected to follow the ethical guidance of ACCA which means that steps will be taken to avoid conflicts of interest or other independence issues such as close personal relationships building up with staff in Octball. Any real or perceived threats to independence will lower the overall trust that can be placed on the internal audit reports produced by T&M.

Skills

T&M must ensure that they have staff with the necessary skills and sufficient time to undertake the internal audit work in Octball. As a firm of auditors, T&M will automatically provide training for its staff as part of the in-house compliance with association regulations (e.g. compulsory CPD). T&M will need to ensure that staff providing the internal audit function to Octball are aware of relevant guidance for internal auditors.

Fee pressure

There may be fee pressure on T&M, either to maintain the cost effectiveness of the internal audit department, or to maintain the competitiveness of the audit fee itself in order to keep the internal audit work.

Knowledge

As external auditors, T&M will already have knowledge of Octball. This will assist in establishing the internal audit department as systems documentation will already be available and the audit firm will already be aware of potential deficiencies in the control systems.

(c) **Controls to maintain the standard of the internal audit department**

- If T&M are appointed, the internal and external audits should be performed by different departments within the firm.

- Performance measures such as cost, areas reviewed, etc. should be set and reviewed. Explanations should be obtained for any significant variances.

- Appropriate audit methodology should be used, including clear documentation of audit work carried out, adequate review, and appropriate conclusions drawn.

- Working papers should be reviewed, ensuring adherence to International Standards on Auditing where appropriate and any in-house standards on auditing.

- The work plan for internal audit should be agreed prior to the work commencing and this should be followed by the outsourcing company.

Test your understanding 3

(1)	C	Internal auditors should not implement new controls as this would create a self-review threat when the controls are tested at a later date.
(2)	D	Internal audit work may be determined by management or the audit committee if there is one. External audits must be conducted in accordance with ISAs.
(3)	B	An audit opinion presented to the shareholders must be expressed by an independent external auditor.
(4)	A	Ethical guidance issued to external auditors requires separate teams to provide internal and external services. Therefore the internal audit staff assigned will not have existing knowledge gained from the external audit.

(5)

	True	False
Internal audit reports must be produced in a standardised format as set out by the financial reporting framework		✓
Internal audit reports are issued to shareholders		✓
There is no legal requirement for companies to have an internal audit department	✓	
The presence of an internal audit function may act as a deterrent for fraud	✓	

Procedures

Chapter learning objectives

This chapter covers syllabus areas:

- D2 – Audit procedures
- D4 – The audit of specific items
- D7 – Not-for-profit organisations

Detailed syllabus objectives are provided in the introduction section of the text book.

PER

One of the PER performance objectives (PO19) is to collect and evaluate evidence for an audit. Carry out an internal or external audit from collecting evidence, through to forming an opinion. You demonstrate professional scepticism and make sure judgements are based on sufficient valid evidence. Working through this chapter should help you understand how to demonstrate that objective.

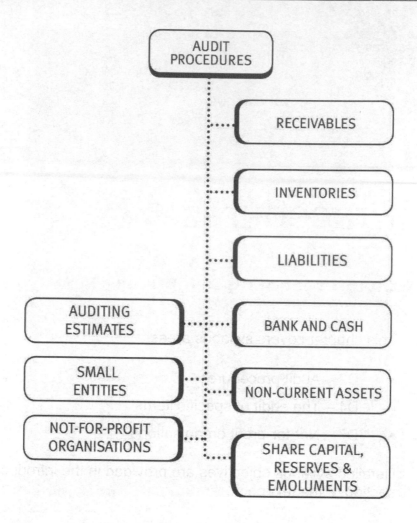

1 Exam focus

We dealt with the principles of audit evidence in an earlier chapter. This chapter deals with the **application** of those principles.

 Audit procedures must be designed to respond to the specific risks of material misstatement identified for each individual client. In the exam, you should make your answers specific to the scenario. It is highly likely the scenario focuses on a specific risk such as valuation of inventory, recoverability of receivables, etc. Therefore audit procedures must focus on these features rather than general audit procedures over inventory or receivables.

 Remember that the auditor's role is to obtain sufficient appropriate evidence that the financial statements are prepared in all material respects with the relevant financial reporting framework. For this reason, you will need to have a good understanding of the accounting standards.

Writing good audit procedures

An audit procedure should be a clear instruction of how the audit evidence is to be gathered.

It should contain an ACTION applied to a SOURCE to achieve an OBJECTIVE.

In other words, it should describe what needs to be done, how it should be done and why it should be done.

 Read the procedure back and consider whether a person with no audit experience will understand it.

Example: Audit objective – Test the existence of non-current assets

Good answer	Bad answer
Select a sample of assets from the non-current asset register and physically inspect them to verify existence.	Check a sample of assets.

Explanation	
The good procedure above clearly states: ➢ from where the sample should be chosen – the non-current asset register ➢ how they should be checked – physically inspect ➢ the objective of the test – existence	The badly worded procedure is not sufficiently described: ➢ From which population should the sample be selected? ➢ How should the auditor 'check' existence? ➢ What are the assets being checked for?

Example: Audit objective – Test the valuation of trade receivables

Good answer	Bad answer
Inspect post year end bank statements to identify if payment has been received post year end. If so, agree the amount to the receivables ledger at the year end.	Perform a receivables circularisation for a sample of customers to confirm the balances are in existence at the year end.

Explanation	
The good answer is a well explained procedure which tests the assertion of valuation in relation to receivables.	The bad answer tests the assertion of existence, not valuation. It is a well written procedure, but not relevant for the stated audit objective.

This chapter is a starting point to help you familiarise yourself with the basic auditing techniques, to allow you to apply them to questions. It is not an exhaustive summary of all audit procedures.

Each section starts with:

Key assertions – these are the assertions most likely to be at risk, however, the auditor must obtain assurance over all relevant assertions.

Sources of evidence – these are the documents that are likely to provide the best evidence over the balance being tested.

2 Directional testing

The concept of directional testing derives from the principle of double-entry bookkeeping, i.e. for every debit there should be a corresponding credit. Therefore any misstatement of a debit entry will also result in a misstatement of a credit entry.

Auditors primarily test debit entries (assets and expenses) for overstatement and credit entries (liabilities and income) for understatement, indirectly testing the corresponding entries at the same time, e.g. directly testing payables for understatement also indirectly tests expenses/cost of sales for understatement.

- Testing for understatement tests completeness.
- Testing for overstatement tests valuation, existence, rights and obligations, and occurrence.

To test for understatement the auditor must select the sample from outside of the accounting system and trace the transaction through to the accounting system.

For example, select a sample of goods despatch notes and trace to the related sales invoice and into the sales day book to confirm completeness.

To test for overstatement the auditor must select the sample from the accounting system and trace the transaction through to the supporting documentation.

For example, from the sales day book, select a sample of sales invoices and trace to the actual sales invoice and related goods despatch note to confirm occurrence.

3 Bank and cash

 The key assertions for bank and cash are existence and valuation.

Sources of evidence:

- Bank confirmation letter
- Bank reconciliation
- Cash book
- Bank statements

The bank and cash included in the financial statements must exist and be included at the appropriate amount. The cash book figure is the balance which should be included in the financial statements. This may differ to the bank statement balance due to timing differences. Therefore the bank reconciliation must be reviewed to ensure the differences can be explained.

The bank confirmation letter provides direct confirmation of bank balances from the bank. It is third party, independent, written evidence and therefore very reliable.

The client must give permission to the bank to release this information to the auditors, as they too have a duty of confidentiality to their clients.

The confirmation request should be sent a minimum of two weeks before the client's year-end. The letter should include enough information to allow the bank to trace the client. The confirmation letter will be sent by the bank directly to the auditor's office.

Test your understanding 1 – Bank and cash

Murray Co

Bank reconciliation as at 31 December 20X4	$
Balance per cash book	(180,345.22)
Add Unpresented cheques	2,223.46
Less Outstanding lodgements	(1,600.34)
Difference	1.34
Balance per bank statement	(179,720.76)

Required:

Describe the substantive procedures the auditor should perform to verify the bank and cash balance of Murray Co.

Illustration 1 – Murray Co Bank confirmation letter

Wimble & Co

14 The Grove

Kingston

KI4 6AP

Manager (Audit Confirmations)

National Bank Anytown Branch

High Street, Anytown, AT1 1 HS

14 December 20X4

Dear Sir,

Re: Murray Co

In accordance with the agreed practice for provision of information to auditors, please forward information on our mutual client as detailed below on behalf of the bank, its branches and subsidiaries. This request and your response will not create any contractual or other duty with us.

Company name: Murray Co

Main account number: 01789311

Sort code: 04-83-12

Information required

- Standard   **x**

- Trade finance   **x**

- Derivative and commodity trading

- Custodian arrangements

- Other information (see attached)

Audit confirmation date: 31/12/X4

The Authority to Disclose Information signed by your customer is already held by you. This is dated 30/11/X4. Please advise us if this Authority is insufficient for you to provide full disclosure of the information requested.

The contact name is: Don Henman (Audit engagement partner)

Telephone: 01234 123456

Yours faithfully,

Wimble & Co

Wimble & Co

Cash counts

Where cash in hand is material, or when fraud is suspected, a cash count should be arranged to verify existence.

The auditor should make sure that all cash balances are counted at the same time to avoid manipulation of the balances between different sites.

The auditor should always be accompanied by a member of the client staff to avoid any allegations from the client of theft by the auditor.

The details of the cash counts should be recorded, such as the locations counted, the amount counted at each location, the client staff present, the auditor performing the tests and the date performed.

Non-current liabilities

The key assertion for liabilities is completeness and valuation.

Sources of evidence:

- Loan agreement
- Cash book
- Bank statements
- Bank confirmation letter

The loan balances must be complete and valued appropriately in the financial statements. Allocation must be assessed as the client should show how much of the loan is due to be paid within one year (included as a current liability) and how much of the loan is due to be paid outside of one year (included as a non-current liability).

The bank confirmation letter will provide details of loans held, the amounts outstanding, accrued interest and any security provided in relation to those loans.

Third party evidence will be available in the form of the bank confirmation letter and the original loan agreement.

Procedures include:

- Obtain a breakdown of all loans outstanding at the year-end, cast to verify arithmetical accuracy and agree the total to the financial statements: **completeness**.

- Agree the balance outstanding to the bank confirmation letter: **accuracy & valuation, rights & obligations**.

- Inspect bank confirmation letters for any loans listed that have not been included in the financial statements: **completeness**.

- Inspect the bank confirmation letter for details of any security over assets and agree the details to the disclosure in the financial statements: **presentation**.

- Inspect financial statements for disclosures of interest rates, and the split of the loan between current and non-current: allocation, classification, **presentation**.

- Recalculate the split between current and non-current liabilities: **allocation, classification, and presentation**.

- Inspect the loan agreement for restrictive covenants (terms) and determine the effect of any loan covenant breaches: **allocation, classification, presentation.** [If loan covenants have been breached the loan may become repayable immediately and should therefore be included as a current liability].

- Inspect the cash book for loan repayments made: **existence, accuracy & valuation**.

- For the related finance cost in the statement of profit or loss, recalculate the interest charge and any interest accrual in accordance with terms within the loan agreement, to ensure mathematical accuracy: **accuracy** of finance costs in the statement of profit or loss, **completeness** of accruals.

4 Non-current assets

 The key assertions for non-current assets are existence, valuation, completeness and rights and obligations.

Sources of evidence:

- Non-current asset register
- Purchase invoices
- Bank statements
- Physical assets
- Depreciation policy and rates
- Ownership documents including title deeds and registration documents
- Capital expenditure budgets / capital replacement plans

Non-current assets must exist, be completely recorded, be valued appropriately and must be owned or controlled by the entity.

The auditor needs to obtain sufficient appropriate evidence over:

- Existing assets i.e. assets purchased in previous periods
- Additions
- Disposals
- Revaluations
- Depreciation
- Related disclosures (the property, plant and equipment note, depreciation policies, useful economic lives, revaluations).

Test your understanding 2 – Non-current assets

Murray Co

Non-current assets: Property, plant and equipment note

	Land & buildings	Fixtures, fittings & equipment	Motor vehicles	Total
	$000	$000	$000	$000
Cost at 1 January 20X4	3,000	2,525	375	5,900
Additions	–	1,050	75	1,125
Disposals	–	(300)	–	(300)
Cost at 31 December 20X4	3,000	3,275	450	6,725
Accumulated depreciation at 1 January 20X4	386	489	125	1,000
Charge for the year	97	338	56	499
Disposals	–	(116)	–	(124)
Accumulated depreciation at 31 December 20X4	483	711	181	1,375
Carrying value at 31 December 20X4	2,517	2,564	269	5,350
Carrying value at 31 December 20X3	2,614	2,036	250	4,900

Required:

Describe the substantive procedures the auditor should perform to confirm the non-current assets included in Murray Co's financial statements.

Illustration 2 – Depreciation proof-in-total

The depreciation charge for fixtures and fittings for the year-ending 31 December 20X4 included in the draft financial statements of Murray Co is $338,000 (to the nearest $000).

Murray Co's depreciation policy is to depreciate fixtures and fittings using the straight line method. The useful economic life for fixtures and fittings is ten years.

Exercise:

Create an expectation of the fixtures and fittings depreciation charge for the year-ending 31 December 20X4.

Solution

The total cost of fixtures and fittings in the draft financial statements of Murray Co is $3,275,000 (to the nearest $000).

We can set an expectation for total depreciation for fixtures and fittings for the year-ending 31 December 20X4 as $3,275,000/10 = $328,000 (to the nearest $000).

The difference of $10,000 is 3% more than our expectation. If this is within an acceptable level of variation (as determined by the judgment of the auditor) the auditor will conclude that depreciation is not materially misstated.

Intangible non-current assets

Development costs

 The key assertion for development costs is existence.

Sources of evidence:

- Breakdown of expenditure during the year
- Purchase invoices
- Bank statements
- Timesheets
- Amortisation policy and rates
- Development expenditure / project plans
- Project test / trial results
- Cash flow forecasts
- Licence agreement
- Third party valuation report e.g. for brand names and trademarks

Development costs should only be capitalised as an intangible asset if the recognition criteria of IAS 38 *Intangible Assets* have been met. The audit procedures suggested below focus on obtaining evidence that the treatment of the relevant item complies with these requirements.

Procedures include:

- Obtain a breakdown of capitalised costs, cast for mathematical accuracy and agree to the amount included in the financial statements **valuation**.

- For a sample of costs included in the breakdown, agree the amount to invoices or timesheets: **valuation**.

- Inspect board minutes for any discussions relating to the intended sale or use of the asset: **existence**.

- Discuss details of the project with the project manager or management to evaluate compliance with IAS 38 criteria: **existence**.

- Inspect project plans and other documentation to evaluate compliance with IAS 38 criteria: **existence**.

- Inspect budgets to confirm financial feasibility: **existence**.

Other intangible assets

- Inspect purchase documentation for the company name and the cost of the purchased intangible assets: **existence, rights and obligations and valuation**.

- Inspect specialist valuation report and agree to the amount included in the general ledger and the financial statements: **valuation**.

Amortisation

- Inspect the budgets/forecasts for the next few years to ascertain the period over which economic benefits are expected to be generated and compare with the amortisation policy, to assess reasonableness of the amortisation period: **valuation**.

- Recalculate the amortisation charge to verify arithmetical accuracy: **accuracy, valuation**.

- For intangibles such as licences, inspect the licence agreement to confirm the amortisation period corresponds to the licence period: **valuation**.

- Inspect the financial statement disclosure in the draft financial statements to ensure compliance with IAS 38: **presentation**.

5 Inventory

The key assertions for inventory are existence, valuation, completeness and rights and obligations.

Sources of evidence:

- Aged inventory listing
- Inventory assets
- Inventory count sheets
- Purchase invoices
- Goods received notes
- Sales invoices
- Goods despatch notes
- Client calculations of overhead allocation, absorption and apportionment

Inventory assets must exist, be completely recorded, be valued appropriately and must be owned or controlled by the entity.

When auditing inventory there are two main factors to consider

- Quantity of inventory – determined by the inventory count
- Valuation of the individual inventory items – usually assessed at the final audit

ISA 501 *Audit Evidence – specific considerations for selected items* requires the auditor to:

- Attend the physical inventory count (unless impracticable), if inventory is material to the financial statements, and
- Perform procedures on the final inventory records to determine whether they accurately reflect the count results.

Attendance at the inventory count is required to:

- Evaluate management's instructions and procedures for the inventory count.
- Observe the performance of the count.
- Inspect the inventory.
- Perform test counts.

[ISA 501, 4]

The inventory count is the responsibility of the client. The auditor does not perform the count.

Test your understanding 3 – Inventory

Murray Co's inventory count instructions are as follows:

(1)   A finance manager must supervise the inventory count.

(2)   No goods are to be received or despatched during the inventory count.

(3)   Each team will consist of two members of staff from the finance department. One person must count the items. The second person will record the count on sequentially numbered count sheets.

(4)   The teams will be allocated a team number and will be provided with a map of the warehouse. Each area of the warehouse is marked on the map with the number of the team that is to count inventory in that area. The warehouse manager will be in attendance to ensure each team is clear about which area they are counting, before it is counted.

(5)   Once a section is counted it must be tagged to confirm it has been counted. Yellow tags are to be used by the first counting team to confirm the count has been performed.

(6)   Once the first count is complete, a second count will take place, with each team counting an area that they were not responsible for on the first count (again according to the warehouse map). Any discrepancies should be notified to the finance director immediately. Green tags are to be used to confirm the count has been checked by a second team.

(7)   Sequentially numbered count sheets will contain the product description from the inventory system but no system quantities.

(8)   Any items of inventory in the warehouse that are not listed on the count sheets should be recorded on a blank, sequentially numbered count sheet.

(9)   Inventory count sheets must be recorded in ink. If a mistake is made, it should be crossed out neatly and the correct information written next to it.

(10)   Any damaged or obsolete items will be moved to a designated area. After the count, an assessment of the goods will be made by the finance manager with advice from a sales manager and the warehouse manager, to determine the allowance appropriate for the condition of the items.

(11)   After the count, the finance manager should review the warehouse to ensure all sections have been tagged with both yellow and green tags to confirm the count is complete.

(12) The count sheets must be signed by each team member responsible for completing the sheets and returned to the finance manager who will perform a sequence check to confirm all count sheets have been returned.

(13) The finance manager will compare the inventory count sheets to the inventory records and any adjustments will be updated by another finance manager not involved in the count.

Required:

(a) **Describe the procedures that should be performed by the auditor before attending the inventory count of Murray Co.**

(b) **Describe the audit procedures that should be performed whilst in attendance at the inventory count of Murray Co.**

(c) **Describe the substantive procedures that should be performed during the final audit of Murray Co.**

Continuous/perpetual inventory systems

A continuous or perpetual inventory system is one which keeps a real time track of inventory records. As a sale is made, the inventory system is updated to reflect the reduction in quantity. As purchases are received, the system is updated to reflect the increase in quantity. This enables the business to know its inventory balance at any point in time.

Over time, the inventory levels stated in the perpetual inventory system may gradually diverge from actual inventory levels, due to unrecorded transactions or theft, so periodically, a count should be performed to compare system balances to actual quantities and the system can be updated accordingly.

Where the client uses a continuous inventory system, lines of inventory are counted periodically (say monthly) throughout the year so that by the end of the year all lines have been counted.

Where the client uses this type of system the auditor should:

- Attend at least one count to ensure adequate controls are applied during the counts (in the same way as for a year-end count).

- Inspect the number and value of adjustments made as a result of the count. If significant adjustments are required after each count, this would indicate that the system figures for inventory cannot be relied upon at the year-end and a full count will be required.

- If the system balance for inventory is deemed reliable as a result of these procedures, further procedures to verify valuation and rights will still be required.

The auditor will still need to perform the audit procedures usually performed at the final audit such as:

- Inspect GRNs and GDNs around the year-end to confirm correct cut-off. Goods received before the year-end should be traced through to inclusion in the inventory listing whilst goods received after the year-end should not be included. Similarly, goods despatched before the year-end should not be included within inventory whereas goods despatched post year-end should be included in the year-end inventory balance.

- Review post year-end sales invoices to ascertain if net realisable value (NRV) is above cost or if an adjustment is required.

- Compare the inventory holding period with prior year to identify slow-moving inventory which needs to be written down to the lower of cost and net realisable value.

- Inspect purchase invoices for the name of the client to confirm rights and obligations.

Advantages and disadvantages of perpetual counts

Advantages

- Reduces time constraints for the auditor, and enables them to attend counts relating to lines at greater risk of material misstatement.

- Slow-moving and damaged inventory is identified and adjusted for in the client's records on a continuous basis meaning the year-end valuation should be more accurate.

Disadvantages

- The auditor will need to obtain sufficient appropriate evidence that the system operates effectively at all times, not just at the time of the count.

- Additional procedures will be necessary to ensure that the amount included for inventory in the financial statements is appropriate, particularly with regard to cut-off and year-end allowances.

Inventory held by third parties

Some companies will not have space to store all of their inventory and may use a third party storage facility. The inventory held at the third party still needs to be counted and included in the client's inventory records. The auditor will need to obtain sufficient appropriate audit evidence that the inventory actually exists and belongs to the client.

Procedures include:

- Where a third party holds inventory on behalf of the client, obtain external confirmation from the third party of the quantity and condition of the goods to confirm **rights and valuation**.

- If the goods held by the third party are material the auditor should attend the inventory count to verify **existence** of the inventory.

- The auditor can also obtain a report from the third party's auditors confirming the reliability of the internal controls at the third party.

Standard costs

Standard costs are often used by manufacturing companies where it would be too time-consuming to collect actual cost information for each individual unit produced. The company establishes an expected cost of producing one item based on a normal level of activity. This is used to value the inventory.

Any difference between actual cost and standard cost is taken to a variance account in the statement of profit or loss. A large variance on the variance account would indicate that the standard costs are not a close approximation of the actual costs and therefore the inventory valuation will not be reliable.

Standard costs are more likely to be reliable if they are updated on a regular basis. How frequently the standard costs should be updated will depend on how often the cost of components used in the manufacturing process increases.

Audit procedures must be performed to assess the reasonableness of the standard costs as a means of valuing inventory, including:

- Obtain the breakdown of the standard cost calculation and agree a sample of costs to invoices.

- Enquire of management the basis for the standard costs and how often they are updated to reflect current costs.

- Inspect the variance account and assess the level of variance for reasonableness. Discuss with management any significant variances arising.

Inventory count: cut-off procedures

The inventory count(s) will be affected by goods despatched and goods received.

During the count, inventory movements should preferably stop to enable the count to be conducted without being affected by deliveries.

For some organisations this won't be possible as they may operate production and deliveries 24 hours a day.

In these types of organisations the client should move the items requiring despatch to a different location to that being counted prior to the count taking place. Any deliveries of goods should be made to a different location while the count is ongoing to enable the count to be conducted without movement of items.

A separate count can then be performed on the items delivered during the count and these can be added to the warehouse items counted.

By having such controls in place, the completeness and existence of inventory at the count date can be verified as well as the cut-off assertion for purchases and sales.

6 Receivables

The focus of testing for receivables is valuation and existence.

Sources of evidence:

- Aged receivables listing

- Sales invoices

- Goods despatch notes

- Receivables circularisation letters

- Post year end bank statements

- Policy for allowance for doubtful receivables

The receivables balance included in the financial statements must exist and be included at the appropriate amount.

Receivables will be overstated if irrecoverable receivables have not been written off or doubtful receivables have not been written down. Audit procedures will therefore obtain evidence regarding the recoverability of amounts outstanding at the year end.

Third party evidence will be obtained in the form of a receivables circularisation letter which will confirm existence of amounts outstanding at the year end.

Receivables circularisations

The auditor will send a circularisation letter to a sample of customers asking them to confirm the balance owed to the client at the year end. This is considered to be a reliable source of evidence because it is documentary evidence sent directly to the auditor from an external source. Circularisation letters can be positive or negative.

A positive receivables circularisation requires customers to respond to the auditor's request for information. The auditor can include the balance per the client's ledger and ask the customer to reply stating whether or not the balance is correct. Alternatively the auditor can ask the customer to respond by stating the balance they believe they owe the client but the auditor does not provide the balance per the client's ledger to the customer.

A **negative receivables circularisation** requests customers to respond only if they disagree with the balance provided by the auditor. This is only suitable if the risk of material misstatement is low as the customer may confirm an incorrect balance if it is in their favour.

Steps in undertaking a positive receivables circularisation

- Obtain consent from the client to perform the circularisation.

- Obtain a list of trade receivables at the year end, cast this and agree it to the receivables ledger control account total.

- Select a sample from the receivables list ensuring that a number of nil, old, credit and large balances are selected.

- Circularisation letters should be prepared on the client's letterhead paper, requesting a confirmation of the year-end receivables balance, and for replies to be sent directly to the auditor's office using a pre-paid envelope.

- An appropriate member of client staff, such as the finance director, should be requested to sign all the letters prior to them being sent out by a member of the audit team.

- Where no response is received, follow this up with another letter or a phone call and where necessary alternative procedures should be performed such as after date cash testing and inspection of sales invoices and GDNs relating to the receivable.

- When replies are received, they should be reconciled to the client's receivables records, and any differences such as cash or goods in transit should be investigated further.

ISA 505 External Confirmations

ISA 505 External Confirmations requires the auditor to maintain control over external confirmation requests when using external confirmations as a source of audit evidence.

This can be achieved by the auditor:

- Preparing the confirmation letters and determining the information to be requested and the information that should be included in the request.

- Selecting the sample of external parties from which to obtain confirmation.

- Sending the requests to the confirming party.

[ISA 505, 7]

Illustration 3 – Murray Co positive confirmation letter

Customer Co

Customer's address

7 January 20X5

Dear Sirs

As part of their normal audit procedures we have been requested by our auditors, Wimble & Co, to ask you to confirm the balance on your account with us at 31 December 20X4, our year-end.

The balance on your account, as shown by our records, is shown below. After comparing this with your records will you please be kind enough to sign the confirmation and return a copy to the auditor in the prepaid envelope enclosed. If the balance is not in agreement with your records, will you please note the items making up the difference in the space provided.

Please note that this request is made for audit purposes only and has no further significance.

Your kind co-operation in this matter will be greatly appreciated.

Yours faithfully

Chief Accountant

Murray Co

Wimble & Co address

> Dear Sirs
>
> We confirm that, except as noted below *, a balance of $XX was owing by us to Murray & Co at 31 December 20X4.
>
> (space for customer's signature)
>
> * Details of differences
>
> ---
>
> *"7 January 20X5":* The confirmation letter should be **sent as soon as possible after the year-end,** to increase the chance of an accurate and timely response.
>
> *"As part of their normal audit procedures, we have been requested by our auditors to confirm the balance on your account with us at 31 December 20X4... please be kind enough to sign the confirmation and return a copy to the auditor...":* It is the **client** who **writes to their customers** requesting the information but the **response** must be sent directly to the auditors to reduce the risk of the client interfering with any response.
>
> *"...in the prepaid envelope enclosed":* Making it as easy as possible to respond increases the chance that sufficient customers will confirm balances for it to be a valid audit test.
>
> *"If the balance is not in agreement with your records, will you please note the items making up the difference in the space provided":* Requesting the customer to complete the reconciliation increases the reliance the auditor can place on this evidence (although the auditor will review the reconciliation and investigate any unreconciled differences or disagreements).

Test your understanding 4 – Receivables

Murray Co

Aged receivables analysis at 31 December 20X4 ($000)

Ref	Customer Name	Total	Current	30–60 days	60–90 days	90–120 days	120 days
A001	Anfield United Shop	176	95	76	5	0	0
B001	Bibs and Balls	0	0	(24)	0	24	0
B002	The Beautiful Game	84	62	0	20	0	2
B003	Beckham's	42	32	10	0	0	0
C001	Cheryl & Coleen Co	12	12	0	0	0	0
D001	Dream Team	45	0	31	14	0	0
E001	Escot Supermarket	235	97	65	0	0	73
G001	Golf is Us	211	0	0	0	100	111
G002	Green Green Grass	61	50	11	0	0	0
H001	HHA Sports	59	40	0	19	0	0
J001	Jilberts	21	11	10	0	0	0
J002	James Smit Partnership	256	73	102	34	45	2
J003	Jockeys	419	278	120	21	0	0
O001	The Oval	92	48	44	0	0	0
P001	Pole Vaulters	76	0	0	76	0	0
P002	Polo Polo	0	0	0	0	0	0
S001	Stayrose Supermarket	97	24	23	23	27	0
T001	Trainers and More	93	73	20	0	0	0
T002	Tike Co	(54)	0	0	0	0	(54)
W001	Wanderers	89	60	29	0	0	0
W002	Whistlers	(9)	645	(654)	0	0	0
W003	Walk Hike Run	4	0	0	0	0	4
W004	Winners	31	21	10	0	0	0
Total		**2,040**	**1,621**	**(127)**	**212**	**196**	**138**

Required:

(a)   Identify, with reasons, four trade receivables balances from the aged receivables analysis that should be selected for further testing.

(b)   Describe substantive procedures that should be performed to confirm the receivables balance of Murray Co.

Prepayments

Prepayments are services or goods which a company has paid for in advance. Therefore the client should include the value of any prepayments as a receivable in the financial statements.

- Inspect bank statements to ensure payment has been made before the year-end: **existence**.

- Inspect invoices to ensure payment relates to goods or services not yet received: **existence**.

- Recalculate the amount prepaid to confirm mathematical accuracy: **valuation**.

- Compare prepayments with the prior year to identify any missing items or any new prepayments which require further testing: **existence, valuation, and completeness. (Analytical procedure)**.

7   Payables and accruals

The focus of testing for liabilities is completeness.

Sources of evidence:

- Aged payables listing

- Purchase invoices

- Goods received notes

- Post year end bank statements

- Supplier statements

- Supplier circularisations (where supplier statements are not available)

The payables balance included in the financial statements must be complete.

Payables will be understated if all liabilities in relation to purchases made have not been recorded.

Third party evidence will be obtained in the form of supplier statements and supplier circularisation letters.

Trade payables

Procedures include:

- Obtain a list of trade payables, cast to verify arithmetical accuracy and agree to the general ledger and the financial statements: verifies **completeness, classification, presentation**.

- Reconcile the total of the individual payables accounts with the control account: verifies **completeness**.

- Obtain supplier statements and reconcile these to the payables balances. Investigate any reconciling items: **existence, completeness, obligations and valuation. Note:** Supplier statement reconciliations provide the most reliable evidence in respect of payables as they provide external confirmation of the balance.

- Inspect after date payments, if they relate to the current year then follow through to the payables ledger or accrual listing: **completeness**.

- Inspect invoices received after the year-end in respect of goods delivered before the year-end and trace through to the accruals listing: **completeness**.

- Enquire of management their process for identifying goods received but not invoiced and ensure that it is reasonable: **completeness**.

- Select a sample of goods received notes immediately before the year-end and follow through to inclusion in the year-end payables balance: **completeness of payables** and **cut-off of purchases**.

- Select a sample of payable balances and perform a trade payables' circularisation, follow up any non-replies and any reconciling items between the balance confirmed and the ledger balance: **completeness and existence**.

- Insect the trade payables ledger for any debit balances, for any significant amounts discuss with management and consider reclassification as current assets: **valuation** of payables and **completeness of receivables, classification**.

- Compare the list of trade payables and accruals against the prior year list to identify any significant omissions: **completeness. (Analytical procedure)**

- Calculate the trade payables payment period and compare to prior year, investigate any significant differences: **completeness** and valuation. **(Analytical procedure)**

Accruals

Procedures include:

- Obtain the list of accruals from the client, cast it to confirm mathematical accuracy and agree to the general ledger and the financial statements: **completeness, classification**.

- Recalculate a sample of accrued costs by reference to contracts and payment schedules (e.g. loan interest): **valuation (accuracy** of purchases and other expenses).

- Inspect invoices received post year-end to confirm the actual amount and assess whether the accrual is reasonable: **valuation**.

- Compare the accruals this year to last year to identify any missing items or unusual fluctuation in amount and discuss this with management: **completeness and valuation. (Analytical procedure)**

Test your understanding 5 – Payables

Murray Co's trade payables balance at 31 December 20X4 is $1,400,000 (to the nearest $000). The total balance has already been agreed to the payables ledger which shows that trade payables consists of fifteen suppliers.

A junior member of the audit team, Rob Cash, has been testing five of these balances by reconciling supplier statements to the balances on the payables ledger. He is unable to reconcile a material balance, relating to Racket Co, who supply Vectran material to Murray Co, for stringing tennis rackets. He has asked for your assistance on the audit work which should be carried out on the differences.

The balance of Racket Co on Murray Co's purchase ledger is shown below:

Payables ledger Supplier: Racket Co

Date	Type	Reference	Status	Dr ($)	Cr ($)	Balance ($)
10.10	Invoice	6004	Paid 1		21,300	
18.10	Invoice	6042	Paid 1		15,250	
23.10	Invoice	6057	Paid 1		26,340	
04.11	Invoice	6080	Paid 2		35,720	
15.11	Invoice	6107	Paid 2		16,320	
26.11	Invoice	6154	Paid 2		9,240	
30.11	Payment	Cheque	Alloc 1	61,630		
	Discount		Alloc 1	1,260		
14.12	Invoice	6285			21,560	
21.12	Invoice	6328			38,240	
31.12	Payment	Cheque	Alloc 2	60,050		
	Discount		Alloc 2	1,230		
31.12	**Balance**					**59,800**

Racket Co have sent the following supplier statement:

Date	Type	Reference	Status	Dr ($)	Cr ($)	Balance ($)
07.10	Invoice	6004		21,300		
16.10	Invoice	6042		15,250		
22.10	Invoice	6057		26,340		
02.11	Invoice	6080		37,520		
13.11	Invoice	6107		16,320		
22.11	Invoice	6154		9,240		
10.12	Receipt	Cheque			61,630	
04.12	Invoice	6210		47,350		
12.12	Invoice	6285		21,560		
18.12	Invoice	6328		38,240		
28.12	Invoice	6355		62,980		
31.12	**Balance**					**234,470**

Racket Co's terms of trade with Murray Co allow a 2% cash discount on invoices where Racket Co receives a cheque from the customer by the end of the month following the date of the invoice (i.e. a 2% discount will be given on November invoices paid by 31 December).

On Murray Co's payables ledger, under 'Status' the cash and discount marked 'Alloc 1' pay invoices marked 'Paid 1' (similarly for 'Alloc 2' and 'Paid 2').

Murray Co's goods received department checks the goods when they arrive and issues a goods received note (GRN). A copy of the GRN and the supplier's advice note is sent to the purchases accounting department.

Required:

(a) **Prepare a statement reconciling the balance on Murray Co's payables ledger to the balance on Racket Co's supplier's statement.**

(b) **Describe the audit work you will carry out on each of the reconciling items you have determined in your answer to part (a) above, in order to determine the balance which should be included in the financial statements.**

8 Provisions and contingencies

 IAS 37 *Provisions, Contingent Liabilities and Contingent Assets* requires an entity to recognise a provision if: a present obligation has arisen as a result of a past event; payment is probable ('more likely than not'); and the amount can be estimated reliably.

If payment is only possible, a contingent liability must be disclosed in the notes to the financial statements.

A contingent asset can only be recognised if it is virtually certain to be received. If it is probable that an inflow of economic benefits will result, a disclosure should be made in the financial statements. If it is only possible, it should be ignored.

Provisions and contingent liabilities

Audit testing will focus on whether an obligation exists, whether payment is probable or possible, and whether the provision is valued appropriately.

Completeness is a key assertion as the company may understate liabilities to improve their financial position.

Contingent assets

Audit testing will focus on whether payment is virtually certain or probable, and whether the receivable is valued appropriately.

Existence is a key assertion as the company may overstate contingent assets to improve their financial position.

Examples of contingent assets include:

- Amounts due to be received from an insurance claim

- Amounts due to be received in respect of a legal claim

- Amounts due to be received from a liquidator in respect of an investment or bankrupt receivable

Provisions and contingent liabilities

Procedures include:

- Obtain a breakdown of the provisions, cast it and agree the figure to the financial statements: **accuracy** and **presentation**.

- Enquire with the directors or inspect relevant supporting documentation to confirm that a present obligation exists at the year-end: **rights and obligations**.

- Inspect relevant board minutes to ascertain whether payment is probable: **existence**.

- Recalculate the liability and agree components of the calculation to supporting documentation: **completeness**.

- Inspect post year-end bank statements to identify whether any payments have been made, compare actual payments to the amounts provided to assess whether the provision is reasonable: **valuation**.

- Inspect the financial statement disclosure of the provisions and contingent liabilities to ensure compliance with IAS 37: **presentation**.

- Obtain a written representation from management that they believe the provisions and contingent liabilities are treated appropriately in the financial statements, are valued appropriately and are complete: **valuation** and **completeness**.

Illustration 4 – Murray Co provisions

The statement of financial position shows that Murray Co has $240,000 provisions for the year ended 31 December 20X4. The majority of the balance relates to provisions for warranties ($200,000). $40,000 of the provision relates to a claim made by an ex-employee of Murray Co who is claiming for unfair dismissal.

The audit plan includes the following audit procedures in relation to these provisions:

Warranty provision procedures

- Obtain a breakdown of the warranty provision and recalculate to verify arithmetical accuracy.

- Enquire of management the basis used for the provision and assess whether this is reasonable.

- Compare previous year actual warranty costs with the amount provided for to assess whether management's process is reasonable.

- Compare warranty claims post year-end to the warranty provision at the year-end to assess whether the provision is adequate.

- Review product returns and complaints to assess whether there is a need for a higher provision than in previous years.

- Calculate warranty costs/revenue and compare with prior year to assess whether the level of provision is consistent with the prior year. Discuss any change in proportion with management.

Legal provision procedures

- Enquire with the directors when the employee was dismissed to confirm that a present obligation exists at the year-end.

- Inspect correspondence between the employee and Murray to verify that the employee was dismissed before the year-end.

- Inspect relevant board minutes to ascertain whether it is probable that the payment will be made to the employee.

- Obtain confirmation from Murray's lawyer about the likely outcome and probability of payment.

- Inspect correspondence received from the lawyer regarding the legal provision to assess whether a provision should be recognised and if so, whether the amount of the provision is adequate.

- Obtain a breakdown of the costs to be provided for and recalculate to ensure completeness.

- Agree the components of the calculation to supporting documentation, e.g. fee estimate from Murray Co's lawyer, claim received from the ex-employee.

- Inspect post year-end bank statements to identify whether any payments have been made and compare actual payments to the amounts provided to assess whether the provision is reasonable.

Procedures relevant to both provisions

- Obtain a written representation from management to confirm the adequacy and reasonableness of the provisions.

- Inspect the financial statement disclosure to ensure compliance with IAS 37 *Provisions, Contingent Liabilities and Contingent Assets*.

Contingent assets

Procedures include:

- Review correspondence from third parties (lawyer, insurance company, insolvency practitioner) regarding the value likely to be received and probability of payment. Agree the figure into the disclosure note relating to the contingent asset: **existence, accuracy & valuation and presentation**.

- Review correspondence from third parties (court, insurance company, insolvency practitioner) confirming the amount awarded to the client. Agree the figure to other receivables and other income within the financial statements: **accuracy & valuation, existence, rights & obligations, and presentation**.

- Review post year end bank statements and cash book to confirm the amount received: **accuracy & valuation, existence, rights & obligations, and presentation**.

ISA 501 Audit Evidence – special considerations for selected items

ISA 501 requires the auditor to design and perform audit procedures in order to identify litigation and claims involving the entity which may give rise to a risk of material misstatement. Procedures include enquiring of management, reviewing meeting minutes and reviewing legal expense accounts. [ISA 501, 9]

9 Accounting estimates

 There are many accounting estimates in the financial statements, e.g. allowances for receivables, depreciation of property, plant and equipment, provisions, etc.

Accounting estimates are inherently risky because they relate to the future and therefore documentary evidence may be limited. This makes it difficult for the auditor to obtain sufficient appropriate evidence regarding the balance.

Inherent risk is increased because management judgement is needed to determine accounting estimates. As a result, estimates may be used to manipulate the financial statements and show a desired result.

Professional scepticism is essential for the auditor to ensure the accounting estimates are reasonable and are not being used to introduce bias into the financial statements.

ISA 540 *Auditing Accounting Estimates, Including Fair Value Accounting Estimates and Related Disclosures* requires the auditor to:

- Obtain an understanding of how management identifies those transactions, events and conditions that give rise to the need for an estimate. [8b]

For each estimate in the financial statements, the auditor must also:

- Enquire of management how the accounting estimate is made and the data on which it is based. [8b]

- Review the outcome of accounting estimates included in the prior period financial statements. [9]

- Determine whether events up to the date of the auditor's report provide additional evidence with regard to the appropriateness of estimates. [13a]

- Test how management made the estimate and evaluate whether the method is appropriate. [13b]

- Test the effectiveness of controls over estimations. [13c]

- Develop a point estimate to use in comparison to managements'. [3d]

- If there are significant risks associated with estimates the auditor should also enquire whether management considered any alternative assumptions and why they rejected them and whether the assumptions used are reasonable in the circumstances. [15]

- Obtain written representations from management confirming that they believe the assumptions used in making estimates are reasonable. [22]

10 Share capital, reserves and director's remuneration

 Each of these areas are material by nature.

Share capital

 Sources of evidence:

- Share register
- Share certificates
- Bank statements and cash book
- Board minutes
- Registrar of companies (e.g. Companies House)

Procedures include:

- Agree authorised share capital and nominal value disclosures to underlying shareholding agreements/statutory constitution documents.
- Inspect cash book for evidence of cash receipts from share issues and ensure amounts not yet received are correctly disclosed as share capital called-up not paid in the financial statements.
- Inspect board minutes to verify the amount of share capital issued during the year.

Dividends

 Sources of evidence:

- Board minutes
- Bank statements and cash book
- Dividend warrant

Procedures include:

- Inspect board minutes to agree dividends declared before the year-end.
- Inspect bank statements to agree dividends paid before the year-end.
- Inspect dividend warrants to agree dividend payment.

Directors' emoluments

 Sources of evidence:

- Directors' service contracts
- Board minutes
- Bank statements and cash book
- Payroll records
- Written representation from management

Procedures include:

- Obtain and cast a schedule of directors' remuneration split between wages, bonuses, benefits, pension contributions and other remuneration, and agree to the financial statement disclosures.

- Inspect payroll records and agree the figures disclosed for wages, bonuses, and pension contributions.

- Inspect bank statements to verify the amounts actually paid to directors.

- Inspect board minutes for discussion and approval of directors' bonus announcements or other additional remuneration.

- Obtain a written representation from directors that they have disclosed all directors' remuneration to the auditor.

Reserves

- Agree opening reserves to prior year closing reserves and reconcile movements.

- Agree movements in reserves to supporting documentation (e.g. revaluation reserve movements to the independent valuer's report).

11 Statement of profit or loss

 The majority of transactions and events in the statement of profit or loss are audited indirectly through the direct tests performed on the corresponding debits or credits in the statement of financial position (directional testing). However, the auditor will normally perform **substantive analytical** procedures on these areas and some specific additional procedures.

Payroll

 The focus of testing for payroll is completeness, accuracy and occurrence.

Sources of evidence:

- Payroll control account
- Payroll payment listing
- Payslips
- Contracts of employment
- Hourly rates of pay
- Timesheets
- Bank statements and cash book
- Starters and leavers forms

Payroll will be understated if all employees who should have been paid have not been paid.

Payroll will be overstated if fictitious employees, or employees who no longer work for the entity, are paid.

Payroll will be misstated if errors are made in the payroll calculations.

Procedures include:

- Agree the total wages and salaries expense per the payroll control account to the general ledger and the financial statements: **completeness and presentation**.

- Cast the monthly payroll listings to verify the accuracy of the payroll expense: **accuracy**.

- Recalculate the gross and net pay for a sample of employees and agree to the payroll records: **accuracy**.

- Recalculate statutory deductions to confirm whether correct deductions for this year have been included within the payroll expense: **accuracy**.

- Select a sample of joiners and leavers, agree their start/leaving date to supporting documentation, recalculate that their first/last pay packet was accurately calculated and recorded: **completeness, occurrence, accuracy**.

- For salaries, agree the total net pay per the payroll records to the bank transfer listing of payments and to the cashbook: **occurrence**.

- For cash wages, agree that the total cash withdrawn for wage payments equates to the weekly wages paid plus any surplus cash subsequently banked: **completeness, occurrence**.

- Agree the year-end tax liability to the payroll records and subsequent payment to the post year-end cash book: **occurrence**.

- For a sample of individuals, agree the amount per the payroll listing to the personnel records, and timesheets if applicable: **accuracy**.

Analytical procedures

- Perform a proof in total of total wages and salaries incorporating joiners and leavers and the pay increase. Compare this to the actual wages and salaries in the financial statements and investigate any significant differences: **completeness, accuracy**.

- Compare the payroll figure for this year to last year to identify any unusual fluctuations and discuss them with management: **completeness, accuracy**.

Illustration 5 – Murray Co payroll proof in total

Total payroll for the year-ending 31 December 20X3 was $1,220,000 (to the nearest $000). At this time Murray Co had 34 employees.

Total payroll for the year-ending 31 December 20X4 is $1,312,000 (to the nearest $000). Murray Co now has 37 employees.

All employees received a 5% pay rise on 31 March 20X4.

Exercise:

Create an expectation of the total payroll cost for year-ending 31 December 20X4.

Solution

The average salary per employee in 20X3 was $35,882 ($1,220,000/34).

We know that all employees received a pay rise of 5% in March. The average value of this pay rise is therefore $1,346 per employee in 20X4 (5% × 9/12 × $35,882).

The average salary for 20X4 should therefore equal $37,228 ($35,882 + $1,346).

We can set an **expectation for total payroll for the year-ending 31 December 20X4** as 37 × $37,228: **$1,377,000** (to the nearest $000).

The **difference** ($65,000) is **less than 5%** more than our expectation. If this is within an acceptable level of variation (as determined by the judgment of the auditor) the auditor will conclude that the payroll cost is not materially misstated.

Revenue

The focus of testing for revenue is completeness, cut-off, occurrence and accuracy.

Sources of evidence:

- Revenue control account
- Sales day book
- Sales invoices
- Customer contracts
- Goods despatch notes
- Sales orders

Revenue will be understated if all sales transactions are not recorded.

Revenue will be overstated if fictitious sales, or sales which have been returned, are recorded.

Revenue will be misstated if errors are made in the sales invoice calculations.

Procedures include:

- Inspect a sample of GDNs before and after the year-end and ensure they have been recorded in the sales day book in the correct period: **cut-off.** In most cases, the despatch of goods indicates that the seller has fulfilled its performance obligations and therefore the sale can be recorded.

- Recalculate discounts and sales tax applied for a sample of large sales invoices: **accuracy.**

- Select a sample of customer orders and agree these to the despatch notes and sales invoices through to inclusion in the sales day book: **completeness**.

- Inspect credit notes issued after the year-end, trace to GDN and invoice and ensure the sale has been reversed: **occurrence.**

Analytical procedures

- Compare revenue against prior year and investigate any significant fluctuations: **cut-off, occurrence, accuracy and completeness.**

- Compare revenue with budget/forecast and investigate any significant fluctuations: **cut-off, occurrence, accuracy and completeness.**

- Calculate the gross profit margin and compare to prior year. Investigate any significant differences: **cut-off, occurrence, accuracy and completeness.**

Purchases and other expenses

 The focus of testing for purchases is completeness, cut-off, occurrence, accuracy and classification.

Sources of evidence:

- Purchase control account

- Purchase day book

- Purchase invoices

- Supplier contracts

- Goods received notes

- Purchase orders

Purchases will be understated if all purchase transactions are not recorded, including around the year-end.

Purchases will be overstated if goods purchased through the business for personal use are recorded, or purchases which have been returned, are recorded.

Purchases will be misstated if errors are made when recording purchase invoices or if purchases have been misclassified.

Procedures include:

- Inspect GRNs before and after the year-end and ensure they have been recorded in the purchase day book in the correct period: **cut-off**.
  In most cases, the company takes ownership for goods when they are received and therefore the purchase expense (and corresponding liability) should be recorded.

- Recalculate discounts and sales tax applied for a sample of purchase invoices: **accuracy**.

- Select a sample of purchase orders and agree these to the GRNs and purchase invoices through to inclusion in the purchases day book: **completeness**.

- Inspect purchase invoices for a sample of purchases/expenses in the ledger for the amount, name of the client and description of the goods: **accuracy, occurrence and classification**.

Analytical procedures

- Compare expenses for each category year on year and investigate any significant fluctuations: **cut-off, accuracy, completeness, classification and occurrence.**

- Compare expenses against budget and investigate any significant fluctuations: **cut-off, accuracy, completeness, classification and occurrence.**

- Calculate gross profit margin and compare with prior year to identify any possible misstatement of purchases. Discuss any significant movement with management: **cut-off, accuracy, completeness, and occurrence.**

- Calculate operating profit margin and compare with prior year. Investigate any significant fluctuations: **cut-off, accuracy, completeness, classification and occurrence.**

12 Audits of smaller entities

The characteristics of smaller entities can lead to both advantages and disadvantages:

- **Lower risk** – Smaller entities may be engaged in relatively simple activities which reduces risk.

- **Direct control by owner managers** – Can be a strength because they know what is going on and have the ability to exercise real control. However, they are also in a strong position to manipulate the figures or put personal transactions through the business.

- **Simpler systems** – Smaller entities are less likely to have sophisticated IT systems, but pure, manual systems are becoming increasingly rare. This is good news in that many of the bookkeeping errors associated with smaller entities may now be less prevalent. However, a system is only as good as the person operating it.

Evidence implications

- The normal rules concerning the relationship between risk and the quality and quantity of evidence apply, irrespective of the size of the entity.

- The quantity of evidence may be less than for a larger organisation due to fewer transactions occurring.

- It may be more efficient to carry out a full substantive audit in a smaller organisation.

Problems

- **Management override** – Smaller entities will have a key director or manager who will have significant power and authority. This could mean controls are lacking in the first place or they are easy to override.

- **No segregation of duties** – Smaller entities tend to have a limited number of accounts clerks who process information. To overcome this, the directors should authorise and review all work performed.

- **Less formal approach** – Smaller entities tend to have simple systems and fewer controls due to reliance on trust and lack of complexity. Therefore, less reliance can be placed on internal controls.

13 Audits of Not-For-Profit Organisations

Not-for-profit (NFP) organisations include charities and public sector entities. Below are some important features of a NFP.

- Profit maximisation is not their main objective. Objectives will be either social or philanthropic.

- There are no shareholders.

- They will not distribute dividends.

Financial statements

NFP organisations, such as charities which are not established as charitable companies, will need to prepare:

- A **statement of financial activities** showing income and expenditure similar to a statement of profit or loss. As the organisation does not exist to make a profit, any additional income over expenditure is known as a surplus and any expenditure in excess of income is a deficit.

- A **balance sheet** showing assets and liabilities, the same as a statement of financial position.

- A **cash flow statement**.

- **Notes to the financial statements**.

Audit risks

Control risk

Some NFP entities, particularly small charities, may have less effective internal control systems due to:

- being controlled by trustees who usually only work on a part-time basis, and are volunteers. They may not devote sufficient time to adequately oversee the strategic direction of the organisation.

- a lack of segregation of duties, as the organisation may not employ many staff in order to keep overheads down.

- the use of volunteers, who are likely to be unqualified and have little awareness of the importance of controls.

- the use of less formalised systems and controls.

Income

With many charities, much of the income received is by way of donation. Some of these transactions will not be accompanied by invoices, orders or despatch notes. For cash donations in particular there is a greater risk of theft.

NFPs may apply for grant income which will only be provided if certain criteria are met, otherwise the money may have to be repaid. There is a risk that grant income may have to be repaid if the organisation does not use the money for its intended purpose.

Restricted funds

Some donations are given with clauses stating the money must be used for a particular purpose. For example, money may be donated to a hospital to purchase a specific piece of equipment, or to be used by a specific department. These restricted funds must be shown separately in the balance sheet and the auditor must review donations to ensure that restricted funds are shown as such.

Going concern

Assessing the going concern status of a NFP entity may also be more difficult, particularly for charities who are reliant on voluntary donations. Many issues, such as economic factors, could impact on their ability to generate income in the short-term. Trends can also have an effect. For example, charities raising money for medical research such as cancer and heart disease are seeing higher numbers of donations, whereas charities such as animal protection are seeing a decline in income.

Complexity of regulations

NFPs may have complex internal and external regulations governing their activities, reporting requirements and taxation system. This means the audit team will need to have knowledge of these regulations, and experience of auditing this type of specialised entity, in order to be able to perform the audit with sufficient competence and due care.

Audit testing

Sufficient appropriate evidence will still need to be obtained through either a mixture of tests of controls and substantive procedures, or substantive procedures only if the controls are ineffective or not in place.

Procedures will still involve enquiries, inspection, analytical procedures, etc.

Other planning activities

In addition to the specific audit risks that need to be considered at the risk assessment stage, the same planning activities are required as for the audit of a company. Differences that will require consideration are:

- The materiality assessment may be lower to compensate for the higher risk, therefore more testing may be required.

- The choice of audit team should include staff with experience of this type of entity and knowledge of the regulations and financial reporting requirements.

Reporting

If sufficient appropriate evidence is not obtained with respect to the above matters, as well as the usual risks of material misstatement faced by any organisation, the auditor will have to modify the audit opinion.

Other reporting responsibilities

Quite often, the scope of the external audit of a NFP is much larger than that for a company.

In addition to the financial statement audit, the following may also be required:

- Value for money audit – assessing whether the organisation is getting the most from the money spent. These are discussed in more detail in the chapter 'Internal audit'.

- Regularity audit – ensuring the expenditure of the organisation is in accordance with the regulations/legislation governing it.

- Audit of performance indicators – auditing the targets of the organisation that have to be reported to stakeholders such as waiting times in an A&E department.

Illustration 6 – Not-for-profit organisation

The Thames Pool Trust (TPT) is a not-for-profit organisation. TPT owns a large area of park space. Within the park is an open-air pool which locals can pay to use. TPT does not employ any staff directly. Day-to-day operations are run by a local organisation, EmCA, under a management agreement, and TPT receives a share of EmCA's operating surplus.

To raise funds to pursue its charitable objective, TPT stages six summer picnic concerts each year. Each event has an audience capacity of 1,200 with a ticket price of $40, and is entirely staffed by volunteers.

Income and expenditure account

	Notes	20X8	20X7
Income:		$000	$000
Share of operating surplus from EmCA	1	49	38
Summer concerts	2	268	275
Total income		317	313
Expenditure:			
Operation of pool	3	(27)	(57)
Summer concerts	4	(242)	(203)
Surplus for year		48	53

Statement of financial position

	Notes	20X8	20X7
		$000	$000
Non-current assets	5	38	55
Current assets:			
Amount due from EmCA		89	102
Cash at bank		877	805
		966	907

Total assets		1,004	962
		———	———
Funds		1,000	952
Non-current liabilities		4	10
		———	———
		1,004	962
		———	———

Notes:

1 Under the management agreement, EmCA submits monthly reports of pool attendance and pool fees received, as well as expense reports. A monthly statement shows TPT's share of EmCA's operating surplus.

2 Income includes ticket sales and the sale of food and drink.

3 Included within pool operation costs are audit fees of $4,000 (20X7: $4,000) and depreciation of $17,000 (20X7: $36,000). The remainder of the costs relate to sundry support costs.

4 Summer concert expenditure includes fees to the bands and the cost of food and drink.

5 The non-current assets note indicates that depreciation expense is the only movement during the year and that the majority of assets are already fully depreciated.

Audit strategy

Audit risk assessment

The greatest risks of material misstatement are:

- Understatement (completeness) of concert income – decreased by $7,000 (2.5%).

- Overstatement of concert expenses – increased by $39,000 (19.2%).

There may be detection risk if adequate accounting records are not maintained for all income and expenditure. For example, if bands are paid cash in hand on the day of the concert there may not be any audit trail for this expense.

Control implications

Controls should be in place to ensure the completeness of income, for example:

- Pre-numbered tickets for each concert

- Recording issues of concert tickets for sale

- Requiring the return of unsold concert tickets

- Reconciling ticket income against the number of tickets sold

- Only allowing admission by ticket. Tickets should be checked at the gate and once scanned/checked, cannot be used again to gain entry. If ticket sales were allowed on the gate, volunteers may pocket the cash.

- Purchase of items within the concert such as food and drink must be by credit or debit card. No cash should be accepted, to reduce the risk of theft by the volunteers.

- Reconciling pool income recorded to the number of visitors on a daily basis.

- Reconciling pool income recorded to the cash/credit card receipts on a daily basis.

Audit plan

Due to the audit risks identified, the audit approach will be substantive.

Share of operating surplus from EmCA and amounts due from EmCA

- Obtain a breakdown by month of the operating surplus from EmCA, cast and agree to the financial statements.

- Agree the monthly surplus amounts to the breakdown to confirm accuracy.

- Using the monthly reports of pool attendance and fees, calculate the expected income for the pool and compare to the amount included in the financial statements.

- Obtain direct confirmation from EmCA of the amount due.

- Agree after-date cash receipts to the amounts due at the year end.

Income from and expenditure on the summer concerts

- Obtain ticket sale data and multiply by the ticket price to confirm the amount of income recorded.

- Compare income for the current year to the prior year and investigate any significant differences e.g. enquire with management why concert income is 2.5% lower this year and consider whether the explanation is reasonable.

- Perform a reasonable test comparing recorded ticket income with maximum revenue $(1,200 \times \$40 \times 6) = \$288,000$.

- Agree the cost of beverages to purchase invoices to confirm accuracy of recording.

- Calculate mark-up on cost to confirm the completeness of income.

- Compare costs by category to the prior year and investigate any significant differences.

- Inspect invoices to confirm the fees paid to the bands, if available.

- Agree amounts paid to bands to the cash book and bank statements.

Pool operating costs

- Obtain a breakdown of operating costs, cast and agree to the financial statements.

- Agree a sample of costs to invoice, cash book and bank statements.

- Perform analytical procedures by comparing the costs to prior year and investigating any significant differences.

Non-current assets

- Obtain the non-current asset register, cast and agree the total to the financial statements.

- Trace a sample of assets from the NCA register to the physical assets to confirm existence.

- Trace a sample of physical assets through to inclusion in the NCA register to confirm completeness.

- Recalculate the depreciation expense to confirm arithmetical accuracy.

Cash at bank

- Obtain a bank confirmation letter confirming the bank balances at the year end.

- Obtain and cast the bank reconciliation and agree the balance per the cash book to the cash book and financial statements.

- Trace reconciling items on the bank reconciliation to the post year end bank statements and pre-year-end cash book.

The procedures above are typical audit procedures that would be used in the audit of a profit making entity. Audits of NFPs are not different to those of a profit making company, however, the audit risks are different due to the nature of the entity.

In addition to the financial statement audit, a value for money audit may be performed to assess whether TPT are getting value for money from the services provided by EMCA. A VFM audit may identify that TFT could obtain a more cost effective service by using another provider or by managing their own activities instead of outsourcing.

Test your understanding 6

(a) List and explain FOUR assertions from ISA 315 *Identifying and Assessing the Risk of Material Misstatement Through Understanding the Entity and its Environment* that relate to the recording of classes of transactions.

(4 marks)

(b) List FOUR assertions relevant to the audit of tangible non-current assets and state one audit procedure which provides appropriate evidence for each assertion.

(4 marks)

(Total: 8 marks)

Test your understanding 7

You are an audit senior working at a medium sized firm of auditors. One of your clients is an exclusive hotel, Numero Uno, situated in the centre of Big City.

Numero Uno prides itself on delivering a first class dining experience and is renowned for its standards of service and cooking that few restaurants in the country come close to. Its inventory therefore consists of the very best foods and beverages from across the globe.

Food products held in inventory are mostly fresh as the head chef will only work with the very best ingredients. Food inventory is stored in the kitchens and managed by the head chef himself.

The majority of beverages held at the hotel are expensive wines that have been sourced from exclusive vineyards. The hotel also stocks a wide range of spirits and mixers. All beverages are stored either in the hotel cellar or behind the bar. The cellar can only be accessed by the duty manager who holds the key. As part of your audit procedures you will attend the year-end inventory count of the hotel's beverages.

Required:

(a) Describe the audit procedures an auditor would conduct before and whilst attending the inventory count of the beverages in the hotel.

(7 marks)

(b) Identify and explain THREE financial statement assertions that are most relevant to inventory.

(3 marks)

(c) Apart from attending the inventory count, describe the substantive procedures an auditor would carry out to confirm the valuation of the wine and spirits held in inventory at the year-end.

(5 marks)

(Total: 15 marks)

Test your understanding 8

(a) Describe the steps an auditor should take when conducting a trade receivables confirmation (circularisation) test.

(4 marks)

(b) Explain why a direct confirmation test may not provide sufficient appropriate audit evidence on its own.

(3 marks)

You are the audit manager in charge of the audit of Builders Mate, a limited liability company. The company's year-end is 31 March, and Builders Mate has been an audit client for three years. Builders Mate sells small tools, plant and equipment exclusively to the building trade. They have 12 warehouse style shops located throughout the country. Builders Mate does not manufacture any products themselves.

The audit fieldwork is due to commence in 3 weeks' time and you are preparing the audit work programme for the trade receivables section of the audit. Extracts from the client's trial balance show the following information.

	$
Trade receivables control account	124,500
General trade receivables allowance	(2,490)
Specific trade receivables allowance	0

From your review of last year's audit file you have determined that last year there were 2 specific allowances of $5,000 and $2,000 as well as a 3% general allowance.

Initial conversations with the client indicate that there are no specific allowances to be made this year, however they intend to reduce the general allowance from 3% to 2%.

You are aware that two of Builders Mate's major customers went into administration during the year and they are likely to be liquidated in the near future. Both of these customers owed material amounts at the year-end.

Required:

(c) **Describe substantive procedures the auditor should perform on the year-end trade receivables of Builders Mate.**

(9 marks)

(d) **Describe how audit software could facilitate the audit of trade receivables.**

(4 marks)

(Total: 20 marks)

Test your understanding 9

You are auditing the revenue section of the financial statements of Ningaloo Co. Internal controls have been evaluated as effective. Substantive procedures have not yet been performed. During the risk assessment you identified that a performance related bonus has been introduced for salesmen who reach a target sales figure each quarter.

(1) **Which of the following statements is correct?**

A   As controls are working effectively within Ningaloo Co the audit plan does not need to contain any substantive procedures as full reliance can be placed on the control system

B   The auditor will perform the same level of substantive procedures as were performed in the prior year

C   The level of substantive procedures may be reduced as a result of the controls being found to work effectively

D   The level of substantive procedures should increase if controls are found to be working effectively

(2) **'Select a sample of goods despatched notes from just before and just after the year-end and trace to the sales day book'. Which financial statement assertion is addressed by this audit procedure?**

    A   Occurrence

    B   Completeness

    C   Cut-off

    D   Accuracy

(3) **Which of the following statements is correct with regard to directional testing?**

    A   A procedure that directly tests receivables for overstatement will indirectly test revenue for understatement

    B   A procedure that directly tests receivables for overstatement will indirectly test revenue for overstatement

    C   To test revenue for overstatement the auditor must choose a sample from outside of the accounting system, such as GDNS, and trace them into the accounting system

    D   To test revenue for understatement the auditor must choose a sample from within the accounting system and trace it to the GDN

(4) **Which of the following is an analytical procedure that can be used to test revenue?**

    A   Comparison of revenue in the current year to revenue in the prior year

    B   Review of credit notes issued post year-end

    C   Inspection of a sample of goods despatch notes and sales invoices

    D   Recalculation of the sales day book

(5) **Sales managers have recorded fictitious sales in order to earn a larger bonus. Which of the following assertions is affected by this?**

    A   Existence

    B   Completeness

    C   Accuracy

    D   Occurrence

Test your understanding 10

You are performing procedures over the non-current assets balance for your client Leveque Co. The balance consists of motor vehicles, fixtures and fittings and land and buildings. Motor vehicles are replaced on a three-year cycle. Fixtures and fittings are replaced as and when required. The company uses the following depreciation rates:

- Land and buildings – no depreciation is charged due to values increasing

- Fixtures and fittings – 10% straight line

- Motor vehicles – 20% straight line.

(1) **Which of the following best describes the audit risk resulting from the depreciation policy used for land and buildings?**

    A   Land and buildings may not exist

    B   Land and buildings may not be completely recorded

    C   Land and buildings may be understated

    D   Land and buildings may be overstated

(2) **Which of the following procedures provides the most reliable evidence to assess whether 10% straight line is an appropriate rate for fixtures and fittings?**

    A   Enquire of the client whether the rate is appropriate and how they chose that rate

    B   Contact the supplier of the fixtures to ask how long the fixtures should last

    C   Review disposals of fixtures and fittings to identify how long the assets had been used by Leveque and whether any significant profit or loss on disposal arose

    D   Compare the rate with other audit clients of your firm

(3) **Which of the following statements is true in respect of Leveque's motor vehicles?**

    A   The depreciation rate is unreasonable as the company only uses the assets for three years therefore depreciation should be charged over three years

    B   Motor vehicles have a useful life of longer than five years therefore depreciation should be charged over a longer period

    C   The depreciation rate is reasonable

    D   The depreciation charge for motor vehicles is unlikely to be material therefore the rate used does not matter

(4) **The audit plan includes a procedure to trace a sample of assets included in the non-current asset register to the physical asset. Which assertion is being tested?**

A   Existence

B   Completeness

C   Valuation

D   Rights and obligations

(5) **Which of the following procedures provides the most reliable evidence when confirming rights and obligations for a non-current asset?**

A   Physical inspection of the assets

B   Inspection of the fixtures and fittings invoice

C   Inspection of a valuation report for land and buildings

D   Written representation from management confirming ownership

Test your understanding 11

You are assigned to the audit team of Carnarvon Co performing testing over non-current assets.

(1) **Which of the following is NOT an audit procedure from ISA 500 *Audit Evidence*?**

A   Inspection

B   Enquiry

C   Check

D   Recalculate

(2) **Which of the following audit procedures would confirm the existence of property, plant and equipment?**

A   Recalculate the depreciation charge using the company's accounting policy

B   Physically inspect a sample of assets listed in the non-current asset register

C   Reconcile the schedule of property, plant and equipment with the general ledger

D   Review the repairs and maintenance expense account in the statement of profit or loss for items of a capital nature

(3) **Which of the following is NOT a financial statement assertion relevant to your testing of non-current assets?**

   A   Occurrence

   B   Completeness

   C   Rights and obligations

   D   Existence

(4) **Which of the following issues would result in a misstatement in the non-current assets balance?**

   (i)   An error in recording the cost of the asset.

   (ii)   A misclassification between fixtures & fittings and motor vehicles.

   (iii)   The depreciation charge has been correctly credited to accumulated depreciation but debited to the irrecoverable debt expense account.

   (iv)   A purchase invoice not being recorded in the asset register.

   A   (ii) and (iv)

   B   (i) and (iii)

   C   (ii) and (iii)

   D   (i) and (iv)

(5) **When testing the assertion of rights and obligations over land and buildings, which of the following would provide the most reliable evidence?**

   A   Inspection of the insurance policy

   B   Physical inspection of the land and buildings

   C   Inspection of the title deeds

   D   Inspection of the non-current asset register

14 Chapter summary

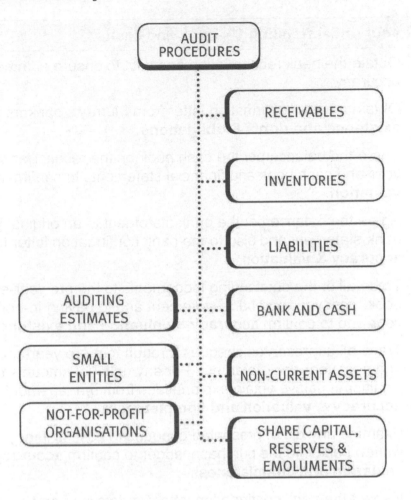

Test your understanding answers

Test your understanding 1 – Bank and cash

- Obtain the bank reconciliation and cast to ensure arithmetical accuracy.

- Obtain a bank confirmation letter from Murray's bankers to confirm **existence and rights & obligations**.

- Agree the balance per the cash book on the reconciliation to the year-end cash book and financial statements to confirm **accuracy & valuation**.

- Agree the balance per the bank statement to an original year-end bank statement and also to the bank confirmation letter to confirm **accuracy & valuation**.

- Trace all of the outstanding lodgements to the pre year-end cash book, post year-end bank statement and to paying-in-book pre year-end to confirm **accuracy & valuation and existence**.

- Trace all unpresented cheques through to a pre year-end cash book and post year-end statement. For any unusual amounts or significant delays obtain explanations from management to confirm **accuracy & valuation and completeness**.

- Examine any old unpresented cheques to assess if they need to be written back into the purchase ledger to confirm **accuracy & valuation and completeness**.

- Inspect the bank confirmation letter for details of any security provided by the company or any legal right of set-off as this may require disclosure to confirm appropriate **presentation**.

- Review the cash book and bank statements for any unusual items or large transfers around the year-end, as this could be evidence of window dressing. This verifies **completeness, existence**.

- Count the petty cash in the cash tin at the year-end and agree the total to the balance included in the financial statements to confirm **accuracy & valuation, and existence**.

Test your understanding 2 – Non-current assets

- Obtain the non-current asset register, cast and agree the totals to the financial statements: verifies **completeness, classification, presentation**.

- Select a sample of assets from the non-current asset register and physically inspect them: verifies **existence**.

- Select a sample of assets visible at the Murray's premises and inspect the asset register to ensure they are included: verifies **completeness**.

- Inspect assets for condition and usage to identify signs of impairment: verifies **valuation**.

- For revalued assets, inspect the independent valuation report and agree the amount stated to the amount included in the general ledger and the financial statements: verifies **valuation**; and ensure that all assets in the same class have been revalued.

- Select a sample of additions and agree the cost to supplier invoice: verifies **valuation**.

- Obtain a list of additions and inspect the description to confirm that they relate to capital expenditure items rather than repairs and maintenance: verifies **existence**.

- Inspect a breakdown of repairs and maintenance expenditure for the year to identify items of a capital nature: verifies **completeness.**

- Inspect supplier invoices (for equipment), title deeds (for property), and registration documents (for motor vehicles) to ensure they are in the name of the client: verifies **rights and obligations**.

- If assets have been constructed by the client, obtain an analysis of the costs incurred, cast for arithmetical accuracy and agree a sample of costs to supporting documentation (e.g. payroll, material invoices): verifies **valuation**.

Disposals

- Obtain a breakdown of disposals, cast the list and agree all assets have been removed from the non-current asset register: verifies **existence**.

- Select a sample of disposals and agree sale proceeds to supporting documentation such as sundry sales invoices: verifies **accuracy of profit on disposal**.

- Recalculate the profit/loss on disposal and agree to the statement of profit or loss: verifies **accuracy of profit on disposal**.

Depreciation

- Inspect the capital expenditure budgets for the next few years to assess the appropriateness of the useful economic lives in light of plans to replace assets: verifies **valuation**.

- Recalculate the depreciation charge for a sample of assets to verify arithmetical accuracy: verifies **accuracy, valuation**.

- Inspect the financial statement disclosure of the depreciation charges and policies in the draft financial statements and compare to the prior year to ensure consistency: verifies **presentation**.

- Recalculate the depreciation charge for revalued assets to ensure the charge is based on the new carrying value: verifies **accuracy, valuation**.

- Review profits and losses on disposal of assets disposed of in the year to assess the reasonableness of the depreciation policies (if depreciation policies are reasonable, there should not be a significant profit or loss): verifies **valuation**.

- Compare depreciation rates to companies with the same type of assets to assess reasonableness: verifies **valuation**.

- Perform a proof in total calculation for the depreciation charged for each category of assets, discuss with management if significant fluctuations arise: verifies **completeness, valuation**. **(Analytical procedure)**

Test your understanding 3 – Inventory

(a) **Before the inventory count**

- Contact the client to obtain a copy of the inventory count instructions to understand how the count will be conducted and assess the effectiveness of the count process.

- Inspect prior year working papers to understand the inventory count process and identify any issues that should be taken into account this year.

- Book audit staff to attend the inventory counts.

- Consider the need for using an expert to assist in valuing the inventory being counted.

- Ascertain whether any inventory is held by third parties, and if possible, make arrangements to visit the third party site to obtain sufficient appropriate evidence.

- Alternatively, send a letter requesting direct confirmation of inventory balances held at the year-end from any third party warehouse providers regarding quantities and condition of inventory held on behalf of the client.

(b) **Audit procedures during the count**

Tests of controls

- Observe the count to ensure that the inventory count instructions are being followed. For example:

  - No movements of inventory occur during the count.

  - Teams of two people perform the count.

  - Sections of inventory are tagged as counted to prevent double counting.

  - Damaged/obsolete items have been separately identified so they can be valued appropriately.

- Inspect the count sheets to ensure they have been completed in pen rather than pencil.

- Inspect the count sheets to ensure they show the description of the goods but do not show the quantities expected to be counted.

- Re-perform the sequence check on the count sheets to ensure none are missing.

- Enquire of the counting staff which department they work in to ensure they are not warehouse staff.

Substantive procedures

- Select a sample of items from the inventory count sheets and physically inspect the items in the warehouse: verifies **existence**.

- Select a sample of physical items from the warehouse and trace to the inventory count sheets to ensure that they are recorded accurately: verifies **completeness**.

- Enquire of management whether goods held on behalf of third parties are segregated and recorded separately: verifies **rights and obligations**.

- Inspect the inventory being counted for evidence of damage or obsolescence that may affect the net realisable value: verifies **valuation**.

- Record details of the last deliveries prior to the year-end. This information will be used in the final audit to ensure that no further amendments have been made: verifies **completeness & existence**.

- Obtain copies of the inventory count sheets at the end of the inventory count, ready for checking against the final inventory listing at the final audit: verifies **completeness** and **existence**.

- Attend the inventory count at the third party warehouses: verifies **completeness** and **existence**.

(c) **Substantive procedures to be performed during the final audit**

- Trace the items counted during the inventory count to the final inventory list to ensure it is the same as the one used at the year-end and to ensure that any errors identified during counting procedures have been rectified: verifies **completeness, presentation**.

- Cast the list (showing inventory categorised between finished goods, WIP and raw materials) to ensure arithmetical accuracy and agree totals to financial statement disclosures: verifies **completeness, classification**.

- Inspect purchase invoices for a sample of inventory items to agree their cost: verifies **valuation**.

- Inspect purchase invoices for the name of the client: verifies **rights and obligations**.

- Inspect post year-end sales invoices for a sample of inventory items to determine if the net realisable value is reasonable. This will also assist in determining if inventory is held at the lower of cost and net realisable value: verifies **valuation**.

- Inspect the ageing of inventory items to identify old/slow-moving amounts that may require an allowance, and discuss these with management: verifies **valuation**.

- Recalculate work-in-progress and finished goods valuations using payroll records for labour costs and utility bills for overhead absorption: verifies **valuation**.

- Trace the good received immediately prior to the year-end to year-end payables and inventory balances: verifies **completeness & existence**.

- Trace goods despatched immediately prior to year-end to the nominal ledgers to ensure the items are not included in inventory and revenue (and receivables where relevant) has been recorded: verifies **completeness & existence**.

- Calculate the inventory holding period and compare this to prior year to identify slow-moving inventory which requires an allowance to bring the value down to the lower of cost and NRV: verifies **valuation**. **(Analytical procedure)**

- Calculate gross profit margin and compare this to prior year, investigate any significant differences that may highlight an error in cost of sales and closing inventory: verifies **valuation**. **(Analytical procedure)**

Test your understanding 4 – Receivables

(a) **Jockeys:** the outstanding balance is over 20% of the total receivables balance at the year-end and is therefore material.

Golf is Us: this large and old balance may require write-off or a specific allowance to be made if the recoverability of the amount is in doubt (similarly for Escot supermarket).

Tike & Co: the large and old credit balance on the listing suggests that an error may have been made. A payment from another customer may have been misallocated to this account or the client may have overpaid an invoice, or paid an invoice twice in error. It may be appropriate to reclassify this balance, along with the balance for Whistlers, as a trade payable.

Whistlers: although the amount is small, the credit balance appears to be due to a difference between a recent large payment and the outstanding balance. This error may indicate other potential errors, and requires further investigation.

There are other balances that could be identified and justified for similar reasons to the above.

(b) **Receivables procedures**

- Obtain the aged receivables listing, cast it and agree the total to the financial statements: verifies **accuracy and presentation**.

– Agree the receivables ledger control account with the receivables ledger list of balances: verifies **completeness** and **existence**.

– Select a sample of year-end receivable balances and agree back to valid supporting documentation of GDN and sales order: verifies **existence**.

– Inspect after date cash receipts and follow through to pre year-end receivable balances: verifies **valuation, rights and obligations** and **existence**.

– Select a sample of goods despatched notes (GDN) before and just after the year-end and follow through to the sales invoice to ensure they are recorded in the correct accounting period: verifies **completeness** and **existence** (**cut-off** of revenue).

– Perform a positive receivables circularisation of a representative sample of Murray Co's year-end balances, for any non-replies, with Murray Co's permission, send a reminder letter to follow-up: verifies **existence** and **rights and obligations**.

– Inspect the **aged receivables report** to identify any slow-moving balances (such as Bibs and Balls, Golf is Us, James Smit Partnership) and discuss these with the credit control manager to assess whether an allowance or write-down is necessary: verifies **valuation** and **allocation**.

– Discuss any significant balances with management (such as Escot, Jockeys, Golf is Us, James Smit Partnership, Stayrose Supermarket) to identify any issues regarding payment: verifies **valuation**.

– Inspect customer correspondence in respect of any slow-moving/aged balances to assess whether there are any invoices in dispute: verifies **valuation**.

– Inspect board minutes of Murray Co to assess whether there are any material disputed receivables that may require write-off: **verifies valuation**.

– Inspect the receivables ledger for any credit balances (such as Whistler and Tike) and discuss with management whether these should be reclassified as payables: verifies **existence of receivables** and **completeness of payables, classification**.

– Inspect a sample of post year-end credit notes to identify any that relate to pre year-end transactions to ensure that they have not been included in receivables: verifies **existence** (**occurrence** of revenue).

– Calculate the average receivables collection period and compare this to prior year, investigate any significant differences: verifies **completeness** and **valuation**. (**Analytical procedure**)

Test your understanding 5 – Payables

Many companies send out monthly statements of account as part of their credit control procedures. It is likely that audit clients will receive a number of these statements from suppliers at the year-end. These can be reconciled to their own payables control account to ensure that their records are correct. This is known as a supplier statement reconciliation and is an important source of audit evidence.

There are two main reasons why there may be a variance:

- **Timing differences,** e.g. invoices sent by the supplier but not yet received by the customer; payments sent by the customer but not yet received by the supplier; returns and credit notes not yet appearing on the supplier's statement; or

- **Errors.**

(a) **Reconciliation of payables ledger balance to balance on supplier's statement:**

		$	$
Balance per payables ledger:			**59,800**
Differences:			
(i)	31.11: Discount not allowed by supplier	1,260	
(ii)	04.11: Transposition error, invoice 6080	1,800	
(iii)	04.12: Invoice 6210 not on payables ledger	47,350	
(iv)	28.12: Invoice 6355 not on payables ledger	62,980	
(v)	31.12: Cash in transit	60,050	
(vi)	Discount not allowed	1,230	
			174,670
Balance per supplier's statement:			**234,470**

(b) **Audit work**

(i) The date of the cash payment for the October invoices suggests that Racket Co will not have received the cheque for $61,630 until after the 30 November and so Murray Co may not be entitled to the 2% cash discount. The entry in Murray Co's ledger suggest the cheque was posted on 30 November however this is not conclusive evidence that the cheque was actually sent to Racket Co on this date.

– The auditor should enquire with Murray Co's payables ledger controller about this item, and inspect correspondence with Racket Co to establish entitlement to the discount.

- If Murray Co is obliged to pay the 2% disallowed discount, this should be added to the payables ledger balance.

- If Racket Co will allow the discount, there is no need to make any adjustments to the payables ledger balance.

(ii) The apparent transposition error on invoice 6080 should be checked by inspecting the invoice.

- If the invoice shows $37,520, then an additional payable of $1,800 should be added at the year-end to correct this error.

- No adjustment will be necessary if Murray Co's figure is correct.

(iii) It appears that invoice 6210 for $47,350 has not been included on Murray Co's payables ledger.

- The auditor should enquire with the warehouse manager whether these goods have been received.

- The GRNs around the expected delivery date should be inspected to identify the relevant GRN.

- Correspondence with Racket Co should be reviewed for discussions relating to a dispute regarding these goods (if relevant).

- If the goods have been received, the purchase invoices file should be inspected to identify if there is a related purchase invoice.

- If there is a purchase invoice, the auditor should enquire with the purchases department why the invoice has not been posted to the payables ledger. This may be because of a dispute (e.g. an incorrect price, the wrong quantity or a fault with the goods).

- If the goods relating to this invoice are in inventory (or have been sold) a purchase accrual should be made for this item (note that the actual quantity of goods received should be accrued for) and correspondence relating to this invoice with Racket Co should be inspected to assess what payment has been agreed.

- If the goods have not been received, no adjustment needs to be made (but a copy of correspondence disputing the delivery/invoice should be placed on file as evidence).

(iv) The appropriate treatment of invoice 6355 depends on whether or not Murray Co received the goods before the year-end.

– The auditor should inspect the GRN for the date to determine if the goods were received before the year-end.

– If the date is before the year-end, Murray Co should be asked to include a purchase accrual at the year-end for this invoice.

(v) The cheque on 31 December appears to be cash in transit.

– The auditor should inspect Murray Co's bank statement to confirm that the cheque was cleared by the bank after the year-end.

– If the cheque cleared within one week of the year-end (with most other cheques issued immediately before the year-end) then this is valid cash in transit.

– If most cheques issued immediately before the year-end take more than a week to clear, this indicates window-dressing of the financial statements (i.e. the cheques were actually sent out after the year-end), in which case the amounts should be credited back to trade payables and debited back to cash.

(iv) If, as appears likely, the cheque for $60,050 is not received by Racket Co until sometime after the year-end, then the discount of $1,230 may be disallowed. If this discount is disallowed, it should be added to payables at the year-end (see (i) above).

Test your understanding 6

(a) **Assertions: classes of transactions**

- **Occurrence**: The transactions and events that have been recorded and disclosed have actually occurred and pertain to the entity.

- **Completeness**: All transactions and events that should have been recorded and disclosed have been recorded and disclosed.

- **Accuracy**: The amounts and other data relating to recorded transactions and events have been recorded appropriately and related disclosures have been appropriately measured and described.

- **Cut-off**: Transactions and events have been recorded in the correct accounting period.

- **Classification**: Transactions and events have been recorded in the proper accounts.

- **Presentation**: Transactions and events are appropriately aggregated or disaggregated and clearly described, and related disclosures are relevant and understandable in the context of the applicable financial reporting framework.

Note: Only four assertions required.

(b) **Tangible non-current assets: assertions and procedures**

- **Completeness:** Agree a sample of assets physically verified on the premises back to the asset register to ensure that all non-current assets are recorded.

- **Existence:** Physically inspect a sample of assets included on the non-current asset register to verify existence.

- **Accuracy, valuation and allocation:** Recalculate the depreciation charge to ensure arithmetical accuracy.

- **Rights and obligations**: Inspect an appropriate document of ownership for example, a purchase invoice, for the client's name to confirm the entity owns or controls the asset.

- **Classification/Presentation:** Inspect the non-current asset disclosure note in the financial statements and agree the figures to the non-current asset register to ensure assets are properly disclosed under the correct headings as required by IAS 16 *Property, Plant and Equipment.*

Test your understanding 7

(a) **Procedures before the count**

- Inspect prior year working papers to understand the inventory count process and identify any issues that should be taken into account this year.

- Contact Numero Uno (client) to obtain inventory count instructions for this year to understand how the count will be conducted and assess the effectiveness of the count process.

- Ascertain whether any inventory is held by third parties. Determine how to gather sufficient appropriate evidence e.g. by visiting the premises or requesting an external confirmation.

- Consider the need for using an expert to assist in valuing the inventory being counted. There may be some specialty wines and spirits that require expert valuation.

During the count

- Observe the count to ensure that the instructions are being followed.

- Inspect the bottles being counted for evidence of damage or obsolescence that may affect the net realisable value and hence overall valuation of inventory.

- Select a sample of beverages from the inventory count sheets and physically inspect the items in the cellar or bar to confirm they exist.

- Select a sample of physical beverages from the cellar or bar and trace to the inventory count sheets to ensure that they are recorded accurately and therefore that the records are complete.

- Record cut-off information by obtaining details of the last deliveries prior to the year-end. This information will be used in final audit to ensure that no further amendments have been made which could result in overstatement or understatement of inventory.

(b) **Inventory assertions**

Identify	Explain
Existence	The inventory recorded actually exists.
Rights and obligations	The company owns or controls the asset and therefore has the right to record the inventories in its financial statements.
Completeness	All inventory balances have been recorded.
Accuracy, valuation and allocation	Inventories are valued appropriately (i.e. at lower of cost and net realisable value).
Cut-off	Inventory movements around the year-end are recorded in the correct period.
Presentation	Inventory is disclosed properly in the financial statements as raw materials, work in progress and finished goods.

(c) **Substantive procedures**

– Trace the items counted during the inventory count to the final inventory listing to ensure the quantities are the same and any errors identified during counting procedures have been rectified.

– Inspect purchases invoices for a sample of beverages to agree their cost, ensuring that the description of goods on the invoice matches the beverage.

– For beverages sold to customers after the year-end, inspect a sample of restaurant bills/invoices back to the final inventory records ensuring that the sales value exceeds the cost. Where sales value is less than cost, ensure that the beverage is stated at the realisable value.

– For high value items such as champagne, vintage wine and exotic spirits, use an expert valuer to review the net realisable value of a sample of items to ensure the value is reasonable.

– Inventory noted during the count as obsolete or damaged should be traced to the inventory records to ensure the valuation has been adjusted to take this into account. The expert valuer may provide assistance with these valuations.

Test your understanding 8

(a) **Trade receivables circularisation**

- Obtain client approval to perform a direct confirmation of trade receivables.

- Obtain the list of receivables balances, and cast it.

- Select a suitable sample from the list of receivables balances using an appropriate sampling technique.

- Prepare the confirmation letters ensuring the contact details are correct and return details clearly state that the reply should be made direct to the auditor. A business reply envelope, addressed to the auditor, could be included for this purpose.

- Ask the client to print the letters on client-headed paper and sign them. The letters should then be returned to the auditor.

- The auditor should send the letters, including any follow-up requests. This process should be controlled by the auditor to ensure the integrity of the test.

- Reconcile replies received to the audit client's receivables accounting records.

- Perform alternative audit procedures on balances where no response to the confirmation letter is received.

(b) **Sufficiency of the evidence from a direct confirmation test**

Several factors influence the sufficiency of evidence gathered during a direct confirmation of trade receivables and other evidence may be required by an auditor to form an opinion in this area:

- There is often a low response rate from trade receivables meaning that other audit procedures will be required for these balances.

- The type of confirmation letter, whether a positive or negative confirmation request, will influence the sufficiency of evidence gathered. Negative confirmations provide less persuasive audit evidence than positive confirmations and it is unlikely that a negative confirmation will provide sufficient evidence on its own.

- The reliability of the responses to the confirmation requests may be in doubt, for example if there is a risk of fraud being perpetrated.

- Mistakes and errors may be present in the accounting records of the trade receivables confirming the balance outstanding.

- Customers may agree with balances containing errors in their favour.

(c) **Substantive procedures for trade receivables**

- Obtain the receivables listing, cast it to verify arithmetical accuracy and agree the total to the financial statements.

- Confirm the trade receivables control account balance matches the sum of the individual trade receivables ledger accounts to confirm completeness.

- For a sample GDNs around the year-end, trace to the sales invoice and ledger accounts to ensure that the transactions have been recorded in the correct accounting period.

- Select a sample of individual trade receivables and perform a direct confirmation test using a positive confirmation letter.

- Inspect the cash book and bank statements for cash received post year-end.

- Recalculate the general allowance based on the 2% figure to ensure arithmetical accuracy.

- Discuss with management why the general allowance has reduced from 3% to 2% and assess the reasonableness of the explanations provided and the reason for not making specific allowances for the two customers in administration who owe material amounts at the year-end.

- Inspect the aged receivables analysis to identify aged debts that may require a specific allowance. Discuss with management any such balances and ensure specific allowances are made if appropriate.

- Confirm that the specific allowances made in the prior year were either written-off or the cash was recovered in the current accounting period.

- Consider and discuss with management the potential implications of failing to make specific allowances on the audit opinion.

(d) **Audit software**

- Audit software can be used to prepare an aged receivables analysis and to identify potential irrecoverable debts using a range of criteria set by the auditor.

- It can be used to quickly identify credit balances or negative balances within the receivables ledger.

- Audit software will be more efficient and accurate at casting the receivables ledger and recalculating figures such as the general allowance.

- It could also select a sample for testing and prepare direct confirmation letters.

Test your understanding 9

(1)	C	Substantive procedures must be performed on all material balances, even if controls are working effectively. This is due to the inherent limitations of controls. However, the level may be reduced if controls are found to be effective.
(2)	C	Selecting transactions around the year-end tests the assertion of cut-off.
(3)	B	If the receivable was overstated the related sale would also be overstated. To test for overstatement the auditor must choose a sample from within the accounting system and trace it back to supporting documentation.
(4)	A	B, C and D are all substantive tests of detail as they focus attention on individual sales transactions. Comparison of sales in the current year to the prior year is an analytical procedure as it is focused on identifying unusual trends or fluctuations which may indicate misstatement.
(5)	D	Occurrence. The transaction will not have occurred if it is fictitious. Existence is not relevant to the statement of profit or loss.

Test your understanding 10

(1)	D	Depreciation affects the valuation assertion therefore options A and B are incorrect. If depreciation has not been charged, the assets will be overvalued therefore option C is incorrect.
(2)	C	Enquiry on its own is not the most reliable form of evidence and should be corroborated with other procedures. The auditor would not contact the supplier and this would not provide evidence of the useful life of the fixtures to Leveque. Comparison with other clients is only useful if those clients are in the same type of industry and using the same type of assets in the same manner as Leveque.
(3)	A	The depreciation rate should match the usage of the asset by the company, therefore the rate should be based on 3 years not 5 years. As no figures are given for the motor vehicles it cannot be said that depreciation will be immaterial.
(4)	A	Testing from the ledger to the source addresses the assertion of existence.
(5)	B	Physical inspection verifies existence. A valuation certificate verifies the valuation of the land and buildings. Neither of these procedures confirms the assets are owned or controlled by Leveque. Written confirmation is not a reliable form of evidence for the assertion of rights and obligations as better procedures can be performed. The purchase invoice for fixtures and fittings should contain the name of the client which would help verify rights and obligations.

		Test your understanding 11
(1)	C	Check is not a valid procedure. Every procedure 'checks' something. The auditor can check through inspection, enquiry, observation, etc.
(2)	B	Option A tests the accuracy of a depreciation charge. Options C and D test the completeness of PPE. Option B confirms existence.
(3)	A	Occurrence is an assertion relevant to the statement of profit or loss, not the statement of financial position.
(4)	D	A misclassification between motor vehicles and fixtures & fittings will not affect the overall non-current assets balance. The depreciation charge has been correctly credited to accumulated depreciation therefore the asset's carrying value will be correctly calculated. The mis-posting to irrecoverable debt expense will mean the classification of the expense in the statement of profit or loss is incorrect. An error recording the cost of the asset will mean the asset is misstated. If the purchase invoice relating to the asset is not recorded, assets will be understated.
(5)	C	The other procedures do not confirm the client owns or controls the assets. The title deeds in the client's name will confirm ownership.

Completion and review

Chapter learning objectives

This chapter covers syllabus areas:

- E1 – Subsequent events

- E2 – Going concern

- E3 – Written representations

- E4 – Audit finalisation and the final review

Detailed syllabus objectives are provided in the introduction section of the text book.

PER

One of the PER performance objectives (PO20) is to review and report on the findings of an audit. You complete an audit, preparing the formal documentation and reporting any control deficiencies to management. You report back to managers in a formal audit report. Working through this chapter should help you understand how to demonstrate that objective.

1 Introduction

After the auditor has completed their substantive testing there are still many procedures that need to be performed before they can sign the auditor's report. These include:

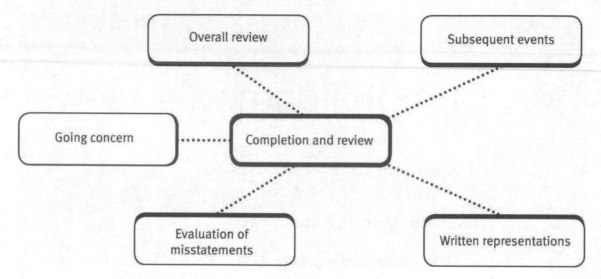

2 Subsequent events

ISA 560 *Subsequent Events,* para 4, requires the auditor to:

- Obtain sufficient appropriate audit evidence about whether events occurring between the date of the financial statements and the date of the auditor's report, that require adjustment or disclosure are appropriately reflected in accordance with the applicable financial reporting framework.

- Respond appropriately to facts that become known to the auditor after the date of the auditor's report.

IAS 10 *Events After the Reporting Period* identifies two types of event after the reporting period:

- Adjusting

- Non-adjusting.

Illustration 1 – Adjusting and non-adjusting events

Adjusting events

These are events that provide additional evidence relating to conditions existing at the reporting date. Such events provide new information about the items included in the financial statements and hence the financial statements should be adjusted to reflect the new information.

Examples of **adjusting** events include:

- Allowances for damaged inventory and doubtful receivables.

- Amounts received or receivable in respect of insurance claims which were being negotiated at the reporting date.

- The determination of the purchase or sale price of non-current assets purchased or sold before the year-end.

- Agreement of a tax liability.

- Discovery of errors/fraud revealing that the financial statements are incorrect.

Non-adjusting events

These are events concerning conditions which arose after the reporting date. If material, disclosure is required in the notes to the financial statements indicating what effect the events may have. Such events, therefore, will not have any effect on items in the statements of financial position or statement of profit or loss for the period.

Examples of **non-adjusting** events include:

- Issue of new share or loan capital.

- Major changes in the composition of the group (for example, mergers, acquisitions or reconstructions).

- Losses of non-current assets or inventory as a result of fires or floods.

- Strikes, government action such as nationalisation.

- Purchases/sales of significant non-current assets.

(IAS 10 *Events After the Reporting Period*)

Auditor responsibilities

Subsequent events

Definition: Subsequent events are events occurring between the date of the financial statements and the date of the auditor's report, and facts that become known to the auditor after the date of the auditor's report

Auditors responsibility

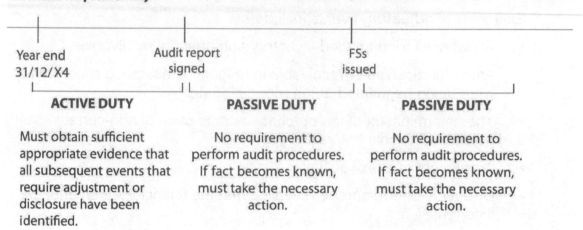

Year end 31/12/X4	Audit report signed	FSs issued
ACTIVE DUTY	**PASSIVE DUTY**	**PASSIVE DUTY**
Must obtain sufficient appropriate evidence that all subsequent events that require adjustment or disclosure have been identified.	No requirement to perform audit procedures. If fact becomes known, must take the necessary action.	No requirement to perform audit procedures. If fact becomes known, must take the necessary action.

Between the date of the financial statements and the date of the auditor's report

- The auditor should perform procedures to identify events that might require adjustment or disclosure in the financial statements.
  [ISA 560, 6]

- If material adjusting events are not adjusted for, or material non-adjusting events are not disclosed, the auditor will ask management to make the necessary amendments to the financial statements.

- If the identified adjustments or disclosures necessary are not made then the auditor should consider the impact on the auditor's report and whether a modification to the opinion is necessary.

Subsequent events procedures

- Enquiring of management if they are aware of any events, adjusting or non-adjusting, that have not yet been included or disclosed in the financial statements.

- Enquiring into management procedures/systems for the identification of events after the reporting period.

- Reading minutes of members' and directors' meetings.

- Reviewing accounting records including budgets, forecasts, cash flows, management accounts and interim information.

[ISA 560, 7]

- Obtaining a written representation from management confirming that they have informed the auditor of all subsequent events and accounted for them appropriately in the financial statements. [ISA 560, 9]

- Inspection of correspondence with legal advisors. [ISA 560, A8]

- Reviewing the progress of known risk areas and contingencies. [ISA 560, A9]

- Considering relevant information which has come to the auditor's attention, from sources outside the entity, including public knowledge, competitors, suppliers and customers.

- Inspecting after date receipts from receivables.

- Inspecting the cash book after the year-end for payments/receipts that were not accrued for at the year-end.

- Inspecting the sales price of inventories after the year-end.

Between the date of the auditor's report and the date the financial statements are issued

- The auditor is under no obligation to perform audit procedures after the auditor's report has been issued, however, if they become aware of a fact which would cause them to amend the auditor's report, they must take action. [ISA 560, 10]

- This will normally be in the form of asking the client to amend the financial statements, auditing the amendments and reissuing the auditor's report.

- If management do not amend the financial statements and the auditor's report has not yet been issued to the client, the auditor can still modify the opinion. [ISA 560, 13a]

- If the auditor's report has been provided to the client, the auditor shall notify management and those charged with governance not to issue the financial statements before the amendments are made.

  If the client issues the financial statements despite being requested not to by the auditor, the auditor shall take action to prevent reliance on the auditor's report. [ISA 560, 13b]

  Legal advice should be sought in this situation as the course of action to prevent reliance on the auditor's report depends on the auditor's legal rights and obligations. [ISA 560, A16]

After the financial statements are issued

- The auditor is under no obligation to perform audit procedures after the financial statements have been issued, however, if they become aware of a fact which would have caused them to amend the auditor's report, they must take action.

- The auditor should discuss the matter with management and consider if the financial statements require amendment. [ISA 560, 14]

- The auditor should perform audit procedures on the amendments to ensure they have been put through correctly. [ISA 560, 15a]

- The auditor should review the steps taken by management to ensure anyone who is in receipt of the previously issued financial statements is informed. [ISA 560, 15b]

- Issue a new auditor's report including an emphasis of matter or other matter paragraph to draw attention to the fact that the financial statements and auditor's report have been reissued. [ISA 560, 16]

- If management refuses to recall and amend the financial statements, the auditor shall take action to prevent reliance on the auditor's report. [ISA 560, 17]

Test your understanding 1

Murray case study: Subsequent events review for the year-ended 31 December 20X4

(1) On 2 January 20X5, Golf is Us, a major customer of Murray Co, was placed into administration owing $211,000.

(2) On 3 January 20X5, the sales director left the company. The sales director is suing Murray Co for constructive dismissal. If successful, the claim amounts to $280,000.

(3) On 5 February 20X5 there was a fire at the premises of the third party warehouse provider, which destroyed all inventory held there. Approximately one half of Murray Co's inventory was stored in these premises. The total value of inventory stored at the premises was $1,054,000.

(4) The financial statements include a $40,000 provision for an unfair dismissal case brought by an ex-employee of Murray Co. On 7 February 20X5 a letter was received from the claimant's solicitors stating that they would be willing to settle out-of-court for $25,000. It is likely the company will agree to this.

Financial statement extracts	31 Dec 20X4	31 Dec 20X3
	$000	$000
Revenue	21,960	19,580
Total assets	9,697	7,288
Profit before tax	1,048	248

Required:

For each of the events above discuss whether the financial statements require amendment in order to avoid a modified audit opinion.

3 Going concern

 The going concern concept

Going concern is the assumption that the entity will continue in business for the foreseeable future.

- The period that management (and therefore the auditor) is required to consider is the period required by the applicable financial reporting framework or by law or regulation if longer.

  Generally the period is a minimum of twelve months from the year-end. In some jurisdictions the period is a minimum of twelve months from the date the financial statements are approved (e.g. the UK).
  [ISA 570, 13]

- Consideration of the foreseeable future involves making a judgment about future events, which are inherently uncertain.

  Uncertainty increases with time and judgments can only be made on the basis of information available at any point. Subsequent events can overturn that judgment.
  [ISA 570, 5]

The going concern concept – significance

Whether or not a company can be classed as a going concern affects how its financial statements are prepared.

Financial statements are prepared using the going concern basis of accounting, unless

- management either intends to liquidate the entity or to cease trading, or

- has no realistic alternative but to do so.

(ISA 570, 2)

- Where the assumption is made that the company will cease trading, the financial statements are prepared using the **break-up or liquidation basis** under which:

  - The basis of preparation and the reason why the entity is not regarded as a going concern are disclosed.

  - Assets are recorded at likely sale values.

  - Inventory and receivables may need to be written down as inventory may be sold for a lower price or may be scrapped, and receivables may not pay if they know the company is ceasing to trade.

  - Additional liabilities may arise (redundancy costs for staff, the costs of closing down facilities, etc.).

Responsibilities for going concern

Director's responsibilities in respect of going concern

- It is the directors' responsibility to assess the company's ability to continue as a going concern when they are preparing the financial statements. [ISA 570, 4]

- In order to do this the directors should prepare forecasts to help assess whether they are likely to be able to continue trading for the next 12 months as a minimum.

- If they are aware of any material uncertainties which may affect this assessment, the directors should disclose these in the financial statements.

- When the directors are performing their assessment they should take into account a number of relevant factors such as:

  - Current and expected profitability

  - Debt repayment

  - Sources (and potential sources) of financing.

Auditor's responsibilities in respect of going concern

ISA 570 *Going Concern*, para 9, states that the auditor shall:

- Obtain sufficient appropriate evidence regarding the appropriateness of management's use of the going concern basis of accounting in the preparation of the financial statements.

- Conclude on whether a material uncertainty exists about the entity's ability to continue as a going concern.

- Report in accordance with ISA 570.

Indicators of going concern problems

Typical indicators and explanations of going concern problems include the following:

- Net current liabilities (or net liabilities overall): indicates an inability to meet debts as they fall due.

- Borrowing facilities not agreed or close to expiry of current agreement: lack of access to cash may make it difficult for a company to manage its operating cycle.

- Defaulted loan agreements: loans normally become repayable on default, the company may find it difficult to repay loan.

- Unplanned sales of non-current assets: indicates an inability to generate cash from other means and as non-current assets generate income, sale of assets will cause a decline in income and therefore profit.

- Missing tax payments: results in fines and penalties, companies normally prioritise tax payments indicating a lack of working capital.

- Failure to pay the staff: indicates a significant lack of working capital.

- Negative cash flow: indicates overtrading.

- Inability to obtain credit from suppliers: suggests failure to pay suppliers on time and working capital problems.

- Major technology changes: inability or insufficient funds to keep up with changes in technology will result in loss of custom and obsolescence of inventory.

- Legal claims: successful legal claims may result in significant cash payments that can only be settled with liquidation.

- Loss of key staff: may result in an inability to trade.

- Over-reliance on a small number of products, staff, suppliers or customers: loss may result in an inability to trade.

- Customers ceasing to trade or having cash flow difficulties: likely to become an irrecoverable debt and therefore payment won't be received.

- Emergence of a successful competitor: will impact revenue if customers switch.

- Uninsured/under-insured catastrophes: the company may not have enough cash to survive.

- Changes in laws and regulations: the cost of compliance may be more than the company can afford.

[ISA 570, A3]

Audit procedures

Audit procedures to assess management's evaluation of going concern

- Evaluate management's assessment of going concern. [ISA 570, 12]

- Assess the same period that management have used in their assessment and if this is less than 12 months, ask management to extend their assessment. [ISA 570, 13]

- Consider whether management's assessment includes all relevant information. [ISA 570, 14]

Audit procedures to perform where there is doubt over going concern

- Analyse and discuss cash flow, profit and other relevant forecasts with management. This should include assessment of the reasonableness of the assumptions used to prepare the forecasts.

- Analyse and discuss the entity's latest available interim financial statements.

- Review the terms of debentures and loan agreements and determining whether any have been breached.

- Read minutes of meetings for reference to financing difficulties.

- Enquire of the entity's lawyer regarding the existence of litigation and claims and the reasonableness of management's assessments of their outcome and the estimate of their financial implications.

- Confirm the existence, legality and enforceability of arrangements to provide or maintain financial support with related and third parties and assess the financial ability of such parties to provide additional funds.

- Review events after the year-end to identify those that either mitigate or otherwise affect the entity's ability to continue as a going concern.

[ISA 570, A16]

- Review correspondence with customers for evidence of any disputes that might impact recoverability of debts and affect future sales.

- Review correspondence with suppliers for evidence of issues regarding payments that might impact the company's ability to obtain supplies or credit.

- Review correspondence with the bank for indication that a bank loan or overdraft may be recalled.

- Obtain written representation from management regarding its plans for the future and how it plans to address the going concern issues.
[ISA 570, 16e]

Exam tip: Audit procedures should focus on cash flows rather than profits. A company can continue to trade as long as it can pay its debts when they fall due. Therefore suggest procedures to obtain evidence about the amount of cash that is likely to be received and the amount of cash that it likely to be paid out and consider whether there is any indication of cash flow difficulties.

Disclosures

Disclosures relating to going concern are required to be made by the directors in the following circumstances:

(1) Where there is any **material uncertainty over the future of a company**, the directors should include disclosure in the financial statements.
A material uncertainty exists when the magnitude of its potential impact and likelihood of occurrence is such that disclosure of the nature and implications of the uncertainty is necessary for the fair presentation of the financial statements and for the financial statements not to be misleading. [ISA 570, 18]

The disclosure should explain:

– the principal events or conditions that cast significant doubt on the entity's ability to continue as a going concern and management's plans to deal with them

– the company may be unable to realise its assets and discharge its liabilities in the normal course of business.

[ISA 570, 19]

(2) Where the directors have been **unable to assess going concern in the usual way** (e.g. for less than one year beyond the date on which they sign the financial statements), this fact should be disclosed.

(3) Where the **financial statements are prepared on a basis other than the going concern basis**, the basis used should be disclosed.

Reporting implications

The auditor should modify the audit opinion if the directors have not made adequate disclosure of any material uncertainty related to going concern or if the directors have not prepared the financial statements on the appropriate basis.

The auditor should issue an unmodified opinion with additional communication if the directors have appropriately disclosed going concern uncertainties or prepared the financial statements on the break-up basis.

Reporting implications in relation to going concern are covered in more detail in the Reporting chapter.

Examination of a cash flow forecast

One way of assessing the client's ability to continue as a going concern is to examine the **reasonableness of the assumptions** used to prepare the cash flow forecast.

The following procedures are typical of those that would be performed in the examination of a cash flow forecast.

Procedures in the examination of a cash forecast would include:

- Agree the opening balance of the cash forecast to the cash book, to ensure accuracy.

- Consider how reasonable company forecasts have been in the past by comparing past forecasts with actual outcomes. If forecasts have been reasonable in the past, this would make it more likely that the current forecast is reliable.

- Determine the assumptions that have been made in the preparation of the cash flow forecast. For example, if the company is operating in a poor economic climate, you would not expect cash flows from sales and realisation of receivables to increase, but either to decrease or remain stable. If costs are rising you would expect payments to increase in the cash flow forecast.

- Agree the timing of receipts from realisation of receivables and payments to suppliers with credit periods and previous trade receivables and payables payment periods.

- Examine the company's detailed budgets for the forecast period and discuss any specific plans with the directors.

- Examine the assessment of the non-current assets required to meet production needs. Agree cash outflows for non-current assets to supplier quotations.

- For acquisitions of buildings, agree the timing and amount of cash outflows to the expected completion date and consideration in the sale and purchase agreement.

- Consider the adequacy of the increased working capital and the working capital cash flows included in the forecast.

- If relevant, compare actual performance in the most recent management accounts to the forecast figures.

- Recalculate the cash flow forecast balances to verify arithmetical accuracy.

- Inspect board minutes for any other relevant issues which should be included within the forecast.

Test your understanding 2

Murray case study: Going concern review for the year-ended 31 December 20X4

On 2 January 20X5, Golf is Us, a major customer of Murray Co, was placed into administration owing $211,000.

On 3 January 20X5, the sales director left the company and has yet to be replaced. The sales director is suing Murray Co for constructive dismissal.

On 5 January 20X5 there was a fire at the premises of the third party warehouse provider, which destroyed all inventory held there. Approximately one half of Murray Co's inventory was stored in these premises.

The assembly line for ergometers (rowing machines) was refurbished during the year at a cost of $1 million. The additional $1.5 million loan facility provided to Murray Co during the year is secured, in part, on the refurbished assembly line. The assembly line broke down during January and six weeks later is still not working.

The company is seeking new funding through an initial public offering of shares in the company (i.e. listing on the stock exchange). In the event that the initial public offering does not proceed, this will require Murray Co's existing banking arrangements to be renegotiated and additional funding to be raised from either existing or new investors.

The financial statements of Murray Co show an overdraft at 31 December 20X4 of $180,000 (20X3: $120,000). The overdraft limit is $250,000. The cash flow forecast shows negative monthly cash flows for the next twelve months. As a result of cash shortages in February 20X5, a number of suppliers were paid late.

Required:

Using the information provided, explain the potential indicators that Murray Co is not a going concern.

4   Overall review of the financial statements

Before forming an opinion on the financial statements and deciding on the wording of the auditor's report, the auditor should conduct **an overall review**.

The auditor should perform the following procedures:

(1)   Review the financial statements to ensure:

– Compliance with accounting standards and local legislation disclosure requirements. This is sometimes performed using a disclosure checklist.

– Accounting policies are sufficiently disclosed and to ensure that they are in accordance with the accounting treatment adopted in the financial statements.

– They adequately reflect the information and explanations previously obtained and conclusions reached during the course of the audit.

(2)   Perform analytical procedures to corroborate conclusions formed during the audit and assist when forming an overall conclusion as to whether the financial statements are consistent with the auditor's understanding of the entity. [ISA 520, 6]

(3)   Review the aggregate of the uncorrected misstatements to assess whether a material misstatement arises. If so, discuss the potential adjustment with management.

The purpose of review procedures

Review forms part of the engagement performance quality control procedures covered in the Planning chapter.

As part of the overall review, the auditor should assess whether:

• The audit work was performed in accordance with professional standards.

• Significant matters have been raised for further consideration and appropriate consultations have taken place.

• There is a need to revise the nature, timing and extent of the work performed.

• The audit evidence gathered by the team is sufficient and appropriate to support the audit opinion.

[ISA 220, A17]

The auditor should ensure that initial assessments made at the start of the audit are still valid in light of the information gathered during the audit and that the audit plan has been flexed to meet any new circumstances.

5 Evaluation of misstatements

The auditor must consider the effect of misstatements on both the audit procedures performed and ultimately, if uncorrected, on the financial statements as a whole. Guidance on how this is performed is given in ISA 450 *Evaluation of Misstatements Identified During the Audit.*

In order to achieve this the auditor must:

- Accumulate a record of all identified misstatements, unless they are clearly trivial. [ISA 450, 5]

- Consider if the existence of such misstatements indicates that others may exist, which, when aggregated with other misstatements, could be considered material. [ISA 450, 6a]

- If so, consider if the audit strategy and plan need to be revised. [ISA 450, 6]

- Communicate all accumulated misstatements to an appropriate level of **management** on a timely basis and request that **all** misstatements are corrected. [ISA 450, 8]

- If management refuses to correct some or all of the misstatements the auditor should consider their reasons for refusal and take these into account when considering if the financial statements are free from material misstatement. [ISA 450, 9]

Evaluation of uncorrected misstatements

If management have failed to correct all of the misstatements reported to them, the auditor should:

- Reassess materiality to determine whether it is still appropriate in the circumstances as the level of risk may be deemed higher as a result of management's refusal. [ISA 450, 10]

- Determine whether the uncorrected misstatements, either individually or in aggregate, are material to the financial statements as a whole, considering both the size and nature of the misstatements and the effect of misstatements related to prior periods (e.g. on corresponding figures, comparatives and opening balances). If an individual misstatement is considered material it cannot be offset by other misstatements. [ISA 450, 11]

- Communicate the uncorrected misstatements to **those charged with governance** and explain the effect this will have on the audit opinion. [ISA 450, 12]

- Request a written representation from management and those charged with governance that they believe the effects of uncorrected misstatements are immaterial. [ISA 450, 14]

Evaluation of misstatements

You are at the completion stage of the audit of Murray Co. The profit before tax for the year is $1,048,000 and total assets are $9,697,000. The following matters have not been corrected by management and have been left for your attention:

(1)   An irrecoverable debt of $211,000 has not been written off.

(2)   An adjustment to a provision relating to the unfair dismissal of an ex-employee of $15,000 has not been made.

(3)   Website development costs of $50,000 were incorrectly capitalised.

(4)   Work in progress was overvalued by $45,000.

All of these misstatements must be communicated to management and requested to be adjusted in accordance with ISA 450.

The irrecoverable debt must be written off to avoid a modified opinion as it is individually material. A material misstatement cannot be off-set by other misstatements.

Even if management agree to write-off the irrecoverable debt, the other uncorrected misstatements are material in aggregate even though they are not material individually.

The adjustments required are:

- Provision: DR Provision (SFP), CR Provision expense (P&L) – $15,000

- Website development costs: DR Expenses (P&L), CR Website development costs (SFP) – $50,000

- Work in progress: DR Closing inventory (P&L), CR Inventory (SFP) – $45,000.

The overall adjustment required to the P&L is $80,000. This represents 7.6% of PBT and is material.

The misstatements will need to be adjusted to avoid a modified opinion.

6   Written representations

 A written representation is: **A written statement by management provided to the auditor to confirm certain matters or to support other audit evidence.** [ISA 580 *Written Representations*, 7].

Purpose of written representations

ISA 580 *Written Representations* requires the auditor to obtain written representations from management:

- That they have fulfilled their responsibility for the preparation of the financial statements. [ISA 580, 6a]

- To support other audit evidence relevant to the financial statements or specific assertions if deemed necessary by the auditor or required by specific ISAs. [ISA 580, 6b]

- That they have provided the auditor with all relevant information. [ISA 580, 11a]

- That all transactions have been recorded and reflected in the financial statements. [ISA 580, 11b]

A representation to support other audit evidence may be appropriate where more reliable forms of evidence are not available, particularly in relation to matters requiring management judgment or knowledge restricted to management. Examples include:

- Whether the selection and application of accounting policies are appropriate.

- Whether the following matters have been measured, presented and disclosed in accordance with the relevant financial reporting framework:

    - Plans or intentions that may affect the carrying value or classification of assets and liabilities.

    - Liabilities, both contingent and actual.

    - Title to, or control over, assets.

    - Aspects of laws, regulations and contractual agreements that may affect the financial statements, including non-compliance.

[ISA 580, A10]

- That the directors have communicated all deficiencies in internal control to the auditor. [ISA 580, A11]

- Specific assertions about classes of transactions, accounts balances and disclosures requiring management judgment. [ISA 580, A13]

Note that written representations cannot be a substitute for more reliable evidence that should be available and do not constitute sufficient appropriate evidence on their own, about any of the matters with which they deal. [ISA 580, 4]

Written representations should only be sought to support other audit evidence.

Process for obtaining a written representation

In practice, the auditor will often draft the wording of the written representation letter but it must be printed on client headed paper, addressed to the auditor and signed by the client.

The letter must be signed by an appropriate senior member of client management, with appropriate responsibilities for the financial statements and knowledge of the matters concerned. This would normally be the chief executive and chief financial officer.

The date of the written representation letter should be the same as the date the financial statements are authorised. It must be obtained and signed before the auditor's report is finalised.

Reliability of written representations

Written representations are client generated, and may be subject to bias. It is therefore, potentially, an unreliable form of audit evidence.

The auditor must consider the reliability of written representations in terms of:

- Concerns about the competence, integrity, ethical values or diligence of management. [ISA 580, 16]

- Inconsistencies with other forms of evidence. [ISA 580, 17]

Steps if written representations are inconsistent with other evidence

- Consider the reliability of representations in general.

- Reconsider the initial risk assessment.

- Consider the need to perform further audit procedures.

[ISA 580, A23]

If there are concerns about the competence, integrity, ethical values or diligence of management:

- The auditor must consider whether the engagement can be conducted effectively.

- If they conclude that it cannot then they should withdraw from the engagement, where permitted by laws and regulations.

- If they are not permitted to withdraw they should consider the impact on the auditor's report. It is likely that this would lead to a disclaimer of opinion.

[ISA 580, A24]

Steps if management refuse to provide written representations

Although possibly unreliable, written representations are a necessary and important source of evidence.

If management refuse to provide requested written representations, the auditor should:

- Discuss the matter with management to understand why they are refusing.

- Re-evaluate the integrity of management and consider the effect that this may have on the reliability of other representations (oral or written) and audit evidence in general.

- Consider the implication for the auditor's report.

[ISA 580, 19]

Audit reporting implications

The auditor should issue a disclaimer of opinion if:

- The auditor concludes there is sufficient doubt about the integrity of management which means the written representations are not reliable, or

- Management does not provide the written representations required in relation to confirming their responsibility to prepare the financial statements and to provide the auditor with information, and confirming completeness of transactions.

[ISA 580, 20]

Illustration 2 – Murray Co-written representation letter

Murray Co

1 Murray Mound, Wimbledon

London WN1 2LN

Wimble & Co

2 Court Lane, Wimbledon

London WN1 2LN

18 February 20X5

Dear Wimble & Co,

This written representation is provided in connection with your audit of the financial statements of Murray Company for the year-ended December 31, 20X4 for the purpose of expressing an opinion as to whether the financial statements give a true and fair view in accordance with International Financial Reporting Standards.

We confirm that:

Financial Statements

- We have fulfilled our responsibilities, as set out in the terms of the audit engagement dated 25 November 20X4, for the preparation of the financial statements in accordance with International Financial Reporting Standards; in particular the financial statements give a true and fair view in accordance therewith.

- Significant assumptions used by us in making accounting estimates, including those measured at fair value, are reasonable. (ISA 540)

- All events subsequent to the date of the financial statements and for which International Financial Reporting Standards require adjustment or disclosure have been adjusted or disclosed. (ISA 560)

- The effects of uncorrected misstatements are immaterial, both individually and in the aggregate, to the financial statements as a whole. A list of the uncorrected misstatements is attached. (ISA 450)

- The basis and amount of the warranty provision are reasonable. (specific matter)

Information provided

- We have provided you with:

    - Access to all information of which we are aware that is relevant to the preparation of the financial statements, such as records, documentation and other matters.

    - Additional information that you have requested from us for the purpose of the audit.

    - Unrestricted access to persons within the entity from whom you determined it necessary to obtain audit evidence.

- All transactions have been recorded in the accounting records and are reflected in the financial statements.

- We have disclosed to you the results of our assessment of the risk that the financial statements may be materially misstated as a result of fraud. (ISA 240)

- We have disclosed to you all information in relation to fraud or suspected fraud that we are aware of and that affects the entity and involves:

    - Management

    - Employees who have significant roles in internal control; or

    - Others where the fraud could have a material effect on the financial statements. (ISA 240)

- We have disclosed to you all information in relation to allegations of fraud, or suspected fraud, affecting the entity's financial statements communicated by employees, former employees, analysts, regulators or others. (ISA 240)

- We have disclosed to you all known instances of non-compliance or suspected non-compliance with laws and regulations whose effects should be considered when preparing financial statements. (ISA 250)

- We have disclosed to you all information in relation to settlement of the unfair dismissal, including our intentions thereon. (specific matter)

- We have disclosed to you all information in relation to the constructive dismissal brought by the previous Sales Director, including our intention thereon. (specific matter)

Ed Perry

Edward Perry

Finance Director, Murray Co

Maria Williams

Maria Williams

Managing Director, Murray Co

Test your understanding 3

Smithson Co provides scientific services to a wide range of clients. Typical assignments range from testing food for illegal additives to providing forensic analysis on items used to commit crimes to assist law enforcement officers.

The annual audit is nearly complete. As audit senior you have reported to the engagement partner that Smithson is having some financial difficulties. Income has fallen due to the adverse effect of two high-profile court cases, following which a number of clients withdrew their contracts with Smithson. A senior employee then left Smithson, stating lack of investment in new analysis machines was increasing the risk of incorrect information being provided by the company. A cash flow forecast prepared internally shows Smithson requiring significant additional cash within the next 12 months to maintain even the current level of services.

Required:

(a) Define 'going concern' and discuss the auditor's and directors' responsibilities in respect of going concern.

(5 marks)

(b) State the audit procedures that may be carried out to try to determine whether or not Smithson Co is a going concern.

(10 marks)

(c) Explain the audit procedures and actions the auditor may take where the auditor has decided that Smithson Co is unlikely to be a going concern.

(5 marks)

(Total: 20 marks)

Test your understanding 4

Potterton is a listed company that manufactures body lotions under the 'ReallyCool' brand. The company's year-end is 31 March 20X2, and today's date is 1 June 20X2. Draft profit before taxation is $4 million.

The audit is nearing completion, but two issues remain outstanding:

(1) On 27 May 20X2 a legal claim was made against the company on behalf of a teenager who suffered severe burns after using 'ReallyCool ExtraZingy Lotion' in July 20X1. Potterton is considering an out-of-court settlement of $100,000 per year for the remaining life of the claimant. However, no adjustment or disclosure has been made in the financial statements.

(2) At a board meeting on 30 April 20X2, the directors of Potterton proposed a dividend of $2 million. It is highly likely that the shareholders will approve the dividend at the annual general meeting on 3 September 20X2. The directors have recorded the dividend in the draft statement of changes in equity for the year-ended 31 March 20X2.

Required:

(a) **Explain whether the two outstanding issues are adjusting or non-adjusting events, in accordance with IAS 10** *Events after the Reporting Period*.

(8 marks)

(b) **Describe appropriate audit procedures in order to reach a conclusion on the two outstanding issues.**

(5 marks)

(c) **Explain the likely impact on the audit opinion if the directors refuse to make any further adjustments or disclosures in the financial statements.**

(4 marks)

(Total: 17 marks)

Test your understanding 5

(a)   List SIX items that could be included in a written representation.

(3 marks)

(b)   List THREE reasons why auditors obtain written representations.

(3 marks)

(Total: 6 marks)

Test your understanding 6

The audit of Leonora Co is nearly complete and you are performing your procedures in respect of going concern. During the audit you have identified several indicators that the company may not be able to continue as a going concern.

(1)   **Which of the following is correct in terms of responsibilities for going concern?**

A   The auditor chooses the basis of preparation for the financial statements.

B   The client should make adequate disclosure of going concern uncertainties and the auditor should assess the adequacy of them.

C   The auditor will make disclosure of going concern uncertainties in the financial statements.

D   The auditor will notify the shareholders immediately of any going concern issues identified during the audit.

(2) **State whether each of the following statements are true or false in respect of assessing the going concern status of Leonora Co.**

		True	False
A	The auditor should prepare forecasts to assess whether Leonora Co are likely to be able to continue trading		
B	The directors of Leonora Co should prepare forecasts for a period of at least 12 months to assess whether the company is likely to be able to continue trading		
C	If the directors of Leonora Co prepare forecasts for a period of less than 12 months, the auditor should ask them to extend their assessment period		
D	If the directors of Leonora Co prepare forecasts for a period of less than 12 months, the auditor should extend the assessment period by preparing a forecast for the additional 6 months		

(3) **Which of the following is correct in respect of going concern?**

A   All companies must prepare their financial statements on the going concern basis.

B   If there are material uncertainties regarding going concern, the financial statements must be prepared on the break up basis.

C   Going concern means the company is no longer profitable.

D   The directors of the company must disclose material uncertainties regarding going concern in the notes to the financial statements.

(4) **Which of the following are indicators of going concern problems?**

(i)   Declining revenues.

(ii)   Significant outstanding receivables.

(iii)   Loan repayments due to be made.

(iv)   Declining current and quick ratios.

A   (i), (ii) and (iii) only

B   (ii), (iii) and (iv) only

C   All of them

D   (iii) only

(5) **Which of the following procedures is not appropriate for obtaining evidence regarding the going concern assumption?**

A   Obtain external confirmation from a customer regarding their outstanding balance.

B   Examine cash flow forecasts.

C   Discuss with management their plans for the future.

D   Inspect correspondence with the bank regarding loan or overdraft facilities.

Test your understanding 7

You are currently performing subsequent events procedures for the audit of Kookynie Co. From a review of the board minutes you identify that a customer is suing the company for an injury they suffered on the client's premises on 5 February 20X0. The client's year-end is 31 January 20X0. The directors are proposing to amend the financial statements to include a provision for the amount of compensation they expect to have to pay to the customer. Legal advice received indicates that the claim is possible to succeed.

(1) **Which of the following statements is true with regard to subsequent events?**

A   The auditor must perform audit procedures to identify events occurring after the date of the financial statements up to the date the auditor's report is signed that could have an effect on the financial statements

B   The auditor does not need to consider any events which occur after the date of the financial statements as it is outside of the reporting period

C   The auditor has no responsibility after the auditor's report has been signed, even if they become aware of events occurring which means the opinion is now incorrect

D   The auditor only needs to consider subsequent events communicated to them by the directors

(2) **Which of the following statements is false in respect of subsequent events?**

A   The auditor must ensure the client has complied with IAS 10 *Events After the Reporting Period* when performing the audit of subsequent events

B   The auditor must comply with IAS 10 *Events After the Reporting Period* when performing the audit of subsequent events

C   The auditor must comply with ISA 560 *Subsequent Events* when performing the audit of subsequent events

D   Events after the reporting period may be adjusting or non-adjusting

(3) **Which of the following is true in respect of adjusting events?**

A   Adjusting events are those events which occur before the auditor's report has been signed

B   Adjusting events are those which occur after the year-end date

C   Adjusting events are those which occur after the year-end date and provide evidence of a condition existing at the year-end date

D   Adjusting events require disclosure in the notes to the financial statements

(4) **In respect of the customer's claim, which of the following statements is true?**

A   If the claim was probable rather than possible, a provision should be recognised in the financial statements dated 31 January 20X0

B   The injury was caused after the year-end therefore was not a condition in existence at the year-end

C   The injury was caused after the year-end therefore has no impact on the financial statements being audited

D   The claim is an adjusting event and the financial statements should reflect the claim

(5) **Which of following procedures would NOT be appropriate in respect of Kookynie Co's subsequent events review?**

A   Inspect correspondence from the lawyers regarding the likely outcome of the case and the estimate of compensation if the claim is successful

B   Discuss with management the details of the accident giving rise to the claim

C   Obtain written representation from management that all known subsequent events have been disclosed to the auditor and reflected in the financial statements.

D   Telephone the lawyer to discuss further details of the case of which the client may not be aware

Test your understanding 8

You are completing the audit of Balladonia Co and you are waiting for the client to sign and return the written representation letter. The directors have expressed concern about signing the letter. They have stated that the auditor has been provided with all of the information they require and therefore do not understand why the representation letter is necessary.

(1) **State whether each of the following statements is true or false in respect of written representations.**

		True	False
A	As you have received all other information during the audit, the decision by management not to provide the written representation letter is not an issue that would affect the auditor's report		
B	A written representation is an important piece of evidence which the auditor must obtain		
C	A written representation does not need to be obtained if the wording would be the same as last year's written representation		
D	Failure by management to provide a written representation letter may cast doubt over management integrity		

KAPLAN PUBLISHING

(2) **Which of the following statements is false?**

A   Written representations include confirmation that management have fulfilled their responsibilities in respect of the financial statements and have provided the auditor will all records and information during the audit.

B   Written representations should only be relied on where there is limited other evidence available such as matters of judgment or matters confined to management.

C   The auditor would obtain a written representation regarding the reasonableness of a depreciation charge as this is an estimate.

D   Failure to obtain a written representation is likely to result in a disclaimer of opinion.

(3) **Which of the following would be the auditor's first course of action after being informed that management are unwilling to provide the written representation?**

A   Discuss the matter with management and try to resolve the issue

B   Discuss the matter with those charged with governance and try to resolve the issue

C   Discuss the matter with the shareholders and try to resolve the issue

D   Modify the audit opinion

(4) **Written representation is required from management to confirm they believe the effects of any uncorrected misstatements are immaterial. Which of the following best describes a misstatement?**

A   An error in the financial statements

B   A fraud which has a material effect on the financial statements

C   An omission of a balance from the financial statements

D   A difference between what has been reported in the financial statements and what should have been reported in the financial statements

(5) **During the audit of Balladonia Co you discovered misstatements totalling $20,000. Profit before tax is $570,000. Which of the following describes the most appropriate course of action?**

A Ignore the misstatements if they are deemed to be immaterial

B Modify the audit opinion as a result of misstatement

C Request the client to correct the misstatements

D Include an Emphasis of Matter paragraph in the auditor's report to highlight that misstatements are present in the financial statements

7 Chapter summary

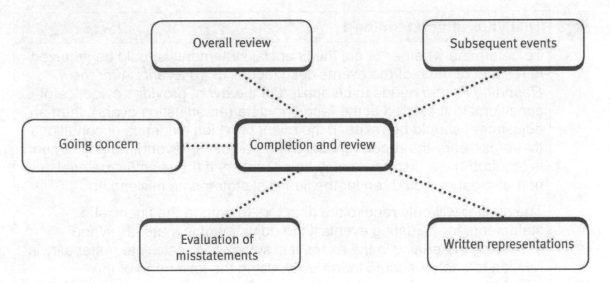

Test your understanding answers

Test your understanding 1

To determine whether or not the financial statements should be adjusted in respect of each of the events described, IAS 10 *Events After the Reporting Period* needs to be applied. If the event provides evidence of conditions that existed at the reporting date (an adjusting event), then an adjustment should be made. If the event provides evidence of conditions that arose after the reporting date (a non-adjusting event), no adjustment is required but a disclosure may be necessary if the event is material and non-disclosure would render the financial statements misleading.

The auditor will only require the directors to amend the financial statements for adjusting events if the adjustment is material. When assessing materiality in the exam, it is sufficient to calculate materiality in relation to each measure individually, using the lower end of the thresholds for prudence. If the item is material to one or more of the measures then it requires adjustment.

(1) Gold is Us was placed into administration after the year-end, which provides evidence of the recoverability of the receivables balance at the year-end. Therefore this is an **adjusting event.** The total value of the balance is $211,000 which is 1% of revenue, 2% of total assets and 20% of profit, and is therefore **material.** The receivables balance should be written off or an allowance for receivables created.

(2) The sales director left the company after the year-end and is suing for constructive dismissal, which is an event that arose after the reporting date. Therefore this is a **non-adjusting event.** The total value of the claim is $280,000, which is 1.3% of revenue, 2.9% of assets and 26.7% of profit before tax and is therefore material. This may also be considered material by nature. The nature of the event and any estimates of the financial impact should therefore be **disclosed**.

(3) A fire destroyed inventory after the year-end, which is therefore a **non-adjusting event** (as the inventory was not damaged at the year-end). The total value of inventory stored at the premises is $1,054,000, which is 5% of revenue, 11% of total assets and 101% of profit and is therefore **material** and the nature of the event and any estimates of the financial impact should be **disclosed**.

(4) After the year-end a letter was received offering to settle a claim for unfair dismissal out-of-court. This is an event that provides evidence of the valuation of the provision at the year-end and is therefore an **adjusting event.** The current provision is for $40,000 and the adjustment would therefore be $15,000. This is **not material** being 0.07% of revenue, 0.15% of total assets and 1.43% profit before tax. Therefore **no adjustment** is necessary.

Test your understanding 2

Going concern indicators at Murray Co:

Indicator	Explanation
A major customer has been placed into administration	Unless the customer can be replaced, this will result in significant loss of future revenues. The debt outstanding is unlikely to be paid resulting in a negative impact on cash flow.
The sales director left the company and has yet to be replaced.	Loss of a key director will impact on the company's sales. As Murray Co has already lost a major customer, without an experienced sales director to generate new sales the company will face significantly reduced sales and cash flows.
The sales director is suing Murray Co for constructive dismissal.	Murray Co will need to pay expensive legal costs in order to defend this litigation, squeezing cash flows even further. In addition, this may damage their reputation and make it difficult to recruit a suitable replacement or other key staff. Any compensation awarded to the sales director will mean further outflow of cash.
Murray Co is seeking new funding through an initial public offering of shares in the company.	If Murray Co does not obtain new funding through a listing, alternative finance will need to be obtained in order to continue to operate. This may not be easy to obtain given their other problems.
Murray Co is operating close to its overdraft limit.	Murray Co is heavily dependent on a short-term source of finance that is repayable on demand. It may be difficult to obtain further sources of finance if the overdraft reaches it limit.

The cash flow forecast shows negative monthly cash flows for the next twelve months.	If the company continues to have cash outflows then the overdraft will increase further and there may be no cash available to pay debts as they fall due.
A number of suppliers have been paid late.	If suppliers are paid late they may refuse to supply Murray Co with goods/components or impose cash on delivery terms which will disrupt production, and delay sales to customers. This may cause them to lose customers altogether.
The loan facility is secured, in part, on the refurbished assembly line which has broken down.	The bank may withdraw the loan facility if the asset on which it is secured is significantly impaired. Murray Co does not have sufficient cash to repay the loan. Unless Murray Co can negotiate with the bank or raise alternative finance (or sell non-current assets), they will have no realistic alternative but to liquidate.
The assembly line broke down during January, and six weeks later is still not working.	If Murray Co cannot meet customer orders due to manufacturing problems, refunds may have to be given and customer goodwill may be lost along with future revenue, which will put further pressure on cash flows.
A fire at the premises of the third party warehouse provider destroyed approximately one half of Murray Co's inventory.	If Murray Co cannot meet customer orders due to this lost revenue. Refunds may have to be given and customer goodwill may be lost along with future revenues which will put further pressure on cash flows. If the losses are not covered by insurance, this will significantly impact profit and cash flow.

Test your understanding 3

(a) **Going concern**

Going concern means that the entity will continue in operational existence for the foreseeable future without the intention or the necessity of liquidation or otherwise ceasing trade. It is one of the accounting principles given in IAS 1 *Presentation of Financial Statements*.

The auditor should consider the appropriateness of management's use of the going concern assumption in the preparation of the financial statements.

The auditor's responsibilities are:

(i) To carry out appropriate audit procedures that will identify whether or not an organisation can continue as a going concern.

(ii) To ensure that the organisation's management have been realistic in their use of the going concern assumption when preparing the financial statements.

(iii) To report to the members where they consider that the going concern assumption has been used inappropriately, for example, when the financial statements indicate that the organisation is a going concern but audit procedures indicate this may not be the case.

It is the directors' responsibility to prepare the financial statements on an appropriate basis, be that either the going concern or the breakup basis.

(b) **Audit procedures regarding going concern**

– Obtain a copy of the cash flow forecast and assess the reasonableness of the assumptions used in the forecast.

– Discuss with the directors their view of whether Smithson can continue as a going concern. Ask for their reasons and try and determine whether these are reasonable.

– Enquire of the directors whether they have considered any other forms of finance for Smithson to make up the cash shortfall identified in the cash flow forecast.

– Obtain a copy of any interim financial statements of Smithson to determine the level of sales/income after the year-end and whether this matches the cash flow forecast.

– Enquire about the possible lack of capital investment within Smithson identified by the employee leaving. Review the purchase policy with the directors.

– Consider the extent to which Smithson rely on the senior employee who recently left the company. Ask the HR department whether the employee will be replaced soon.

– Obtain a solicitor's letter and review to identify any legal claims against Smithson related to below standard services being provided to clients. Where possible, consider the financial impact on Smithson and whether insurance is available to mitigate any claims.

– Review Smithson's order book to try and determine the value of future orders compared to previous years.

– Review the bank letter to determine the extent of any bank loans and whether repayments due in the next 12 months can be made without further borrowing.

– Review other events after the end of the financial year and determine whether these have an impact on Smithson.

– Obtain a written representation confirming the directors' opinion that Smithson is a going concern.

(c) **Audit procedures and actions if Smithson is not considered to be a going concern**

– Discuss the situation again with directors. Consider whether additional disclosures are required in the financial statements or whether the financial statements should be prepared on the break-up basis.

– Explain to the directors that if additional disclosure or restatement of the financial statements is not made then the auditor will have to modify the auditor's report and opinion.

– Consider implications for the auditor's report. Where the directors provide adequate disclosure of the going concern situation of Smithson, then a section should be included in the auditor's report headed 'Material Uncertainty Related to Going Concern' to draw attention to the going concern disclosures.

– Where the directors do not make adequate disclosure of the going concern situation then modify the audit opinion due to material misstatement from inadequate disclosure.

– The modification will be an 'except for' qualification or an adverse opinion depending on whether the issue is material or material and pervasive.

– The 'Basis for Opinion' section will be amended to 'Basis for Adverse Opinion' or 'Basis for Qualified Opinion' to explain the reason for the modified opinion.

– If Smithson is a listed company, the Key Audit Matters section will reference the 'Basis for Adverse/Qualified Opinion' section.

Test your understanding 4

(a) **Analysis of events**

Legal claim: The legal claim is an adjusting event because it provides evidence of a condition existing at the end of the reporting period. As at 31 March 20X2, the claimant had purchased and used the product, and the damage to the claimant's skin had already occurred.

The legal claim is material, because, if the claimant lived for, say, another 40 years, the company would owe him/her $4 million. This is 100% of the current year draft profit before tax.

Therefore profit should be reduced and liabilities increased by the expected value of the claim.

Proposed dividend: The proposed dividend is a non-adjusting event because the condition arose after the end of the reporting period. No liability for the dividend can exist until the shareholders approve the dividend.

The proposed dividend is material because it constitutes 50% ($2m/$4m × 100) of the company's profit before tax, as well as being material by nature.

Therefore the dividend should not be recognised in the financial statements for the year-ended 31 March 20X2. However, the proposed dividend should be disclosed in a note to the financial statements.

(b) **Audit procedures**

Legal claim:

– Review legal correspondence in order to understand the likely outcome of the legal claim.

– Review customer correspondence/legal files in order to identify other similar claims which could give rise to additional liabilities.

– Discuss with the production director the likely cause of the burns (e.g. allergy in user or inadequate printed instructions on product use) to determine the likelihood of any claim being successful in court.

– Review trade/consumer press to identify whether the claim might damage Reallycool's reputation which could impact future revenues or even create a going concern threat.

– Propose adjustment of the financial statements to the directors.

Proposed dividend:

- Inspect board minutes in order to confirm the amount of the proposed dividend.

- Propose an adjustment to the financial statements to remove the dividend from being recognised in the statement of changes in equity but ensure that the dividend proposal is disclosed within the notes.

(c) **Impact on audit opinion**

- The auditor must modify the audit opinion if the directors refuse to make the relevant adjustments in the financial statements requested by the auditors.

- Both the legal claim (which should have been recognised) and the proposed dividend (which should have been disclosed rather than recognised) are materially misstated.

- The auditor must express a qualified ('except for') opinion if they conclude that the misstatements are material, but not pervasive, to the financial statements.

- The auditor must express an adverse opinion if they conclude that misstatements are both material and pervasive to the financial statements.

- Given the size of the amounts involved, an adverse opinion may be appropriate in these circumstances.

Tutorial note: If the requirement asked for implications for the auditor's report, the following points should also be included in the answer:

- The 'Basis for Opinion' section will be amended to 'Basis for Adverse' or 'Basis for Qualified Opinion' to explain the reason for the modified opinion.

- As Potterton is listed, the Key Audit Matters section will reference the 'Basis for Adverse/Qualified Opinion' section.

Test your understanding 5

(a) **Items to be included in a written representation letter**

- All books, records and relevant information have been made available to the auditors.

- Financial statements have been prepared in accordance with an applicable financial reporting framework.

- All transactions have been recorded and reflected in the financial statements.

- The effects of uncorrected misstatements are immaterial to the financial statements.

- Any instances of non-compliance with laws and regulations have been disclosed to the auditor.

- The directors believe the company can continue to trade as a going concern.

- The directors have no plans that will materially alter the carrying value or classification of assets or liabilities in the financial statements.

- No plans to abandon any product lines that will result in any excess or obsolete inventory.

- All subsequent events have been disclosed to the auditor and reflected appropriately in the financial statements.

- No irregularities involving management or employees that could have a material effect on the financial statements.

(b) **Reasons why the auditor obtains written representations**

- Formal confirmation by management of their responsibilities.

- To support other evidence relevant to the financial statements if determined necessary by the auditor, e.g. matters requiring management judgment.

- Required by ISA 580 and other ISAs.

Test your understanding 6		
(1)	B	The directors (client) must make the disclosures in the financial statements. The auditor will audit them.
(2)	A – False	The auditor should review the forecasts prepared by the directors. The auditor should not prepare them.
	B – True	The directors (client) should prepare the forecasts to assist with their assessment of going concern in order to determine the appropriate basis on which to prepare the financial statements.
	C – True	The directors are required to consider at least a 12 month period for their going concern assessment. The auditor must ask them to extend their assessment if they fail to consider at least 12 months.
	D – False	The auditor should not extend the assessment or prepare forecasts for the client.
(3)	D	The financial statements should be prepared on the break up basis if the company is not a going concern. If there are material uncertainties regarding going concern, these must be disclosed by the directors. A company may be profitable but not have the cash to pay its debts when they fall due.
(4)	C	All are indicators of going concern problems.
(5)	A	Obtaining external confirmation from a customer may confirm the balance owed but does not provide evidence that the money will be received.

Test your understanding 7

(1)	A	The auditor has an active duty up to the date the auditor's report is signed. If they become aware of events after this date that would cause them to modify their opinion they must take action.
(2)	B	IAS 10 *Events After the Reporting Period* refers to the accounting treatment the client should comply with. The auditor must comply with ISA 560 *Subsequent Events*.
(3)	C	Adjusting events provide evidence of conditions existing at the year-end (IAS 10, 3a).
(4)	B	As the injury was suffered after the year-end it is a non-adjusting event. Therefore a provision is not required at 31 January 20X0. If it is material, disclosure should be made.
(5)	D	The auditor has no right to contact the lawyer in this manner. A lawyer confirmation letter may be sent with client permission. It would not be professional for the lawyer to discuss details of the case that are not known to the client with the auditor.

Test your understanding 8

(1)	A – False	Written representations are required by ISA 580. Without it the auditor does not have sufficient appropriate evidence and as such must modify the auditor's report.
	B – True	
	C – False	The written representation must be dated just before the date of the auditor's report. Even if the wording is the same, a written representation must be obtained each year.
	D – True	Management are informed in the engagement letter that written representations will be required.
		Failure to provide one indicates management are trying to conceal information from the auditor which casts doubt over their integrity.
(2)	C	Sufficient other evidence is available to assess the reasonableness of depreciation.
(3)	A	The first course of action would be to try and resolve the issue with management. If that failed the auditor could discuss the matter with those charged with governance. The shareholders would not be involved in this issue. The audit opinion would be modified if the issue could not be resolved with management or those charged with governance.
(4)	D	Errors, frauds and omissions are all types of misstatement. Therefore the best description of a misstatement is answer D. A difference between what should be reported and what has been reported can be caused by an error, fraud or omission.
(5)	C	Even if misstatements are immaterial they should not be ignored altogether. The client will be asked to correct them. There is no need to modify the auditor's report or opinion if they remain uncorrected provided the refusal to correct does not indicate the presence of other misstatements. An Emphasis of Matter paragraph is not appropriate in this situation. There is no need to communicate immaterial matters to the users of the financial statements.

Reporting

Chapter learning objectives

This chapter covers syllabus areas:

- E5 – The Independent Auditor's Report

- C4c – Communicating with those charged with governance

Detailed syllabus objectives are provided in the introduction section of the text book.

PER

One of the PER performance objectives (PO20) is to review and report on the findings of an audit. You complete an audit, preparing the formal documentation and reporting any control deficiencies to management. You report back to managers in a formal audit report. Working through this chapter should help you understand how to demonstrate that objective.

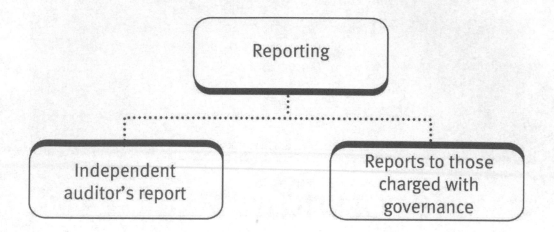

Reporting

Independent auditor's report

Reports to those charged with governance

1 The independent auditor's report

The objectives of the auditor are:

- To form an opinion on the financial statements based on an evaluation of the conclusions drawn from the audit evidence obtained, and

- To express clearly that opinion through a written report.

[ISA 700 *Forming an Opinion and Reporting on Financial Statements*, 6]

The auditor forms an opinion on whether the financial statements are prepared, in all material respects, in accordance with the applicable financial reporting framework.

Illustration 1 – Auditor's report with unmodified opinion

INDEPENDENT AUDITOR'S REPORT

To the Shareholders of Murray Company

Report on the Audit of the Financial Statements [sub-title is not included if there is no separate Report on Other Legal and Regulatory Requirements]

Opinion

We have audited the financial statements of the Murray Company (the Company), which comprise the statement of financial position as at 31 December, 20X4, and the statement of comprehensive income, statement of changes in equity and statement of cash flows for the year then ended, and notes to the financial statements, including a summary of significant accounting policies.

In our opinion, the accompanying financial statements present fairly, in all material respects, (or give a true and fair view of) the financial position of the Company as at December 31, 20X4, and its performance and its cash flows for the year then ended in accordance with International Financial Reporting Standards.

Basis for Opinion

We conducted our audit in accordance with International Standards on Auditing (ISAs). Our responsibilities under those standards are further described in the Auditor's Responsibilities for the Audit of the Financial Statements section of our report. We are independent of the Company in accordance with the ethical requirements that are relevant to our audit of the financial statements in [jurisdiction], and we have fulfilled our other ethical responsibilities in accordance with these requirements. We believe that the audit evidence we have obtained is sufficient and appropriate to provide a basis for our opinion.

Key audit matters [listed companies only]

Key audit matters are those matters that, in our professional judgment, were of most significance in our audit of the financial statements of the current period. These matters were addressed in the context of our audit of the financial statements as a whole, and in forming our opinion thereon, and we do not provide a separate opinion on these matters.

[Description of each key audit matter in accordance with ISA 701]

Other information

Management is responsible for the other information. The other information comprises the Chairman's statement, but does not include the financial statements and the auditor's report thereon.

Our opinion on the financial statements does not cover the other information and we do not express any form of assurance conclusion thereon.

In connection with our audit of the financial statements, our responsibility is to read the other information and, in doing so, consider whether the other information is materially inconsistent with the financial statements or our knowledge obtained in the audit or otherwise appears to be materially misstated. If, based on the work we have performed, we conclude that there is a material misstatement of this information, we are required to report that fact. We have nothing to report in this regard.

Responsibilities of Management and Those Charged With Governance for the Financial Statements

Management is responsible for the preparation and fair presentation of these financial statements in accordance with International Financial Reporting Standards, and for such internal control as management determines is necessary to enable the preparation of financial statements that are free from material misstatement, whether due to fraud or error.

In preparing the financial statements, management is responsible for assessing the Company's ability to continue as a going concern, disclosing as applicable, matters related to going concern and using the going concern basis of accounting unless management either intends to liquidate the Company or to cease operations, or has no realistic alternative but to do so.

Those charged with governance are responsible for overseeing the Company's financial reporting process.

Auditor's Responsibilities for the Audit of the Financial Statements

Our objectives are to obtain reasonable assurance about whether the financial statements as a whole are free from material misstatement, whether due to fraud or error, and to issue an auditor's report that includes our opinion. Reasonable assurance is a high level of assurance, but is not a guarantee that an audit conducted in accordance with ISAs will always detect a material misstatement when it exists. Misstatements can arise from fraud or error and are considered material if, individually or in the aggregate, they could reasonably be expected to influence the economic decisions of users taken on the basis of these financial statements.

As part of an audit in accordance with ISAs, we exercise professional judgment and maintain professional scepticism throughout the audit. We also:

- Identify and assess the risks of material misstatement of the financial statements, whether due to fraud or error, design and perform audit procedures responsive to those risks, and obtain audit evidence that is sufficient and appropriate to provide a basis for our opinion. The risk of not detecting a material misstatement resulting from fraud is higher than for one resulting from error, as fraud may involve collusion, forgery, intentional omissions, misrepresentations, or the override of internal control.

- Obtain an understanding of internal control relevant to the audit in order to design audit procedures that are appropriate in the circumstances, but not for the purpose of expressing an opinion on the effectiveness of the Company's internal control.

- Evaluate the appropriateness of accounting policies used and the reasonableness of accounting estimates and related disclosures made by management.

- Conclude on the appropriateness of management's use of the going concern basis of accounting and, based on the audit evidence obtained, whether a material uncertainty exists related to events or conditions that may cast significant doubt on the Company's ability to continue as a going concern. If we conclude that a material uncertainty exists, we are required to draw attention in our auditor's report to the related disclosures in the financial statements or, if such disclosures are inadequate, to modify our opinion. Our conclusions are based on the audit evidence obtained up to the date of our auditor's report. However, future events or conditions may cause the Company to cease trading as a going concern.

- Evaluate the overall presentation, structure and content of the financial statements, including the disclosures, and whether the financial statements represent the underlying transactions and events in a manner that achieves fair presentation.

We communicate with those charged with governance regarding, among other matters, the planned scope and timing of the audit and significant findings, including any significant deficiencies in internal control that we identify during our audit.

We also provide those charged with governance with a statement that we have complied with relevant ethical requirements regarding independence, and to communicate with them all relationships and other matters that may reasonably be thought to bear on our independence, and where applicable, related safeguards.

From the matters communicated with those charged with governance, we determine those matters that were of most significance in the audit of the financial statements of the current period and are therefore the key audit matters. We describe these matters in our auditor's report unless law or regulation precludes public disclosure about the matter or when, in extremely rare circumstances, we determine that a matter should not be communicated in our report because the adverse consequences of doing so would reasonably be expected to outweigh the public interest benefits of such communication.

Report on Other Legal and Regulatory Requirements

[As required by local law, regulation or national auditing standards]

Wimble & Co

Wimble & Co, London

18 February 20X5

[ISA 700, Appendix]

Explanations of the sections

	Section	Purpose
1	Title	To clearly identify the report as an Independent Auditor's Report.
2	Addressee	To identify the intended user of the report.
3	Auditor's Opinion	Provides the auditor's conclusion as to whether the financial statements give a true and fair view.
4	Basis for Opinion	Provides a description of the professional standards applied during the audit to provide confidence to users that the report can be relied upon.
5	Key Audit Matters	To draw attention to any other significant matters of which the users should be aware, to aid their understanding of the entity. (**Note:** This section is only compulsory for listed entities.)
6	Other Information	To clarify that management are responsible for the other information such as the Chairman's statement. The auditor's opinion does not cover the other information and the auditor's responsibility is only to read the other information and report in accordance with ISA 720.
7	Responsibilities of Management and Those Charged with Governance for the Financial Statements	To clarify that management are responsible for preparing the financial statements and for the internal controls. Included to help minimise the expectation gap.

8	Auditor's Responsibilities for the Audit of the Financial Statements	To clarify that the auditor is responsible for expressing reasonable assurance as to whether the financial statements give a true and fair view and express that opinion in the auditor's report. The section also describes the auditor's responsibilities in respect of risk assessment, internal controls, going concern and accounting policies. Included to help minimise the expectations gap.
9	Report on Other Legal and Regulatory Requirements	To highlight any additional reporting responsibilities, if applicable. This may include responsibilities in some jurisdictions to report on the adequacy of accounting records, internal controls over financial reporting, or other information published with the financial statements.
10	Signature	Identifies the audit firm responsible for the auditor's report and opinion.
		If Murray Co was a listed company, the report would include the name of the engagement partner.
11	Auditor's address	Identifies the specific office of the engagement partner responsible for the report in case of any queries.
12	Date	To identify the date up to which the audit work has been performed. Any information that comes to light after this date will not have been considered by the auditor when forming their opinion. The report must be signed and dated after the date the directors approved the financial statements. Often, the financial statements are approved and the auditor's report signed on the same day.

2 Forming an opinion

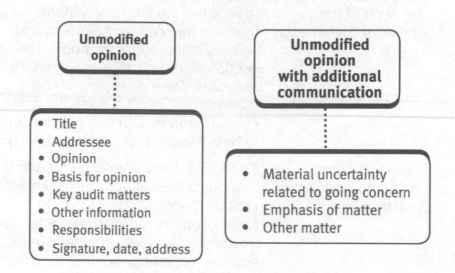

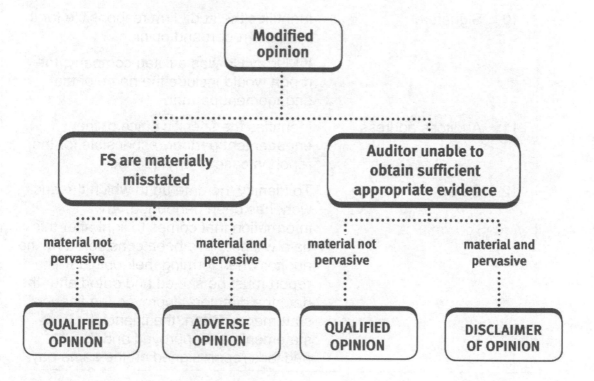

As can be seen from the diagram above, the report can include:

- **An unmodified opinion**

  The financial statements give a true and fair view. (ISA 700)

- **An unmodified opinion but the report contains additional communication**

  The financial statements give a true and fair view but there is additional communication required to bring something to the attention of the user.

- **A modified opinion**

  The financial statements don't fully give a true and fair view or the auditor has not obtained sufficient appropriate evidence to make that conclusion. (ISA 705 *Modifications to the Opinion in the Independent Auditor's Report*).

3 Unmodified opinion

When the auditor concludes that the financial statements are prepared, in all material respects, in accordance with the applicable financial reporting framework they issue an **unmodified opinion** in the auditor's report.
[ISA 700, 16]

This will mean:

- The financial statements adequately disclose the significant accounting policies.

- The accounting policies selected are consistently applied and appropriate.

- Accounting estimates made by management are reasonable.

- Information is relevant, reliable, comparable and understandable.

- The financial statements provide adequate disclosures to enable the users to understand the effects of material transactions and events.

- The terminology used is appropriate.

[ISA 700, 13]

Other Information

A separate section is included in the auditor's report under the heading 'Other Information'. [ISA 720, 21]

 Other information refers to financial or non-financial information, other than the financial statements and auditor's report thereon, included in the entity's annual report. [ISA 720, 12c]

Examples of other information include:

- Chairman's report

- Operating and financial review

- Social and environmental reports

- Corporate governance statements.

The Other Information section:

- Identifies the other information obtained by the auditor prior to the date of the auditor's report.

- States that the auditor has not audited the other information and accordingly does not express an opinion or conclusion on that information.

- Includes a description of the auditor's responsibilities with respect to the other information.

- States either that the auditor has nothing to report or provides a description of the material misstatement if applicable.

[ISA 720, 22]

Purpose

The auditor must not be knowingly associated with information which is misleading. [ISA 720, 4]

Misstatement of other information exists when the other information is incorrectly stated or otherwise misleading (including because it omits or obscures information necessary for a proper understanding of a matter).

Material misstatements or inconsistencies in the other information may undermine the credibility of the financial statements and the auditor's report.

If the auditor obtains the final version of the other information before the date of the auditor's report, they must read it to identify any material inconsistencies with the financial statements or the auditor's knowledge obtained during the audit. [ISA 720, 3]

If the auditor identifies a material inconsistency they should:

- Perform limited procedures to evaluate the inconsistency. The auditor should consider whether it is the financial statements or the other information that requires amendment. [ISA 720, 16]

- Discuss the matter with management and ask them to make the correction. [ISA 720, 17a]

- If management refuse to make the correction, communicate the matter to those charged with governance. [ISA 720, 17b]

- If the matter remains uncorrected the auditor must describe the material misstatement in the auditor's report. [ISA 720, 18a]

- Alternatively, the auditor should withdraw from the engagement if possible under applicable law or regulation as the issue casts doubt over management integrity. [ISA 720, 18b]

Position in the auditor's report

The Other Information section is included in the auditor's report below the Basis for Opinion and Key Audit Matters section (if applicable) and above the Responsibilities of Management.

 Tutorial notes

The auditor must retain a copy of the final version of the other information on the audit file. [ISA 720, 25b]

If the auditor issues a disclaimer of opinion on the financial statements, the Other Information section should not be included in the auditor's report as to do so may overshadow the disclaimer of opinion. [ISA 720, A58]

Key Audit Matters – Listed companies only

ISA 701 *Communicating Key Audit Matters in the Independent Auditor's Report* requires auditors of **listed companies** to determine key audit matters and to communicate those matters in the auditor's report. [ISA 701, 5]

Auditors of non-listed entities may voluntarily, or at the request of management or those charged with governance, include key audit matters in the auditor's report.

 Key audit matters are those that in the auditor's professional judgment were of most significance in the audit and are selected from matters communicated to those charged with governance.
[ISA 701, 8]

The purpose of including these matters is to assist users in understanding the entity, and to provide a basis for the users to engage with management and those charged with governance about matters relating to the entity and the financial statements. [ISA 701, 3]

Each key audit matter should describe why the matter was considered to be significant and how it was addressed in the audit.

Key audit matters include:

- Areas of higher assessed risk of material misstatement, or significant risks identified in accordance with ISA 315 *Identifying and Assessing the Risks of Material Misstatement through Understanding the Entity and Its Environment.*

- Significant auditor judgments relating to areas in the financial statements that involved significant management judgment, including accounting estimates that have been identified as having high estimation uncertainty.

- The effect on the audit of significant events or transactions that occurred during the period.

[ISA 701, 9]

Specific examples include:

- Significant fraud risk
- Goodwill
- Valuation of financial instruments
- Fair values
- Effects of new accounting standards
- Revenue recognition
- Material provisions such as a restructuring provision
- Implementation of a new IT system, or significant changes to an existing system.

Note that a matter giving rise to a qualified or adverse opinion, or a material uncertainty related to going concern are by their nature key audit matters. However, they would not be described in this section of the report. Instead, a reference to the Basis for qualified or adverse opinion or the going concern section would be included. [ISA 701, 15]

If there are no key audit matters to communicate, the auditor shall:

- Discuss this with the engagement quality control reviewer, if one has been appointed.

- Communicate this conclusion to those charged with governance. [ISA 701, 17b]

- Explain in the key audit matters section of the auditor's report that there are no matters to report. [ISA 701, 16]

4 Unmodified opinion with additional communication

In certain circumstances auditors are required to make additional communications in the auditor's report even though the financial statements show a true and fair view. Issues requiring communication include:

- **Material Uncertainty Related to Going Concern** (ISA 570 *Going Concern*)

- **Emphasis of Matter paragraph** (ISA 706 *Emphasis of Matter Paragraphs and Other Matter Paragraphs in an Auditor's Report*)

- **Other Matter paragraph** (ISA 706)

It is important to note that these **do not impact the wording of the opinion** and do not constitute either a qualified, adverse or disclaimer of opinion.

Material Uncertainty Related to Going Concern

Purpose

This section is included when there is a material uncertainty regarding the going concern status which the directors have adequately disclosed in the financial statements. The auditor uses this section to draw the attention of the user to the client's disclosure note. [ISA 570, 22]

Position in the auditor's report

Below the Basis for Opinion section.

Emphasis of Matter paragraph

Purpose

An Emphasis of Matter paragraph is used to refer to **a matter that has been appropriately presented or disclosed in the financial statements** by the directors. The auditor's judgment is that these matters are **of such fundamental importance to the users' understanding** of the financial statements that the auditor should emphasise the disclosure. [ISA 706, 7a]

Examples of such fundamental matters include:

- Where the financial statements have been prepared on a basis other than the going concern basis.

- An uncertainty relating to the future outcome of exceptional litigation or regulatory action.

- A significant subsequent event occurs between the date of the financial statements and the date of the auditor's report.

- Early application of a new accounting standard.

- Major catastrophes that have had a significant effect on the entity's financial position.

- Where the corresponding figures have been restated.

- Where the financial statements have been recalled and reissued or when the auditor provides an amended auditor's report.

[ISA 706, A5]

Position in the auditor's report

Below the Basis for Opinion section.

When a Key Audit Matters section is presented in the auditor's report, an Emphasis of Matter paragraph may be presented either directly before or after the Key Audit Matters section, based on the auditor's judgment as to the relative significance of the information included in the Emphasis of Matter paragraph.

The heading of the paragraph can be amended to provide further context, for example, Emphasis of Matter – Subsequent event. [ISA 706, A16]

 Tutorial notes

An Emphasis of Matter paragraph is not used to draw attention to immaterial misstatements. The fact that they are immaterial means they do not warrant the attention of the shareholders.

An Emphasis of Matter paragraph can only be used when adequate disclosure has been made of the matters mentioned above. The auditor can only emphasise something that is already included.

Where adequate disclosure has not been made the opinion will need to be modified and an Emphasis of Matter paragraph should NOT be used.

An Emphasis of Matter should not be used to highlight an issue already included in the Key Audit Matters section. The auditor must use judgment to determine which section they consider is the most appropriate to highlight the issue.

Other Matter paragraph

Purpose

An Other Matter paragraph is included in the auditor's report if the auditor considers it necessary to communicate to the users regarding **matters other than those presented or disclosed in the financial statements** that, in the auditor's judgment, are **relevant to understanding the audit, the auditor's responsibilities, or the auditor's report**.
[ISA 706, 7b]

Examples of its use include:

- To communicate that the auditor's report is intended solely for the intended users, and should not be distributed to or used by other parties. [ISA 706, A14]

- When law, regulation or generally accepted practice requires or permits the auditor to provide further explanation of their responsibilities. [ISA 706, A11]

- To explain why the auditor has not resigned, when a pervasive inability to obtain sufficient appropriate evidence is imposed by management (e.g. denying the auditor access to books and records) but the auditor is unable to withdraw from the engagement due to legal restrictions. [ISA 706, A10]

- To communicate audit planning and scoping matters where laws or regulations require. [ISA 706, A9]

- Where an entity prepares one set of accounts in accordance with a general purpose framework and another set in accordance with a different one (e.g. one according to UK and one according to International standards) and engages the auditor to report on both sets. [ISA 706, A13]

Position in the auditor's report

When an Other Matter paragraph is included to draw the users' attention to a matter relating to other reporting responsibilities addressed in the auditor's report, the paragraph may be included in the Report on Other Legal and Regulatory Requirements section.

When relevant to all auditor's responsibilities or users' understanding of the auditor's report, the Other Matter paragraph may be included as a separate section following the Report on the Other Legal and Regulatory Requirements.

The heading may be amended to provide further context, for example, Other Matter – Scope of the audit.
[ISA 706, A16]

 Tutorial notes

An Other Matter paragraph does not include confidential information or information required to be provided by management. [ISA 706, A15]

5   Modified opinions

Modifications to the audit opinion

The auditor may decide they need to modify the opinion when they conclude that:

- Based upon the evidence obtained **the financial statements** as a whole **are not free from material misstatement**. This is where the client has not complied with the applicable financial reporting framework.

- They have been **unable to obtain sufficient appropriate evidence** to be able to conclude that the financial statements as a whole are free from material misstatement. This is evidence the auditor would expect to exist to support the figures in the financial statements.

[ISA 705, 6]

The nature of the modification depends upon whether the auditor considers the matter to be material but not pervasive, or material and pervasive, to the financial statements.

Material but not pervasive – Qualified opinion

- If the misstatement or lack of sufficient appropriate evidence is **material but not pervasive**, a **qualified opinion** will be issued. [ISA 705, 7]

- This means the matter is material to the area of the financial statements affected but does not affect the remainder of the financial statements.

- **'Except for'** this matter, the financial statements give a true and fair view.

- Whilst significant to users' decision making, a material matter can be isolated whilst the remainder of the financial statements may be relied upon.

Material and pervasive

A matter is considered '**pervasive**' if, in the auditor's judgment:

- The effects are not confined to specific elements, accounts or items of the financial statements

- If so confined, represent or could represent a substantial proportion of the financial statements, or

- In relation to disclosures, are fundamental to users' understanding of the financial statements.

[ISA 705, 5a]

In brief, a pervasive matter must be fundamental to the financial statements, therefore rendering them unreliable as a whole.

Adverse opinion

An **adverse opinion** is issued when a misstatement is considered material and pervasive. [ISA 705, 8]

This will mean the financial statements **do not give a true and fair view**. Examples include:

- Preparation of the financial statements on the wrong basis.

- Non-consolidation of a subsidiary.

- Material misstatement of a balance which represents a substantial proportion of the assets or profits e.g. would change a profit to a loss.

Disclaimer of opinion

A **disclaimer of opinion** is issued when the auditor has not obtained sufficient appropriate evidence and the effects of any possible misstatements could be pervasive. [ISA 705, 9]

The auditor **does not express an opinion** on the financial statements in this situation.

Examples include:

- Failure by the client to keep adequate accounting records.

- Refusal by the directors to provide written representation.

- Failure by the client to provide evidence over a single balance which represents a substantial proportion of the assets or profits or over multiple balances in the financial statements.

Impact of a disclaimer of opinion

Where a disclaimer of opinion is being issued:

- The statement that sufficient appropriate evidence to provide a basis for the auditor's opinion has been obtained is not included.

- The statement that the financial statements have been audited is changed to 'we were engaged to audit the financial statements'.

[ISA 705, 19]

- The statements regarding the audit being conducted in accordance with ISAs, and independence and other ethical responsibilities, are positioned within the Auditor Responsibilities section rather than the Basis for Disclaimer of Opinion section. [ISA 705, A25]

- The Key Audit Matters section is not included in the report as to do so would suggest the financial statements are more credible in relation to those matters which would be inconsistent with the disclaimer of opinion on the financial statements as a whole. [ISA 705, 29]

Basis for modified opinion

When the auditor decides to modify the opinion, they must amend the heading 'Basis for Opinion' to 'Basis for Qualified Opinion', 'Basis for Adverse Opinion' or 'Basis for Disclaimer of Opinion', as appropriate. [ISA 705, 20a]

Where a qualified or adverse opinion is being issued, the auditor must amend the statement '...the audit evidence is sufficient and appropriate to provide a basis for the auditor's qualified/adverse opinion.' [ISA 705, 25]

The section will explain the reason why the opinion is modified e.g. which balances are misstated, which disclosures are missing or inadequate, which balances the auditor was unable to obtain sufficient appropriate evidence over and why. [ISA 705, 20b]

If possible, a quantification of the financial effect of the modification will be included. [ISA 705, 21]

If the material misstatement relates to narrative disclosures, an explanation of how the disclosures are misstated should be included, or in the case of omitted disclosures, the disclosure should be included if the information is readily available. [ISA 705, 22]

The following table illustrates the impact on the audit opinion and auditor's report. [ISA 705, A1]

	Material but Not Pervasive	Material & Pervasive
Financial statements are materially misstated	Qualified Opinion Except for ... Basis for qualified opinion	Adverse Opinion FS do not give a true and fair view Basis for adverse opinion
Inability to obtain sufficient appropriate audit evidence	Qualified Opinion Except for ... Basis for qualified opinion	Disclaimer of Opinion Do not express an opinion Basis for disclaimer of opinion

Management imposed limitation of scope

- If after accepting the engagement management impose a limitation of scope that will result in a modified opinion, the auditor will request that management remove the limitation. [ISA 705, 11]

- If management refuse, the matter must be communicated with those charged with governance. [ISA 705, 12]

- The auditor should perform alternative audit procedures to obtain sufficient appropriate evidence, if possible. [ISA 705, 12]

- If the auditor is unable to obtain sufficient appropriate evidence and the matter is material but not pervasive, the auditor must issue a qualified audit opinion. [ISA 705, 13a]
  If the matter is considered pervasive, the auditor must withdraw from the audit. [ISA 705, 13bi]

- If withdrawal is not possible before issuing the auditor's report, a disclaimer of opinion should be issued. [ISA 705, 13bii]

- If the auditor decides to withdraw from the audit, the auditor must communicate any material misstatements identified during the audit to those charged with governance before withdrawing.
  [ISA 705, 14]

Going concern reporting implications

Situation	Impact on audit opinion	Impact on auditor's report
No material uncertainty exists regarding going concern.	Unmodified – Financial statements give a true and fair view.	No impact
Material uncertainty exists and is adequately disclosed by management.	Unmodified – Financial statements give a true and fair view.	Additional communication: 'Material Uncertainty Related to Going Concern'.
Material uncertainty exists which is not adequately disclosed or is omitted altogether.	Modified – qualified or adverse.	Basis for qualified/adverse opinion explaining the going concern issues management have failed to disclose adequately.
Company is not a going concern and has prepared the financial statements on the break up basis appropriately and made adequate disclosure of this fact.	Unmodified – Financial statements give a true and fair view.	Additional communication: Emphasis of matter paragraph.
Company is not a going concern and has prepared the financial statements using the going concern basis of accounting.	Modified – adverse opinion.	Basis for modified opinion explaining the going concern issues management have failed to account for appropriately.
The period assessed by management is less than twelve months from the statement of financial position date and management is unwilling to extend the assessment.	Modified – qualified or disclaimer due to an inability to obtain sufficient appropriate audit evidence regarding the use of the going concern assumption.	Basis for qualified/disclaimer opinion explaining that sufficient appropriate evidence was not obtained to form a conclusion on the going concern assumption.

6 Illustrations

Illustration 2 – Material Uncertainty Related to Going Concern

We draw attention to Note 6 in the financial statements, concerning the uncertainty of Murray Company's future funding. The Company is seeking new funding through an initial public offering of shares. In the event that the initial public offering does not proceed, this will require the Company's existing banking arrangements to be renegotiated and additional funding to be raised from either existing or new investors. This condition indicates the existence of a material uncertainty which may cast significant doubt on the Company's ability to continue as a going concern. The financial statements do not include any adjustments that would result if the Company was unable to continue as a going concern. Our opinion is not modified in respect of this matter.

Illustration 3 – Emphasis of Matter Paragraph

We draw attention to Note 12 of the financial statements, which describes the effects of a fire at the premises of a third party warehouse provider. Our opinion is not modified in respect of this matter.

Illustration 4 – Other Matter Paragraph

The financial statements of Murray Co for the year ended December 31, 20X3, were audited by another auditor who expressed an unmodified opinion on those statements on May 31, 20X4.

Illustration 5 – Murray Co Qualified opinion 1

Example where the auditor concludes that the financial statements are materially (but not pervasively) misstated:

Qualified Opinion

We have audited the financial statements of Murray Company (the Company), which comprise the statement of financial position as at 31 December, 20X4, and the statement of comprehensive income, statement of changes in equity and statement of cash flows for the year then ended, and notes to the financial statements, including a summary of significant accounting policies.

In our opinion, **except for the effects of the matter described in the Basis for Qualified Opinion section of our report, the accompanying financial statements give a true and fair view**.................. *(remainder of wording as per an unmodified opinion).*

Basis for Qualified Opinion

No allowance has been provided in the financial statements for a receivable for which recoverability is in doubt, which, in our opinion, is not in accordance with International Financial Reporting Standards. The allowance for the year ended 31 December 20X4 should be $211,000 based on the value of the receivable in current assets and the likely recoverability of the amount. Accordingly, current assets should be reduced by an allowance of $211,000 and the profit for the year and accumulated profit should be decreased by the same amount.

We conducted our audit in accordance with International Standards on Auditing (ISAs). Our responsibilities under those standards are further described in the Auditor's Responsibilities for the Audit of the Financial Statements section of our report. We are independent of the Company in accordance with the ethical requirements that are relevant to our audit of the financial statements in [jurisdiction], and we have fulfilled our other ethical responsibilities in accordance with these requirements. **We believe that the audit evidence we have obtained is sufficient and appropriate to provide a basis for our qualified opinion.**

Key Audit Matters

Except for the matter described in the Basis for Qualified Opinion section, we have determined that there are no other key audit matters to communicate in our report.

Illustration 6 – Murray Co Qualified opinion 2

Example where the auditor concludes that they have been unable to gather sufficient appropriate evidence and the possible effects are deemed to be material but not pervasive:

Qualified Opinion

We have audited the financial statements of the Murray Company (the Company), which comprise the statement of financial position as at 31 December, 20X4, and the statement of comprehensive income, statement of changes in equity and statement of cash flows for the year then ended, and notes to the financial statements, including a summary of significant accounting policies.

In our opinion, **except for the possible effects of the matter described in the Basis for Qualified Opinion section of our report, the accompanying financial statements give a true and fair view**...............(remainder of wording as per an unmodified opinion).

Basis for Qualified Opinion

As described in note 8 to the financial statements, Murray Company is the defendant in a lawsuit alleging constructive dismissal. The Company has filed a counter action, and preliminary hearings and discovery proceedings on both actions are in progress. The liability has been disclosed as contingent in accordance IAS 37 *Provisions, Contingent Liabilities and Contingent Assets*. We have been unable to obtain a response to our request for information from the solicitors representing Murray Company in the case. We were unable to confirm or verify by alternative means the likely success of the lawsuit and therefore unable to determine whether disclosure of a contingent liability is appropriate, or whether a provision for the value of the claim of $280,000 should be included in the statement of financial position as at 31 December 20X4 and an associated expense included in the statement of profit or loss for the year ended 31 December 20X4. Consequently, we were unable to determine whether any adjustments to these amounts were necessary.

We conducted our audit in accordance with International Standards on Auditing (ISAs). Our responsibilities under those standards are further described in the Auditor's Responsibilities for the Audit of the Financial Statements section of our report. We are independent of the Company in accordance with the ethical requirements that are relevant to our audit of the financial statements in [jurisdiction], and we have fulfilled our other ethical responsibilities in accordance with these requirements. **We believe that the audit evidence we have obtained is sufficient and appropriate to provide a basis for our qualified opinion.**

Key Audit Matters

Except for the matter described in the Basis for Qualified Opinion section, we have determined that there are no other key audit matters to communicate in our report.

Illustration 7 – Murray Co Adverse opinion

Example where the auditor concludes that the financial statements are materially and pervasively misstated:

Adverse Opinion

We have audited the financial statements of the Murray Company (the Company), which comprise the statement of financial position as at 31 December, 20X4, and the statement of comprehensive income, statement of changes in equity and statement of cash flows for the year then ended, and notes to the financial statements, including a summary of significant accounting policies.

In our opinion, **because of the significance of the matter discussed in the Basis for Adverse Opinion section of our report, the accompanying financial statements do not give a true and fair view**.......... (remainder of wording as per an unmodified opinion).

Basis for Adverse Opinion

As explained in note 12 to the financial statements, the financial statements have been prepared on the going concern basis. However, in our opinion, due to the number and significance of the material uncertainties, Murray Co is not a going concern in accordance with IAS 1 *Presentation of Financial Statements* and therefore the financial statements should not be prepared on the going concern basis.... [explanation of the various effects on the amounts presented in the financial statements].

We conducted our audit in accordance with International Standards on Auditing (ISAs). Our responsibilities under those standards are further described in the Auditor's Responsibilities for the Audit of the Financial Statements section of our report. We are independent of the Company in accordance with the ethical requirements that are relevant to our audit of the financial statements in [jurisdiction], and we have fulfilled our other ethical responsibilities in accordance with these requirements. **We believe that the audit evidence we have obtained is sufficient and appropriate to provide a basis for our adverse opinion.**

Key Audit Matters

Except for the matter described in the Basis for Adverse Opinion section, we have determined that there are no other key audit matters to communicate in our report.

Illustration 8 – Murray Co Disclaimer of opinion

Example where the auditor concludes that they have been unable to gather sufficient appropriate evidence and the possible effects are deemed to be both material and pervasive.

Disclaimer of Opinion

We were engaged to audit the financial statements of Murray Company (the Company), which comprise the statement of financial position as at 31 December, 20X4, and the statement of comprehensive income, statement of changes in equity and statement of cash flows for the year then ended, and notes to the financial statements, including a summary of significant accounting policies.

We do not express an opinion on the accompanying financial statements. Because of the significance of the matter described in the Basis for Disclaimer of Opinion section of our report, **we have not been able to obtain sufficient appropriate evidence to provide a basis for an audit opinion on these financial statements**.

Basis for Disclaimer of Opinion

Due to a fire at a third party warehouse provider's premises, the records relating to inventory held there were destroyed. We were unable to confirm or verify by alternative means closing inventory of $1,054,000 deducted from cost of sales included in the statement of profit or loss for the year ended 31 December 20X4, and the inventory balance of $1,054,000 included in the statement of financial position as at 31 December 20X4.

As a result, we were unable to determine whether any adjustments to the financial statements might have been necessary in respect of recorded or unrecorded inventory or cost of sales, and the associated elements of the statement of changes in equity and statement of cash flows.

Responsibilities of Management and Those Charged With Governance for the Financial Statements

[Wording as per ISA 700]

Auditor's Responsibilities for the Audit of the Financial Statements

Our responsibility is to conduct an audit of the financial statements in accordance with International Standards on Auditing and to issue an auditor's report. However, because of the matter described in the Basis for Disclaimer of Opinion section of our report, we were not able to obtain sufficient appropriate evidence to provide a basis for an audit opinion on these financial statements.

We are independent of the Company in accordance with ethical requirements that are relevant to our audit of the financial statements in [jurisdiction], and we have fulfilled our other ethical responsibilities in accordance with these requirements.

Illustration 9 – Key Audit Matter

Integrated website and finance systems	How our audit addressed the Key Audit Matter
During the year the company introduced a new website which enables customers to order online. The website is integrated with the finance system. There is a risk of material misstatement in relation to completeness of revenue.	• Obtaining an understanding of the new system and the controls management implemented to ensure the system works effectively. • Testing controls over the new website and finance system. • Performing substantive tests of detail over completeness of income.

Exam question approach

The exam will regularly feature a requirement asking for the implications for the auditor's report if issues identified during the audit are not resolved. The following approach should be taken to answer this type of requirement.

Explain the implications for the auditor's report

(1) Materiality assessment – if the issue is not material it won't affect the auditor's report. Calculate the percentage of assets and profit the issue represents and state whether this is material or not material.

(2) Identify the type of issue

– Material misstatement – non-compliance with an accounting standard.

– Inability to obtain sufficient appropriate evidence – evidence the auditor would expect to obtain hasn't been obtained.

– Material uncertainty – significant events where the outcome will only be known in the future.

– Inconsistency with the other published information – contradiction between the financial statements and the other information which is not subject to audit e.g. directors' report, chairman's statement, CSR report, etc.

– A matter that is of importance to the scope of the audit, the auditor's assessment of materiality, assessment of risk of material misstatement or other key audit matter that the auditor should specifically refer to in their report.

(3) Comment on the issue

- Which accounting standard has not been complied with and why?

- Which piece of evidence has not been obtained and why?

- What event/outcome is uncertain?

- What is the contradiction in the unaudited information?

- Explain why the auditor focused specifically on the key audit matters described in greater detail in the auditor's report e.g. involved a high degree of management judgment, required complex accounting treatment creating significant risk of material misstatement.

(4) State whether the issue is material but not pervasive or material and pervasive. If it is isolated or relatively small in impact it will be material but not pervasive. If it makes the financial statements as a whole unreliable it will be material and pervasive.

(5) Conclude on the opinion

- Unmodified if there are no material misstatements and sufficient appropriate evidence has been obtained, or

- Modified if there is material misstatement or the auditor has been unable to obtain sufficient appropriate evidence.

(6) State the name of opinion and the key wording of that opinion

- Unmodified – 'The financial statements give a true and fair view'

- Qualified – 'Except for the matter described in the basis for opinion, the financial statements give a true and fair view'

- Adverse – 'The financial statements do not give a true and fair view'

- Disclaimer – 'The auditor does not express an opinion'

(7) State any other reporting implications

- Basis for modified opinion if the opinion is modified

- Material Uncertainty Related to Going concern section

- Emphasis of Matter paragraph

- Other Matter paragraph

- An inconsistency needs to be described in the Other Information section

- Requires inclusion in the Key Audit Matters section for a listed entity.

7 Reporting to those charged with governance

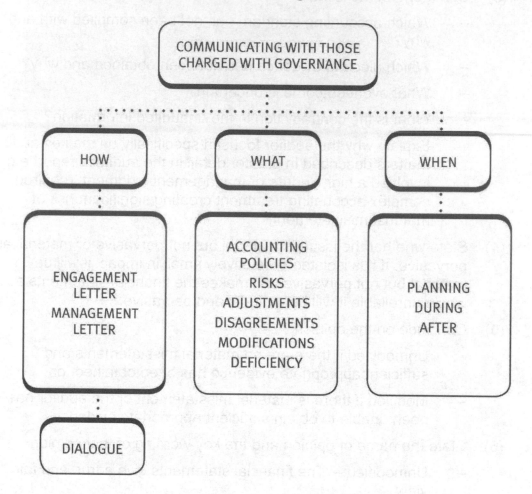

ISA 260 *Communication with Those Charged with Governance* and ISA 265 *Communicating Deficiencies in Internal Control to Those Charged with Governance and Management*, require the external auditor to engage in communications with management.

The main forms of formal communication between the auditors and management are: the engagement letter (see 'Ethics and Acceptance' chapter); and another written communication, usually sent at the end of the audit, which is often referred to as 'the management letter.'

In addition, the auditor will communicate with those charged with governance throughout the audit as required.

Reasons for communicating to those charged with governance

- To communicate responsibilities of the auditor and an overview of the scope and timing of the audit.

- To obtain information relevant to the audit.

- To report matters from the audit on a timely basis.

- To promote effective two-way communication.

[ISA 260, 9]

Matters that should be reported to those charged with governance

- The auditor's responsibilities in relation to the financial statements audit. [ISA 260, 14]

- The planned scope and timing of the audit including, for example:

  - The auditor's approach to internal control relevant to the audit

  - The extent to which the auditor is planning to use the work of internal audit and the arrangements for so doing

  - Business risks that may result in material misstatements

  - Communications with regulators.

[ISA 260, 15 & A14]

- Significant findings from the audit, such as:

  - The auditor's views about qualitative aspects of the entity's accounting practices/policies

  - Significant difficulties encountered during the audit

  - Significant matters arising during the audit that were discussed with management

  - Written representations the auditor is requesting

  - Circumstances that affect the form and content of the auditor's report, if any. This includes any expected modifications to the report and key audit matters to be communicated in accordance with ISA 701 *Communicating Key Audit Matters in the Independent Auditor's Report*

  - Other matters that, in the auditor's opinion, are significant to the oversight of the reporting process.

[ISA 260, 16 & A24]

- Matters of auditor independence. [ISA 260, 17]

Ultimately what constitutes a matter requiring the attention of those charged with governance is a matter of professional judgment. Typical examples include:

- Delays in obtaining information for the audit.

- An unreasonably brief time within which to complete the audit.

- Expected limitations on the audit, either imposed by management or other circumstances.

- The potential effect on the financial statements of any material risks and exposures, such as pending litigation, that are required to be disclosed in the financial statements.

- A summary of identified misstatements, whether corrected or not by the entity and a request that they are adjusted.

- Material uncertainties related to events and conditions that may cast significant doubt on the entity's ability to continue as a going concern.

- Any other matters agreed upon in the terms of the audit engagement.

Timing of communication with those charged with governance	
Stage of audit	**Communication required**
Planning	Significant risks identified by the auditor
	How the auditor plans to address the risks
	Auditor's approach to internal control relevant to the audit
	Application of materiality in the context of an audit
During the audit	If any situation occurs and it would not be appropriate to delay communication until the audit is concluded
Conclusion of the audit	Major findings from the audit work.
	Delays caused by management

The auditor must take care not to compromise the effectiveness of the audit by communicating too much information about the planned scope and timing of the audit to such an extent that procedures become too predictable.

Test your understanding 1

Murray case study: Auditor's report

As a result of the going concern review undertaken at the completion stage, the audit engagement partner has decided that there is a material uncertainty regarding the going concern status of Murray Co. He has requested that the directors make adequate disclosure in the final version of the financial statements for the year ended 31 December 20X4.

Required:

Describe the impact on the auditor's report for the year ended 31 December 20X4 if:

(i)   The directors include disclosure regarding the material uncertainty over going concern, which in the partner's view is adequate.

(3 marks)

(ii)   The directors refuse to include any disclosure on the matter.

(3 marks)

(Total: 6 marks)

Test your understanding 2

ISA 260 *Communication with Those Charged with Governance* deals with the auditor's responsibility to communicate with those charged with governance in relation to an audit of financial statements.

Required:

(i)   Describe TWO specific responsibilities of those charged with governance.

(2 marks)

(ii)   Explain FOUR examples of matters that might be communicated to them by the auditor.

(4 marks)

(Total: 6 marks)

Test your understanding 3

Henry

(a) Aragon Co operates a perpetual inventory system. No year-end count is performed. You have reviewed the level of adjustments made each month after each perpetual count and concluded that due to the significance of the adjustments, the inventory system is not reliable. You have requested that a full year-end count is performed but management have refused saying it would be too disruptive. The inventory balance is $4 million. Sales revenue is $50 million and profit for the year is $15 million.

(b) Boleyn Co has not made allowance for an irrecoverable debt of $50,000 in respect of a customer declared bankrupt just after the year-end. Profit for the year is $500,000.

(c) Seymour Co is being sued by a competitor for the theft of intellectual property. The amount of the claim is material and the case could go either way. The claim is not mentioned anywhere in the financial statements.

(d) Howard Co is a cash retailer. There is no system to confirm the accuracy of cash sales.

(e) Cleves Co has neglected to include a statement of profit or loss in its financial statements.

(f) Parr Co is involved in a major court case that would bankrupt the company if lost. The directors assess and disclose the case as a contingent liability in the accounts. The auditors agree with the treatment and disclosure.

Required:

For each of the above situations describe the implications for the independent auditor's report.

(18 marks)

Test your understanding 4

You are the audit manager of Brakes Co, a listed client. Brakes Co is a global manufacturer of braking systems for use in domestic and commercial motor vehicles. $250,000 was raised through a new share issue in the year. Draft profit before tax is $9m and total assets are $37m. The audit is nearly complete and you are undertaking an overall review of the audit evidence on file.

(a) **Explain the importance of the overall review of evidence obtained.**

(3 marks)

(b) During your review you notice that the section of the file relating to share capital and reserves is incomplete.

Required:

Describe audit procedures that should be performed in respect of Brake's share capital and reserves.

(4 marks)

(c) The following matters arising during the audit of Brakes Co have been noted on file for your attention:

(i) A customer of Brakes Co had to withdraw one of their family car models this year due to concerns over the safety of the braking system. The customer has lodged a legal claim against Brakes Co for $10 million for the negligent supply of faulty braking systems. The company's lawyers believe that there is an 80% chance that Brakes Co will lose the case but the directors believe that their quality control procedures have always been robust and that the braking systems will be proven to have been safe. They have however decided to disclose the matter in the financial statements as a contingent liability.

(5 marks)

(ii) Brakes Co also produces and sells brake fluid. Another customer has recently returned a small batch of brake fluid because the fluid appeared to be contaminated with oil. Brakes Co issued the customer with a credit note for the full value of $137,500 and correctly accounted for this in the draft financial statements. As the brake fluid was returned before the year-end, Brakes Co has included it in the year-end inventory listing at cost of $125,000. Brakes Co may be able to re-filter and re-sell the brake fluid at the original selling price, but filtering will cost a further $62,500.

(4 marks)

(iii) Four months ago, Brakes Co began renting some additional warehouse space from a third party storage provider, Wheels Co. At the year end, raw materials with a value of $3.2 million belonging to Brakes were stored at Wheels Co's premises. The directors of Brakes Co did not make you aware of the new third party storage facility. Consequently, no audit procedures were performed to verify the raw materials.

(4 marks)

Required:

Discuss each of these issues and describe the impact on the independent auditor's report if the above issues remain unresolved.

Note: The mark allocation is shown against each of the three issues above.

(13 marks)

(Total: 20 marks)

Test your understanding 5

You are about to issue the auditor's report for Exmouth Co, a listed client. Half way through the year the company suffered a major computer systems failure which destroyed the accounting records for the year to date. Backups had not been kept and so the company has had to reconstruct the figures for the first six months.

(1) **Which opinions are most appropriate for Exmouth Co?**

    A   Qualified or adverse

    B   Unmodified or adverse

    C   Unmodified or disclaimer

    D   Qualified or disclaimer

(2) **What is the purpose of the Basis for Opinion paragraph in an auditor's report which contains an unmodified opinion?**

    A   To state the opinion on the financial statements

    B   To confirm the audit has been conducted in accordance with ISAs and ethical requirements

    C   To highlight a material uncertainty relating to going concern which has been adequately disclosed

    D   To highlight management's responsibilities to the users of the financial statements

(3) **Which of the following shows the correct order of the elements to be included in the auditor's report of Exmouth Co?**

    A   Opinion, date, auditor's address, signature

    B   Title, opinion, signature, key audit matters

    C   Addressee, opinion, auditor's responsibilities, date

    D   Responsibilities of management, basis for opinion, date, addressee

(4) **Which of the following describes the wording of a disclaimer of opinion?**

    A   The financial statements give a true and fair view

    B   The financial statements do not give a true and fair view

    C   The auditor does not express an opinion on the financial statements

    D   Except for the matter described, the financial statements give a true and fair view

(5) **Which of the following statements is correct in relation to the auditor's report of Exmouth Co?**

    A   The Key Audit Matters section should be used to describe the matter giving rise to the modified opinion, in this case that the auditor has been unable to obtain sufficient appropriate evidence

    B   If a disclaimer of opinion is to be issued, the Key Audit Matters section should not be included in the auditor's report as to do so may suggest other aspects of the financial statements are reliable

    C   An Emphasis of Matter paragraph should be included to draw attention to the inability to obtain sufficient appropriate evidence

    D   The auditor will conclude that the financial statements do not give a true and fair view

Test your understanding 6

You are about to issue the auditor's report for two listed clients, Kalgoorlie Co and Cundeelee Co. The financial statements show the following:

	Kalgoorlie	Cundeelee
	$000	$000
Profit before tax	10	245
Total assets	2,300	6,500

Uncorrected misstatements:

	Kalgoorlie	Cundeelee
Overstatement of receivables due to an irrecoverable debt not being written off	15	
Overstatement of inventory due to failure to value at lower of cost and NRV		85

(1) **Which of the following is the most appropriate opinion for Kalgoorlie Co?**

    A   Adverse

    B   Disclaimer

    C   Qualified

    D   Unmodified

(2) **Which of the following is the most appropriate opinion for Cundeelee Co?**

    A   Adverse

    B   Disclaimer

    C   Qualified

    D   Unmodified

(3) **How would your answer change for Cundeelee Co if the misstatement of inventory had been $10,000 instead of $85,000?**

    A   Adverse opinion

    B   Unmodified opinion with emphasis of matter

    C   Qualified opinion

    D   Unmodified opinion

(4) **You have also identified material uncertainties relating to going concern during your audit of Kalgoorlie Co. These have been adequately disclosed by management. How will this impact the auditor's report?**

   A   The report should include a section titled 'Emphasis of Matter' which will refer to the management's disclosure note

   B   The report should include a section titled 'Material Uncertainty Related to Going Concern' which will refer to the management's disclosure note

   C   The report should include a section titled 'Going concern issues' which will refer to the management's disclosure note

   D   As management have adequately disclosed the uncertainties relating to going concern, the auditor does not need to modify the report as the financial statements include the appropriate information

(5) Included within the financial statements of Cundeelee Co is a provision for a legal case of which the outcome is uncertain at this date. Adequate disclosure of the matter has been included by management. The case represents a significant uncertainty and you have included an emphasis of matter in the auditor's report to refer to the client's disclosure of the uncertainty.

   What other modifications, if any, will be required to the report in respect of this matter?

   A   The opinion should be modified as a result of the significant uncertainty

   B   No further modifications to the report are required

   C   The Key Audit Matters section should describe the uncertainty

   D   The Basis for Opinion section should describe the uncertainty

8 Chapter summary

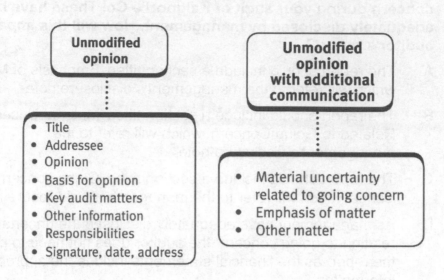

- Title
- Addressee
- Opinion
- Basis for opinion
- Key audit matters
- Other information
- Responsibilities
- Signature, date, address

Unmodified opinion with additional communication

- Material uncertainty related to going concern
- Emphasis of matter
- Other matter

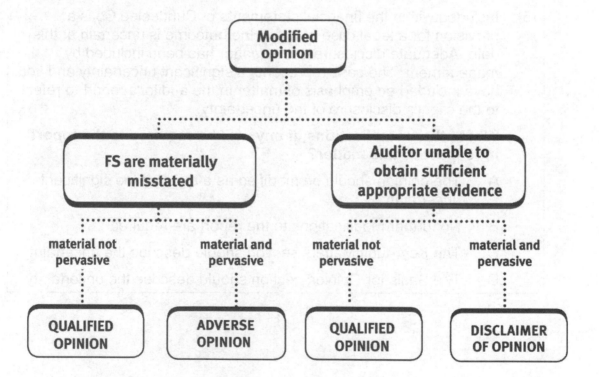

Modified opinion

FS are materially misstated

Auditor unable to obtain sufficient appropriate evidence

material not pervasive | material and pervasive | material not pervasive | material and pervasive

QUALIFIED OPINION | ADVERSE OPINION | QUALIFIED OPINION | DISCLAIMER OF OPINION

Test your understanding answers

Test your understanding 1

(i) If the directors make adequate disclosures regarding the material uncertainty over the going concern status of Murray Co, the financial statements will show a true and fair view.

   As there is no material misstatement, or lack of sufficient appropriate evidence on this matter, the audit opinion can remain unmodified.

   Additional communication will be required in the form of a Material Uncertainty Related to Going Concern paragraph. This will draw the shareholder's attention to the disclosure note.

   The paragraph would state that our opinion is not modified in this respect.

   The paragraph would be inserted below the basis for opinion paragraph.

(ii) If the directors refuse to make any disclosures, then in the auditor's opinion, the financial statements are materially misstated.

   The audit opinion will need to be modified due to this material misstatement.

   The type of opinion given would depend on whether the auditor considers the misstatement to be material and pervasive or material but not pervasive.

   If it is pervasive, an adverse opinion will be given. The opinion will state 'In our opinion the financial statements do not give a true and fair view/are not fairly presented'.

   If it is not considered pervasive, a qualified opinion can be given. The opinion would state 'Except for the matter described in the basis for qualified opinion paragraph below, in our opinion the financial statements show a true and fair view/are fairly presented'.

   The basis for opinion paragraph will need to change to a basis for qualified/adverse opinion and will explain the reason for the modified opinion.

Test your understanding 2

(i)   Those charged with governance are responsible for overseeing:

- The strategic direction of the entity

- Obligations related to the accountability of the entity. This includes overseeing the financial reporting process

- Promotion of good corporate governance

- Risk assessment processes

- The establishment and monitoring of internal controls

- Compliance with applicable law and regulations

- Implementation of controls to prevent and detect fraud and errors.

(ii)   General audit matters that might be communicated to those charged with governance are:

(1)   The auditor's responsibilities in relation to financial statement audit. This would include:

- A statement that the auditor is responsible for forming and expressing an opinion on the financial statements.

- That the auditor's work is carried out in accordance with ISAs and in accordance with local laws and regulations.

(2)   Planned scope and timing of the audit. This would include:

- The audit approach to assessing the risk of serious misstatement, whether arising from fraud or error.

- The audit approach to the internal control system and whether reliance will be placed on it.

- The timing of interim and final audits, including reporting deadlines.

(3)   Significant findings from the audit. This could include:

- Significant difficulties encountered during the audit, including delays in obtaining information from management.

- Significant deficiencies in internal control and recommendations for improvement.

- Audit adjustments, whether or not recorded by the entity, that have, or could have, a material effect on the entity's financial statements. For example, the bankruptcy of a material receivable shortly after the year-end that should result in an adjusting entry.

> (4) A statement on independence issues affecting the audit. This would include:
>
> – That the audit firm has ensured that all members of the audit team have complied with the ethical standards of ACCA.
>
> – That appropriate safeguards are in place where a potential threat to independence has been identified.

Test your understanding 3

(a) Aragon

– Inventory is material as it represents 8% of sales revenue and 27% of profit.

– There is a lack of sufficient appropriate audit evidence over inventory. The auditor cannot form a conclusion as to whether inventory is materially misstated or free from material misstatement.

– The audit opinion will be modified.

– A qualified opinion using the 'except for' wording will be issued as the matter is material but not pervasive.

– The basis for opinion section will be amended to basis for qualified opinion.

– The basis for qualified opinion section will explain the reason for the qualified opinion and quantify the effect of the issue on the financial statements.

(b) Boleyn

– The balance is material as it represents 10% of profit.

– An irrecoverable debt has not been written off. The financial statements will be materially misstated due to overstatement of receivables.

– The audit opinion will be modified.

– A qualified opinion using the 'except for' wording will be issued as the matter is material but not pervasive.

– The basis for opinion section will be amended to basis for qualified opinion.

– The basis for qualified opinion section will explain the reason for the qualified opinion and quantify the effect of the issue on the financial statements.

(c) **Seymour**

- The claim is material and represents an uncertainty that should be communicated to the users of the financial statements.

- As the claim could go either way, a contingent liability should be disclosed. Failure to do this will mean the financial statements are materially misstated.

- The audit opinion will be modified.

- A qualified opinion using the 'except for' wording will be issued as the matter is material but not pervasive.

- The basis for opinion section will be amended to basis for qualified opinion.

- The basis for qualified opinion section will explain the reason for the qualified opinion and quantify the effect of the issue on the financial statements.

(d) **Howard**

- There is no system to confirm cash sales therefore the auditor cannot form a conclusion as to whether revenue is materially misstated or free from material misstatement.

- The auditor is unable to obtain sufficient appropriate evidence for a significant class of transactions in the financial statements.

- The issue is material and pervasive.

- The audit opinion will be modified.

- A disclaimer of opinion will be issued stating that the auditor does not express an opinion on the financial statements.

- The basis for opinion section will be amended to a basis for disclaimer of opinion.

- The basis for disclaimer of opinion section will explain the reason for the disclaimer and quantify the effect of the issue on the financial statements.

- The statement referring to the audit being conducted in accordance with ISAs and ethical requirements will be moved from the basis for opinion section and included in the Auditor responsibilities section.

- The statement within the auditor's report that sufficient appropriate evidence has been obtained will be removed.

- The statement that the financial statements have been audited will be changed to the auditor was engaged to audit the financial statements.

(e) Cleves

- The financial statements do not contain a statement of profit or loss which is one of the primary financial statements and must be presented.

- The financial statements are misstated and the effect is pervasive.

- The audit opinion will be modified.

- An adverse opinion will be issued stating that the financial statements do not give a true and fair view.

- The basis for opinion section will be amended to a basis for adverse opinion.

- The basis for adverse opinion section will explain the reason for the adverse opinion and quantify the effect of the issue on the financial statements.

(f) Parr

- The claim is material and represents an uncertainty that should be communicated to the users of the financial statements.

- The directors have correctly disclosed the matter in the financial statements.

- The audit opinion will be unmodified as the financial statements give a true and fair view.

- Additional communication will be required to highlight the disclosure made by the client to the user.

- This could be achieved by including an emphasis of matter paragraph. The emphasis of matter paragraph will refer to the client's disclosure of the court case to make the users aware of it.

- Alternatively, the auditor may consider the issue a material uncertainty related to going concern and refer to the court case by including a going concern section in the report instead of an emphasis of matter.

- The choice of how the auditor should refer to the matter in the auditor's report is a matter of professional judgment.

An adverse opinion will be issued stating that the financial statements do not give a true and fair view.

The basis for opinion section will be amended to a basis for adverse opinion.

The basis for adverse opinion section will explain the reason for the adverse opinion and quantify the effect of the issue on the financial statements.

The Key Audit Matters section will reference the 'Basis for Adverse Opinion'.

(ii) Contaminated brake fluid

Inventory should be valued at the lower of cost and net **realisable value** (IAS 2 Inventories, 9).

The contaminated brake fluid cost $125,000. If sold at the original price charged of $137,500, the net realisable value will be $75,000 ($137,500 less $62,500 re-filtering costs). Inventory is therefore overstated by $50,000.

$50,000 is not material at 0.6% of profit ($50,000/$9m) and 0.1% of total assets ($50,000/$37m).

As the misstatement is not material, the audit opinion will not be modified in respect of this matter and no reference to the misstatement would be made in the auditor's report.

The misstatement should be brought to the attention of management and they should be asked to correct it.

(iii) Inventory held at third party premises

The auditor has not obtained sufficient appropriate evidence over the inventory held at third party premises.

The inventory is material to the statement of profit or loss at 36% of profit ($3.2m/$9m) and the statement of financial position at 8.6% of total assets ($3.2m/$37m).

If alternative sources of evidence cannot be obtained, it will be necessary to modify the audit opinion due to an inability to obtain sufficient appropriate evidence.

A qualified opinion using the 'except for' wording will be necessary.

The basis for opinion section will be amended to a basis for qualified opinion.

The basis for qualified opinion section will explain the reason for the qualified opinion and quantify the effect of the issue on the financial statements.

The Key Audit Matters section will reference the 'Basis for Qualified Opinion'.

Test your understanding 4

(a) Overall review of evidence is important as it enables the auditor to ensure:

- sufficient appropriate evidence has been obtained.

- the evidence supports the conclusions reached, and is appropriately documented.

- work has been performed in accordance with professional standards.

For the appraisal and development of staff.

(b) Audit procedures: Share capital

- Agree authorised share capital and nominal value disclosures to underlying shareholding agreements/statutory constitution documents.

- Inspect the cash book for evidence of cash receipts from share issues and ensure amounts not yet received are correctly disclosed as share capital called-up not paid in the financial statements.

- Inspect board minutes to verify the issue of share capital during the year.

Audit procedures: Reserves

- Agree opening reserves to prior-year closing reserves and reconcile movements.

- Agree movements in reserves to supporting documentation (e.g. agree revaluation reserve movements to an independent valuer's report).

(c) Impact on auditor's report:

(i) Faulty brake systems

The amount of $10m is 111% ($10m/$9m) of profit before tax and is therefore material.

The $10m provision would turn a profit of $9m into a loss of $1m and is also therefore pervasive.

It is probable that Brakes Co will lose the legal case and therefore the claim of $10m should be provided for in the financial statements in accordance with IAS 37 *Provisions, Contingent Liabilities and Contingent Assets*.

The audit opinion will be modified as the financial statements are materially misstated.

Test your understanding 5

(1)	D	Qualified or disclaimer. Six months of accounting records have been lost meaning sufficient appropriate evidence will not be available. Whether the matter is deemed material or material and pervasive will depend on the auditor's assessment of the reconstruction of figures for the first six months.
(2)	B	A 'basis for opinion' paragraph confirms the audit has been conducted in accordance with ISAs and ethical requirements.
(3)	C	Addressee, opinion, auditor's responsibilities, date.
(4)	C	A disclaimer of opinion is where the auditor does not express an opinion.
(5)	B	ISA 705 states that where a disclaimer of opinion is issued, the Key Audit Matters section should not be included in the auditor's report.

Test your understanding 6

(1)	A	Whilst the misstatement represents less than 1% of total assets, it represents 150% of PBT and would turn the profit to a loss which is pervasive. Therefore an adverse opinion would be appropriate.
(2)	C	The misstatement represents 35% of PBT and 1.3% of total assets. This is material but not pervasive. A qualified opinion is appropriate.
(3)	D	The misstatement would represent 4.1% of PBT and 0.15% of total assets. This is not material. An unmodified opinion would be appropriate.
(4)	B	A section titled 'Material Uncertainty Related to Going Concern' will be included in the auditor's report.
(5)	B	No further modifications are required. The Key Audit Matters section should not describe matters already described in an Emphasis of Matter paragraph. The Basis for Opinion section would only describe matters giving rise to a modified opinion. As management have included the provision and disclosure of the legal case in the financial statements there is no reason to modify the audit opinion.

Summary of key ISAs

Chapter learning objectives

This section is designed to help you with the key requirements of the International Auditing Standards.

200 series: General principles and responsibilities

ISA 200 *Overall Objectives of the Independent Auditor and the Conduct of an Audit in Accordance with International Standards on Auditing*

Objectives of the auditor [11]:

- To obtain reasonable assurance about whether the financial statements as a whole are free from material misstatement, whether due to fraud or error.

- To express an opinion on whether the financial statements are prepared, in all material respects, in accordance with an applicable financial reporting framework.

- To report on the financial statements, and communicate as required by the ISAs, in accordance with the auditor's findings.

Responsibilities of management [A2]:

- Preparation of the financial statements in accordance with the applicable financial reporting framework, including their fair presentation.

- Internal control necessary to enable preparation of financial statements that are free from material misstatement, whether due to fraud or error.

- To provide the auditor with:

  - Access to all information relevant to the preparation of the financial statements

  - Unrestricted access to persons from within the entity from whom the auditor determines it necessary to obtain evidence.

Risk:

- Audit: the risk of issuing an inappropriate opinion. [13c]

- Inherent: the susceptibility of an assertion about a class of transaction (e.g. revenue) or account balance (e.g. receivables) to material misstatement before the consideration of any related internal controls. [13ni]

- Control: the risk that material misstatement will not be prevented, detected or corrected by entity's internal control. [13nii]

- Detection: the risk that audit procedures do not detect material misstatements. [13e]

An auditor must perform the audit with professional scepticism: an attitude that includes a questioning mind, being alert to conditions which indicate possible misstatement due to error or fraud, and a critical assessment of audit evidence. [13l]

Inherent limitations of audit [A47]:

Audit evidence is persuasive rather than conclusive because of:

- The nature of financial reporting
- The nature of audit procedures
- The need to conduct audit a within reasonable time and at reasonable cost.

ISA 210 Agreeing the Terms of Audit Engagements

The auditor should establish whether the preconditions for an audit are present [6]:

- Determine whether an acceptable financial reporting framework is to be applied in the preparation of the financial statements; and
- Obtain agreement of management that it acknowledges and understands its responsibility.

Contents of engagement letter [10]:

- The objective and scope of the audit.
- The responsibilities of the auditor.
- The responsibilities of management.
- The identification of the applicable financial reporting framework.
- The expected form and content of any reports to be issued.

ISA 220 Quality Control for an Audit of Financial Statements

The firm should have a system of quality control to ensure [2]:

- Compliance with professional standards, and
- Reports issued are appropriate in the circumstances.

The engagement partner takes overall responsibility for the overall quality of the engagement including the direction, supervision and performance of the engagement. [8 & 15]

An engagement quality control reviewer must be assigned for listed entities and high risk engagements focusing on significant matters and areas involving significant judgment. [19 & 20]

The firm's quality control processes must be monitored to ensure they are relevant, adequate and operating effectively. [23]

ISA 230 *Audit Documentation*

Objective of documentation [2]:

- Evidence of the basis for the independent auditor's report

- Evidence that audit planned and performed in accordance with ISAs and legal/regulatory requirements.

Audit documentation should enable an experienced independent auditor with no previous connection to the audit to understand [8]:

- Nature, timing & extent of audit procedures performed:
    - Specific items tested.
    - Who performed work and when.
    - Who reviewed work and when.

- Results of audit procedures performed.

- Significant conclusions and professional judgments made in reaching those conclusions.

ISA 240 The Auditor's Responsibilities Relating to Fraud in an Audit of Financial Statements

Objectives of the auditor [10]:

- Identify risks of material misstatement due to fraud.

- Obtain sufficient appropriate evidence regarding assessed risks.

- Respond appropriately to fraud or suspected fraud identified.

Definition [11a]: An intentional act involving use of deception to obtain unjust/illegal advantage.

Two types of fraud [3]:

- Fraudulent financial reporting.

- Misappropriation of assets.

Audit procedures must be performed to: [32]:

- Test the appropriateness of journal entries.

- Review accounting estimates for bias.

- Identify significant transactions outside the normal course of business.

ISA 250 Consideration of Laws and Regulations in an Audit of Financial Statements

Auditor's objectives [11]:

- Obtain sufficient appropriate evidence regarding compliance with provisions of laws/regulations that may materially affect FS.

- Perform audit procedures to identify instances of non-compliance that may materially affect FS.

- Respond appropriately to identified or suspected non-compliance during the audit.

ISA 260 Communication With Those Charged With Governance

Those charged with governance [10a]:

- Those with responsibility for overseeing the strategic direction of the entity.

Matters to be communicated:

- Auditor's responsibility in relation to the FS audit [14]

- Planned scope and timing of audit [15]

- Significant findings from audit [16]

- Auditor's independence (listed companies). [17]

ISA 265 Communicating Deficiencies in Internal Control to Those Charged With Governance and Management

Reporting responsibilities:

- Significant deficiencies, to those charged with governance [9]

- Significant deficiencies and other deficiencies, to an appropriate level of management. [10]

What makes deficiencies significant [A6]:

- Likelihood of material misstatement in the FS.

- Susceptibility to loss or fraud of the related asset.

- Volume of activity in the related account balance.

- Interaction of the deficiency with other deficiencies.

300 & 400 series: Assessment and response to assessed risks

ISA 300 *Planning an Audit of Financial Statements*

Benefits of planning [2]:

- Helps the auditor to devote appropriate attention to important areas of audit.

- Helps identify and resolve potential problems on a timely basis.

- Assists in the selection of a suitable audit team.

- Helps the direction and supervision of the audit team.

Content of audit strategy [8]:

- Characteristics of the engagement

- Reporting objectives (e.g. reporting timetable)

- Factors significant in directing the team's efforts

- Results of preliminary engagement activities

- Nature, timing and extent of resources.

Content of audit plan [9]:

Nature, timing and extent of:

- Planned risk assessment procedures.

- Planned further audit procedures at the assertion level.

ISA 315 Identifying and Assessing the Risks of Material Misstatement Through Understanding the Entity and its Environment

Required understanding of entity and environment [11]:

- Industry/regulatory factors affecting FS

- Nature of the entity:
    - operations
    - ownership and governance
    - how it is financed.

- Accounting policies

- Objectives and strategies

- Review of financial performance.

Components of internal control:

- Control environment [14]
- Entity's risk assessment process [15]
- Information system relevant to financial reporting [18]
- Control activities [20]
- Monitoring of controls. [22]

Financial statement assertions [A129]:

- Transactions and events and related disclosures: Occurrence; completeness; accuracy; cut-off; classification; presentation.
- Account balances and related disclosures: Existence; rights & obligations; completeness; accuracy, valuation & allocation; classification; presentation.

ISA 320 Materiality in Planning and Performing an Audit

Materiality: Misstatements, including omissions, are considered to be material if they, individually or in the aggregate, could reasonably be expected to influence the economic decisions of users taken on the basis of the financial statements. [2]

Performance materiality: an amount set at less than materiality for the FS as a whole, to reduce to an appropriately low level the probability that the aggregate of uncorrected and undetected misstatements exceeds materiality for the FS as a whole. [9]

ISA 330 The Auditor's Responses to Assessed Risks

The auditor shall design and perform audit procedures whose nature, timing and extent are based on and are responsive to the assessed risks of material misstatement. [6]

Substantive procedures: to detect material misstatements at assertion level, comprising tests of details and analytical procedures. [4a]

Test of controls: to evaluate operating effectiveness of controls in preventing, or detecting and correcting material misstatements at the assertion level. [4b]

ISA 402 *Audit Considerations Relating to an Entity Using a Service Organisation*

The auditor of the user entity must obtain an understanding of the services provided by the service organisation and their effect on the user entity's internal control relevant to audit, sufficient to identify and assess the risks of material misstatement and perform audit procedures responsive to those risks. [7]

An understanding may be obtained by [12]:

- Obtaining a type 1 or type 2 report

- Contacting the service organisation

- Visiting the service organisation and performing tests of controls

- Using another auditor to perform procedures and provide information about the relevant controls.

ISA 450 Evaluation of Misstatements Identified During the Audit

A misstatement is: A difference between the amount, classification, presentation, or disclosure of a reported financial statement item and the amount, classification, presentation, or disclosure that is required for the item to be in accordance with the applicable financial reporting framework. Misstatements can arise from error or fraud. [4a]

Requirements:

- Accumulate misstatements identified during the audit. [5]

- Determine whether audit strategy and audit plan needs to be revised. [6]

- Communicate all misstatements accumulated with the appropriate level of management on a timely basis. [8]

- Evaluate effect of uncorrected misstatements. [10]

- Request a written representation that uncorrected misstatements are not material. A summary of the uncorrected misstatements shall be included in the written representation. [14]

500 series: Evidence

ISA 500 *Audit Evidence*

Characteristics:

- Sufficiency: measure of quantity, affected by quality of evidence and risk of material misstatement. [5e]

- Appropriateness: measure of quality, linked to relevance and reliability. [5b]

Relevance: linked to FS assertions. [A27]

Reliability [A31]:

- Independent evidence more reliable than client generated.

- Evidence obtained directly by the auditor is more reliable than indirectly obtained.

- Documentary evidence more reliable than oral.

- Original documents more reliable than copies or documents transformed into electronic form.

Procedures:

- Inspection [A14]

- Observation [A17]

- External confirmation [A18]

- Recalculation [A19]

- Re-performance [A20]

- Analytical procedures [A21]

- Enquiry. [A22]

ISA 501 Audit Evidence – Specific Considerations for Selected Items

The auditor should obtain sufficient appropriate evidence regarding [3]:

- Existence and condition of inventory.

- Completeness of litigation and claims involving the entity.

- Presentation and disclosure of segment information.

ISA 505 *External Confirmations*

External confirmations provide more persuasive evidence as the evidence is obtained directly by the auditor from an independent source. This is important where there is a higher assessment of audit risk. [3]

Definitions:

External confirmation – audit evidence obtained by the auditor directly from a third party in paper form or by electronic or other medium. [6a]

Positive confirmation request – a request for the third party to confirm whether they agree or disagree with the information in the request, or provide the requested information. [6b]

Negative confirmation request – a request for the third party to respond directly to the auditor only if they disagree with the information provided in the request. [6c]

ISA 520 *Analytical Procedures*

Definition: Evaluation of financial information through analysis of plausible relationships among both financial and non-financial data. [4]

May be used as a substantive procedure. [5]

Must be used at the completion stage when forming an overall conclusion to ensure the financial statements are consistent with the auditor's understanding of the entity. [6]

ISA 530 *Audit Sampling*

Definitions:

- Audit sampling: The application of audit procedures to less than 100% of a population to provide the auditor with a reasonable basis to draw conclusions on entire population. [5a]

- Sampling risk: The risk the auditor's conclusion based on the sample is different from the conclusion if the entire population were subjected to the same audit procedure. [5c]

- Non-sampling risk: The risk the auditor reaches an erroneous conclusion for any reason not related to sampling risk. [5d]

- Statistical sampling: random selection of the sample and the use of probability theory to evaluate results. [5g]

- Tolerable misstatement: A monetary amount set by the auditor in respect of which the auditor seeks to obtain an appropriate level of assurance that the monetary amount set by the auditor is not exceeded by the actual misstatement in the population. [5i]

Factors increasing sample size for substantive procedures [Appendix 3]:

- Increase in the assessed risk of material misstatement.

- Decrease in tolerable misstatement.

- Increase in expected misstatement.

ISA 540 Auditing Accounting Estimates, Including Fair Value Accounting Estimates and Related Disclosures

Audit approach:

- Review events after the reporting period [13a]

- Test management's estimate:
  - Appropriateness of method [13bi]
  - Reasonableness of assumptions [13bii]

- Test the effectiveness of controls over the estimate [13c]

- Develop an independent estimate [13d]

- Obtain evidence from an expert. [14]

ISA 560 *Subsequent Events*

Obtain sufficient appropriate evidence about whether events occurring between the date of the financial statements and the date of the auditor's report that require adjustment of or disclosure in the financial statements are appropriately reflected in those financial statements. [4]

ISA 570 *Going Concern*

Auditor must [9]:

- Obtain sufficient appropriate evidence regarding the appropriateness of management's use of the going concern basis of accounting.

- Conclude whether a material uncertainty exists about the entity's ability to continue as a going concern.

- Report in accordance with ISA 570.

ISA 580 *Written Representations*

Contents:

- Management responsibility for preparation of FS. [10]

- Completeness of information provided to the auditor. [11a]

- All transactions recorded in FS. [11b]

- Plans that may affect the carrying value of the assets. [A10]

- As required by other ISAs e.g. ISA 240, 250, 450, 560, 570, 580. [Appendix 1]

600 series: Using the work of others

ISA 610 *Using the Work of Internal Auditors*

Evaluating the internal audit function [15]:

- The extent to which the internal audit function's **organisational status** and relevant policies and procedures support the **objectivity** of the internal auditors.

- The level of **competence** of the internal audit function.

- Whether the internal audit function applies a systematic and disciplined **approach,** including quality control.

Evaluating the internal audit work [23]:

- The work was properly planned, performed, supervised, reviewed and documented.

- Sufficient appropriate evidence has been obtained.

- The conclusions reached are appropriate in the circumstances.

- The reports prepared are consistent with the work performed.

Using internal audit to provide direct assistance

The external auditor may use the internal audit function to provide direct assistance with the external audit under the supervision and review of the external auditor.

- Direct assistance cannot be provided in countries where national law prohibits such assistance. [26]

- Internal auditor must be objective and competent. [27]

- External auditor must not assign work which is judgmental, a high risk of material misstatement or with which the internal auditor has been involved. [30]

- External auditor must not use the internal auditor excessively. [31]

- Management must agree not to intervene with the work. [33a]

- Internal auditor must observe confidentiality. [33b]

ISA 620 Using the Work of an Auditor's Expert

The auditor must:

- Evaluate the competence, capability and objectivity of the expert. [9]

- Obtain an understanding of the field of expertise. [10]

- Agree in writing the work to be performed. [11]

- Evaluate the adequacy of the expert's work for audit purposes. [12]

700 series: Audit conclusions and reporting

ISA 700 (Revised) Forming an Opinion and Reporting on Financial Statements

Content of an independent auditor's report:

- Title: [21]
  - reference to independent auditor
- Addressee: [22]
  - shareholders/members
- Auditor's Opinion: [23]
  - Identifies the entity, subject matter and reporting date [24]
  - FS prepared in accordance with the applicable FR framework [25a]
  - FS give true and fair view [25b]
- Basis for Opinion: [28]
  - Audit conducted in accordance with ISAs and ethical requirements
  - States whether the auditor believes that the audit evidence obtained is sufficient and appropriate for forming an opinion
- Going Concern: [29]
  - Reference to any going concern disclosures made by management
- Key Audit Matters [30]
- Other Information [32]
- Responsibilities of Management for the Financial Statements: [34]
  - Preparation of FS
  - Internal controls
  - Assessing the entity's ability to continue as a going concern
- Auditor Responsibilities for the Audit of the Financial Statements: [38]
  - The objectives of the auditor are to obtain reasonable assurance about the FS and issue an auditor's report containing an opinion
- Name of Engagement Partner (listed entities) [46]
- Signature of the Auditor [47]
- Auditor's address [48]
- Date of the Auditor's Report [49]

ISA 701 *Communicating Key Audit Matters in the Independent Auditor's Report*

Key audit matters (KAM) are those that in the auditor's professional judgment were of most significance in the audit and are selected from matters communicated with those charged with governance. [8]

KAM include: [9]

- Areas of higher assessed risk of material misstatement
- Significant auditor judgments relating to areas of significant management judgment
- Significant events of transactions that occurred during the period.

The description of each KAM will consider: [13]

- Why it is considered a key audit matter
- How the matter was addressed in the audit.

ISA 705 Modifications to the Audit Opinion in the Independent Auditor's Report

Definitions:

- Modified opinion: qualified, adverse or disclaimer of opinion [5b]
- Pervasive: not confined to specific elements or representing a substantial proportion of a single element [5a]

Modifications:

- FS as a whole not free from material misstatement [6a]
    - Material but not pervasive: qualified [7a]
    - Pervasive and pervasive: adverse [8]
- Unable to obtain sufficient appropriate evidence [6b]
    - Material but not pervasive: qualified [7b]
    - Pervasive and pervasive: disclaimer [9]

When the auditor modifies the opinion, the basis for opinion is amended to 'Basis for Qualified Opinion', 'Basis for Adverse Opinion' or 'Basis for Disclaimer of Opinion' as appropriate. [20a]

The 'Basis for...' section includes a description of the matter giving rise to the modification. [20b]

ISA 706 *Emphasis of Matter Paragraphs and Other Matter Paragraphs in the Independent Auditor's Report*

Emphasis of matter

- Refers to matters fundamental to the user's understanding of the FS. [7a]

- Used to draw attention to a matter already presented or disclosed in the FS. [8]

Other matter

- Refers to matters relevant to the user's understanding of the audit, the auditor's responsibilities or the auditor's report. [7b]

ISA 720 The Auditor's Responsibilities Relating to Other Information in Documents Containing Audited Financial Statements

Auditor responsibilities:

- Read other information to identify material inconsistencies with the FS or the auditor's knowledge which indicates material misstatement of the FS or the other information. [3]

- If inconsistencies identified:

  - Perform procedures to conclude whether it is the financial statements or the other information that requires amendment. [16]

  - If other information is wrong, ask management to correct it. [17]

  - If matter remains uncorrected, describe the inconsistency in the Other Information section of the auditor's report or withdraw from the engagement where withdrawal is possible. [18]

Financial reporting revision

Chapter learning objectives

This section is designed to help you with the key requirements of the accounting standards examinable for this exam.

IAS 1 Presentation of Financial Statements

This standard provides formats for the statement of profit or loss and other comprehensive income, statement of financial position, and statement of changes in equity.

Accounting policies should be selected so that the financial statements comply with all international standards and interpretations.

IAS 1 requires that other comprehensive income is presented in two categories, namely items that:

- will not be reclassified to profit or loss, and
- may be reclassified to profit or loss in future reporting periods.

IAS 2 Inventories

Inventories should be valued 'at the lower of cost and net realisable value' (IAS 2, para 9).

IAS 2 says that the cost of inventory includes:

- Purchase price including import duties, transport and handling costs
- Direct production costs e.g. direct labour
- Direct expenses and subcontracted work
- Production overheads (based on the normal levels of activity)
- Other overheads, if attributable to bringing the product or service to its present location and condition.

IAS 2 specifies that cost excludes:

- Abnormal waste
- Storage costs
- Indirect administrative overheads
- Selling costs.

Some entities can identify individual units of inventory (e.g. vehicles can be identified by a chassis number). Those that cannot should keep track of costs using either the first in, first out (FIFO) or the weighted average cost (AVCO) assumption.

Some entities may use standard costing for valuing inventory. Standard costs may be used for convenience if it is a close approximation to actual cost, and is regularly reviewed and revised.

IAS 7 Statement of Cash Flows

IAS 7 requires a statement of cash flow that shows cash flows generated from:

- Operating activities
- Investing activities
- Financing activities.

IAS 10 Events After the Reporting Period

Definitions

Events after the reporting period are **'those events, favourable and unfavourable, that occur between the statement of financial position date and the date when the financial statements are authorised for issue'** (IAS 10, para 3).

Adjusting events after the reporting period are those that 'provide evidence of conditions that existed at the reporting date' (IAS 10, para 3a).

Non-adjusting events after the reporting period are **'those that are indicative of conditions that arose after the reporting period'** (IAS 10, para 3b).

Accounting treatment

Adjusting events affect the amounts stated in the financial statements so they must be adjusted.

Non-adjusting events do not concern the position as at the reporting date so the financial statements are not adjusted. If the event is material then the nature and its financial effect must be disclosed.

IAS 16 Property Plant and Equipment

Cost and depreciation of an asset

IAS 16 states that property, plant and equipment is initially recognised at cost.

An asset's cost is its purchase price, less any trade discounts or rebates, plus any further costs directly attributable to bringing it into working condition for its intended use.

Subsequent expenditure on non-current assets is capitalised if it:

- Enhances the economic benefits of the asset e.g. adding a new wing to a building.

- Replaces part of an asset that has been separately depreciated and has been fully depreciated; e.g. a furnace that requires new linings periodically.

- Replaces economic benefits previously consumed, e.g. a major inspection of aircraft.

The aim of depreciation is to spread the cost of the asset over its life in the business.

- IAS 16 requires that the depreciation method and useful life of an asset should be reviewed at the end of each year and revised where necessary. This is not a change in accounting policy, but a change of accounting estimate.

- If an asset has parts with different lives, (e.g. a building with a flat roof), the component parts should be capitalised and depreciated separately.

Revaluation of property, plant and equipment

Revaluation of PPE is optional. If one asset is revalued, all assets in that class must be revalued.

Valuations should be kept up to date to ensure that the carrying amount does not differ materially from the fair value at each statement of financial position date.

Revaluation gains are credited to **other comprehensive income** unless the gain reverses a previous revaluation loss of the same asset previously recognised in the statement of profit or loss.

Revaluation losses are debited to the statement of profit or loss unless the loss relates to a previous revaluation surplus, in which case the decrease should be debited to other comprehensive income to the extent of any credit balance existing in the revaluation surplus relating to that asset.

Depreciation is charged on the revalued amount less residual value (if any) over the **remaining useful life** of the asset.

An entity may choose to make an annual transfer of excess depreciation from revaluation reserve to retained earnings. If this is done, it should be applied consistently each year.

IAS 27 Separate Financial Statements

This standard applies when an entity has interests in subsidiaries, joint ventures or associates and either elects to, or is required to, prepare separate **non-consolidated financial statements**.

If separate financial statements are produced, investments in subsidiaries, associates or joint ventures can be measured:

- at cost

- using the equity method

- in accordance with IFRS 9 *Financial Instruments*.

IAS 28 Investments in associates and joint ventures

Joint ventures

A joint venture is a **'joint arrangement whereby the parties that have joint control of the arrangement have rights to the net assets of the arrangement'** (IAS 28, para 3). This will normally be established in the form of a separate entity to conduct the joint venture activities.

Associates

An associate is defined as an entity **'over which the investor has significant influence'** (IAS 28, para 3).

Significant influence is the **'power to participate in the financial and operating policy decisions of the investee but is not control or joint control over those policies'** (IAS 28, para 3).

It is normally assumed that significant influence exists if the holding company has a shareholding of 20% to 50%.

Equity accounting

In the consolidated financial statements of a group, an investment in an associate or joint venture is accounted for using the equity method.

The **consolidated statement of profit or loss** will show a single figure in respect of the associate or joint venture. This is calculated as the investor's share of the associate or joint venture's profit for the period.

In the **consolidated statement of financial position**, the 'investment in the associate/joint venture' is presented in non-current assets. It is calculated as the initial cost of the investment plus/(minus) the investor's share of the post-acquisition reserve increase/(decrease).

The associate or joint venture is outside the group. Therefore transactions and balances between group companies and the associate or joint venture are not eliminated from the consolidated financial statements.

IAS 37 Provisions, Contingent Liabilities and Contingent Assets

IAS 37 provides the following definitions:

- A provision is **'a liability of uncertain timing or** amount' (IAS 37, para 10).

- A contingent liability is a possible obligation arising from past events whose existence will only be confirmed by an uncertain future event outside of the entity's control.

- A contingent asset is a possible asset that arises from past events and whose existence will only be confirmed by an uncertain future event outside of the entity's control.

Provisions

Provisions should be recognised when:

- An entity has a present obligation (legal or constructive) as a result of a past event

- It is probable that an outflow of economic benefits will be required to settle the obligation, and

- A reliable estimate can be made of the amount of the obligation.

Measurement of provisions:

- The provision amount should be the best estimate of the expenditure required to settle the present obligation.

- Where the time value of money is material, the provision should be discounted to present value.

Restructuring provisions:

- Provisions can only be recognised where an entity has a constructive obligation to carry out the restructuring.

- A constructive obligation arises when there is a detailed formal plan which identifies:

  - The business concerned

  - The principal location, function and approximate number of employees being made redundant

  - The expenditures that will be incurred

  - When the plan will be implemented

  - There is a valid expectation that the plan will be carried out by either implementing the plan or announcing it to those affected.

Specific guidance:

- Future operating losses should not be recognised.

- Onerous contracts should be recognised for the present obligation under the contract.

Contingent liabilities should not be recognised. They should be disclosed unless the possibility of a transfer of economic benefits is remote.

Contingent assets should not be recognised. If the possibility of an inflow of economic benefits is probable they should be disclosed.

IAS 38 Intangible Assets

IAS 38 says that an intangible asset is **'an identifiable non-monetary asset without physical substance'** (IAS 38, para 8).

Initial recognition

IAS 38 states that an intangible asset is initially recognised at cost if all of the following criteria are met.

(1) It is identifiable – it could be disposed of without disposing of the business at the same time.

(2) It is controlled by the entity – the entity has the power to obtain economic benefits from it, for example patents and copyrights give legal rights to future economic benefits.

(3) It will generate probable future economic benefits for the entity – this could be by a reduction in costs or increasing revenues.

(4) The cost can be measured reliably.

If an intangible does not meet the recognition criteria, then it should be charged to the statement of profit or loss as expenditure is incurred. Items that do not meet the criteria are internally generated goodwill, brands, mastheads, publishing titles, customer lists, research, advertising, start-up costs and training.

Subsequent treatment

Intangible assets should be amortised over their useful lives.

If it can be demonstrated that the useful life is indefinite no amortisation should be charged, but an annual impairment review must be carried out.

Intangible assets can be revalued but fair values must be determined with reference to an active market. Active markets have homogenous products, willing buyers and sellers at all times and published prices. In practical terms, most intangible assets are likely to be valued using the cost model.

Research and development

The recognition of internally generated intangible assets is split into a research phase and a development phase.

Costs incurred in the research phase must be charged to the statement of profit or loss as they are incurred.

IAS 38 says that costs incurred in the development phase should be recognised as an intangible asset if they meet the following criteria:

(a) The project is technically feasible

(b) The asset will be completed then used or sold

(c) The entity is able to use or sell the asset

(d) The asset will generate future economic benefits (either because of internal use or because there is a market for it)

(e) The entity has adequate technical, financial and other resources to complete the project

(f) The expenditure on the project can be reliably measured.

Amortisation of development costs will occur over the period that benefits are expected.

IFRS® 3 Business Combinations

On acquisition of a subsidiary, the purchase consideration transferred and the identifiable net assets acquired are recorded at fair value.

Fair value is **'the price that would be received to sell an asset or paid to transfer a liability in an orderly transaction between market participants at the measurement date'** (IFRS 13, para 9).

Purchase consideration

Purchase consideration is measured at fair value. Note that:

- Deferred cash consideration should be discounted to present value using a rate at which the acquirer could obtain similar borrowing.

- The fair value of the acquirer's own shares is the market price at the acquisition date.

- Contingent consideration is included as part of the consideration at its fair value, even if payment is not probable.

Goodwill and the non-controlling interest

The non-controlling interest (NCI) at acquisition is measured at either:

- Fair value, or

- The NCI's proportionate share of the fair value of the subsidiary's identifiable net assets.

Gain on bargain purchase

If the net assets acquired exceed the fair value of consideration, then a gain on bargain purchase (negative goodwill) arises.

After checking that the calculations have been done correctly, the gain on bargain purchase is credited to profit or loss.

Other adjustments

Other consolidation adjustments need to be made in order to present the parent and its subsidiaries as a single economic entity. Transactions that require adjustments include:

- Interest on intragroup loans

- Intragroup management charges

- Intragroup sales, purchases and unrealised profit in inventory

- Intragroup transfer of non-current assets and unrealised profit on transfer

- Intragroup receivables, payables and loans.

 IFRS 10 Consolidated Financial Statements

IFRS 10 states that consolidated financial statements must be prepared if one company controls another company.

Control, according to IFRS 10, consists of three components:

(1) **Power** over the investee: this is normally exercised through the **majority of voting rights,** but could also arise through other contractual arrangements.

(2) **Exposure** or rights to variable returns (positive and/or negative), and

(3) The **ability to use power** to affect the investor's returns.

It is normally assumed that control exists when one company owns more than half of the ordinary shares in another company.

IFRS 15 Revenue from Contracts with Customers

Revenue recognition is a five step process.

(1) **Identify the contract**

A contract is an agreement between two or more parties that creates rights and obligations.

(2) **Identify the separate performance obligations within a contract**

Performance obligations are, essentially, promises made to a customer.

(3) **Determine the transaction price**

The transaction price is the amount the entity expects to be entitled in exchange for satisfying all performance obligations. Amounts collected on behalf of third parties (such as sales tax) are excluded.

(4) **Allocate the transaction price to the performance obligations in the contract**

The total transaction price should be allocated to each performance obligation in proportion to stand-alone selling prices.

(5) **Recognise revenue when (or as) a performance obligation is satisfied.**

For each performance obligation an entity must determine whether it satisfies the performance obligation over time or at a point in time.

An entity satisfies a performance obligation over time if one of the following criteria is met:

(a) **'the customer simultaneously receives and consumes the benefits provided by the entity's performance as the entity performs**

(b) **the entity's performance creates or enhances an asset (for example, work in progress) that the customer controls as the asset is created or enhanced, or**

(c) **the entity's performance does not create an asset with an alternative use to the entity and the entity has an enforceable right to payment for performance completed to date'** (IFRS 15, para 35).

For a performance obligation satisfied over time, an entity recognises revenue based on progress towards satisfaction of that performance obligation.

If a performance obligation is not satisfied over time then it is satisfied at a point in time. The entity must determine the point in time at which a customer obtains control of the promised asset.

Questions and Answers

Test your understanding 1 – Confidentiality

Client confidentiality underpins the relationship between Chartered Certified Accountants in practice and their clients. It is a core element of ACCA's Code of Ethics.

Required:

(a) **Explain the circumstances in which external auditors are permitted or required to disclose information relating to their clients to third parties without the knowledge or consent of the client.**

(4 marks)

(b) A waste disposal company has breached tax regulations, environmental regulations and health and safety regulations. The auditor has been approached by the tax authorities, the government body supervising the award of licences to such companies and a trade union representative. All of them have asked the auditor to provide them with information about the company. The auditor has also been approached by the police. They are investigating a suspected fraud perpetrated by the managing director of the company and they wish to ask the auditor certain questions about him.

Describe how the auditor should respond to these types of request.

(6 marks)

(Total: 10 marks)

Test your understanding 2 – Ethical threats

You are a manager in the audit firm of JT & Co and this is your first time you have worked on one of the firm's established clients, Pink Co. The main activity of Pink Co is providing investment advice to individuals regarding saving for retirement, purchase of shares and securities and investing in tax efficient savings schemes. Pink Co is a listed company regulated by the relevant financial services authority.

You have been asked to start the audit planning for Pink Co, by Mrs Goodall, a partner in JT & Co. Mrs Goodall has been the engagement partner for Pink Co, for the previous seven years and so has a sound knowledge of the client. Mrs Goodall has informed you that she would like her son Simon to be part of the audit team this year; Simon is currently studying for his first set of papers for his ACCA qualification. Mrs Goodall also informs you that Mr Supper, the audit senior, received investment advice from Pink Co during the year and intends to do the same next year.

In an initial meeting with the finance director of Pink Co, you learn that the audit team will not be entertained on Pink Co's yacht this year as this could appear to be an attempt to influence the audit opinion. Instead, he has arranged a day at the horse races costing less than two fifths of the expense of using the yacht and hopes this will be acceptable.

JT & Co have done some consulting work previously and the invoice is still outstanding.

Required:

Identify and explain the threats to independence in relation to the audit of Pink Co by JT & Co. For each threat, recommend how the threat can be managed.

(10 marks)

Test your understanding 3 – Analytical risk assessment

(a) **With reference to ISA 520 *Analytical Procedures* explain:**

(i) **what is meant by the term 'analytical procedures'**

(1 mark)

(ii) **the different types of analytical procedures available to the auditor**

(3 marks)

(iii) **the situations in the audit when analytical procedures are used.**

(3 marks)

Tribe Co sells bathrooms from 15 retail outlets. Sales are made to individuals, with income being in the form of cash and debit cards. All items purchased are delivered to the customer using Tribe's own delivery vans as most bathrooms are too big for individuals to transport in their own motor vehicles. The directors of Tribe indicate that the company has had a difficult year, but are pleased to present some acceptable results to the members.

The statement of profit or loss for the last two financial years are shown below:

Statement of profit or loss

	31 March 20X4	31 March 20X3
	$000	$000
Revenue	11,223	9,546
Cost of sales	(5,280)	(6,380)
	5,943	3,166
Operating expenses		
Administration	(1,853)	(1,980)
Selling and distribution	(1,472)	(1,034)
Interest payable	(152)	(158)
Investment income	218	–
	2,684	(6)

Statement of financial position extract

Cash and bank	380	(1,425)

Required:

(b)   **As part of your risk assessment procedures for Tribe Co, identify and provide a possible explanation for unusual changes in the statement of profit or loss.**

(8 marks)

(Total: 15 marks)

Test your understanding 4 – Audit risk

You are an audit senior in Staple and Co and you are commencing the planning of the audit of Smoothbrush Paints Co (Smoothbrush) for the year ending 31 August 20X0. Smoothbrush is a paint manufacturer and has been trading for over 50 years. It operates from one central site which includes the production facility, warehouse and administration offices.

Smoothbrush sells all of its goods to large home improvement stores, with 60% being to one large chain store Homewares. The company has a one-year contract to be the sole supplier of paint to Homewares. It secured the contract through significantly reducing prices and offering a four-month credit period, the company's normal credit period is one month.

Goods in/purchases

In recent years, Smoothbrush has reduced the level of goods directly manufactured and instead started to import paint from South Asia. Approximately 60% is imported and 40% manufactured. Within the production facility is a large amount of old plant and equipment that is now redundant and has minimal scrap value. Purchase orders for overseas paint are made six months in advance and goods can be in transit for up to two months. Smoothbrush accounts for the inventory when it receives the goods.

To avoid the disruption of a year-end inventory count, Smoothbrush has this year introduced a continuous/perpetual inventory counting system. The warehouse has been divided into 12 areas and these are each to be counted once over the year. At the year-end it is proposed that the inventory will be based on the underlying records. Traditionally Smoothbrush has maintained an inventory allowance based on 1% of the inventory value, but management feels that as inventory is being reviewed more regularly it no longer needs this allowance.

Finance Director

In May 20X0 Smoothbrush had a dispute with its finance director (FD) and he immediately left the company. The company has temporarily asked the financial controller to take over the role while they recruit a permanent replacement. The old FD has notified Smoothbrush that he intends to sue for unfair dismissal. The directors are not proposing to make any provision or disclosure for this, as they are confident the claim has no merit.

Required:

(a) Explain the audit risks identified at the planning stage of the audit of Smoothbrush Paints Co.

(8 marks)

(b) Discuss the importance of assessing risks at the planning stage of an audit.

(6 marks)

(c) Describe THREE substantive procedures the auditor of Smoothbrush Paints Co should perform at the year-end in confirming each of the following:

(i) The valuation of inventory

(ii) The completeness of provisions or contingent liabilities.

(6 marks)

(Total: 20 marks)

Test your understanding 5 – Fraud

Fraud and error present risks to an entity. Both internal and external auditors are required to deal with risks to the entity. However, the responsibilities of internal and external auditors in relation to the risk of fraud and error differ.

Required:

(a) **Explain how the internal audit function helps an entity deal with the risk of fraud and error.**

(5 marks)

(b) **Explain the responsibilities of external auditors in respect of the risk of fraud and error in an audit of financial statements.**

(5 marks)

(c) Stone Holidays is an independent travel agency. It takes commission on holidays sold to customers through its chain of high street shops. Staff are partly paid on a commission basis. Well-established tour operators run the holidays that Stone Holidays sells. The networked reservations system through which holidays are booked, and the computerised accounting system, are both well-established systems used by many independent travel agencies.

Payments by customers, including deposits, are accepted in cash and by debit and credit card. Stone Holidays is legally required to pay an amount of money (based on its total sales for the year) into a central fund maintained to compensate customers if the agency should cease operations.

Describe the nature of the risks to which Stone Holidays is subject arising from fraud and error.

(5 marks)

(Total: 15 marks)

Test your understanding 6 – Quality control

You are the partner responsible for quality control within your firm. You are reviewing the findings from a recent post-issuance (cold) review performed by your firm's compliance department. The following issues were identified on a number of audits:

Client A

A review of working papers found that some working papers had not been signed off by the team member who completed the work. Some working papers were not dated and some did not have a signature confirming they had been reviewed.

Client B

A mandatory procedure included in the audit plan which required a written representation letter to be obtained, had not been completed. A comment had been added by the audit manager stating that there were no issues requiring a written representation from management.

Client C

An audit test over purchases required a sample of 30 invoices to be tested. 27 had been tested and found to be recorded accurately and completely. 3 invoices could not be found. No further invoices were identified for testing and a conclusion was drawn based on the 27 items tested.

Client D

The audit of a material provision was performed by the audit junior as the audit manager was too busy finishing off work for the previous audit client on which they had been working.

Client E

The planning section of the file has not been completed. The audit procedures performed were copied over from the previous year's file and the same approach and sample sizes have been used for this year's audit.

Required:

Describe the quality control issues arising from each of the findings.

(10 marks)

Test your understanding 7 – Controls

You are carrying out the audit of the purchases system of Spondon Furniture. The company has revenue of $10 million and all the shares are owned by Mr and Mrs Fisher, who are non-executive directors and are not involved in the day-to-day running of the company.

The bookkeeper maintains all the accounting records and prepares the annual financial statements.

The company uses a standard computerised accounting package.

You have determined that the purchases system operates as follows:

- When materials are required for production, the production manager sends a handwritten note to the buying manager. For orders of other items, the department manager or managing director sends handwritten notes to the buying manager. The buying manager finds a suitable supplier and raises a purchase order. The purchase order is signed by the managing director. Purchase orders are not issued for all goods and services received by the company.

- Materials for production are received by the goods received department, who issue a goods received note (GRN), and send a copy to the bookkeeper. There is no system for recording receipt of other goods and services.

- The bookkeeper receives the purchase invoice and matches it with the goods received note and purchase order (if available). The managing director authorises the invoice for posting to the purchase ledger.

- The bookkeeper analyses the invoice into relevant nominal ledger account codes and then posts it.

- At the end of each month, the bookkeeper prepares a list of payables to be paid. This is approved by the managing director.

- The bookkeeper prepares the cheques and remittances and posts the cheques to the purchase ledger and cashbook.

- The managing director signs the cheques and the bookkeeper sends the cheques and remittances to the payables.

Mr and Mrs Fisher are aware that there may be weaknesses in the above system and have asked for advice.

Explain the control deficiencies in Spondon's purchases system and suggest improvements to overcome the deficiencies.

(10 marks)

Test your understanding 8 – Inventory count

DinZee Co assembles fridges, microwaves, washing machines and other similar domestic appliances from parts procured from a large number of suppliers. As part of the interim audit work two weeks prior to the company year-end, you are testing the procurement and purchases systems and attending the inventory count.

On the day of the inventory count, you attended depot nine at DinZee. You observed the following activities:

Pre-numbered count sheets were being issued to client staff carrying out the count. The count sheets showed the inventory ledger balances for checking against physical inventory.

All count staff were drawn from the inventory warehouse and were counting in teams of two.

Three counting teams were allocated to each area of the stores to count, although the teams were allowed to decide which pair of staff counted which inventory within each area. Staff were warned that they had to remember which inventory had been counted.

Information was recorded on the count sheets in pencil so amendments could be made easily as required.

Any inventory not located on the pre-numbered inventory sheets was recorded on separate inventory sheets which were numbered by staff as they were used.

At the end of the count, all count sheets were collected and the numeric sequence of the sheets checked. The sheets were not signed.

Required:

(a) Describe FOUR audit procedures that an auditor will normally perform prior to attending the client's premises on the day of the inventory count.

(4 marks)

(b) Identify the deficiencies in the control system for counting inventory, explain why it is a deficiency and state how each deficiency can be overcome.

(12 marks)

(c) State the aim of a test of control and the aim of a substantive procedure and in respect of your attendance at DinZee Co's inventory count, state one test of control and one substantive procedure that you should perform.

(4 marks)

(Total: 20 marks)

Test your understanding 9 – Evidence and procedures

You are the auditor of BearsWorld, a company which manufactures and sells small cuddly toys by mail order. The company is managed by Mr Kyto although due to other business commitments Mr Kyto only visits the office once a week. BearsWorld employs two assistants. One assistant maintains the payables ledger, orders inventory and pays suppliers. The other assistant receives customer orders and despatches cuddly toys. Mr Kyto authorises important transactions such as wages and large orders.

At any time, about 100 different types of cuddly toys are available for sale. All sales are paid for at the time of ordering. Customers pay using credit cards and occasionally by sending cash. Revenue is over $5.2 million.

You are planning the audit of BearsWorld and are considering using some of the procedures for gathering audit evidence recommended by ISA 500 *Audit Evidence* as follows:

- Analytical procedures

- Inquiry

- Inspection

- Observation

- Recalculation.

Required:

For each of the above procedures in relation to the audit of Bearsworld:

(i) Explain its use in gathering audit evidence.

(ii) Describe one example how it could be used.

(iii) Explain the benefits of each procedure.

(iv) Explain the limitations of each procedure.

(20 marks)

Test your understanding 10 – Procedures

(i) Describe FIVE types of procedures for obtaining audit evidence; and

(ii) For each type of procedure, describe an example relevant to the audit of BANK balances.

Note: The total marks will be split equally between each part.

(10 marks)

Test your understanding 11 – Audit risk NFP

(a) Explain the term 'audit risk' and the three elements of risk that contribute to total audit risk.

(4 marks)

The EuKaRe charity was established in 1960. The charity's aim is to provide support to children from disadvantaged backgrounds who wish to take part in sports such as tennis, badminton and football.

EuKaRe has a detailed constitution which explains how the charity's income can be spent. The constitution also notes that administration expenditure cannot exceed 10% of income in any year.

The charity's income is derived wholly from voluntary donations. Sources of donations include:

- Cash collected by volunteers asking the public for donations in shopping areas.

- Cheques sent to the charity's head office.

- Donations from generous individuals. Some of these donations have specific clauses attached to them indicating that the initial amount donated (capital) cannot be spent and that the income (interest) from the donation must be spent on specific activities, for example, provision of sports equipment.

The rules regarding the taxation of charities in the country EuKaRe is based are complicated, with only certain expenditure being allowable for taxation purposes and donations of capital being treated as income in some situations.

Required:

(b) Identify areas of inherent risk in the EuKaRe charity and explain the effect of each of these risks on the audit approach.

(12 marks)

(c) Explain why the control environment may be weak at the charity EuKaRe.

(4 marks)

(Total: 20 marks)

Test your understanding 12 – NFP audit

Ajio is a charity whose constitution requires that it raises funds for educational projects. These projects seek to educate children and support teachers in certain countries. Charities in the country from which Ajio operates have recently become subject to new audit and accounting regulations. Charity income consists of cash collections at fundraising events, telephone appeals, and bequests (money left to the charity by deceased persons). The charity is small and the trustees do not consider that the charity can afford to employ a qualified accountant. The charity employs a part-time bookkeeper and relies on volunteers for fundraising. Your firm has been appointed as accountants and auditors to this charity. Accounts have been prepared in the past by a volunteer who is a recently retired Chartered Certified Accountant but these accounts have not been audited.

Required:

(a) **Explain the audit risks associated with the audit of Ajio.**

(4 marks)

(b) **Describe the audit procedures to be performed on income and expenditure from fund raising events.**

(6 marks)

Note: You are not required to deal with the detail of accounting for charities in either part of the question.

(Total: 10 marks)

Test your understanding 13 – Subsequent events

Grains 4U Co (Grains) manufactures breakfast cereals and has three factories, four warehouses and three distribution depots spread across North America. The audit for the year ended 31 December 20X5 is almost complete and the financial statements and auditor's report are due to be signed shortly. Profit before taxation is $7.9 million. The following events have occurred subsequent to the year-end and no amendments or disclosures have been made in the financial statements.

Event 1 – Fire

On 15 February 20X6, a fire occurred at the largest of the distribution depots. The fire resulted in extensive damage to 40% of the company's vehicles used for dispatching goods to customers, however, there have been no significant delays to customer deliveries. The company estimates the level of damage to the vehicles to be in excess of $650,000. Only a minimal level of inventory, approximately $25,000, was damaged. Grain's insurance company has started to investigate the fire to assess the likelihood and level of payment, however, there are concerns the fire was started deliberately, and if true, would invalidate any insurance cover.

(5 marks)

Event 2 – Inventory

On 18 February 20X6, it was discovered that a large batch of Grain's new cereal brand 'Loopy Green Loops' held in inventory at the year end was defective, as the cereal contained too much green food colouring. To date no sales of this new cereal have been made. The cost of the defective batch of inventory is $915,000 and the defects cannot be corrected. However, the scrapped cereal can be utilised as a raw material for an alternative cereal brand at a value of $50,000.

(5 marks)

Required:

For each of the two subsequent events described above:

(i)   **Based on the information provided, explain whether the financial statements require amendment, and**

(ii)   **Describe audit procedures which should now be performed in order to form a conclusion on any required amendment.**

(Total: 10 marks)

Test your understanding 14 – Written representations

(a) Explain the purpose of a written representation.

(3 marks)

(b) You are the manager in charge of the audit of Crighton-Ward, a public limited liability company which manufactures specialist cars and other motor vehicles for use in films. Audited revenue is $140 million with profit before tax of $7.5 million.

All audit work up to, but not including, the obtaining of written representations has been completed. A review of the audit file has disclosed the following outstanding points:

Lion's Roar

The company is facing a potential legal claim from the Lion's Roar company in respect of a defective vehicle that was supplied for one of their films. Lion's Roar maintains that the vehicle built was not strong enough while the directors of Crighton-Ward argue that the specification was not sufficiently detailed. Dropping a vehicle 50 metres into a river and expecting it to continue to remain in working condition would be unusual, but this is what Lion's Roar expected.

Solicitors are unable to determine liability at the present time. A claim for $4 million being the cost of a replacement vehicle and lost production time has been received by Crighton-Ward from Lions' Roar. The directors' opinion is that the claim is not justified.

Depreciation

Depreciation of specialist production equipment has been included in the financial statements at the amount of 10% per annum using the reducing balance method. The treatment is consistent with prior accounting periods (which received an unmodified audit opinion) and other companies in the same industry. Sales of old equipment show negligible profit or loss on sale. The audit senior, who is new to the audit, feels that depreciation is being undercharged in the financial statements.

Required:

(b) Discuss whether or not a paragraph is required in the written representation for each of the above matters.

(4 marks)

(c) A suggested format for the written representation has been sent by the auditors to the directors of Crighton-Ward. The directors have stated that they will not sign the written representation this year on the grounds that they believe the additional evidence that it provides is not required by the auditor.

Required:

Discuss the actions the auditor may take as a result of the decision made by the directors not to sign the written representation.

(3 marks)

(Total: 10 marks)

Test your understanding 15 – Auditors' reports

You are currently reviewing the working papers of several audit assignments recently carried out by your audit firm. Each of the audit engagements is nearing completion, but certain matters have recently come to light which may affect your audit opinion on each of the engagements. In each case the year-end of the company is 30 September 20X2.

(a) **Jones** (Profit before tax $150,000)

On 3 October 20X2 a letter was received informing the company that a customer, who owed the company $30,000 as at the year-end had been declared bankrupt on 30 September. At the time of the audit it was expected that unsecured creditors, such as Jones, would receive nothing in respect of this debt. The directors refuse to change the financial statements to provide for the loss, on the grounds that the notification was not received by the statement of financial position date.

Total debts shown in the statement of financial position amounted to $700,000. **(5 marks)**

(b) **Roberts** (Profit before tax $500,000)

On 31 July 20X2 a customer sued the company for personal damages arising from a defect in one of its products. Shortly before the year-end the company made an out-of-court settlement with the customer of $10,000, although this agreement is not reflected in the financial statements. Further, the matter subsequently became known to the press and was extensively reported. The company's legal advisers have now informed you that further claims have been received following the publicity, although they are unable to place a figure on the potential liability arising. The company has referred to the claims in a note to the financial statements stating that no provision has been made because the claims are not expected to be material. **(5 marks)**

(c) Griffiths (Profit before tax $250,000)

The audit work revealed that a trade investment stated in the statement of financial position at $500,000 has suffered a permanent fall in value of $300,000. The company has refused to put an impairment charge through for it on the grounds that other investments (not held for resale) have risen in value and are stated at amounts considerably below their realisable values.

(5 marks)

(d) Evans (Profit before tax $100,000)

This client is a construction company, currently building a warehouse on its own premises and using some of its own workforce. The labour cost has been included in the cost of the non-current asset in the statement of financial position at a value of $10,000. During the audit it was discovered that the direct labour cost records for the early part of the year have been accidentally destroyed.

(5 marks)

Required:

Discuss each of the cases outlined above, referring to materiality considerations and, where appropriate, relevant accounting principles and appropriate accounting standards. Explain the audit reporting implications in each case.

(Total: 20 marks)

Test your understanding 16 – Corporate Governance 1

You are an audit manager of Satsuma & Co and have been assigned to the audit of Tangerine Tech Co (Tangerine), a company which is planning to list on a stock exchange within six months. The listing rules of the stock exchange require compliance with corporate governance principles, and the directors are unsure whether they are following best practice in relation to this. They have asked the audit engagement partner for their view on this matter.

Tangerine's board comprises six executive directors, a non-executive chair and three other non-executive directors (NEDs). The chair and one of the NEDs are former executive directors of Tangerine and on reaching retirement age were asked to take on non-executive roles. The company has established an audit committee, and all NEDs are members including the chair who chairs the committee. All four members of the audit committee were previously involved in sales or production related roles.

All of the directors have been members of the board for at least four years. As the chair does not have an executive role, he has sole responsibility for liaising with the shareholders and answering any of their questions. The company has not established an internal audit function to monitor internal controls.

Required:

Using the information above describe FIVE corporate governance weaknesses faced by Tangerine Tech Co and provide a recommendation to address each weakness to ensure compliance with corporate governance principles.

(10 marks)

Test your understanding 17 – Corporate Governance 2

(1) **What is meant by corporate governance?**

(2 marks)

(2) **Why are external auditors interested in corporate governance?**

(2 marks)

(3) **Who should make up a typical audit committee?**

(1 mark)

(4) **What is the audit committee's role?**

(5 marks)

(5) **Why does a company need an audit committee if it has a good relationship with its external auditors?**

(2 marks)

(6) **A company has identified one of its major risks as loss of key staff.**

Explain:

- **What they should do as a result of this?**

- **How they might reduce or even eliminate the risk?**

- **Why the auditor is interested in this, given that it is not a direct financial risk?**

(3 marks)

(Total: 15 marks)

Test your understanding 18 – Internal audit

Flylo is an airline. The company owns some of its fleet of aircraft. Other aircraft are leased from third parties. Flylo has an internal audit function that has recently been expanded. Your firm is the external auditor of Flylo. Your firm has been asked to investigate the extent to which it may be able to rely on the work of internal audit in the following areas:

- Sales and ticketing

- Fleet acquisition and maintenance

- Trade payables and long-term debt financing (borrowings).

Required:

(a) **Explain why the work of the internal auditors, in the three areas noted above, is likely to be useful to you as the external auditor.**

(6 marks)

(b) **Explain the matters that should be considered by the external auditor when evaluating the internal audit function and whether reliance can be placed on their work.**

(4 marks)

(Total: 10 marks)

Test your understanding answers

| Test your understanding 1 – Confidentiality |

(a) **Disclosure of information relating to clients to third parties**

- Auditors are permitted or required to disclose information about their clients to third parties without their knowledge or consent in very limited circumstances.

- Generally, auditors can be required to, or are permitted to, disclose information to certain regulatory bodies, including certain specialist units under legislation. Examples include legislation covering financial services companies such as banks, money laundering and investigation of serious fraud or tax evasion.

- Auditors may disclose information where they are personally involved in litigation, including litigation that involves the recovery of fees from clients, or where they are subject to disciplinary proceedings brought by ACCA or other, similar professional bodies.

- Auditors are permitted to disclose information where they consider it to be in the 'public interest' or in the interests of national security. Factors to take into account include the seriousness of the matter, the likelihood of repetition and the extent to which the public is involved.

(b) **Response to requests**

- The auditor must not disclose information without the consent of the client or unless the necessary statutory documentation is provided by the person(s) requesting the information.

- Unless the auditor has reason to believe that there is a statutory duty not to inform the client that an approach has been made, the client should first be approached to see if consent can be obtained, and to see if the client is aware of the investigations. The auditor should ensure that the client is aware of the fact the voluntary disclosure may work in the client's favour. If the client refuses, the auditor should inform the client if the auditor has a statutory duty of disclosure.

- Legal advice should be sought in all of the cases described.

- Where the auditor is made aware of potential actions against the client that may have an effect on the financial statements, the auditor must consider the effect on the auditor's report. If the client is aware of the investigation, the auditor will be able to seek audit evidence to support any necessary provisions or disclosures in the financial statements.

- The auditor should consider whether the suspected fraud relating to the managing director relates to the company and affects the financial statements.

- The auditor will be in a very difficult situation if they become aware of an action that may materially affect the financial statements, but where the client is not, and where auditors are under a statutory duty not to inform the client. This situation will not be improved by the resignation of auditors as they may be obliged to make a statement on resignation. Legal advice is essential in such circumstances.

- Tax authorities normally have powers to ask clients to disclose information voluntarily. Such voluntary disclosure is often looked on favourably by the tax authorities and the courts. Tax authorities normally also have statutory powers to demand information from both clients and auditors. The same is generally true of environmental and health and safety inspectors.

- The power of the police to demand information is sometimes less clear and auditors and clients should take care to ensure that the appropriate authorities are in place. Those sections of the police investigating serious frauds usually have more powers than the general police.

- It is unlikely that trade union representatives have any statutory powers to demand information.

Test your understanding 2 – Ethical threats

Threat	Managing the threat
Mrs Goodall has been the engagement partner for the last seven years. This creates a familiarity threat. Mrs Goodall may be too trusting of or too close to the client to be able to make objective decisions due to this long association.	Mrs Goodall should be rotated from the engagement team. It may be possible to allow Mrs Goodall to continue as engagement partner for one further year in order to safeguard audit quality. Audit committee approval must be obtained in order to allow this and an independent partner review of the audit files for Pink Co should be arranged.

There may be the impression of lack of independence as Simon is related to the engagement partner. Simon could be tempted not to identify errors in case this prejudiced his Mum's relationship with the client. In addition, if Mrs Goodall was reviewing Simon's work, she may not review it as thoroughly as the other audit staff due to their relationship.	To demonstrate complete independence, Simon should not be part of any audit or assurance team for which Mrs Goodall is partner.
As long as Mr Supper paid a full fee to Pink Co for the investment advice (i.e. it is on normal commercial terms) there is no ethical threat as investment advice is in the normal course of business for Pink Co. However, if Mr Supper received a discount on the services or preferential rates, as a benefit of being part of the audit team, this would create a self-interest threat. Mr Supper may feel he has to overlook issues identified during the audit because of the preferential treatment.	Mr Supper should be asked not to use the services of Pink Co again unless this is first agreed with the engagement partner.
The audit team has been offered a day at the horse races at the end of the audit which creates a self-interest threat. Unless the value is trivial and inconsequential, hospitality is not allowed. The fact that the horse race day costs less than the yacht expense is irrelevant. The auditors may feel indebted to the client and therefore overlook issues identified during the audit.	The day out should not be accepted. The rationale for accepting hospitality in previous years should be investigated.
There are outstanding fees creating a self-interest threat. JT & Co may be reluctant to identify misstatements for fear of not getting paid. In addition, outstanding fees may be considered to be a loan. Loans to clients are not permitted.	Payment for work should be arranged before the audit is commenced, or a payment plan agreed.

Test your understanding 3 – Analytical risk assessment

(a) (i) Explanation of analytical procedures

'Analytical procedures' means the evaluation of financial and other information and the review of plausible relationships in that information. The review also includes identifying fluctuations and relationships that do not appear consistent with other relevant information or results.

(ii) Types of analytical procedures

Analytical procedures can be used as:

– Comparison of comparable information to prior periods to identify unusual changes or fluctuations in amounts.

– Comparison of actual or anticipated results of the entity with budgets and/or forecasts, or the expectations of the auditor in order to determine the potential accuracy of those results.

– Comparison to industry information either for the industry as a whole or by comparison to entities of similar size to the client to determine whether the receivable collection period, for example, are reasonable.

(iii) Use of analytical procedures

Risk assessment procedures

Analytical procedures are used at the beginning of the audit to help the auditor obtain an understanding of the entity and assess the risk of material misstatement. Audit procedures can then be directed to these risky areas.

Analytical procedures as substantive procedures

Analytical procedures can be used as substantive procedures in determining the risk of material misstatement at the assertion level during work on the statement of profit or loss and statement of financial position.

Analytical procedures in the overall review at the end of the audit

Analytical procedures help the auditor at the end of the audit in forming an overall conclusion as to whether the financial statements as a whole are consistent with the auditor's understanding of the entity.

(b)   Net profit

Overall, Tribe's result has changed from a net loss to a net profit. Given that revenue has only increased by 17% and that expenses, at least administration expenses, appear low, then there is the possibility that expenditure may be understated.

Revenue – increase 17%

According to the directors, Tribe has had a difficult year. Reasons for the increase in revenue must be ascertained as the change does not conform to the directors' comments. It is possible that the industry as a whole, has been growing allowing Tribe to produce this good result. Alternatively, incorrect revenue recognition may have been applied.

Cost of sales – fall 17%

A fall in cost of sales is unusual given that revenue has increased significantly. This may have been caused by an incorrect inventory valuation and the use of different (cheaper) suppliers which may cause problems with faulty goods in the next year.

Gross profit (GP) – increase 88%

This is a significant increase with the GP% changing from 33% last year to 53% this year. Identifying reasons for this change will need to focus initially on the change in revenue and cost of sales.

Administration – fall 6%

A fall is unusual given that revenue is increasing and so an increase in administration to support those sales would be expected. Expenditure may be understated, or there has been a decrease in the number of administration staff.

Selling and distribution – increase 42%

This increase does not appear to be in line with the increase in revenue as selling and distribution would be expected to increase in line with revenue. There may be misallocation of expenses from administration or the age of Tribe's delivery vans is increasing resulting in additional service costs.

Investment income – new this year

This is expected given the cash surplus in the year, although the amount is still very high indicating possible errors in the amount or other income generating assets not disclosed on the statement of financial position extract.

Interest payable – small fall

Given that Tribe has a considerable cash surplus this year, continuing to pay interest is surprising. The amount may be overstated.

Reasons for the lack of fall in interest payment e.g. loans that cannot be repaid early, must be determined. If the interest is associated with the overdraft that was in the SOFP last year, this may have only been paid off just before the year-end.

Test your understanding 4 – Audit risk

(a) **Audit risks**

Inventory valuation

Smoothbrush supplies 60% of its goods to Homewares at a significantly reduced selling price. Inventory may be overvalued if the net realisable value is lower than cost.

Receivables

Smoothbrush has extended its credit terms to Homewares from one month to four months. There is an increased risk as balances outstanding become older that they may be irrecoverable resulting in overstatement of receivables.

Plant and equipment

The production facility has a large amount of unused plant and equipment. This plant and equipment should be stated at the lower of its carrying value and recoverable amount, which may be at scrap value depending on its age and condition. Plant and equipment may be overvalued.

Cut-off

Smoothbrush imports goods from South Asia and the paint can be in transit for up to two months. The company accounts for goods when they receive them. Therefore at the year-end only goods that have been received into the warehouse should be included in the inventory balance and a respective payables balance recognised. Cut-off of purchases and inventory may not be accurate.

Inventory system

A new inventory system was introduced in the year. This could result in inventory balances being misstated if the records and new system have not initially been set up correctly.

Inventory allowance

Smoothbrush previously maintained an inventory allowance of 1%, however, this year it has decided to remove this. Unless all slow-moving/obsolete items are identified at the year-end and their value adjusted, there is a risk that the overall value of inventory may be overstated.

Legal action

The company's finance director (FD) has left and is intending to sue Smoothbrush for unfair dismissal. However, the company does not intend to make any provision or disclosure for any potential payment to the FD. Provisions or contingent liability disclosures may not be complete.

Lack of FD

Inherent risk is higher due to the changes in the finance department. The financial controller has been appointed as temporary FD and this lack of experience could result in increased risk of errors arising in the financial statement. In addition, the previous FD is not available to help with the audit.

Perpetual inventory system

Inventory may be misstated if the perpetual inventory counts are not complete and accurate. The inventory counts should cover all of the inventory lines but if any of the warehouses are not counted then this will need to be done at the year-end. In addition, inventory adjustments arising from the counts must be verified and updated by an appropriate member of the finance team to ensure the records are accurate.

(b) **Importance of assessing risks**

- Assessing engagement risk at the planning stage will ensure that attention is focused early on the areas most likely to cause material misstatements.

- A thorough risk assessment will also help the auditor to fully understand the entity, which enables an effective audit to be performed. Any unusual transactions or balances would also be identified early, so that these could be addressed in a timely manner.

- As auditors adopt a risk based audit approach, these risks need to be assessed early in order for the audit strategy and detailed work programmes to be developed.

- Assessing risks early should also result in an efficient audit. The team will only focus their time and effort on key areas as opposed to balances or transactions that might be immaterial or unlikely to contain errors.

- Assessing risk early should ensure that the most appropriate team is selected with more experienced staff allocated to higher risk areas and high risk balances.

- A thorough risk analysis should ultimately reduce the risk of an inappropriate audit opinion being given. The audit would have focused on the main risk areas and hence any material misstatements should have been identified.

- It should enable the auditor to have a good understanding of the risks of fraud, money laundering, etc. Assessing risk should enable the auditor to assess whether the client is a going concern.

(c) **Substantive procedures to confirm valuation of inventory**

- Select a representative sample of goods in inventory at the year-end, agree the cost per the records to a recent purchase invoice and ensure that the cost is correctly stated in the inventory records.

- Select a sample of inventory from the inventory listing and review post year-end sales invoices to ascertain if NRV is above cost or if an adjustment is required.

- For a sample of manufactured items obtain cost sheets and confirm:

    - raw material costs to recent purchase invoices

    - labour costs to time sheets or wage records

    - overheads allocated are of a production nature.

- Review aged inventory reports and identify any slow-moving goods. Discuss with management why these items have not been written down.

- Compare the level/value of aged product lines to the total inventory value to assess whether the allowance for slow-moving goods of 1% should be reinstated.

- Review the inventory records to identify the level of adjustments made throughout the year for damaged/obsolete items. If significant, consider whether the year-end records require further adjustments and discuss with management whether any further write downs/allowance may be required.

- Follow up on any damaged/obsolete items noted by the auditor at the inventory counts attended, to ensure that the inventory records have been updated correctly.

- Calculate the average inventory holding period for the current year and compare to prior year. Discuss any significant variations with management.

- Compare the gross margin for current year with prior year. Fluctuations in gross margin could be due to inventory valuation issues. Discuss significant variations in the margin with management.

Substantive procedures to confirm completeness of provisions or contingent liabilities

- Discuss with management the nature of the dispute between Smoothbrush and the former FD, to ensure that a full understanding of the issue is obtained and to assess whether an obligation exists.

- Review any correspondence with the former FD to assess if a reliable estimate of any potential payments can be made.

- Review correspondence with the company's lawyers to obtain their views as to the probability of the FD's claim being successful.

- Review board minutes and any company correspondence to assess whether there is any evidence to support the former FD's claims of unfair dismissal.

- Obtain a written representation from the directors of Smoothbrush confirming their view that the former FD's chances of a successful claim are remote, and hence no provision or contingent liability is required.

Test your understanding 5 – Fraud

(a) **Internal audit function: risk of fraud and error**

Internal audit can help management manage risks in relation to fraud and error, and exercise proper stewardship by:

– Commenting on the process used by management to identify and classify the specific fraud and error risks to which the entity is subject (and in some cases helping management develop and implement that process).

– Periodically auditing or reviewing systems or operations to determine whether the risks of fraud and error are being effectively managed.

– Where deficiencies are identified which provides opportunity for fraud and error, making recommendations for improvements.

– Monitoring the incidence of fraud and error and investigating serious cases.

In practice, the work of internal audit often focuses on the adequacy and effectiveness of internal control procedures for the prevention, detection and reporting of fraud and error. Routine internal controls (such as the controls over computer systems and the production of routine financial information) and non-routine controls (such as controls over year-end adjustments to the financial statements) are relevant.

It should be recognised however that many significant frauds bypass normal internal control systems and that in the case of management fraud in particular, much higher level controls (those relating to the high level governance of the entity) need to be reviewed by internal audit in order to establish the nature of the risks, and to manage them effectively.

(b) **External auditors: fraud and error in an audit of financial statements**

– External auditors are required by ISA 240 *The Auditor's Responsibilities Relating to Fraud in an Audit of Financial Statements* to consider the risks of material misstatements in the financial statements due to fraud. Their audit procedures will then be based on that risk assessment.

– Regardless of the risk assessment, auditors are required to be alert to the possibility of fraud throughout the audit and maintain an attitude of professional scepticism, notwithstanding the auditors' past experience of the honesty and integrity of management and those charged with governance.

- Members of the engagement team should discuss the susceptibility of the entity's financial statements to material misstatements due to fraud.

- Auditors should make enquiries of management regarding management's assessment of fraud risk, its process for dealing with risk, and its communications with those charged with governance and employees. They should enquire of those charged with governance about the oversight process.

- Auditors should also enquire of management and those charged with governance about any suspected or actual instance of fraud.

- Auditors should consider fraud risk factors, unusual or unexpected relationships, and assess the risk of misstatements due to fraud, identifying any significant risks. Auditors should evaluate the design of relevant internal controls, and determine whether they have been implemented.

- Auditors should determine an overall response to the assessed risk of material misstatements due to fraud and develop appropriate audit procedures, including testing certain journal entries, reviewing estimates for bias, and obtaining an understanding of the business rationale of significant transactions outside the normal course of business.

- Appropriate written representations should be obtained from management confirming they have informed the auditor of all known or suspected frauds.

- External auditors are only concerned with risks that might cause material error in the financial statements. External auditors might therefore pay less attention than internal auditors to small frauds (and errors), although they must always consider whether evidence of single instances of fraud (or error) are indicative of more systematic problems.

- It is accepted that because of the hidden nature of fraud, an audit properly conducted in accordance with ISAs might not detect a material misstatement in the financial statements arising from fraud. In practice, routine errors are much easier to detect than frauds.

- Where auditors encounter suspicions or actual instances of fraud (or error), they must consider the effect on the financial statements, which will usually involve further investigations.

- They should also consider the need to report to management and those charged with governance.

- Where serious frauds (or errors) are encountered, auditors need also to consider the effect on the going concern status of the entity, and the possible need to report externally to third parties, either in the public interest or for regulatory reasons. Many entities in the financial services sector are subject to this type of regulatory reporting and many countries have legislation relating to the reporting of money laundering activities, for example.

(c) **Nature of risks arising from fraud and error: Stone Holidays**

- Stone Holidays is subject to all of the risks of error arising from the use of computer systems. If programmed controls do not operate properly, for example, the information produced may be incomplete or incorrect.

- Inadequate controls also give rise to the risk of fraud by those who understand the system and are able to manipulate it in order to hide the misappropriation of assets such as receipts from customers.

- All networked systems are also subject to the risk of error because of the possibility of the loss or corruption of data in transit. They are also subject to the risk of fraud where the transmission of data is not securely encrypted.

- All entities that employ staff who handle company assets (such as receipts from customers) are subject to the risk that staff may make mistakes (error) or that they may misappropriate those assets (fraud) and then seek to hide the error or fraud by falsifying the records.

- Stone Holidays is subject to problems arising from the risk of fraud perpetrated by customers using stolen credit or debit cards or even cash. Whilst credit card companies may be liable for such frauds, attempts to use stolen cards can cause considerable inconvenience.

- There is a risk of fraud perpetrated by senior management who might seek to lower the amount of money payable to the central fund (and the company's tax liability) by falsifying the company's sales figures, particularly if a large proportion of holidays are paid for in cash.

- There is a risk that staff may seek to maximise the commission they are paid by entering false transactions into the computer system that are then reversed after the commission has been paid.

Test your understanding 6 – Quality control

Client A

Failure to sign off a working paper makes it difficult to identify the person responsible for the work in case of any query. If the working papers had been reviewed, the reviewer should have identified this issue and investigated who had performed the work and asked them to sign the working papers.

Completion dates of audit work are essential in order to identify the information that would have been available to the auditor at the time the procedures were completed. With the passage of time, more information can come to light which would change the conclusion. If the working papers had been reviewed the reviewer should have identified this issue and asked the preparer to date the working papers.

Review of the working papers is an important quality control procedure. Every team member's work should be reviewed by someone more senior to ensure it has been performed properly and to the appropriate standard. If a review has not been performed there could be material misstatements that have not been detected during the audit which could result in an inappropriate auditor's report being issued.

Client B

The comment on the file stating that there are no matters requiring written representation would indicate that the audit manager does not understand the professional standards that should be followed during an audit, specifically the requirements of ISA 580 *Written Representations*.

Written representations are required by ISA 580. By not obtaining a written representation the audit firm does not have sufficient appropriate evidence to support the audit opinion.

Written representations should include matters such as the management confirming they have prepared financial statements that give a true and fair view and that they have provided the auditor with all of the information required for the audit.

The audit partner should not have signed the auditor's report without the written representation being on file.

Client C

A sample of 30 was chosen for a purchases test yet only 27 were tested and a conclusion drawn from those items.

Sample sizes are chosen to ensure sufficient appropriate evidence has been obtained. As only 27 items were tested instead of 30, sufficient appropriate evidence has not been obtained in this instance.

The three missing invoices could be evidence of a wider control deficiency or a material fraud. Further investigation should have been performed to discover the reason for the missing invoices.

The issue may indicate a lack of supervision if the audit team member was unsure how to proceed after discovering the issue.

The issue would also indicate a lack of review as the matter was not identified during the review process.

Client D

Provisions are inherently risky as they are often determined by the judgment of management. As such they should be audited by someone with suitable experience and judgment.

An audit junior should not have performed this task. Tasks should be allocated to team members of appropriate experience and competence. Junior members of staff are usually allocated lower risk areas which require little experience and judgment. More senior members of the team should be assigned the riskier areas of the audit.

It is stated that the audit manager was too busy to perform the audit of the provision due to other client work. This may indicate that the workload of staff is not manageable. Audit quality could have been affected on both clients as work may be rushed to get it completed which may result in material misstatements going undetected.

Client E

Planning is an important and compulsory part of the audit process. ISA 300 *Planning an Audit of Financial Statements* requires the audit to be planned in order to ensure that the audit is performed in an efficient and effective manner and an appropriate audit approach is taken which addresses the risks of the audit.

The auditor should not simply copy last year's procedures and approach as this may not be appropriate for this year's circumstances.

By failing to plan the audit properly, ISA 300 has not been complied with and therefore the audit has not been performed in accordance with professional standards.

General points

The quality control issues identified raise doubts over the performance of several audits conducted by the firm.

If it is discovered that an inappropriate auditor's report was issued in any of these cases the firm could face action by the ACCA and by the client.

Any action taken against the firm could damage their reputation as well as result in a loss of clients and financial penalties.

The firm's policies and procedures should be communicated again to staff to remind them of the requirements and the importance of them.

Further training is recommended to ensure staff are aware of how to comply with the requirements.

Disciplinary action may be necessary in respect of staff who have been found to be deliberately disregarding company policy.

Test your understanding 7 – Controls

Deficiency (1 mark)	Recommendation (1 mark)
(1) Hand written orders are not sequentially numbered. Orders could be placed for goods not required resulting in overspending which will reduce profit. Alternatively, orders could be lost and not placed leading to potential stock outs. This will mean customer orders cannot be fulfilled leading to customer dissatisfaction.	Orders should be sequentially pre-numbered. A sequence check should be performed on a regular basis to ensure completeness. Orders should be authorised by a manager before being placed to ensure the goods are required.
(2) Purchase orders are not issued for all goods and services. Goods/services could be purchased that are not legitimate. This will increase costs for the company.	Purchase orders should be required for all goods. For services, a budget should be set and quotes obtained. Purchase orders should be authorised by someone other than the person requesting the goods to ensure they are for business use.

(3)	There is no system for recording receipt of other goods and services.	A goods received note should be completed and used to update the inventory records on a daily basis.
	Failure to record goods received could lead to over-ordering as inventory levels will be inaccurate. This will result in additional cost for the company and poor cash flow management.	
(4)	Goods received are not checked against the purchase order.	Agree the GRN to the purchase order to ensure the correct goods are being delivered.
	Goods could be received that have not been ordered. Incorrect quantities could be received. This will lead to production delays if the wrong goods have been received and delays in fulfilling customer orders leading to customer dissatisfaction.	
(5)	There is no review of the bookkeeper's work e.g. posting of invoices into the nominal ledger.	A review of the nominal ledger postings by a manager should be performed on a regular basis.
	Errors could go undetected resulting in suppliers being paid incorrect amounts. This will affect the company's relationship with the supplier affecting credit terms or discounts received.	
(6)	A list of payables is given to the managing director without supporting documentation.	The managing director should also review source documents before signing the list to ensure payments are for a valid business use.
	The managing director will not know if payables are valid or correct therefore could be paying incorrect amounts resulting in poor cash flow management.	
(7)	There is a lack of segregation of duties as the managing director authorises invoices, approves payment and signs cheques.	Segregate duties by sharing the responsibility with another manager.
	Fraud could occur and go undetected as the managing director could create a fictitious purchase invoice to support a payment to himself. This will cause loss for the company.	

Test your understanding 8 – Inventory count

(a) **Audit procedures prior to inventory count attendance**

- Review prior year working papers to identify any issues encountered which the auditor should be prepared for this year.

- Obtain inventory count instructions from the client to ascertain whether appropriate controls and procedures will be in place during the count.

- Enquire with management whether there have been any control issues relating to inventory during the year.

- Enquire of the client whether any inventory is held at third parties and assess whether attendance is required at those sites.

(b) **Deficiencies in counting inventory**

Deficiency	Explanation	How to overcome deficiency
Inventory sheets stated the quantity of items expected to be found in the store	Count teams will focus on finding that number of items making undercounting of inventory more likely – teams may stop counting when 'correct' number of items found.	Count sheets should not state the quantity of items so as not to pre-judge how many units will be found.
Count staff were all drawn from the stores	Count staff are also responsible for the inventory. There could be a temptation to hide errors or missing inventory that they have removed from the store illegally.	Count teams should include staff who are not responsible for inventory to provide independence in the count.
Count teams are allowed to decide which areas to count	There is a danger that teams will either omit inventory from the count or even count inventory twice due to lack of precise instructions on where to count.	Each team should be given a precise area of the store to count.
Count sheets were not signed by the staff carrying out the count	Lack of signature makes it difficult to raise queries regarding items counted because the actual staff carrying out the count are not known.	All count sheets should be signed to confirm who actually carried out the count of individual items.

Inventory is not marked to indicate it has been counted	As above, there is a danger that inventory will be either omitted or included twice in the count.	Inventory should be marked in some way to show that it has been counted to avoid this error.
Recording information on the count sheets in pencil	Recording in pencil means that the count sheets could be amended after the count has taken place, not just during the count. The inventory balances will then be incorrectly recorded.	Count sheets should be completed in ink.
Count sheets for inventory not on the pre-numbered count sheets were only numbered when used	It is possible that the additional inventory sheets could be lost as there is no overall control of the sheets actually being used. Sheets may not be numbered by the teams, again giving rise to the possibility of loss.	All inventory sheets, including those for 'extra' inventory, should be pre-numbered.

(c) **Tests of controls and substantive procedures**

The aim of a test of control is to check that an audit client's internal control systems are operating effectively.

Example: Observe the count teams ensuring that they are counting in accordance with the client's inventory count instructions.

The aim of a substantive procedure is to ensure that there are no material errors at the assertion level in the client's financial statements.

Example: Record the condition of items of inventory to ensure that the valuation of those items is appropriate on the final inventory listing.

Test your understanding 9 – Evidence and procedures

Audit procedures

(i) *Analytical procedures* consist of evaluations of financial information made by a study of plausible relationships among both financial and non-financial data.

Inquiry means to seek relevant information from sources, both financial and non-financial, either inside or outside the company being audited. Evidence may be obtained orally or in writing.

Inspection is the examination of records, documents and tangible assets.

Observation involves looking at a process or procedure as it is being performed to ensure that the process actually works as documented.

Recalculation means the checking of the mathematical accuracy of documents or records.

(ii) *Analytical procedures*

Compare revenue year on year to try to identify whether income has been understated, possibly by cash being taken prior to banking. There is no control over the opening of post so cash could be withdrawn by one assistant, and the deficit made up by a fraud on customers.

Inquiry

Obtain statements from suppliers to check the completeness of liabilities at the end of the year. As there is no control over purchases, invoices could have been misplaced resulting in a lower purchases and trade payables figure.

Inspection

The assets of the company, namely cuddly toys in inventory at the end of the year, can be inspected to ensure the inventory exists and that the toys are saleable in their current condition.

Observation

Procedures such as the opening of the post and recording of customer orders can be observed to ensure that all orders are recorded in the sales day book and cash book.

Recalculation

Recalculating the cash book to confirm that the total amount of cash recorded is accurate and can be included in the revenue figure (cash receipts should equal revenue as there are no receivables).

(iii) *Analytical procedures*

This method of collecting evidence will be useful in BearsWorld because it will help to identify unusual changes in income and expenditure. As BearsWorld is a relatively small company, monitoring gross profit will show relatively small changes in sales margin or purchasing costs. Decisions by Mr Kyto to amend margins can therefore be traced into the actual sales made.

Enquiry

Enquiry evidence will be very useful in the audit of BearsWorld, especially where this is derived from third parties. Third party evidence is generally more reliable than client originated evidence as there is a decreased likelihood of bias. Trade payables can therefore be verified using supplier statement reconciliations. A review of any customer complaints file (if these letters are kept) will also help to identify any orders that have not been despatched.

Inspection

Inspection of documents within BearsWorld will be useful, particularly regarding checking whether expenses are bona fide. All purchase invoices, for example, should be addressed to BearsWorld and relate to purchases expected from that company, e.g. cuddly toys for resale, office expenses, etc.

Observation

Observation may be useful because it will show how the assistants perform their work and whether there are any obvious deficiencies in the processes of the company.

Recalculation

Recalculation evidence is very useful for checking additions on invoices, balancing of control accounts, etc. This means that the arithmetical accuracy of the books and records in BearsWorld can be confirmed.

(iv) *Analytical procedures*

The technique may be limited in its application because it will not detect errors or omissions made consistently year on year. If either assistant is defrauding the company (for example by removing cash) each year, then analytical procedures will not detect this. Analytical procedures will also not detect misstatements which cancel each other out, i.e. one misstatement may overstate the balance but another may understate the balance. The auditor would not detect these misstatements using analytical procedures.

Enquiry

External inquiry evidence will be less useful in the audit of sales and receivables because there are no receivables as goods are paid for prior to despatch. Internal evidence will be available from Mr Kyto and the assistant, however the lack of segregation of duties means that this may not be so reliable.

Inspection

Inspection of documents can be time consuming. However, given the poor internal control system within BearsWorld, the auditor may have no choice but to use this method of gathering evidence.

The fact that an invoice is addressed to the company does not confirm completeness of recording so inspection of the cash book for unusual payments verified by checking the purchase invoice will also be required. Additional substantive testing would also be required due to poor controls.

Observation

Observation tests will be of limited usefulness because the assistants may act differently when an auditor is present. The same problem will apply to any observation checking carried out by Mr Kyto.

Recalculation

The main weakness of recalculation checking is that calculations can only be carried out on figures that have been recorded. If there are any omissions then checks cannot be carried out.

Test your understanding 10 – Procedures

Inspection

Inspection involves examining records or documents, whether internal or external, in paper form, electronic form, or other media, or a physical examination of an asset.

Inspect the bank reconciliation for any outstanding lodgements and agree to the pre year-end cash book, post year-end bank statement and also to paying-in-book pre year-end.

Observation

Observation consists of looking at a process or procedure being performed by others.

Observe the process for the opening of mail and logging of any cheques received from customers to ensure adequate segregation of duties.

Analytical procedures

Analytical procedures consist of evaluations of financial information through analysis of plausible relationships among both financial and non-financial data. Analytical procedures also encompass such investigation as is necessary of identified fluctuations or relationships which are inconsistent with other relevant information or which differ from expected values by a significant amount.

Review the year-end bank balance against prior year to identify any significant fluctuations as these could be evidence of window dressing and discuss with management.

Inquiry

Inquiry consists of seeking information from knowledgeable persons, both financial and non-financial, within the entity or outside the entity.

Inquire of management as to whether the company has opened/closed any bank accounts during the period.

Recalculation

Recalculation consists of checking the mathematical accuracy of documents or records. Recalculation may be performed manually or electronically.

Recalculate the additions in the cash book to confirm accuracy of the amount.

External confirmation

An external confirmation represents audit evidence obtained by the auditor as a direct written response to the auditor from a third party, in paper form, electronic form or by other medium.

Obtain a standard bank confirmation from each bank the company has undertaken banking transactions with during the year.

Re-performance

Re-performance involves the auditor's independent execution of procedures or controls which were originally performed as part of the entity's internal control.

Re-perform the year-end bank reconciliation to ensure the process was undertaken accurately.

Test your understanding 11 – Audit risk NFP

(a) **Audit risk**

Audit risk is the risk that an auditor gives an inappropriate opinion on the financial statements being audited.

Inherent risk is the susceptibility of an assertion to a misstatement that could be material individually or when aggregated with misstatements, before considering any related controls.

Control risk is the risk that a material misstatement could occur in an assertion that could be material, individually or when aggregated with other misstatements, and will not be prevented or detected on a timely basis by the company's internal control systems.

Detection risk is the risk that the auditors' procedures will not detect a misstatement that exists in an assertion that could be material, individually or when aggregated with other misstatements.

(b)   **Inherent risks and effect on audit approach**

Area of inherent risk	Effect on audit approach
Income is from voluntary donations only. It will be difficult to estimate future income. There is a risk that disclosure of going concern issues is not adequate in the financial statements.	Review forecasts and enquire with the trustees and management of the charity about their fundraising plans for the future. Obtain written representation from the trustees that they believe the charity can continue in existence for the foreseeable future.
Risk to completeness of income as cash donations may be stolen in the absence of any controls. No invoices will be raised and therefore there will be no evidence of the income received.	Assess what controls exist over cash donations (if any). Test the effectiveness of the controls in place. There may need to be a modified opinion due to lack of sufficient appropriate evidence.
There is a risk that the funds are not spent in accordance with the aims of the charity (regularity audit).	Inspect the constitution of the charity to understand its aims. Review a breakdown of expenditure to ensure it is in line with the constitution.
The taxation rules are quite complex for the charity resulting in a risk to the reasonableness of the tax accrual at the year-end.	Consult with a tax expert or audit staff with relevant knowledge to assess the tax rules and recalculate the tax charge and liability to ensure arithmetical accuracy.
According to the constitution of the charity, only 10% of expenditure can be on administration. There is a risk that administration costs are deliberately misstated to ensure this restriction is met.	Inspect the constitution of the charity to understand its aims. Review the breakdown of other types of expenditure to identify any admin costs incorrectly classified if the 10% limit has been exceeded.
Some donations are made for an intended purpose. There is a risk that these restricted funds are not disclosed as such in the financial statements.	Obtain supporting documentation for any donations and agree the expenditure to the terms of the donation. Any discrepancies should be reported to management.

(c) **Weak control environment**

Lack of segregation of duties

There is normally a limited number of staff working in the charity meaning that a full system of internal control including segregation of duties cannot be implemented.

Volunteer staff

Many staff are volunteers and so will only work at the charity on an occasional basis. Controls will be performed by different staff on different days making the system potentially unreliable.

Lack of qualified staff

As staff are mainly volunteers they may not have professional qualifications or experience to implement or maintain good control systems.

No internal audit department

Any control system will not be monitored effectively, mainly due to the lack of any internal audit department. The charity will not have the funds or experience to establish internal audit.

Attitude of the trustees

Where trustees are not professionally trained or have little time to devote to the charity, there may be a perception that controls are not important. The overall control environment may therefore be weak as other charity workers may not appreciate the importance of maintaining good controls.

 Test your understanding 12 – NFP audit

(a) **Audit risks**

– Charities can be viewed as inherently risky because they are often managed by non-professionals and are susceptible to fraud, although many charities and the volunteers that run them are people of the highest integrity who take a great deal of care over their work.

– Charities are also at risk of being in violation of their constitutions, which is important where funds are raised from public or private donors who may object strongly if funds are not used in the manner expected. Other charities and regulatory bodies supervising charities may also object.

- Most small charities have a high level of control risk because formal internal controls are expensive and are not often in place. This means that donations may be susceptible to misappropriation. Charities have to rely on the trustworthiness of volunteers.

- Ajio is a new client and as a result detection risk is higher due to a lack of cumulative knowledge and experience.

(b) **Audit procedures: fundraising events**

- Attend a fundraising event and observe the procedures employed in collecting, counting, banking and recording the cash. This will help provide audit evidence that funds have not been misappropriated and that all income from such events has been recorded. Sealed boxes or tins that are opened in the presence of two volunteers are often used for these purposes.

- Perform cash counts at the events to provide evidence that cash has been counted correctly and that there is no collusion between volunteers to misappropriate funds.

- Examine bank paying-in slips, bank statements and bank reconciliations and ensure that these agree with records made at events. This also provides evidence as to the completeness of income.

- Examine the records of expenditure for fundraising events (hire of equipment, entertainers, purchase of refreshments, etc.) and ensure that these have been properly authorised (where appropriate) and that receipts have been obtained for all expenditure. This provides evidence as to the completeness and accuracy of expenditure.

- Review the income and expenditure of fundraising events against any budgets that have been prepared and investigate any significant discrepancies.

- Ensure that all necessary licences (such as public entertainment licences) have been obtained by the trustees for such events in order to ensure that no action is likely to be taken against the charity or volunteers.

- Obtain written representation from the trustees to the effect that there are no outstanding unrecorded liabilities for such events for completeness of expenditure and liabilities.

Test your understanding 13 – Subsequent events

Event 1 – Fire

This event occurred after the reporting period and is not an event which provides evidence of a condition at the year-end and hence this is a non-adjusting event.

Normally as the company is insured, only uninsured losses suffered by Grains 4U Co (Grains) would need to be accounted for, which in the normal course of events would be an immaterial amount. However, the insurance company is investigating, as there is a possibility the fire was started deliberately, and this would invalidate the insurance policy.

If this is the case, the total damaged assets of $675,000 (650 + 25) would be material as they represent 8.5% (675/7,900) of profit before tax.

Therefore as a material non-adjusting event, the assets should not be written down to their scrap value in the current year financial statements. However, the directors should include a disclosure note detailing the fire and the total value of assets which may be impacted due to the possibility of a lack of an insurance settlement.

Procedures

- Obtain a schedule showing the damaged property, plant and equipment and agree the net book value to the non-current assets register to confirm the total value of affected assets.

- Obtain a breakdown of the inventory stored at the distribution centre on 15 February 20X6 and compare to earlier records or despatch documents to ascertain the likely level of inventory at the time of the fire.

- Review any correspondence from the insurance company confirming the amount of the claim, and the current status of their investigation into the fire and any likely payments to assess the extent of any uninsured amounts.

- Discuss with the directors whether they will disclose the effect of the fire in the financial statements.

Event 2 – Inventory

Grains has identified that inventory at the year-end with a cost of $915,000 is defective. This information was obtained after the year-end but provides further evidence of the net realisable value of inventory at the year-end and hence is an adjusting event.

The inventory of $915,000 must be written down to its net realisable value of $50,000.

The write down of $865,000 (915 – 50) is material as it represents 10.9% (865/7,900) of profit before tax.

Hence, the directors should amend the financial statements by writing down the inventory to $50,000.

Procedures

- Discuss the matter with the directors and enquire if they are prepared to write down the cost of the inventory to net realisable value.

- Review the board minutes to assess whether this event was the only case of defective inventory as there could potentially be other inventory which requires writing down.

- Obtain a schedule showing the defective inventory and agree to supporting production documentation that it was produced prior to 31 December, as otherwise it would not require a write down at the year end.

- Discuss with management how they have assessed the scrap value of $50,000 and agree this amount to any supporting documentation to confirm the value.

Test your understanding 14 – Written representations

(a) Written representations are a form of audit evidence. They are written by the company's directors and sent to the auditor, just before the auditor's report is signed.

Written representations are required for two reasons:

- For the directors to acknowledge their collective responsibility for the preparation of the financial statements and to confirm that they have approved those statements.

- To confirm any matters which are material to the financial statements where representations are crucial to obtaining sufficient and appropriate audit evidence.

In the latter situation, other forms of audit evidence are normally limited because knowledge of the facts is confined to management and the matter is one of judgment or opinion.

Obtaining written representations does not mean that other evidence does not have to be obtained. Audit evidence will still be collected and the representation will support that evidence. Any contradiction between sources of evidence should be investigated.

(b) *Lion's Roar*

It is appropriate to include the claim in the written representation.

The amount of the claim is material being 50% of profit before taxation.

There is also a lack of definitive supporting evidence for the claim. The two main pieces of evidence available are the claim from Lion's Roar itself and the legal advice from Crighton Ward's solicitors. However, any claim amount cannot be accurately determined because the dispute has not been settled.

The directors have stated that they believe the claim not to be justified, which is one possible outcome of the dispute. However, in order to obtain sufficient evidence to show how the treatment of the potential claim was decided for the financial statements, the auditor must obtain this opinion in writing.

Depreciation

Including the point in the written representation is inappropriate because the auditor appears to have obtained sufficient evidence to confirm the accounting treatment.

The lack of profit or loss on sale confirms that the depreciation charge is appropriate. Large profits would indicate over-depreciation and large losses would indicate under-depreciation. The amount also meets industry standards confirming that Crighton-Ward's accounting policy is acceptable.

(c) Lack of written representation

- Discuss the situation with the directors to try and resolve the issue that the directors have raised. Ascertain exact reasons why the directors will not sign the letter.

- Explain the need for the written representation again and note that the requirement to obtain a written representation letter was included in the engagement letter.

- Consider whether amendments can be made to the letter to incorporate the directors' concerns that will still provide the auditor with appropriate and sufficient audit evidence.

- Explain that if the auditor does not receive sufficient and appropriate audit evidence, then the audit opinion will have to be modified due to an inability to obtain sufficient appropriate evidence.

Test your understanding 15 – Auditor's report

(a) Jones

Materiality

The receivable of $30,000 represents 20% of profit and more than 4% of receivables therefore is material.

Relevant accounting principles

The bankruptcy of the customer provides evidence of a condition existing at the statement of financial position date. It should therefore be treated as an adjusting event in accordance with IAS 10 *Events After the Reporting Period*. The receivable should be written off in full in the financial statements at 30 September 20X2.

The company has overstated receivables and profit by $30,000.

Impact on the auditor's report

– The financial statements are materially misstated.

– The matter is material but not pervasive.

– A qualified opinion should be issued with the 'except for' wording.

– The 'Basis for Opinion' section will be amended to a 'Basis for Qualified Opinion' to explain the reason for the qualified opinion.

– **Tutorial note:** If the company is listed the Key Audit Matters section will reference the Basis for Qualified Opinion.

(b) Roberts

Materiality

The amount of $10,000 represents only 2% of the stated profit before tax and therefore is not material.

The potential losses may be more significant than the figure of $10,000 since other claims are now pending. The auditor may conclude that the whole legal matter is potentially material.

Relevant accounting principles

There is uncertainty with regard to the outcome of the pending claims and the potential liability which may arise as a result of the product defect. The appropriate accounting treatment will depend on whether the chance of loss is probable, possible or remote. If it is probable a provision should be recognised. If it is possible a contingent liability should be disclosed. If it is remote the financial statements will not be affected. (IAS 37 *Provisions, Contingent Liabilities and Contingent Assets*).

Liabilities may be understated or contingent liabilities may not be adequately disclosed.

Impact on the auditor's report

– Management has chosen to ignore both the actual loss (which is not individually material) and the potential loss (which may be material). If the auditor does not believe that the management's view is acceptable, or does not think that the disclosure is adequate, the financial statements will be materially misstated.

– If the potential claims are considered material, a qualified opinion with the 'except for' wording should be issued.

– If the auditor believes that the claims are likely to be successful and are likely to be substantial then an adverse opinion should be issued stating that the financial statements do not show a true and fair view.

– The 'Basis for Opinion' section will be amended to a 'Basis for Qualified Opinion' or 'Basis for Adverse Opinion' to explain the reason for the modified opinion.

– **Tutorial note:** If the company is listed the Key Audit Matters section will reference the Basis for Qualified/Adverse Opinion.

(c) **Griffiths**

Materiality

The fall in value is material and pervasive as the adjustment would have the effect of turning a profit before tax of $250,000 into a loss of $50,000.

Relevant accounting principles

Investments should be written down if they are impaired. A fall in the value of one asset must not be offset against an increase in the value of another asset. Each asset has to be considered separately.

As the company admits that a permanent fall in value has taken place it should write the value of the assets down otherwise assets will be overstated.

Impact on the auditor's report

- The financial statements are materially misstated.

- The matter is material and pervasive.

- An adverse opinion should be issued stating that the financial statements do not show a true and fair view.

- The 'Basis for Opinion' section will be amended to a 'Basis for Adverse Opinion' to explain the reason for the adverse opinion.

- **Tutorial note:** If the company is listed the Key Audit Matters section will reference the Basis for Adverse Opinion.

(d) **Evans**

Materiality

The $10,000 represents 10% of profit before tax, and so would appear to be material.

Since the accounting records were only destroyed for the early part of the year, the auditor would still be able to confirm the calculations for the later part of the year. In these particular circumstances the auditor may consider that the amount of any error (which is likely to be considerably less than $10,000) is not material.

Relevant accounting principles

The company must include the cost of its own labour and materials in the construction of the warehouse, since these have been used to create a capital asset.

Impact on the auditor's report

- There is a lack of sufficient appropriate evidence to support the treatment of the $10,000 labour costs therefore the auditor does not know whether the costs are materially misstated.

- Assuming that the extent of any potential misstatement is considered not material, an unmodified opinion will be issued stating that the financial statements give a true and fair view.

- If the possible misstatement is considered material, a qualified opinion with the 'except for' wording will be required.

- If modified, the 'Basis for Opinion' section will be amended to a 'Basis for Qualified Opinion' to explain the reason for the qualified opinion.

Tutorial note: If the company is listed the Key Audit Matters section will reference the Basis for Qualified Opinion.

Test your understanding 16 – Corporate governance 1

The board comprises six executives and only four non-executive directors (NEDs). There should be an appropriate balance of executives and NEDs, to ensure that the board makes the correct objective decisions, which are in the best interest of the stakeholders of the company, and no individual or group of individuals dominates the board's decision-making.	At least half of the board should be NEDs. Hence the board of Tangerine Tech Co (Tangerine) should consider recruiting and appointing additional independent NEDs to satisfy this requirement.
One of the NEDs and the chair are former executive directors of Tangerine who were asked to take on their existing roles following retirement. As former executive directors, they were previously employed by the company and so will not bring the required level of independence and objective judgement to the role as is necessary. The independence of the other NEDs cannot be assessed.	Only independent non-executives with relevant experience and skills should be appointed to the board of Tangerine. A review should be under taken of the independence of all existing NEDs. Any who are not independent should ideally be replaced or supplemented by independent NEDs.
The board chair, who is a NED, also has the role of audit committee chair. The chair of the board should not be a member of the audit committee as this will compromise the independence of the audit committee and give too much power to the board chair.	The board chair should cease to be a member of audit committee. One of the newly appointed independent NEDs should be appointed as audit committee chair.

All four members of the audit committee were previously involved in sales or production related roles. At least one member of the audit committee should have recent and relevant financial experience. None of the NEDs were former finance directors and so it is unlikely they possess the required financial experience.	The company should ensure when they recruit the new independent NEDs that at least one of them has the required recent and relevant financial experience.
All of the directors have been members of the board for at least four years. The shareholders should review on a regular basis that the composition of the board of directors is appropriate, and that there is an appropriate re-election process in place to ensure this can be achieved.	The directors should be subject to re-election annually by the shareholders. At the current year's annual general meeting it should be proposed that a number of the directors are subject to re-election. The remaining directors could then be subject to re-election next year.
The chair has sole responsibility for liaising with the shareholders and answering any of their questions. However, this is a role which the board as a whole should undertake.	All members of the board should be involved in ensuring that satisfactory dialogue occurs with shareholders, for example, all should attend meetings with shareholders such as the annual general meeting. The board should state in the annual report the steps they have taken to ensure that the members of the board, and in particular the non-executive directors, develop an understanding of the views of major shareholders about the company.
Currently Tangerine has not established an internal audit function. The audit committee should consider the effectiveness of internal controls and internal audit could support this role. Where there is no internal audit function, the audit committee is required to consider annually the need for one.	Further consideration should be given to establishing an internal audit function. Having an internal audit function will help the audit committee to discharge their responsibility for monitoring internal controls. However, the costs of establishing an internal audit function should be considered against the benefits.

Test your understanding 17 – Corporate governance 2

(1) Corporate governance definition

The term corporate governance refers to the means by which a company is directed and controlled in the interests of all stakeholders. It will include consideration of:

– Directors' responsibilities

– Composition of the board of directors

– Audit requirements (internal and external).

(2) External auditors and corporate governance

If a company has good standards of corporate governance and is managed well in the interests of all stakeholders, the auditors are likely to conclude that control risk is lower and therefore audit risk is reduced. As a result of this they may be able to reduce the extent of the audit procedures they carry out.

The audit committee should take responsibility for ensuring the external auditor is independent and for monitoring and assessing the quality and effectiveness of the external audit.

The external auditor may have to report on whether the company is compliant with corporate governance requirements.

(3) Composition of the audit committee

The audit committee should be made up of independent non-executive directors and include at least one person with recent and relevant financial experience.

(4) Role of the audit committee

– Monitoring the integrity of the financial statements.

– Reviewing the company's internal financial controls.

– Monitoring and reviewing the effectiveness of the internal audit function.

– If no internal audit function is in place, they should consider annually whether there is a need for one and make a recommendation to the board. The reasons for there being no internal audit function should be explained in the annual report.

– Making recommendations in relation to the appointment and removal of the external auditor and their remuneration.

– Reviewing and monitoring the external auditor's independence and objectivity and the effectiveness of the audit process.

– Developing and implementing policy on the engagement of the external auditor to supply non-audit services.

(5) **Need for an audit committee**

The existence of an audit committee will enhance the company's corporate governance profile by:

- Improving public confidence

- Providing further support to directors

- Strengthening the independence of the external auditor

- Improving internal controls.

(6) **Risk management**

The risk committee should discuss the issue and assess its seriousness in relation to its likelihood and potential impact. They should then decide what action is appropriate in order to manage the risk.

This risk might be reduced by:

- Ensuring favourable employment packages for such individuals

- Ensuring training for other staff assists in case of succession issues

- Ensure key tasks are not carried out by just one person.

The auditor must consider the possible impact of all significant risks as any of these could ultimately have financial consequences or going concern issues, hence impacting on the audit opinion.

Test your understanding 18 – Internal audit

(a) **Use of the work of the internal auditors by external auditors**

Sales and ticketing

– The sales function is likely to be integrated with the accounting and internal control system used to produce the figure in the financial statements for revenue, on which the external auditor reports and is therefore useful.

– The internal auditors' work on the ticketing system relates to an operational area which does not have a direct impact on the financial statements. Ticketing may have an indirect effect because it is likely to be integrated with the sales system and there is likely to be some crossover between the controls over ticketing and controls over sales generally. The work of the internal auditors is therefore likely to be of some use to the external auditor.

Fleet acquisition and maintenance

– The internal auditors' work on the fleet acquisition system is likely to be relevant to the external auditor because owned aircraft and leased aircraft will constitute a substantial element of statement of financial position assets and liabilities. The related depreciation and finance charges will be included in the statement of profit or loss.

– Much of the internal auditors' work is likely to relate to ensuring that company policy has been complied with. Company policy will relate to the authorisation for and acquisition of aircraft and ensuring the appropriate accounting treatment is being used. The external auditor will want to ensure that the company's policies are both appropriate and complied with.

– It is also possible that the internal auditors' work may involve some verification of the statement of profit and loss and statement of financial position figures. Given the likely materiality of the amounts involved, this work will also be of interest to the external auditor.

– It is possible that the internal auditors' work may also relate to the quality of aircraft, and other operational aspects of fleet management. These issues may also be relevant to the external auditor, insofar as they relate to compliance with laws and regulations.

– Maintenance expenditure in the statement of profit or loss may be material and the work of the internal auditors is therefore of interest to external auditors. The internal auditors' work is likely to relate to the authorisation and correct accounting for maintenance expenditure (capitalisation or expensing) which will affect the financial statements.

Trade payables and long term debt financing

– The extent of the external auditor's interest in the internal auditors' work on trade payables and long term financing will depend on the materiality of the amounts involved. Trade payables (for certain types of routine maintenance, and payables due to the service organisations, for example) may be material. Long term debt financing is very likely to be material as many airlines have substantial debt financing.–

Internal audit work on trade payables is likely to involve ensuring that routine internal controls are properly designed and are operating effectively. This will be relevant to the external auditor.

– There are substantial financial statement disclosures required for debt financing. The internal auditors' assistance with ensuring that disclosures are properly made, as well as with ensuring that any covenants have been complied with and that the accounting for the financing is appropriate, may also be helpful to the external auditor.

(b) Evaluating the internal audit function

– The firm will seek to ensure that there is an appropriate structure within the department itself, with appropriate reporting lines outside of the department, preferably reporting into the audit committee.

– The internal audit function has recently been expanded and there are likely to be changes in the way it is organised. The function should have operational independence within the organisation and formal terms of reference that encompass the recent changes made.

– The function should have a systematic and disciplined approach to its work including quality control procedures.

– Staff should be appropriately trained, experienced and qualified. The head of the internal audit department should preferably be professionally qualified.

References

The Board (2018) IAS 1 *Presentation of Financial Statements. London*: IFRS Foundation.

The Board (2018) IAS 2 *Inventories*. London: IFRS Foundation.

The Board (2018) IAS 7 *Statement of Cash Flows*. London: IFRS Foundation.

The Board (2018) IAS 10 *Events after the Reporting Period*. London: IFRS Foundation.

The Board (2018) IAS 16 *Property, Plant and Equipment*. London: IFRS Foundation.

The Board (2018) IAS 27 *Separate Financial Statements*. London: IFRS Foundation.

The Board (2018) IAS 28 *Investments in Associates and Joint Ventures*. London: IFRS Foundation.

The Board (2018) IAS 37 *Provisions, Contingent Liabilities and Contingent Assets*. London: IFRS Foundation.

The Board (2018) IAS 38 *Intangible Assets*. London: IFRS Foundation.

The Board (2018) IFRS 3 *Business Combinations*. London: IFRS Foundation.

The Board (2018) IFRS 10 *Consolidated Financial Statements*. London: IFRS Foundation.

The Board (2018) IFRS 15 *Revenue from Contracts with Customers*. London: IFRS Foundation.

KAPLAN PUBLISHING